More praise for
The Hunt for Bin Laden

"*The Hunt for Bin Laden* transports you inside the beating heart of America's war on terror, then spirals you down a main artery onto the front lines with a Special Forces detachment cutting down al Qaeda terrorists. . . . By the time I finished reading *The Hunt for Bin Laden*, I was in awe of this force America had unleashed against our enemies. . . . *The Hunt for Bin Laden* has the epic style and reality of *We Were Soldiers Once . . . and Young*."

—MASTER SERGEANT THOMAS R. BUMBACK (Ret.)
U.S. Army Special Operations
Soldier of Fortune magazine

"Swashbuckling . . . [Moore reaches] a kind of ground truth in his narrative of Special Forces at war: the dangerous, sometimes thrilling but unpredictable nature of combat that makes soldiers laugh bitterly at the phrase 'military precision.' "

—*The Washington Post Book World*

"Robin Moore is back in his element. . . . *The Hunt for Bin Laden* offers valuable insights into the war."

—*San Diego Union-Tribune*

Also by Robin Moore
THE GREEN BERETS
THE FRENCH CONNECTION

THE HUNT FOR BIN LADEN

TASK FORCE DAGGER

ROBIN MOORE

BALLANTINE BOOKS • NEW YORK

A Presidio Press Book
Published by The Random House Publishing Group

Copyright © 2003 by Robin Moore
Maps copyright © 2003 by David Lindroth

Presidio Press and colophon are trademarks of Random House, Inc.

www.presidiopress.com

ISBN 0-89141-838-5

This edition published by arrangement with Random House, Inc.

Cover photo courtesy of the Northern Alliance Advisor Group
Cover photo Osama bin Laden © Reuters-NewMedia/Corbis
Inside front cover photo courtesy of Sherry Bolduc and
Theresa Morehead

Manufactured in the United States of America

First Mass Market Edition: December 2003

OPM   10   9   8   7   6   5   4   3   2   1

To Commander Ahmad Shah Massoud,
who warned America and perished on September 9, 2001.

To the men, women, and children
who perished on September 11, 2001.

To the New York City firefighters and police officers,
and Port Authority police officers who perished
trying to save them.

And to the Green Berets
who perished avenging them . . .

Acknowledgments

The story of TASK FORCE DAGGER could not have been written without the guidance and wisdom of Bob Loomis, vice-president and executive editor at Random House. For many years I wanted to do a book with him, and the story of the Green Berets in Afghanistan finally provided that opportunity. I cannot thank him enough for his steadfastness through endless rewrites and corrections, including several last-minute revisions and two total rewrites.

I must also thank my wonderful literary agent, Marianne "Mimi" Strong, who stuck with me through thick and thin and remained loyal throughout it all, with supportive letters and a strong sense of justice.

Many thanks are in order for Major General Geoffrey Lambert, commander of the Green Berets at Fort Bragg and a stalwart soldier and friend. Without General Lambert's assistance and the support of his staff, it would have been impossible even to start writing this book. And thanks also to his Special Forces sergeants, for without them, and their will to win, there would be no story of Afghanistan's liberation to write.

Only weeks before we were to finalize the book, *Newsweek* printed its skewed account of General Dostum's alleged "container deaths." We found official sources virtually closed—no one in Special Operations wanted to trust journalists anymore. To get the story, I had to use my unofficial sources and my influence as the only civilian in history to become Special Forces qualified. With loose ends still hanging, the task of finishing this book became even more daunting.

This book in its present form owes much to the hard work and diligence of my project coordinator, Chris Thompson. Countless hours turned into months and months of writing, editing, rewriting, and contacting the people involved in the War on Terror to verify information. Before *The Hunt for bin Laden* entered its final stages of publication, Chris and I traveled to places such as New York City; Fort Bragg, North Carolina; and Fort Campbell, Kentucky.

Chris served for six years in the U.S. Army as a light infantryman before studying journalism at the University of Massachusetts, Amherst. Before coming on as my full-time writing assistant, he worked as a newspaper correspondent in Massachusetts.

No stranger to Special Ops, Chris's father, Lynn Thompson, was a member of the Special Forces' supersecret MACV-SOG program in Vietnam, which operated deep behind enemy lines. His uncle also served as a Green Beret in Vietnam and in Delta Force, the Army's elite counterterrorist unit. A great Thompson family friend, retired MACV-SOG Sergeant Major William D. "Billy" Boggs, always had good input on the subject matter and ice-cold beers in his "team room."

Great insight into the workings and politics of the Northern Alliance was obtained from a special advisor to the United Front Military Forces of Afghanistan, known as "Jack." He also helped us ferret out countless factual errors and the revisionist history set forth by official sources. Since the start of the war, Jack has personally waged his own vicious battle against al-Qaida. He has lived with the Northern Alliance since the war began and is a fierce advocate for American support of these vehemently anti-Taliban and anti–al-Qaida fighters.

Thanks also to Chief Warrant Officer 5 Larry Plesser, the highest-ranking warrant officer in the U.S. Army Special Forces, who accompanied me to TASK FORCE DAGGER's secret base, known as K2, and from there into Afghanistan, where I experienced the greatest Christmas adventure of my life.

I returned to Bagram and we took off for K2. Due to the weather in the north, we landed in Pakistan instead. I woke up at the U.S. Air Force base in the early morning. A friendly communications officer made sure I had e-mail access, and a short time later we landed at a barely functional Bagram airfield north of Kabul, where I checked in with Major Nero's Green Beret B-Team.

I spent Christmas Eve in Kabul, where I met Master Sergeant Diaz and the Triple Nickel (ODA 555). They presented me with a white-and-gold Taliban battle banner that had recently been captured from the enemy. I couldn't leave Kabul without visiting my longtime Green Beret friend Keith Idema. In Kabul's Intercontinental Hotel, where we met that day, there were more guns, from both the Northern Alliance and the Special Forces, than ever before. Needless to say, I was well protected.

From there I flew back to K2, where the most meaningful Christmas dinner of my life was consumed with the men and women of TASK FORCE DAGGER. Like many others at this memorable Christmas feast, I had a spouse at home missing me, my beautiful and patient wife, Mary Olga Moore. In fact, the entire writing team owes her a debt of gratitude for welcoming the invasion of our house, as Green Berets returning from Afghanistan came and went to assist with our work.

As I sat among the Special Forces warriors returning to K2 and leaving from K2 to Afghanistan, I was overwhelmed by their compassion and intensity—there was no doubt they wanted Osama bin Laden and his al-Qaida terrorists, and they wanted them bad. Unlike the Green Berets in Vietnam, they were America's avenging angels in this war, but that didn't make them completely different from the ones who had gone before them.

When I visited Bagram air base, I found out exactly how true that was. I gave out more than one hundred copies of my book *The Green Berets* over the Christmas holidays. As one of the Special Forces soldiers at Bagram airfield north of Kabul prepared to leave the chilly, unheated tent where I had just interviewed him, he thrust an autographed copy of the book into his rucksack. The Green Beret was back at his base camp after spending thirty days in combat. He had thoroughly enjoyed the warm makeshift shower, had been given hot meals, and was issued a few new items of equipment to replace those that were worn out. Outfitted with ammunition, batteries, and the like, he was moving back out to the front-lines the next day along with the rest of his A-Team.

I had just completed taping an hour-long conversation with the sergeant. I punched the button on my microcassette recorder, jotted a note on the tape, and carefully sealed it in a Ziploc bag before dropping it into my kit bag, which was full of similar interview tapes.

I had been a machine gunner on B-17s during World War II, one of the most dangerous jobs in the war. Years later, as a journalist in Vietnam, I had traveled from Green Beret base camp to base camp, living with the men, sharing the fight, the honor, glory, and sorrow. Now I was capturing, via the interviews, the modern-day Special Forces soldier. I found that the uniform had changed from tiger-striped fatigues, and that the fight was in high deserts and mountains instead of jungles and mangrove swamps, yet the men were the same great chaps as their fathers. American soldiers had remained American soldiers, and those of the Greatest Generation would be proud.

As the young man stood to leave, I asked the staff officers in the freezing room, who were using Army cots as chairs, to leave me for a quiet moment alone with the Green Beret and his fellow warrior sergeants.

I knew that the men were obligated to obey General Order Number One, which was a terrible tradition started back in Desert Storm: a ban on drinking alcoholic beverages in defined areas of a war zone. The same thing had been done in the Balkans, and now it had become institutionalized practice, particularly in Muslim nations. It seemed odd to me that those willing to die couldn't be trusted with an occasional "cold one."

I soon found out it was all hogwash. General Order Number One in Afghanistan meant as much as General Order Number Two in Vietnam, and El Salvador, and Somalia, and everywhere else the Green Berets had fought and died. The simple fact was that the Green Berets would fight hard and party hard, no matter where they were, and one hundred General Orders would not get in the way of either endeavor.

Reaching for my cane, I rose to my feet and unscrewed the top of my stout walking stick. Inside was a long, spring-loaded, padded glass flask. I removed the tube and asked the Green Berets if they would like "a touch of the cane."

The sergeants knew this was a moment for those who had been bathed in fire and blood. They realized I knew that getting a drink was virtually impossible, and if there was one thing I wanted to do, it was to have a private drink with these twenty-first-century heroes. We each took a sip of bourbon, which glistened golden in the dim light. When the tube was empty, I recapped it and slid it back into my cane. As I secured the top once again, each of the men gave me a hug.

I also owe a debt of gratitude to Colonel John Mulholland, who put me into the isolation area of K2, where I met so many Special Forces men just back from operations against the Taliban. Also, how can I forget Sergeant First Class Brian Sutton, who worked hard to help me in Afghanistan and to get information cleared by the various commands? And there was Captain Chang, K2's supply officer, who provided the refills for the cane, which had been given to me by Ranger Colonel Bob Morris from Fort Benning, Georgia.

Major Kathleen "Kaz" Culp, the speechwriter for Lieutenant General Doug Brown at U.S. Army Special Operations Command, was my gracious and gorgeous escort while I spent the week in Fort Bragg, North Carolina, for the fiftieth anniversary of the Special Forces.

And again, thanks to Chris Thompson and an "anonymous" Green Beret for their day-and-night rewrites in the final months.

Although the soldiers themselves helped me immensely, it wasn't all a bed of roses when dealing with the staff officers. More often than not, the USASOC PAOs and CENTCOM staff officers stonewalled us as we tried to tell the true story. As I got deeper into the real story, things got more complicated—some of the tapes I made at K2 of the Green Berets telling me their stories disappeared, and others ended up with numerous sections erased after they had been "officially reviewed."

Most of the dialogue comes from the memories of the people there, and on rare occasions we filled in the blanks with the help of third parties or Northern Alliance sources. In some cases, dialogue was derived from tapes or written accounts. It was necessary for us to change a few minor facts and names to protect confidential sources and secret material, and to maintain certain aspects of the Green Berets' OPSEC— operational security.

Thanks also to my publicist, Viktoria RunningWolf, for long nights of proofreading and for helping to keep my writing team together.

In the end, we finally finished the book on September 11, 2002, three months later than planned, not by design or intent, but merely by necessity and with much effort.

Robin Moore
September 11, 2002

Contents

Introduction

*". . . a symbol of excellence, a badge of courage, a mark of
distinction in the fight for freedom."*
> —JOHN F. KENNEDY describing the Green Beret
> on December 10, 1961. This became a
> Presidential Executive Order that would
> forever protect the Green Beret as the official
> headgear of the U.S. Army Special Forces.

It started early the evening of Friday, September 7, 2001, at Fort
Bragg, North Carolina. Major General Geoffrey C. Lambert
was having a party for friends and family at his on-post quarters. I brought with me a carton of books, *The Green Berets,*
to sign for guests. In the front of each book was pasted a seal
that read:

> TO COMMEMORATE THE CHANGE OF COMMAND CEREMONY
> 8 SEPTEMBER 2001
> MAJOR GENERAL GEOFFREY C. LAMBERT BECOMING
> COMMANDING GENERAL OF THE UNITED STATES ARMY
> SPECIAL FORCES,
> FORT BRAGG, NC

"The Ballad of the Green Berets" was played on the stereo
and everyone wanted my autograph inside each book cover.
The next day, Saturday, dawned a beautiful September morn,
and promptly at 10 A.M. we watched as Lambert joined a list

Afghanistan

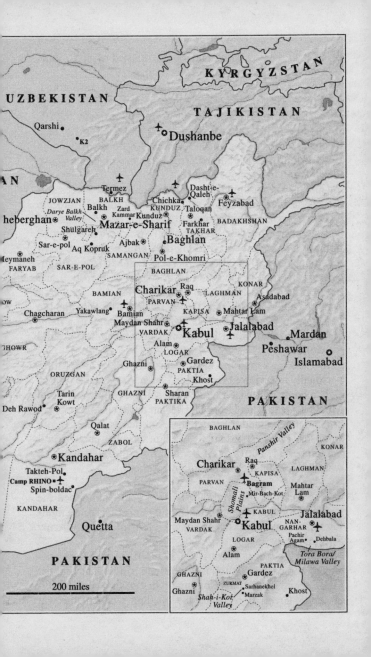

of Special Forces commanders that started with Colonel
Aaron Bank, who first formed the group in 1952.

Ten years later, Lieutenant General William P. Yarborough
made the Green Beret headgear an official part of the Special
Forces uniform when he wore it to meet President John F.
Kennedy, who gave his approval on the spot. To this day, Jack
Kennedy's presidential decree serves to protect the Green
Beret from the conventional army officers who circle above
the elite unit like jealous vultures.

General Yarborough once described a Special Forces soldier as "a man who could be dropped by himself into the
wilderness with nothing but a knife and his own devices, and
emerge sometime later, leading a fully-trained and equipped
fighting force." Just two working days after he became commanding general of Special Forces, Lambert found himself and his men in the type of war for which their unit had
been originally designed. The September 11, 2001, attack on
America at the World Trade Center in New York City and the
Pentagon in Washington, D.C., was the beginning of a *jihad*
on Western civilization by Islamic fundamentalists around
the world.

In 1998, in a mud hut in Afghanistan, ABC's John Miller
personally interviewed Osama bin Laden. As described in *The
Cell,* a book Miller later wrote with Michael Stone and Chris
Mitchell, Osama bin Laden had declared war on America, but
bin Laden remained frustrated that America wouldn't declare
war back. The West just didn't take him seriously enough until
September 11, 2001. As Miller and his colleagues wrote, it
was that day that the sleeping giant awoke.

Awake America did, and the sleeping giant summoned the
strength, the honor, and the skill of the most fearsome fighting unit the world has ever known, the United States Army
Special Forces.

This is the story of how TASK FORCE DAGGER was designed and carried out by Colonel John Mulholland and the
U.S. Special Operations Command. In just six months, Mulholland's Green Berets won the opening phase of the war

against terrorism in Afghanistan, defeating an entrenched army of religious fanatics sworn to die for Allah and Osama bin Laden. By even conservative accounts, the Green Berets sent more than 31,000 Islamic fundamentalists to their after-life. Whether or not Allah and his multitude of virgins ever welcomed them upon arrival is a moot point.

Such a military feat had never before been carried out. The Russians failed to overcome Afghanistan in ten years of dev-astating warfare. The British Imperial military forces had also learned hard lessons in Afghanistan. Of course Russia did not have the Green Berets on the ground. It has now been well acknowledged by reports and military experts that the trained, seasoned, and diplomatic Green Berets, soldiers in their mid-to-late twenties, thirties, and early forties, once left to their own devices, were responsible for wrapping up the first phase of the war in just under six months. The capture of every Taliban-occupied Afghan city beginning with Taloqan, Kunduz, and Mazar-e-Sharif in the north and spreading out across the mountainous country's cities and military targets was indeed the secret work of the Special Forces. Most peo-ple think it took 5,000 to 40,000 U.S. troops to free Kabul. They are vastly mistaken—fewer than 100 American soldiers were on the ground when Kabul fell. Not since Kublai Khan's Mangudai and the 300 Spartans had so few men fought so many.

The Green Berets were back in the business of destroying America's enemies, just as they had done in Vietnam, Central America, and Desert Storm. And business was good . . .

PROLOGUE:

The War on Terror

*"Muslims must prepare all possible might to repel the enemy:
military, economically, through missionary activity and all
other areas . . . to unite our ranks so that we can repel the
greater Kufr [the unbeliever, the United States]."*
—OSAMA BIN LADEN in *Nida 'ul Islam*, 1996

WORLD TRADE CENTER, 1993
MOGADISHU, SOMALIA, 1993
KHOBAR TOWERS, 1996
AMERICAN EMBASSY, KENYA, 1998
AMERICAN EMBASSY, TANZANIA, 1998
USS *COLE*, 2000
WORLD TRADE CENTER, 2001
PENTAGON, 2001

*"Apocalyptic terrorists, no matter their rhetoric, seek your de-
struction and must be killed to the last man. The apt metaphor
is cancer: you cannot hope for success if you only cut out part
of the tumor. . . . For a superpower to think small, which has
been our habit across the last decade, at least, is self-defeating
folly. Our responses to terrorist acts should make the world
gasp."*

—RALPH PETERS in *When Devils Walk the Earth*

September 11, 2001
Fort Campbell, Kentucky

John Bolduc called his wife Sherry at 0800 hours.

"Well, I finally did it, my retirement was accepted."

"Are you sad?" Sherry asked.

"Just a little. Look, I've done my job for twenty years, and I feel proud about that. But I'm gonna miss the guys." John Bolduc was talking about his teammates in the 5th Special Forces Group (Airborne).

"Just think about that house we always wanted to build, and Holly." Sherry Bolduc was referring to their daughter.

"Yeah, I've been running hard for a long time, I guess it's time to kick back for awhile and see what the real world is like. I'll see you tonight."

"Love you, John."

"Me too, Sherry."

Master Sergeant John Bolduc had been a Ranger, and then a Ranger instructor, and finally, a Green Beret. As a team sergeant in 5th Special Forces Group, Bolduc was loved by his men, and his command. He was also loved by Sherry and Holly, and they were quietly thrilled that the long months of deployments, dangerous missions, and secret operations were finally over.

September 11, 2001
Almaty, Kazakhstan

A handful of Green Berets from the 5th Special Forces Group had just spent their summer training an airborne unit of the Kazakhstani Army, and they were almost halfway into their final month as advisors in the former Soviet republic.

The president of Kazakhstan was always proud to say that Mary Hemingway, the wife of the famous American writer, once called its capital city, Almaty, "the most beautiful city in the world." The snow-covered peaks of the Alatau Mountains serve as Almaty's backdrop, with the highest, Khan Tengri, reaching over twenty thousand feet into the heavens. Gardens of apricot and other fruit trees surround the city, which has an Alpine flair.

A pizza parlor in the center of Almaty had been the nightly haunt for the Green Berets, who would socialize over slices of pie after long days spent with the paratroopers of Kazakhstan's 34th Airborne Brigade. One of the special operators, Sergeant First Class Mike McElhiney, answered the cell phone that began vibrating on his hip. McElhiney was a towering, dark-haired Green Beret who looked as much like an All-American quarterback as a hardened commando. As he listened, his steel-square jaw lost its smile, and he dropped his slice of pepperoni back onto his plate. After a few moments, McElhiney closed the flip phone and called out to the restaurant's owner: "Holy shit! Turn the television to the BBC!"

The gruff ex-Soviet pizza maker quickly flipped through the stations.

"Mike, what's going on?" one of the other Green Berets seated at the table questioned.

"Dan Petithory just told me that an aircraft has just crashed into the World Trade Center." Petithory was their in-country liaison and logistics (L&L) man at the U.S. embassy in Almaty.

As the Green Berets watched the screen in disbelief, they saw the second plane hit the Twin Towers. After several reruns of the destruction of the world's foremost cityscape, they began to discuss who could be responsible for such an atrocity. All of the Green Berets had the same opinion: Osama bin Laden.

McElhiney's phone rang again, and this time it was Green Beret headquarters at Fort Campbell, Kentucky.

"Right, right, roger that!" McElhiney hung up the phone.

"Fucking A, guys, we're going to war."

September 11, 2001
Los Angeles, California

His wife rolled over and gently woke him up. They had just started making love when the phone rang. It was 0600 local time, 9 A.M. on the East Coast.

TIGER 02—northern Afghanistan

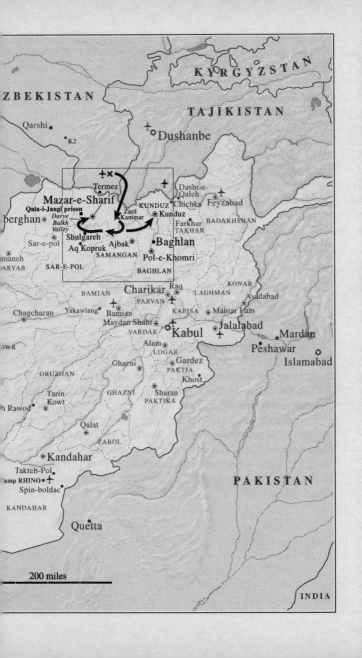

"Turn on your TV, they just blew up the World Trade Center," the voice at the other end announced.

"Fuck you, it's six A.M.," Idema said as he slammed the phone onto its receiver. The phone rang again, the same announcement. "This isn't funny, call me later," Idema said as he hung the phone up again.

It was Todd Friedman, an attorney and friend. After the fourth call, he turned on the TV just in time to see the second plane hit the World Trade Center.

"We're going to war. I have to get back to Bragg ASAP," he calmly exclaimed to his wife as he watched the attacks in awe.

September 11, 2001
Stirling Lines
Herefordshire, England

"Blimey, the fucking A-rabs have just attacked America," the troop commander exclaimed as rushed into the Regimental Headquarters and headed for the television, "Quick, put on BBC."

"Put the lads on full alert, bring them all in, notify the Territorials all three Regiments are going to full alert. I want options, plans, backgrounds, and possible targets in six hours, get the MI-6 liaison in here immediately," the Regimental Commander ordered.

"I've already got a FLASH message from our lads at Delta, and they're saying the entire U.S. Special Ops Command has gone to immediate full alert." The troop commander was referring to the two SAS operators that they kept at Fort Bragg at all times, working as liaisons with the American's Delta Force.

CHAPTER 1

The Tiger
Roars

"On my orders, the United States military has begun strikes against al-Qaida terrorist training camps and military installations of the Taliban regime in Afghanistan. These carefully targeted actions are designed to disrupt the use of Afghanistan as a terrorist base of operations and to attack the military capability of the Taliban regime."

—PRESIDENT GEORGE W. BUSH,
address to the nation, October 7, 2001

Darye Suf Valley, northern Afghanistan
November 5, 2001
Late morning

It was dawn when the two dark matte-green Special Operations MH-47 Chinook helicopters landed on the alien moonscape of the Darye Suf Valley floor in northern Afghanistan. One dropped off half of the twelve-man A-Team that would be known as TIGER 02. The other held the quick-reaction force (QRF) that would be needed if the insertion turned out to be hot.

Flaring out above the desert sands, the long, fat chopper reduced the power to its rear rotor blades and brought its nose slightly up. Thick, coarse sand blacked out the windshield's view as the Green Berets on board checked the magazines on their weapons, made sure a round was chambered, and took off their safeties. The first two ran off the tailgate and took up security positions in the sand as the others threw off their rucksacks and bags of equipment. A fine-tuned killing machine had just been inserted into northern Afghanistan, and the prey would be Osama bin Laden and his terrorists.

Once the twelve Green Berets touched down, Captain Mark Nutsch, the team leader, had his team sergeant, Paul Evans, split the A-Team in half once again. Six of the twelve-man team separated into two three-man close air support teams. Close air support, also known as CAS, or "calling air strikes," would be one of the key components in fewer than four hundred Green Berets winning the war in Afghanistan in just under six months. In fact, in the first ninety days of the war, there were fewer than 120 Green Berets on the ground, augmented by about forty SAS commandos, fighting a Taliban and al-Qaida (AQ) army composed of tens of thousands of hardened "holy warriors."

Nutsch and Evans had been assigned in early October to General Abdul Rashid Dostum, the Northern Alliance warlord commanding the troops who would bear the brunt of the fighting. The young captain and the tough master sergeant were preparing to advise and assist Dostum in taking back the key northern city of Mazar-e-Sharif before Christmas, when the Afghan winter would turn its worst. The Taliban forces were arrayed against the Northern Alliance in vastly superior numbers, and they held defensive posts all along Dostum's intended route of attack.

General Dostum was a big man, over six feet tall, and ethnically, he was Uzbek. He had been trained by the Soviet Army to fight against the Afghans, but defected after becoming disenchanted with the Soviets' methods. Dostum spoke almost no Arabic, but communicated in a smattering of Dari, Russian, and Uzbek. He was viewed by his enemies as a brutal military commander, with an intense hatred of Islamic fundamentalists that was documented back to the 1980s, before the Taliban's rise to power in Afghanistan. With his crew-cut graying hair, barrel chest, and imposing presence, Dostum was a gregarious commander who had changed sides many times.

As the press spent their time hypothesizing about America's tactics, the Green Berets laughed at the notion that the war would take a hiatus during the terrible Afghan winter and, of course, Ramadan, the Muslim month-long period of fasting, contemplation, and prayer. So did their ultimate commander, President George W. Bush.

Two Air Force personnel were assigned to each of the Special Forces' twelve-man A-Teams, after Green Berets were already on the ground. The Air Force combat controllers were experts at calling in air strikes and performing air traffic control functions. But, according to the Green Berets, the greatest benefit of the additional two Air Force personnel was that they brought two extra satellite radios with them. This allowed Evans and the other team sergeants to break their teams into four three-man elements during close air support missions. They could form a half-moon shape with their teams, effectively controlling and overlapping their fire support, drastically improving the already devastating firepower they called in.

Master Sergeant Evans picked one of the Air Force CAS specialists for his three-man CAS team, so he could see firsthand what all the fuss was about. He never had a problem calling in CAS, and there had never been a case of a Green Beret sergeant calling in friendly fire on his own team. The only such cases they had heard about had involved officers, who were not as adept at such tasks. Evans, Staff Sergeant Mike Elmore, and the Air Force sergeant were dressed in the local garb worn by the Northern Alliance. They wore long checkered scarves and round brownish-tan or gray wool *pakols,* also known as "Massoud" caps, named after Ahmad Shah Massoud, the assassinated legend and former leader of the Northern Alliance. Their attire allowed the Green Berets to blend in with the locals from a distance. The three men also all sported beards they had started growing in mid-September back in the States, when they were first alerted for their deployment to Afghanistan.

The three special operators crouched behind a mound of dirt in an old bomb crater and set up their equipment. The first piece was a large, olive-green, rubberized spotting scope, and the second piece resembled something akin to a giant pair of olive drab binoculars mounted on a small tripod, with a trigger attached to a coiled length of cable. It was called a SOFLAM. SOFLAM (Special Operation Forces' Laser Marker) is special-ops lingo for a laser designator, which shoots out a laser beam to mark the enemy target so that a laser-guided bomb can strike it. With a range of 200 to 10,000 meters, the twelve-pound SOFLAM, using an integrated Global Positioning System would be used to mark and designate terrorist targets for the aircraft circling above.

"Scanning for targets," announced Air Force Staff Sergeant Matt Leinhard over his satellite radio. Evans stared through the lens of the spotting scope, scanning from left to right across the face of the barren, rocky ridgelines that lay ahead. Evans abruptly stopped his scan. "I've got eyes on a target!" he exclaimed.

Staff Sergeant Elmore, the team's weapons sergeant, began punching data into the Panasonic "Toughbook" laptop computer lying open in front of him. All of their information would be useful with the reports they would be delivering later to TASK FORCE DAGGER headquarters.

"Good to go! SOFLAM ready," the towering six-foot-plus Elmore replied.

The Taliban and al-Qaida forces would never quite understand the concept of smart bombs or the lasers that targeted them, and in the weeks ahead, a rumor began wildly circulating among them that the Special Forces possessed a "Death Ray" that would destroy anything they aimed it at. The Death Ray was about to unleash a healthy dose of American vengeance.

Sergeant Elmore aimed the laser marker at the front of a Taliban bunker built into the face of the hillside half a kilometer away. Inside the firing ports of the enemy bunker he could see the muzzle flashes of automatic weapons. Bul-

lets cracked overhead as the Berets began taking enemy
fire. Sergeant Leinhard picked up the satellite radio and began speaking into it. The snapping of automatic rifle fire
raked the shelter just above their heads and made it difficult to hear. The three special operators ducked down behind the berm as the enemy bullets showered dirt onto their
backs.

"We have two F/A-18s on deck," Sergeant Leinhard announced, his ear pressed to the LST-5 satellite radio.

"Target is marked," Sergeant Elmore replied, squeezing
the trigger that shot the invisible, infrared laser beam into
the front opening of the enemy bunker.

A pair of Navy F/A-18 fighters streaked across the sky
twenty thousand feet in the air above the scene, so high they
were virtually invisible to the naked eye. One of the planes
banked sharply and swooped down, letting loose a thousand-
pound laser-guided bomb. As the smart bomb whistled through
the air, its internal computer homed in on the laser signature. The bomb's tail fins directed it on its collision course
with the enemy bunker. The three special operators braced
themselves, keeping their mouths open so the force of the
blast wouldn't rupture their eardrums.

About half a minute passed, then BOOM!

The earth shook as the bomb detonated directly over the
top of the bunker, throwing a giant brown cloud of dirt, fire,
and black smoke high into the sky. Master Sergeant Evans
waited for the aftershock to pass by them and then peered
out through the scope. In place of the bunker was a huge,
smoking crater. He could see the body parts of slain Taliban
soldiers scattered around it.

"Target destroyed!" Evans shouted to his partners as he
peered through the spotting scope, a wide grin on his stub-
bly face.

For a long moment there was silence once again, then
the entire hillside erupted into a fierce volley of fire. Now,
through the spotting scope, Evans could see the muzzle flash

of machine-gun fire coming from another bunker on the Taliban-controlled hillside.

"I've got eyes on another bunker!" Evans cried out, tapping his partner's shoulder and pointing toward it.

Something streaking through the air caught their attention. It looked like the Taliban were shooting Roman candles into the sky above their heads. The smoke trails from the objects began to fall toward the earth in front of the Americans' position.

"RPGs!" Elmore exclaimed. The Taliban were shooting rocket-propelled grenades toward them, but instead of aiming them directly at the Americans' position, they were lobbing them skyward like mortar rounds, hoping to land one behind the mound of dirt in the crater that was protecting the American advisors to the Northern Alliance.

The pair of Green Berets manning the spotting scope and the laser marker slid backward on their bellies, seeking as much overhead cover as they could find. The RPGs exploded on the ground in front of their position, showering them with rocks and rubble, and filling the air with black smoke and the smell of cordite. Leinhard was crouched nearby, his hands clamped over his radio headphones. They glanced behind them, down the ridgeline to their rear, to see if any of the rocket-propelled grenades had flown that far.

About a hundred men crouched below them, hidden among the rough boulders. From a distance, they looked the same as the three special operators, but they were in fact Northern Alliance freedom fighters, called *mujahadeen,* most of them clutching a variety of old AK-47 assault rifles. They looked up at the two Green Berets and their Air Force sergeant with a mixture of fear and nervousness.

"It looks like these guys want to leave," Elmore said to his partners, chuckling. One of the crouching Northern Alliance militiamen yelled up to them in Dari, the native dialect, barely distinguishable over the roar of enemy fire and the thuds of detonating grenades.

"The *muj* want to get out before the Taliban can launch a counterattack," Leinhard shouted over the gunfire. The *muj*

were scared, but not of the Taliban. General Dostum had
warned his soldiers that he would personally kill every one
of them and their families if an American were so much as
superficially wounded.

"Tell them we're going to hold tight, we've got the high
ground," Evans responded.

Ignoring the danger, the three soldiers low-crawled up to
the top of the berm yet again. The hailstorm of gunfire continued, peppering the ground in front of them and cracking
through the air overhead.

The glint of metal caught the three soldiers' eyes as they
saw something large rolling out from behind a hidden position on the Taliban-held ridgeline. For a second they thought
it was a Russian T-55 tank, but in the place of a main gun
there were four smaller barrels. It was a ZSU-23-4, a Russian antiaircraft gun left over from the Soviet invasion of
Afghanistan. Through the spotting scope, Evans could see
the operator's head sticking up out of the turret, and as the
enemy soldier swung the turret toward them, the four 23mm
barrels bristling out of the turret's center began flashing
rapidly, throwing out clouds of smoke.

"I've got two more F/A-18s on deck!" Leinhard shouted.

By this time, the ZSU, or "Zeus," as the Afghans call it,
began throwing a volley of rounds in their direction. To them
it sounded like the chugging of a steam locomotive, and the
rounds blasted rocks and dirt into the air all around them.

Sergeant Elmore aimed the laser marker at the ZSU's turret. At the same time, the Zeus began rolling backward toward
cover. Elmore held the laser beam steady on the front of the
berm the antiaircraft vehicle now hid behind. The only thing
that gave away its position was the black puffs of diesel
smoke that rose from behind the berm.

BOOM! Another thousand-pound bomb exploded, throwing a mushroom cloud of dust and thick black smoke high
into the sky.

"I can't tell, but I think we neutralized the ZSU," Sergeant
Leinhard called out on his radio.

The 23mm cannon fire from the Zeus had just been

eliminated, but the Taliban rifle and RPG fire were increasing. It was a constant barrage, and down the hill on the friendly side, the Northern Alliance soldiers began to grow even more nervous and weary.

"Tell them if they can hang on another ten minutes, I've got a B-52 on the way!" Leinhard shouted to his partners over the roar of the battle as he held his ear to the radio headset.

"Hoo-ah!" shouted Sergeant Elmore, unable to contain his excitement, and then he relayed the message to the cowering *muj* hunkered down behind them.

"It better be quick," Sergeant Evans replied, "because we've got enemy troops in the open out here!"

The Green Berets were carrying the M-4, a special version of the M-16 assault rifle, shortened, with a collapsible stock and outfitted with a scope, laser designator, and an improved 5.56mm boat-tailed 70-grain bullet. It was a twenty-first-century version of the old XM177E2 the SOG (Studies and Observation Group) recon teams had carried in Vietnam.

A stream of charging Taliban began running down the enemy hillside toward them. The two Green Berets returned fire, picking off Taliban fighters, who tumbled down the slope like rag dolls after being hit by the special operators' bullets. Ten minutes seemed to stretch into an eternity as the wave of charging Taliban grew closer. The terrorists were closing the gap, now running up the front of the friendly hillside, less than two football fields away from the Americans' position.

The Green Berets looked to their rear, and saw the *muj* behind them starting to beat a hasty retreat back toward the east, to their original position. The Northern Alliance commander waved for the Americans to follow and grabbed some of the Green Berets' equipment, throwing it on his horse and galloping away. It appeared now as though the *muj* were scared of both Dostum and the Taliban, and with good reason.

At that instant, the B-52 bomber checked in, and Evans

smiled skyward and gave a thumbs-up. He mouthed the phrase "Bombs away!" and dove for cover. The two other special operators hastily followed his example.

The earlier set of explosions was puny compared with the devastation that was unleashed as the rolling thunder of twelve 500-pound bombs carpeted the hillside with a cascade of brilliant fireballs. The shock wave bounced the three special operators up off the ground, and covered them in dust and debris. For the first time in what seemed like forever, the enemy fire began to subside. As the dust settled, they scrambled back up the berm at the crater's edge to assess what had happened.

Having assumed the banzai charge of the frenzied Taliban would be stopped completely by the B-52 strike, they were amazed to see a large number of enemy soldiers still advancing up the hill. They were so close now the Americans could see their faces: some Arab, some Chechen, some Pakistani, but all fighting under the banner of Osama bin Laden's Taliban and al-Qaida network.

The close air support team emptied the thirty round magazines in their M-4s before deciding to follow their partisans down the hill to the east. Glancing backward as they ran, they saw the first of the Taliban and al-Qaida fighters were already cresting the hill, standing on the position the Americans had just abandoned. Elmore, Evans, and Leinhard ducked behind a boulder, and Leinhard got on the radio once again. A Navy F-14 Tomcat checked in with the team, and the Air Force sergeant quickly explained the situation to the pilot.

"We're about to be fucking overrun. . . . I need ordnance quick!" Leinhard shouted into the radio.

The F-14 pilot responded by saying he could see plenty of enemy troops out in the open, advancing on their position. He could also see several trucks, and tracked enemy vehicles coming out of hiding in covered positions, starting to roll down the ridgeline toward them. The pilot announced to the team that he would do a "gun run" for them. A gun run is a low sweep over the enemy, in which the fighter strafes the enemy with cannons, rockets, machine guns, and everything else it can turn loose, all at once.

The Tomcat swooped down out of the sky in a roar, destroying everything in sight with a volley of automatic cannon fire. After three more high-speed passes from the F-14, every single one of the enemy vehicles was reduced to a smoking hulk of twisted metal.

With the Taliban offensive momentarily halted, the three special operators took the opportunity to run down the hill and into the riverbed, taking temporary shelter behind a rocky outcropping, where the CAS team took up a defensive position and caught their breath for a minute. Sergeant Elmore glanced at his watch. It was 1400 hours (2 P.M.) already. The sun was high in the sky, and the shade of the outcropping felt good.

A short whistle drew their attention to the rocks on their left. A Northern Alliance soldier was hiding behind an adjacent boulder, holding the tethers to three Afghan horses. He waved the trio over and they jumped on the horses, following the stay-behind *muj* down a ravine and up an incline toward a ridgeline adjacent to the one that had just been overrun by the Taliban. The two Green Berets and their Air Force sergeant smiled at him and then went back to business. They again set up their spotting scope and laser marker, staring out at their previous and hastily abandoned observation post (OP). The place they had just evacuated was now swarming with Taliban fighters.

Sergeant Elmore called out to his partners, "Holy shit, we were just on that ridgeline. We must still have the GPS coordinates of where we just were on the computer." Evans punched a few buttons on the GPS and cried out triumphantly, "Got it!"

Matt Leinhard opened a channel on his radio and was informed that the B-52 Stratofortress was still in the area. The B-52's navigator asked Elmore to be sure that they were no longer in or near the coordinates. "We wouldn't want to drop an egg on where you happen to be standing right now," the navigator explained.

Leinhard cringed at the concept and asked if they had any satellite-guided bombs on board.

"Roger that," the bombardier called back over the headset.

Sergeant Evans smiled again, and repeated the coordinates of the ridgeline position from which they had been surveying the enemy until they had to retreat.

The B-52 bombardier radioed to the team over their radio that he was on station and called out, "Bombs away!"

As they waited for the necessary two minutes it took the bomb to impact, they watched the Taliban and for the first time realized just how many there were, scurrying around like ants trying to dig bodies of their fallen comrades out of the rubble with their rifle butts.

The three special operators watched as the two-thousand-pound satellite-guided bomb detonated exactly fifty feet over the heads of the Taliban.

"Holy shit! Un-fucking-believable!" one of the Americans screamed. He couldn't believe his eyes; it was amazing. They witnessed a tremendous explosion in the air and the bodies of maybe a hundred Taliban and AQ troops drawn from the ground upward, arms and legs kicking for a fraction of a second before disappearing into a pink haze without a trace of solid matter left of their bodies or clothing. America's enemies had literally been obliterated.

That single bomb killed everybody on the hill, as well as the Taliban fighters behind it. Not one enemy soldier was left alive. Most of the bodies were completely vaporized by the intensity of the explosion.

The Northern Alliance soldiers stormed back up over the ridgeline, retaking the smoky, ruined hilltop and cheering in victory. With only three special ops personnel, they had just won their first key battle over the Taliban without sustaining any major casualties. They had never seen anything like it. The *muj* congregated around the three Americans, patting their backs and praising them.

The offensive push to the city of Mazar-e-Sharif was just two days northwest through the Darye Suf Valley. As the two Green Berets rode their wiry little Afghan horses over the rocky, uneven terrain, they sang a song together, a song that both of them knew by heart. Even Leinhard, the Air Force sergeant from the Special Tactics Squadron, knew it. They often sang this during parties and reunions, but no matter how many times they sang it, it always made them feel proud of their chosen profession.

> Fighting soldiers from the sky,
>   Fearless men who jump and die.
> Men who mean just what they say,
>   The brave men of the Green Beret.
>
> Trained to live off nature's land,
>   Trained in combat, hand-to-hand.
> Men who fight by night and day,
>   Courage take from the Green Beret.
>
> Silver wings upon their chests,
>   These are men, America's best.
> One hundred men we'll test today,
>   But only three win the Green Beret.
>
> Back at home a young wife waits,
>   Her Green Beret has met his fate.
> He has died for those oppressed,
>   Leaving her this last request:
>
> Put silver wings on my son's chest,
>   Make him one of America's best,
> He'll be a man they'll test one day—
>   **Have him win the Green Beret!**

Men Who Mean Just What They Say

Those lines and the music that accompanied them, written by me and Sergeant Barry Sadler early in the Vietnam War days, inspired an entire generation of patriotic young Americans from pre–high school age onward to win the Green Beret. Even today, thirty-six years later, men both young and middle-aged tell how they read the book, saw the movie, heard the song, and became Green Berets—"which changed my life forever—for the better," they always add.

As TIGER 02/A-Team 595 was galloping across the desert northwest of Mazar-e-Sharif singing "The Ballad of the Green Berets," the same inspiring tune was guiding another Green Beret into the eye of the storm just one hundred miles away.

He had already been in Afghanistan for weeks, but in 1968, he was a youngster in upstate New York who read *The Green Berets*, saw John Wayne in the 1968 movie, and played the ballad on his Fender electric guitar. He was twelve years old then. By the time he graduated from high school he had been accepted to three colleges but instead joined the Army shortly after his seventeenth birthday with an enlistment option to try out for Special Forces. The Vietnam War was winding down, and he knew if anyone would stay there, it would be the Green Berets. After basic training and jump school, young "Jack" was introduced to the incredible rigors of the grueling Q course, the Special Forces Qualification Course. Colonel Charles (Chargin' Charlie) Beckwith addressed more than one thousand recruits in 1975, telling them to look around and realize that none of the men beside them would graduate; in fact, he expected to graduate only sixteen of the scores of men standing before him that day.

One of the first tests was a swimming trial in Fort Bragg's Brian L. Buker pool, named for a Special Forces sergeant who won the Medal of Honor in Vietnam in 1970. Each man was given a forty-pound pack and a rifle, and told to swim the length of the pool and back in his fatigues and boots. The contestants had to jump off the diving board and struggle to make the two lengths. Jack dived in with the pack on his back and didn't come up, swimming underwater with a powerful breaststroke to the end of the pool. And, as the onlookers watched, expecting him to surface, he pushed off the bulkhead without coming up for air and continued to swim underwater back to the end of the pool where he had started. Slamming into the concrete wall headfirst, he struggled to the surface and on the verge of unconsciousness, he felt a strong arm haul him, breathless, out of the pool. It was none other than the colonel, Chargin' Charlie, silently congratulating this promising young recruit with an expression of elation at the feat performed by one of his charges.

"Boy, where'd you learn to swim like that?" Colonel Beckwith growled with his southern-Texas drawl.

"My dad's backyard," the skinny private responded.

"You're in the program, son!" Beckwith turned to the first sergeant. "Sign this man into the Q course."

"But sir," the first sergeant protested, "he's just turned eighteen. The recruiters signed him into the Army with a Special Forces option, but he can't attend the course until he meets the age limit."

"Goddammit, Sergeant!" Beckwith thundered. "This man is in!"

Some twenty-plus weeks later, Jack was one of the sixteen men, out of the twelve hundred who started the course, to win their berets, presented to them by the legendary colonel.

After graduating Phase I, and being awarded the coveted Green Beret, Jack had many more courses and schools to attend. Jack learned everything the top instructors in Special Forces had to teach. Mike Echanis, the infamous hand-to-hand-combat specialist, trained the five-foot-nine fighting man day and night. Echanis congratulated his newly adept Hwa-Rang-Do warrior into the most elite and closed society of Green Berets after another three months of training, again thanks to Jack's mentor, Beckwith. Beckwith also arranged for the young special-warfare student to receive cross-training in other areas before being assigned to regular Special Forces duties. By 1979, Jack was working the British Special Air Service regiments, first training them at Fort Devens, Massachussetts, in Special Forces operations, then learning anti-terrorism and SAS tactics from the lads in England.

Jack would become an extremely controversial figure in Special Forces. A quarter of a century later, CBS' Dan Rather would voice his own opinion of Jack when he met him in Afghanistan, saying he was "politically incorrect, abrasive, unconventional, and unquestionably heroic." Jack had missed Vietnam by the time his Special Forces training ended, but he wasn't about to miss Afghanistan and a crack at bin Laden, even if he was officially out of the Army.

On September 12, he told his friends he was going to war and two weeks later he was packing to leave for Afghanistan—like the rest of the Green Berets, he meant just what he said.

CHAPTER 2

Striking at the Heart of Evil

"I firmly believe that this is the most important tasking the U.S. military has been handed since the Second World War. . . . They passed the weapons-of-mass-destruction barrier on September 11 for sure, at least in my mind, and it's global in scale, and it's going to be a tough fight."
— GENERAL RICHARD MYERS,
chairman of the Joint Chiefs of Staff,
Department of Defense briefing, October 18, 2001

September 2001
Washington, D.C.

George W. Bush had it right and his administration followed through: "Give us bin Laden and we will not trouble you further." That was his simple ultimatum presented to the Taliban.

Fortunately for Afghanistan and the free world, the Taliban fundamentalist extremists never heard of the old Mafia saying, "Make them an offer they can't refuse."

Miller's Finest Hour

September 2001
Tampa, Florida

Before the end of the day on September 11, 2001, a meeting was already taking place in Tampa, at the headquarters of SOCOM (Special Operations Command) and CENTCOM

(Central Command). Every officer in attendance at this emergency meeting prayed to God that the Taliban would refuse the United States' offer to turn over Osama bin Laden for trial. Dozens of stone-faced career officers, known as the "silent professionals," were planning the total annihilation of the Taliban and bin Laden's AQ terrorists.

Al-Qaida was mostly composed of fanatical young Pakistanis, Chechens, Arabs, and Egyptians who were for the most part despised by the native Afghans. Al-Qaida and the Taliban represented a foreign influence that the Afghans wanted no part of. The Afghans hated foreign invaders, and the penalty for enemy soldiers captured by the Northern Alliance, if they were not of Afghan descent, would be a slow, miserable death.

The key to taking down the Taliban, especially at the beginning of the hostilities, was the Northern Alliance's "resistance potential." Ripe for combat—they had already been fighting the Taliban for many years—the Northern Alliance was a loose organization of Afghan warlords. Despite the lack of any great degree of external sponsorship or support, they still held on to more than 10 percent of Afghanistan's landmass. They were Tajiks, Uzbeks, Hazaras, and other Dari-speaking minorities that fought against their Pashto-speaking "brothers" from southern Afghanistan as well as the hated foreign AQ. In many ways they were similar to the Montagnards of Vietnam, in that they were fiercely independent, courageous, and historical underdogs.

In Vietnam, the enemy was the VC, or Viet Cong. They were crafty, devious, and brutal. In Afghanistan, it was the AQ who took the inhuman side of the VC and intensified it a hundredfold.

Lieutenant Colonel Dave Miller of the U.S. Special Operations Command examined the resistance potential of the Northern Alliance and concluded that the Taliban government might be brought to its knees if several sequential actions could be accomplished. Miller knew what had to be done, and he explained it to those who didn't.

First, dialogue and connections had to be established with what special ops referred to as the "host nation" resistance.

Second, personal relationships and trust between the leaders of the resistance and Special Forces teams had to be developed.

Third, the resources to fight had to be delivered in bulk to the resisters, many holed up behind enemy lines, to allow for the creation of an adequate force to conduct maneuver warfare against the Taliban.

Fourth, U.S. air power would have to be available in support of the Special Forces advisors.

And finally, Special Forces would need Defense Secretary Donald Rumsfeld's persistent backing, since guerrilla or unconventional warfare (UW) was always speculative, reliant on delicate personal relationships among the guerrillas and the rapport between the guerrillas and their Green Beret advisors.

The alternatives to using guerrilla warfare to destroy the Taliban regime were not necessarily attractive. The Afghans had soundly trounced the Soviets by fighting a protracted and particularly vicious partisan war for over a decade. The Soviets suffered countless casualties in the frustrating effort to defeat the warlords. The Afghan tribes simply hated foreigners. In fact, no one, including the British, had ever successfully occupied the savage land.

The use of guerrilla warfare/unconventional warfare as an indirect approach to unseat the Taliban would therefore be the key to success. The Green Berets, men who took naturally to being America's "stone-cold killers" when combating the enemy, were the only ones who could do this.

Forty years before, General William P. Yarborough had trained every officer and enlisted man in Special Forces to become experts at unconventional warfare during exhaustive exercises in Florida jungles; in the Uwharrie National Forest, spreading north and west near Fort Bragg, North Carolina; and in Panama. Urban warfare training was conducted in mock cities in the mountains of Pennsylvania and upstate New York, all the way to Washington State, Texas, and the Philippines.

Miller explained how the Special Forces A-Team was an incredible composite of military skills. Commanded by a Special Forces–qualified captain, with a warrant officer as the executive officer and second in command, it is embedded with highly trained and gifted noncommissioned officers, more commonly known as sergeants. The backbone of the team is two intelligence sergeants, two weapons sergeants, two medical specialists, two demolition sergeants, and two communication specialists—each of them cross-trained in at least one other skill to ensure a mission can continue in spite of combat casualties.

Once dropped in behind enemy lines, Green Berets can survive and fight indefinitely. They are parachute qualified and experts in water operations, desert warfare, mountain warfare, espionage, clandestine operations, Morse code, hand-to-hand combat, and a myriad of other skills. They can ride horses, repair vehicles, pick locks, set up drop zones and landing zones, interrogate prisoners, and change their identities. They can "lock out" of nuclear submarines while submerged and infiltrate beaches with underwater operations gear, skydive into a foreign country from forty thousand feet, and infiltrate enemy territory by plane, helicopter, boat, or foot. Some of them can even drive Soviet tanks, fly airplanes, and repair computers. Everyone on a twelve-man A-Team is fluent in the tongues spoken in their area of operations. Some of them speak more than two languages.

There is no fighting unit in the world like the U.S. Army Special Forces A-Team. If enemy attrition is your goal, i.e., killing the bad guys, then Special Forces are the men for the job. The U.S. Army Special Forces are able to field the most completely cross-trained fighting men and diplomats of any military unit in the history of warfare. They could have won the war in Vietnam had they been permitted to do so by the successors of President John F. Kennedy. Even then–Secretary of Defense Robert McNamara, in his mea culpa written thirty years after the fact, admitted that we should either have gracefully withdrawn or gone ahead and won the war in Vietnam using Special Forces in their guerrilla capacity rather than their counterinsurgency capability. Fighting a war of attrition until we were forced to abandon our allies in the rout at the U.S. embassy in Saigon was obviously fruitless.

The core of special operators in the U.S. Army, whose motto is *De Oppresso Liber* ("Free the Oppressed"), could win the opening phase of this war of liberation against the forces of the Taliban with not only their unconventional warfare skills, but with the unique advantage of twenty-first-century smart weapons, which had been greatly improved since they were first fielded on a large scale in the Gulf War. The information age had also brought forth unprecedented visibility of the battlefield and unique precision weaponry. Special Forces, with their chameleonlike ability to be everywhere and nowhere at once, could now be the nation's best "deep targeteers." Their specialty would be finding and flushing out targets that would increasingly have to hide from the United States' big eyes in the sky.

Miller's prebriefings had discussed changing Special Forces from one principal vector, that of unconventional warfare, to two vectors: unconventional warfare and the "terminal guidance of precision ordnance" to destroy deep, difficult, and obscure targets on the battlefield. Another proposal included permanently changing the size of the revered A-Team to fourteen men instead of the traditional twelve, a mix of intelligence, weapons, engineer, medical, and communications experts. This meant adding two Air Force sergeants, one a targeteer/observer, and a senior targeteer/observer. The men would not just be forward observers; they would also be information experts, nominators of targets for psychological attack, and coordinators of humanitarian relief by way of food and medical supplies. The two new Air Force men would eliminate the problem of unproven and unknown fire-support personnel from the USAF joining the Special Forces A-Teams at the last minute prior to combat operations. It was difficult to remain invisible when teams were forced to accept attachments that didn't know the culture, the language, or the team's well-rehearsed and synchronized actions for how to react in combat.

The new, fourteen-man teams were given the name Interim Special Forces Group. Reception to the new idea by Special Forces Command was not good at first. Six weeks after the Tampa meeting, in Afghanistan, the reception by the Taliban of Special Forces teams directing close air support was even worse. The Taliban and al-Qaida would be destroyed by the synergistic effects of old-fashioned unconventional warfare combined with the latest state-of-the-art, precision fire support.

But in the end, the Interim Special Forces Group was not the answer. Like the Navy SEALs, the Air Force wanted to be on the ground, even if it wasn't their forte. No one wanted the Green Berets to seize all the glory, and there were still conventional military officers that hated them as much as the old Vietnam-era generals. In spite of the fact that the Taliban and AQ would be destroyed with the help of CAS, by the time the battles were over, the Green Beret sergeants would prove they needed no one on the ground with them— not the combat controllers, not the Navy SEALs, and not the Marines. The Green Berets were just fine doing the killing all by themselves.

By the end of the day, when it was all hashed out, Miller had won his chance to map the future of SF. The briefing room at CENTCOM in Tampa opened its doors to the first joint command meeting after the attacks of September 11 and was filled with Special Operations officers, led by Rear Admiral Albert M. Calland III, the Special Operations commander for all ops between the Horn of Africa and the Hindu Kush. Shortly before the briefing, the deputy commander in chief for Central Command, Lieutenant General Michael P. DeLong, entered the room, followed by General Tommy Franks.

Franks was the regional CINC. Pronounced *sink,* it means commander in chief of the Central Command. Central Command would exercise overall operational control (OPCON) in the Central Asia theater of war. Basically, that meant that an infantry and aviation officer who was not even airborne qualified was going to make operational decisions that would directly impact the U.S. Army Special Operations Forces and the most unconventional war in American history.

Luckily, although the regional CINC had operational combat control, General Franks would be working closely with General Charles R. Holland. General Holland was a four-star who commanded the U.S. Special Operations Command in Tampa, Florida. Silver-haired and handsome, Holland was an Air Force general. But he had extensive experience in Special Operations, flying as far back as the Vietnam era when he piloted 130's out of Ubon Royal Thai Air Force Base. He also flew AC-130 Spectre gunships, which would be used throughout the war in Afghanistan to support the SF teams on the ground. The generals' offices were literally next door to each other, and they would be able to see each other every day as they planned the war.

But the most important general in the war would be Lieutenant General Doug Brown, commander of the U.S. Army Special Operations Command. General Brown was "as good as it gets," according to the operators in the field. He had been a former commander of JSOC, the Joint Special Operations Command, and had vast experience exercising operational control over the Green Berets, the Navy SEALs, Delta Force, and virtually every other covert unit in the SOF community. It would be Brown's task to command and coordinate everything from Green Berets to Army Aviation, including secret commando and military intelligence groups. Because U.S. Army Special Operations Command was not considered a combat command, only a resource command, the ultimate battlefield control would still lie with Franks. Throughout the war, it would be a constant source of frustration for General Brown and the Green Berets.

No one was certain how a room full of conventional officers would receive the pitch for a plan of unconventional warfare, especially since the briefer was Lieutenant Colonel Dave Miller. One of the last Vietnam veterans on active duty at his rank, Miller had a year left in the Special Forces before retirement, and was fed up with bureaucracy and political correctness. He was a staunch unconventional warfare advocate, frequently driving his more conventional-minded, "heavy metal" bosses to distraction.

Miller knew that all the anti-Taliban movements in Afghanistan were basically the same, since they all flew under the banner of slain Northern Alliance hero Ahmad Shah Massoud, even if they did have different political parties. Fort Bragg's analysis, on the other hand, was that each disparate group of Northern Alliance resistance leaders had its own set of local political, military, and logistical conditions that would allow some to be "kick-started" in short order. Others at Fort Bragg were concerned that the U.S. Army would not be prepared enough to build an Afghan host-nation resistance force among the *muj*.

As the briefing began, those who were not at the head table held their breath, not knowing what Miller was about to say. There had been great debate over whether to turn Miller loose in "public" forum. The critical briefing turned out to be Miller's finest hour. In simple terms, he explained that unconventional warfare could be the key to victory and that Special Operations Forces were available and trained to the task. Miller enlightened the room with a plan beginning with the sending of Green Berets behind the lines to recruit forces, followed by a slow buildup of capability that would bring the Northern Alliance up to speed by spring of 2002.

After Miller was finished, General Franks took over the briefing. Franks assumed he had solid intelligence that even the special operators lacked. He had the private debriefings of all the Soviet generals who had lost thousands of men to the *mujahadeen* in Afghanistan. Franks had also examined the logistical nightmares and political obstructions to effectively basing large troop formations in the AO, or area of operations. He knew what a drawn-out, protracted war would mean for American troops and their families. Most important, Franks knew the conventional American Army was simply not ready for immediate war.

What Franks didn't know was that he was not the only expert on the Soviet's Afghan experience. There were few Green Berets operating in that part of the world that hadn't seen two books printed by the U.S. Marine Corps Combat Development Command. The first was *The Other Side of the*

Mountain, which focused on *mujahadeen* tactics against the Soviets. The second, *The Bear Went over the Mountain,* focused on Soviet tactics against the *mujahadeen.* The books contained basically the same "classified" interviews the CIA had given Franks. The lesson was that you had better get up pretty early to outthink the Green Berets.

Holland and Brown knew America was not ready for a protracted war. Clinton's press op war in Bosnia had depleted military arsenals. Under Clinton, U.S. military capabilities had been reduced by 40 percent, and the U.S. military was desperately trying to rebuild under Bush. Franks knew he didn't have enough cruise missiles, smart bombs, and ammunition to back a conventional war like Desert Storm. George W. Bush wanted exactly what the rest of America wanted, he wanted revenge, and he wanted it quickly. Defense Secretary Donald Rumsfeld wanted the same thing Bush wanted—except he also wanted bin Laden's head on a stake. Franks knew it would be political suicide to tell the White House and Rumsfeld he wasn't ready for war. Besides, the Green Berets insisted they *were* ready for war.

"We're underfunded, underpaid, underequipped, and undermanned. Unleash one hundred of our Dogs of War with no rules and no orders, and we'll bring down the whole fucking Taliban and al-Qaida Afghan empire in just a hundred days," said a gruff Green Beret officer from New York who took a private call from the White House during the briefing.

With Rumsfeld demanding the military quit talking and start fighting, General Franks reluctantly accepted Miller's briefing as the only option that made sense: the Green Berets would be the ones to take on the brunt of the war in Afghanistan. Besides, one Green Beret commented after the briefing, putting SF on the ground would give Holland a chance to show off the Air Force's precision air strike capability.

After the briefing Lieutenant General DeLong told the Special Operations staff that gaining General Franks' support so easily was a compliment to Miller's genius, knowledge, and preparation. DeLong was a stone-faced, square-jawed jarhead Marine with almost as many medals as Chesty Puller.

With more than eight hundred hours of helicopter combat, as far back as Vietnam, DeLong was not about to pass out his approval lightly. He smiled, winked one of his ice-blue eyes, and shook Miller's hand on the way out of the briefing room.

"Gentlemen, it doesn't get any better than this!" one of the officers commented to his peers as they exited.

Final Tweaks

The meeting was hardly over before the secure lines to the Special Forces Command were lit up with the news, and they were delighted. The Special Forces had rarely been charged with the main effort of a war, although they had participated in virtually all of the small conflicts in the latter part of the twentieth century. The last time the Green Berets had been unleashed as the principal element of change had been in 1983 in El Salvador.

Each of the SMU's, Special Mission Units, were notified to start preparations, for what no one knew, but they knew there would be a mission, and there would be a war. Official word went out to the British Ministry of Defence, but there had already been more than a dozen secure phone calls back and forth between the British Special Air Service and the British Special Boat Service, both of which were "unofficially" invited into the fray. The bonds between the British Special Forces and the American Special Forces went back fifty years, to the days of the 1st Special Service Force; the OSS (Office of Strategic Services) and the SOE (Special Operations Executive), both of whom had conducted joint operations during World War II. Those bonds were still deep, kept strong by exchange programs, joint training exercises, attendance at each other's special schools, and common enemies.

Generals Holland and Brown had some serious work ahead of them to execute the plan Miller had laid the groundwork for in the briefing. There was no base that would be able to support the unconventional warfare effort inside Afghanistan. The size and weight of the force required to conduct and resupply sustained combat precluded operations off Navy platforms such as aircraft carriers.

In addition, there was no infrastructure to support the supply effort needed to sustain the combat operations and confront the Taliban. It had taken six months to build up a force to confront Saddam Hussein in Desert Storm. The White House had given Special Forces just a few weeks.

Franks immediately began working with the State Department and the CIA, and promised aid and money to find foreign bases that could fulfill such a requirement. Several former Soviet Socialist Republics along Afghanistan's northern border were surprisingly receptive, as was Pakistan along the southern border, once sovereignty and other legal issues were resolved. According to General Lambert, the welcome of U.S. forces was partly due to the fact that Franks and his staff "drank a lot of tea." However, inside information revealed that substantial bribes were paid to officials from Uzbekistan and Tajikistan to secure their cooperation.

"Drinking tea" with leaders of the independent states in the unconventional warfare arena literally meant that U.S. generals spent a lot of time with their peers drinking tea and simply listening. Some key players, particularly President Musharraf of Pakistan, would be taking a risk in the eyes of their people by supporting the United States' war efforts. Bush directed the State Department to supply a list of demands to Pakistan—they could either be with us or against us—and Pakistan was forced to accept unconditionally.

While various commands worked on the deployment of other forces and the building of a base, Special Forces Command selected the 5th Special Forces Group as the first Green Beret unit to be deployed to Afghanistan. These men were intensively indoctrinated in that part of the world, in language training and cultural study, and had been involved in classified missions designed to keep Saddam Hussein in check. The A-Teams frequently spent weeks in the desert in Kuwait, and were active in the formerly Russian "Stans": Uzbekistan, Kazakhstan, Kyrgyzstan, Tajikistan, and Turkmenistan. It was their "theater of operations," and they were the best desert fighters that the Special Operations Command possessed.

Franks drank even more tea in Tashkent in the weeks ahead, promising military aid and money; he got the go-ahead from Uzbekistan's chief of state, Islam Karimov, to create the covert American base that would be known as K2.

To effectively defeat the Taliban and AQ, a secret and unas-sailable base was needed for staging Special Forces opera-tions against the enemy. A deserted muddy expanse of flat land with a large man-made berm down the middle separat-ing the concrete runway of a former Soviet air base from a former barracks area provided the best possible headquarters for TASK FORCE DAGGER.

Once the United States made final arrangements with Ka-rimov, the Sheraton Hotel in Tashkent, Uzbekistan's capital, became the construction office for K2. By late September a caravan of construction supplies was transported from Tash-kent to the Soviet's old Khanabad air base in Qarshi, just one hundred miles north of the Afghan border. The six-hour drive was along good highways through the fields of one of the most extensive cotton-producing areas on earth.

Looming above K2 and indeed the entire border area be-tween Uzbekistan and Afghanistan were mountain ranges up to fourteen thousand feet high that separated the Stans. Uzbekistan was a former member of the USSR and had been a staging area for Soviet operations, and the other, Afghani-stan to the south, had savagely battled the Soviet Army for ten years. With the help of the United States the *mujahadeen,* along with the then-CIA-backed al-Qaida forces and what was to become the Taliban, defeated the Soviet initiative. In the 1980s, one Agency man, Billy Waugh, a former Green Beret sergeant major in Vietnam, reported seeing Osama bin Laden almost every day while he was instructing the Afghans in the use of the advanced surface-to-air missiles that brought down Soviet helicopters and warplanes during the eighties.

In mid-October the teams from 5th Group at Fort Camp-bell began to arrive at K2 and found themselves in the most primitive of conditions. Meanwhile, the construction officers working from Tashkent were busy night and day ordering supplies and picking up whatever could be purchased locally. For the first month electricity was at a premium but then generators were installed along with hot-water showers and chemical latrines. K2 became a livable and reasonably comfortable tent city as the headquarters of TASK FORCE DAGGER.

The U.S. Army Special Forces with the combined air armadas of the Army, Navy, Marines, and the Air Force would reach halfway around the world almost overnight as they launched their plan to destroy bin Laden and his terrorists. One predicament, however, was not solved before two helicopters were lost. This was how to cross the high mountain range between K2 and the combat zones in Afghanistan to which the Special Forces A-Teams had to be transported. When a team had to put down at high altitude destinations, or a chopper had to settle in and try to land at fourteen thousand feet, there was the problem of the rotor blades having enough power to lift the helicopter back up into the thin atmosphere of the mountains. The engines couldn't get enough oxygen to produce the necessary thrust, and the air was so thin that the rotors couldn't effectively lift the chopper. This was particularly true in the case of a medevac or with personnel pickup with a crew aboard. If a helicopter had to land and then take off again at high altitudes with an even heavier load, the rotors had to struggle and sometimes just couldn't get off the ground, or if they did rise a bit they came down hard, damaging the aircraft and injuring those inside. Once the helo (helicopter) was in the air the rotors could maintain altitude. The problem was getting airborne with a heavy load. Gasoline weighed six pounds per gallon and it took at least two hundred gallons of gasoline for the helicopter to get safely out of the mountains and home again. This added up to more than twelve hundred pounds of extra weight on top of the passengers, crew, and cargo.

A brilliant mechanic-pilot finally came up with a solution to the problem: Why not get rid of the gasoline, take off, and refuel in the air? Great idea, his superiors commented, but how do you refuel in the mountains at an altitude of over two miles?

The solution was simple: The helicopter would carry a large empty rubber bladder aboard when a mountain landing was anticipated. Upon landing, the fuel in the chopper would be pumped into the bladder laid out on the ground through a rubber hose. Then when the bird took off, well over a thousand pounds lighter and safely hovering, it could suck the fuel back into its tanks and fly away. It was precisely these types of improvised solutions that allowed a few hundred men to succeed in winning a war in an environment that had helped to defeat the entire Soviet Army.

After these problems were resolved, the European Command (EUCOM) stepped in to help by handling the logistical nightmare of supplying the Green Berets and the Afghan UW forces. The task ultimately fell on the shoulders of General Montgomery Meigs, commanding general of United States Army, Europe, which would furnish the massive airdrop of supplies into Afghanistan. The air component for dropping most of the bundles would be coming from the aircraft under the command of U.S. Air Force, Europe.

The Taliban had frequently said that the U.S. lacked the national will to fight them face-to-face, frequently deriding President Clinton's use of TLAM cruise missiles from hundreds of miles away to attack al-Qaida training facilities and Baghdad as cowardly. A much-publicized comment from an AQ source was that the only thing the United States would do when attacked is "sue someone."

George W. Bush was going to surprise the Taliban by changing that perception early on. The U.S. Army Ranger intelligence officers at Fort Benning, Georgia, were working day and night studying target folders and satellite photos supplied by the National Reconnaissance Office (NRO) and the CIA. After assessing the photos, angles of trajectory for the satellites, and times of day, they used shadows and digital 3D maps to determine the heights of walls, the sizes of buildings, and the locations of heavy weapons and ground-to-air-missile emplacements.

Four weeks later, they were ready to launch a U.S. Army Airborne Ranger raid deep into the interior of southern Afghanistan. Those attacks on Kandahar and at the guarded airfield south of it would severely shock a complacent enemy. The Department of Defense preplanned to broadcast the Army's combat footage of the Rangers parachuting onto their objective on worldwide television.

On the night of October 19, the United States conducted its first ground-combat operations in Afghanistan. The new moon had passed four days before and the desert was dark. Four MC-130 Combat Talon aircraft parachute-dropped more than two hundred Rangers from the Army's 75th Ranger Regiment, commanded by Colonel Joe Votel, on an isolated airstrip code-named OBJECTIVE RHINO. Just a few minutes before parachuting into the night, the Rangers had stood in the aircraft aisles and recited the Ranger Creed. As they said, "I will never leave a fallen comrade to fall into the hands of the enemy," the tears welled up in their eyes, and adrenaline flowed.

OBJECTIVE RHINO was sixty miles southwest of Kandahar. The Ranger operations resulted in the death of over forty Taliban defenders at the airfield. The Rangers had been "hot to kill something" ever since September 11, and they had finally been given their chance.

Back home, the television images were firmly entrenched in all Americans' memory. The dull green view through night-vision scopes of the Rangers assaulting the Kandahar airfield sent a clear message to Americans and the international community: The U.S. was not casualty-averse and was capable and willing to reach out and touch the al-Qaida or Taliban anywhere in the world. Bin Laden had attacked America, expecting us to surrender through inaction. America had responded with words derived from the Ranger Creed: "Surrender is not an option."

That same night an AC-130 Spectre gunship killed more than thirty Taliban soldiers who had made contact with a small group of other Americans—Delta Force. SFOD-D, Special Forces Operational Detachment-Delta, as it was officially known, was working as part of a new operational element called TASK FORCE 11, named in memory of September 11. The Rangers called them "the D-boys." Delta had come in by helicopters to raid a Taliban compound at the edge of the city. The compound was that of Mullah Mohammed Omar. Osama bin Laden had married the only daughter of Mullah Omar's tenth wife. That alone made Omar a hot target.

An additional target, believed to contain several high-ranking members of the Taliban and al-Qaida network, was hit by the Counter-Revolutionary Warfare Wing of the 22nd SAS. Operating in four-man bricks, or teams, more than forty SAS commandos hit their target simultaneously, killing and wounding more than 25 enemy, and capturing several enemy soldiers. One important aspect of using the SAS so early was that they had Pashto speakers, which was the southern dialect in the Kandahar region.

The mission was not without problems. Conventional generals had turned it into a larger-than-needed operation. Almost an entire squadron of Delta had landed near Omar's house, gone in, and picked up significant intelligence material, but Omar was not there. On their way out, a dozen Delta operators were wounded when Taliban and al-Qaida forces hit them hard with scores of RPG rockets. The Delta boys slaughtered everything in their path, but took heavy casualties. The SAS also took casualties, with several of their assaulters wounded.

Even still, American forces in Kandahar went in fast, accomplished their mission, which was to send a message, and came out fast.

But, by the time it was over, no one was pleased about General Franks having OPCON over the Green Berets in Afghanistan. Some operators believed that Franks had already screwed up the OBJECTIVE RHINO mission by making it "too heavy, too slow, and too stupid." Several senior Special Forces officers suggested that "Franks needs adult supervision." One journalist reported that a senior military officer said, "Franks is clueless." The SAS command sent word back that they would operate independently of CENTCOM micro-management, preferring to be given a task and left alone to complete it. The next day Franks was complaining that using special ops was a mistake, and that the war in Afghanistan was not for Special Operations, it was for "heavy metal conventional units."

But it was too late. Rumsfeld wanted "Special Forces boots on the ground," and General Doug Brown was happy to accommodate him. Two more Special Forces teams were already infiltrating the north of Afghanistan.

The Clinton-era hesitancy and hand-wringing were over. Poststrike statements from Mullah Mohammed Omar's Taliban government clearly revealed that the message had been received.

Bin Laden just didn't get it. He didn't understand history, the history of Omaha Beach, Iwo Jima, Tarawa, Gettysburg, the Ardennes. Americans were willing to die for their cause—they would run into a hailstorm of bullets in a New York minute if they believed in the cause—especially if that cause was good against evil. It was the classic battle of eternity.

In fact, little did the world know that within minutes of the attack on the World Trade Center, Air Force Colonel Robert K. Marr, Jr., commander of the Northeast Air Defense Sector, was preparing to send *unarmed* U.S. fighter planes into combat as battering rams. National Guard Fighter jets already in the air on training missions over Michigan were on the verge of being deployed against bin Laden's "airline missiles." The pilots would be ordered to smash into the terrorist's jetliners and destroy them in the air before they reached their targets. Marr justified his plans accordingly: sending a pilot to his certain death to save American civilians was no different than sending a soldier to his death on Normandy Beach in 1944.

The U.S. Army Special Operations Command and the Green Berets were ready to send a similar message: that the United States would take on the Taliban and al-Qaida anywhere, anytime, any way, including American suicide missions if necessary.

CHAPTER 3

The Ranchers

"Everybody in Afghanistan ought to know we're coming in and hell's coming with us."

— former National Security Advisor
ROBERT MCFARLANE
on CBS' *Face the Nation*,
October 28, 2001

Cheyenne, Wyoming
September 10, 2001

Two men stepped out of the clothing store next to the old railroad depot in Cheyenne, Wyoming. It was a bitter day, the first light snow had already fallen in late August, and it was clear winter would come early. The men had purchased new rattlesnake-skin boots to wear home the next morning on the airplane to Fort Campbell, Kentucky.

They planned to break in their boots by going to a nearby dance hall to learn the Cotton-eyed Joe. They were gaining cultural nuances (i.e., scoping out the chicks) and noted that in Cheyenne, men were never asked to remove their hats indoors, particularly in liquor-laced environments.

Using their A-Team nicknames of "Dutch" and "Randy," they were posing as two East Coast businessmen looking for an adventure. The cadre from a horsemanship and pack animal school in town had taken to the urban cowboys, particularly since they seemed so eager to learn and were willing to put in extra hours to optimize the short time they would be at the school.

Both men had been sent to Romania to build rapport with the newly independent state right after the Berlin Wall had come down. They had found a gold mine. Ski troops and a mountain regiment still existed in the Romanian Army, even after the Soviets had ordered a formation of the men in the mid-fifties and burned all of their skis, and changed the regimental history.

The Romanians had their own arms industry, and ingenious ideas on how to pack mortars, ammunition, heavy weapons, rations, and other equipment on the backs of horses and mules. Of particular note was a carefully bred pack animal, a small but incredibly sturdy horse, developed by the Romanian military over the years. Dutch called them "pack-animals on steroids." The two Special Forces sergeants had a great time learning mountaineering techniques and listening to stories about the evils of Communism and how the Drac, or the devil himself, Nicolae Ceauşescu, had ruined a great nation.

Now, over ten years later, Randy and Dutch still were sent out periodically to refresh their skills. The use of beasts of burden in combat had been stressed less and less in Special Forces since the conflicts in Central America, and fewer men were being trained in the skill. Yet Special Forces Command in Fort Bragg encouraged its units to keep a few men trained, just in case.

The country-western dance lessons ran from 6 till 7 P.M. at the local saloon. It was the best way to meet local girls. Randy and Dutch had just enough time to shower, attend the dance lessons, grab a buffalo steak, be back at the bar to bust a move on the dance floor by nine, and be shit-faced drunk by midnight. After all, it was "nickel night."

It had been a great night. The beds had rocked. They were both comfortable in their warm beds with down comforters and an extra pair of feet for each of them. Their two cowgirls were still passed out—it had been an exhausting night.

They were sleeping snugly with sweat-drenched hair when the phone rang.

Randy picked it up. It was the 5th Special Forces Group command sergeant major. Randy listened intently, ending the conversation by saying, "Got it," trying to be excessively nonchalant. He slowly hung up the phone, tossed his head back and looked upward, and gave silent thanks to God.

The command sergeant major had told Randy and Dutch to start growing a beard and to hurry home to Fort Campbell. The Green Berets were going to war.

Next to the phone, Randy had a copy of Special Forces School's Field Manual 31-27, *Pack Animals in Support of Army Special Operations Forces,* dated February 2000. He chuckled to himself about the naysayers that said publishing the manual was a waste of time and money. Afghanistan and bin Laden were the likely targets; he couldn't think of a better place to apply the lessons in the manual, especially after the success of the highly classified Special Forces mule program for the *mujahadeen* during the 1980s. Working out of a covert base in western Pakistan, SF had supplied the *mujahadeen* with mules, weapons, and ammunition.

It was time for the Ranchers to head into "Indian country," and they wouldn't be carrying six-guns.

CHAPTER 4

The Dogs
of War

"They [senior members of al-Qaida] are dead. They just don't know it yet."

—unnamed U.S. official quoted in
The New York Times, October 10, 2001

Bosnia
Late September 2001

General Doug Brown's U.S. Army Special Operations Command was boldly planning the first military strikes against the forces of terror linked to the World Trade Center and Pentagon attacks. The lads at Stirling Lines were also on the roll. The counter-revolutionary warfare section, known as the CRW Wing, was preparing target folders on every Arab terrorist that might have an even remote link to Osama bin Laden, and MI6 headquarters, at Vauxhall Cross in London, had secretly informed the Regiment that preemptive lethal strikes were about to be authorized on a wide variety of known terrorists.

First, Green Berets from the 10th Special Forces Group, stationed in Germany, started hitting locations suspected to hold components used for chemical warfare attacks; the reconnaissance team slowly worked its way down the sidewalk, smoking nonchalantly, speaking in whispers. Given their clothing, gait, and two-day-old stubble, they blended in perfectly. One donned a black civilian beret, customarily worn by middle-age Muslim men. Their earjacks and wires were hidden so they could speak to each other and broadcast their situation to the command-and-control element hidden in a nondescript Toyota a few blocks away. Underneath their clothes they had concealed weapons, flex cuffs, minifragmentation grenades, and other gear that could come in handy during the operation.

A second team of Green Berets, similarly outfitted, were working the back of their target, which was a newly refurbished hotel.

Two cars entered the neighborhood, slowly moving down the narrow streets. The men in the first car were the assaulting element of the team, and wired to both the "walkers" doing the final checks around the hotel, as well as to the command-and-control element in the SUV behind them.

One of the walkers entered the hotel and went casually up to the second floor, while his mate covered his back and watched the bottom of the stairs. The code word relayed from upstairs was simple: "Clear, I say again, clear."

The command-and-control element in the Toyota immediately gave the men the command they had hoped for: "Go, Go, Go!" Those words released all elements into motion simultaneously, including a quick-reaction force (QRF) loaded to the gills with ammo, just in case something went awry.

The assault team's SUV came to a stop in front of the hotel and the men sprang out, moving with purpose and completely under control. The A-Team's demolitions man walked quietly up to the entrance, quickly taping his special C-4 explosive cutting charge on the door. The men stepped back, knowing exactly how far away they needed to be to take prompt advantage of the explosive entry, yet be safe from its effects. This would be it: spaced surprise and violence of action.

The demo sergeant gave a thumbs-up, which started the count. The team paused, each man whispering, "One, two, three . . ."

BOOM!

The door went flying into the apartment, the assault team

right behind it. Two men were sitting in the apartment's small living room. One started to run and two Green Berets took him down quickly without firing a shot. The other stood up and challenged the assaulters. He had no weapon, but he reached quickly for a cardboard box on the coffee table. One of the raiders struck him in the chest with a full thrust of his rifle barrel, enough to rock a normal man. He simply reared back and charged with his bare hands.

Subduing him was not easy. The terrorist would need over a dozen stitches by the time he was cuffed and moved out of the apartment. He appeared to be over fifty, but was in tremendous physical condition, and he fought like a trapped animal.

The walkers stayed behind as the special operators whisked the prisoners out of the hotel. They needed to guard the room for the investigators. One man watched the entryway, which was now a hole in the wall after the demise of the door and most of the frame. The other Green Beret looked at the floor, littered with the items knocked from the top of the coffee table during the scuffle with the assaulters. Looking down on the carpet his eyes widened. He called out to his partner, "Jesus H. Christ! Box cutters!"

The "take-down" in the apartment had been Mohammed Atta's roommate in Germany and part of the infamous Hamburg cell in Germany. The notorious Atta was one of the suicide pilots that had flown into the World Trade Center; he had been working for Osama bin Laden.

Born on June 28, 1957, bin Laden joined an Islamic fundamentalist group in Saudi Arabia at the age of sixteen. In December 1979 he left for Afghanistan to fight the Soviets. Successful in that quest, he relocated to the Sudan in 1989 to begin assembling what he called a "United Islamic State," which would include fifty countries united against the infidel. In 1990 he formed al-Qaida, which meant "the Basis," a radical Islamic terrorist group. It was to be the foundation of his New World order for Islam. The U.S. government referred to it as "al-Qaeda" and "the Base," which meant bin Laden's base for terrorism.

In 1993, bin Laden financed the first attack on the World Trade Center. In 1994, under threats against the stability of their regime, Saudi Arabia stripped bin Laden of his citizenship. In 1995 he was implicated in the bombing of U.S. military facilities in Saudi Arabia and the murder of five U.S. soldiers. By 1996 bin Laden had begun his allegiance with the Taliban. Over the next five years he would continue attacks against the U.S. in Africa and other areas, announcing in 1998 the creation of a "global Islamic force" against the "Judaists" and "Christian crusaders." There was to be no distinction between military and civilian American targets. Women and children would be fair game for his terrorist forces. Something bin Laden made all too clear in his speeches time and again.

The fifty-second child of Mohamed Avad bin Laden, he was born into one of the wealthiest families in the Middle East. The only son of his father's tenth wife, he took over the family business when Mohamed Avad died in 1975. With billions of dollars at his disposal, bin Laden would be able to merge big business and terrorism into a new breed of violence against the infidel. Relying on his business skills and experience obtained through his father's multibillion dollar construction company, The Bin Laden Construction Group corporation, Osama bin Laden built his terrorist organization in the image of a multinational corporation. There were be a CEO, or Chief Executive Officer, a Chief Financial Officer (CFO), a Chief Operations Officer (COO), and even a public affairs group, led by a CIO, or Chief Information Officer.

With Egyptian Ayman Al-Zawahiri as the CEO; Mohammed Atef, another Egyptian as the Executive Vice President in charge of military operation; Khalid Shaikh Mohammed, a Kuwaiti, as the COO; and Omar Al-Faruq as a Branch Manager in Southeast Asia and an area CFO, al-Qaida was truly an international terrorist corporation. The corporate levels started with the leadership section, underneath it the management section, and below that the cells that conduct operations.

When additional corporate assets or local talent is needed, al-Qaida can draw on its private contractors—terrorists who have been trained in the AQ camps, but are not necessarily permanent employees of the group.

Bin Laden, of course, would be the Chairman of the Board. If one corporate officer retired, by being captured or killed, then another would be appointed from the ranks below.

It would be called *megaterrorism,* and would engulf more than sixty countries. The group would form "the Basis" for a worldwide *jihad,* which would permanently seize the world's attention on September 11, 2001.

Shortly after the Green Berets hit the apartment, an al-Qaida Saudi front organization was also busted in Sarajevo. Computer files were uncovered detailing the entry methods for U.S.-bound terrorists. Also discovered were fake U.S. government identification badges and credit cards, and photos of the World Trade Center, the Pentagon, the USS *Cole,* and the U.S. embassies in Kenya and Tanzania. There were two photos of each site, one before and one after the attacks.

The message was clear: The United States wanted Osama bin Laden and his al-Qaida network. TASK FORCE 11 would concentrate on POW snatches, grabbing suspected and known terrorists and taking them into custody, kidnapping AQ leaders, and killing individual terrorist threats. TASK FORCE DAGGER would focus on destroying the Taliban and al-Qaida's Afghanistan sanctuary to put bin Laden on the run, as well as destroying his infrastructure and permanently eliminating bin Laden's elite terrorist training camps. TASK FORCE 160 would deliver the Special Operations commandos into the storm wherever it raged, and the mysterious rogue TASK FORCE SABER would support U.S. forces and the Northern Alliance with human intelligence and "collateral issues." The terrorists would have nowhere to run and nowhere to hide—only a barren desert to die in.

The 22 SAS brought all four 60-man operational squadrons online twenty-four hours a day. One would be kicking doors around the world in coordination with the American Special Operations Forces, two would prepare for full deployment to Afghanistan, and one would remain in England, to counter any threat that might occur on home ground. The reserve squadron would be used to fill in under-strength teams, since the SAS, like the Green Berets, were always under-strength. Although they were Territorials, they were *always* ready to deploy anywhere, and looked forward to such times.

The hunted had now become the hunters. At the same time the Sarajevo missions were going down, covert Special Forces, Delta Force, and SAS CRW teams were hitting locations all over the world in violent assaults on Osama bin Laden's terrorist cells and policing up suspected terrorists throughout Europe.

Rumsfeld had now unleashed his Dogs of War.

CHAPTER 5

Isolation

"More than two weeks ago, I gave Taliban leaders a series of clear and specific demands: close terrorist training camps; hand over leaders of the al-Qaida network; and return all foreign nationals, including American citizens, unjustly detained in your country. None of these demands were met. And now the Taliban will pay a price."

—PRESIDENT GEORGE W. BUSH,
address to the nation,
October 7, 2001

Fort Campbell, Kentucky
Late September 2001

The Green Berets have a well-developed technique for mission preparation, now adopted by the entire Special Operations community. A-Teams are locked down, away from their families, in a location that is guarded from the outside. Phones are off-limits. Meals, exercise, and all mission preparations are done on a schedule where no A-Team has contact with any other. The facility is called an isolation facility, or ISOFAC.

The teams are given intelligence, equipment, and are taken to low-visibility rehearsal sites and training areas to practice and prepare for their missions. At times human assets are brought in for debriefing by the teams. Human assets include citizens, foreigners, natives, or spies who are familiar with the target area, its culture and local customs—they are immensely important in tuning up the teams to operate in another culture.

The Green Beret team members are also encouraged to ask for whatever material or intelligence they need to accomplish their mission. It is the Special Forces Command hierarchy's job to try and fulfill all of their requests.

One 5th Special Forces Group battalion commander had been in isolation for forty-eight hours along with the A-Teams under his command. The lieutenant colonel was frustrated because he had received no intelligence of value. 5th Group, as the Green Berets referred to it, had received deployment orders from Special Operations Command Central, but little else, just a list of doctrinal missions they *might* perform. They couldn't tie anything to a specific point on the ground. They knew neither where they would be inserted nor what the specific mission would be.

The good news was that new Army equipment, particularly cold-weather gear and test laser designators from the Army labs, was flowing into the ISOFAC. Each room in the ISO-FAC was small, cramped, and claustrophobic. At one end were the cots for the men. Three computers were wired into the corner of the room, linked to a closed, classified system that gave them access to DIA (Defense Intelligence Agency) and CIA information databases, target folders, and satellite maps. The rest of the space was filled with two large planning tables and what seemed to be fifty large footlockers. The lockers, called team boxes, were full of M-4 assault rifles; sniper rifles; Mark-19 grenade launchers; M249 SAW machine guns, M9 Beretta pistols and suppressors, six kinds of radios for UHF, HF, VHF, and satellite communication; extreme-cold-weather clothing to defeat the bitter cold and wind they would encounter; night-vision goggles; laser markers; engineering equipment; and demolition kits. Also included were individualized medical kits, put together in the last two days, to increase the men's chances of survival deep inside Afghanistan.

The walls were covered with satellite imagery and maps of all sorts with special elevation, weather, and other unique data. However, normal ISOFAC checklists couldn't be followed until the men received information on their specific area of operations, concept of employment, enemy situation, and designated Northern Alliance or Pashtun allies. Throughout isolation it was important to maintain operational security "so plans didn't get blown and people didn't get killed." Yet in just days, each member of the teams would have to wade through a staggering amount of information, assimilating as much as they could.

The lieutenant colonel kept his men occupied with their training on new equipment and preparing for the C-17 and C-5 aircraft that were soon to arrive and transport them in the dead of night to their secret forward operations base, known as the FOB.

What Is the Mission?

During the November 1970 Son Tay Raid, where a handful of Green Berets went deep into North Vietnam to rescue POWs and kill Chinese and Russian military advisors, they developed a special patch in isolation. The mission was called OPERATION KINGPIN, but the patch had a mushroom embroidered on it and said "KITD/FOHS." It meant "Kept in the Dark/Fed on Horse Shit." Nothing had changed thirty years later. The men who would soon infiltrate Afghanistan hoped that when their commanding general showed up, more detailed information would be available. They would be disappointed. Major General Geoffrey Lambert had flown in from Fort Bragg to visit the ISOFAC. New in command, he had never visited the unit. In fact, it was the first time he had ever visited Fort Campbell. Lambert entered the lieutenant colonel's isolation room, shook hands with those at the table, and sat down to begin discussing some points he had scribbled on a desk pad prior to leaving his office.

"I want to have an open discussion with you about your upcoming deployment to Afghanistan. I want you all to participate. First of all, what is your mission?" Lambert questioned.

One of the team members raised his hand and said, "Unconventional warfare, sir."

Lambert replied softly, "Put unconventional warfare, a fuzzy concept in today's Army, aside, and tell me what your mission-essential tasks are. Forget doctrine, and forget current operations plans; start with a blank piece of paper. What will you do first?"

Several men immediately piped up, saying, "The first thing we have to do is infiltrate the operational area." Lambert agreed and responded, "Okay, our first task is to *infiltrate.* Be prepared, then, to parachute in or to be put on the ground by the 160th." The 160th SOAR (Special Operations Aviation Regiment) was the regiment highlighted in *Black Hawk Down.* The 160th Nightstalkers, as they call themselves, are perhaps one of the most secret units in the U.S. military and the most technologically advanced organization in the Special Operations Command. Flying a variety of heavily modified helicopters, such as the MH-47D/E Chinook, the MH-60K/L Pave Hawk, the AH-60K Attack Black Hawk, and the A/M/TH-6 "Little Bird"—a complete family of assault, surveillance and light attack helicopters—the 160th would deliver the Green Berets into the hellstorm wherever it raged.

Lambert asked what would be the second mission. The answer from the men was easy. "Link up and build rapport with the designated guerrilla elements."

"Third?" Lambert asked.

"Kill the enemy with precision weapons [bombs and close air support] and our long barrels [sniper rifles]," the team's operations sergeant answered.

"Fourth?" Lambert questioned.

"Equip the Afghans, who will be our guerrilla force, as well as possible," the team sergeant answered. "I worked with some of these boys back in the mid-eighties with the Agency. All of the teams need to remember that only fifteen percent of the men we will fight with are literate."

"You need to be prepared for challenges. Be ready to get new equipment via airdrop. There will be no training bases or camps in the traditional sense," Lambert said. The Green Berets were up for any challenge, but the idea of having new equipment, like sat phones and radios, airdropped in to them after they were on the ground really pissed them off. For years money that should have been used to equip the men had been diverted to exotic weapons platforms and aircraft.

"I know the plan is to train these guys up like the Sals or the Yards," the team sergeant said, referring to the Salvadoran units and Montagnard fighters SF had trained in the past, "but the fact is, Afghan warriors consider training an insult. They learn to fight by doing and observing," the team sergeant emphasized, having worked with the Afghan resistance against the Soviets.

"Good, excellent. Fifth?" Lambert questioned and then answered himself, "Recruit and build the force until it can maneuver sizable units against the Taliban. And sixth? Be combat advisors for the war of movement and help plan, develop orders, and coordinate the battles. And seventh, provide ground truth to the U.S. commanders and senior leaders. Special Forces will be the eyes and ears for the generals."

Lambert ended with "Eighth? *Survive.*"

"Sir, with all due respect . . . ," the sergeant began.

"Go ahead," Lambert said.

"I didn't think we were going into another survival course. I thought the point was to kill these bastards. If it's all the same to you, we'll be leaving our survival kits home and bringing more ammo."

The general smiled.

Lambert was pleased with their comments and observations. It was clear that the lieutenant colonel and his men were "switched on," as Lambert referred to being ready.

"Anything else you boys need?" the general asked before leaving.

"Yes, sir," the team leader answered, "we need some Afghan dictionaries and Soviet intel reports."

"We have sent two books into each isolation room from the Army's Military History Institute; the best is a collection of stories from *mujahadeen* commanders with detailed accounts of their tactics against the Russians. It is invaluable. The Army's mini-dictionaries for Pashto and Dari will be here in a few hours."

The general surprised some of the men with his next question. "What should you be reading in the latrine?" He again provided the answer: "It should be FM [Field Manual] 7-10 or FM 7-20, *How Conventional Companies and Battalions Fight.* Remember, you will be fighting infantry and tank battles with some ambushes thrown in.

"Take your Special Forces and unconventional warfare training, bank it, and then combine it with what you see as necessary to fight a conventional fight. It will lead to unique and creative problem solving, our forte."

The team knew what had to be done. They had two weapons sergeants that were experts on conventional tactics, and were prepared to outsmart any conventional tactic the bad guys could throw at them. They were also brushing up on Soviet armor tactics, since many of the Taliban armor commanders had either worked for or fought the Soviets. Most had also been to Ranger School, and as worthless as that was for a Green Beret, it did have one redeeming quality: it taught the unconventional guerrilla fighters how the conventional army patrolled, moved, worked, and thought.

Lambert went on. "Let me give you an example. When we patrol and cross a danger area and the enemy sees us, what do we do? We break contact with or without fire so we can run away. What if you are looking for the Taliban and are trying to regain contact with him so you can take it to him? Then, getting shot at is a good thing because you can engage and destroy the enemy. Don't be trapped by your special reconnaissance and direct-action skills. I want you to think about battlefield effects and to not be impeded by how you have been trained for other missions."

Every Green Beret knew the way to break contact if they were vastly outnumbered. It was called IADs, immediate action drills—dumping every bullet they had in their weapons into the enemy and running like hell.

How Are You Going to Die?

General Lambert paused, ready to discuss what he thought some of the men might be hesitant to address. He asked, "How are you going to die?"

The men responded quickly and soon came up with a likely order of probability: Taliban artillery, sniper fire, enemy ambush, and vehicle accident, which had been the biggest killer in Bosnia and Desert Storm.

One staff sergeant cut in, laughing when vehicle accidents came up and said, "Going down shooting and taking as many of those motherfucking ragheads with me as I possibly can." Waiting patiently until after the laughter died down, Lambert continued.

Land mines were seen as a serious concern, but their intelligence showed that the *muj* generally knew how to walk through the minefields still in existence from the war with the Soviets. The men then discussed how to mitigate other threats: artillery could be countered by moving at night and in existing trench lines, as well as maintaining dispersion on the battlefield. Lambert quickly agreed that enemy sniper fire could be countered by purchasing local garb and dressing like the *muj,* including growing beards. Counterambush techniques included lead and flank security, dispersion, crossloading of key personnel and equipment, and good battle drills. As for dealing with accidents, the consensus was for the teams to do their own driving, since for over two decades, no programs had existed for licensing Afghans, and Afghan men with poor eyesight not only rarely wore glasses, they barely knew what they were.

Prisoners of War

The Special Forces SERE (Survival, Evasion, Resistance, and Escape) committee had viewed films from the al-Qaida and Chechens recording how they tortured and murdered prisoners of war in Bosnia and Chechnya. The John F. Kennedy Special Warfare Center and School was the proponent agency for all Special Forces training. There had been good years and bad years for JFKSWCS. The conventional army had desperately tried to subvert and degrade the training. SWC commanders like General Sidney Shacknow, a former POW during World War II and Lithuanian national who fought the Soviets; General Ken Bowra, a Vietnam-era Green Beret who had worked for the Agency; and General Bill Garrison, the former commander of Delta, all fought the conventional "Green Army" to keep Special Forces special. It was men like them who had put the Special Warfare Center back on track over the last ten years.

JFKSWCS sent almost all Green Berets to SERE School, which specialized in training Green Berets to survive in hostile environments, such as being trapped behind enemy lines, or as a prisoner of war. They trained Special Forces to prepare for the possibility of beheadings on international television as an example of what could happen to Americans who had been captured.

A-Teams accepted being captured simply as part of the operating environment, spending little time on the issue. Their plan was to fight to the death; capture was not an option. Every operator going in had already decided their course of action. No Green Beret was going to be captured alive, that was their pact, their sworn oath, their commitment to America, and their duty. Like everything else that brought pain and death, it was just part of the job.

"Good Old-Fashioned Conventional War"

General Lambert looked at his watch. He had to keep moving in order to see every team in isolation before they deployed. As he moved down through the ISOFAC, visiting one A-Team after the next, he was pleased how "tightly wrapped" the 5th Group soldiers were. Of all the teams he saw that day, only one didn't pass muster. General Lambert mentioned it to his escort, the deputy commander of the 5th Special Forces Group, saying, "I'm not sure that the boys in this isolation room understand what they are going to have to do. You need to do some 'headspace and timing' checks when you get to K2 in Uzbekistan." Several weeks later, Lambert was informed that Colonel Mulholland, the 5th Special Forces Group commander, after putting the suspect A-Team into final preparation for overseas, had made the same observation. He took the men on the suspect team off-line and put them to work on his staff.

As General Lambert prepared to leave the final A-Team he said, "Remember, once you are on the ground, you are engaged in World War II–type combat. It's a good old-fashioned conventional war. There are frontlines. You don't need elaborate evasion plans. If you are injured, call for a medevac. Buy your way out or to safety if you really get in trouble. This is your grandfather's war in Europe or in Korea, so stay on your toes and maintain situational awareness. You will be okay. Dominate the environment. Think." Lambert thanked the men for their time.

The Green Berets chuckled at the naivete of conventional thinking. It might have been good old-fashioned war for the Taliban, with their armor, their artillery, their trenches, and their frontlines, but for the Green Berets it was going be unconventional war and guerrilla tactics. Being good with weapons and military gear wasn't enough for the conduct of unconventional warfare. The men had to be able to outthink the enemy. And they were about to show American generals exactly how futile conventional warfare initiatives were against well-trained, highly experienced unconventional killing machines. They would not fight their grandfather's war in Europe or Korea. They would strike from the shadows, like their Revolutionary predecessors, Roger's Rangers. There would be no safe haven for America's enemies as they appeared and disappeared at will. They would bring the terror of unrestrained, violent guerrilla warfare to the doorstep of the Taliban and the al-Qaida, giving bin Laden a taste of his own medicine. Two Green Berets considered packing samurai swords, telling their team leaders that a few public beheadings of the Taliban might be in order. As far as the Green Beret sergeants were concerned, this war was going to be anything but conventional.

The ultimate goal was still Osama bin Laden. Taking Afghanistan was just a stop along the way. The Green Berets knew they must control bin Laden's sanctuary in order to destroy his terrorist apparatus. In spite of the broad mission to liberate Afghanistan, one personal mission remained at the forefront of every Green Beret's consciousness: they had to kill the senior leaders of al-Qaida, and they had to kill bin Laden.

Isolation was now in its final phase, and deployment was on the immediate horizon.

CHAPTER 6

The Flag and the Ring

"For states that support terror, it is not enough that the consequences be costly—they must be devastating."
— PRESIDENT GEORGE W. BUSH,
speech at the Citadel,
December 11, 2001

"We're going to need the ring for this one."
— unidentified Special Forces ground commander
upon learning that fewer than one hundred Green Berets
would fight the entire northern war

The Flag

5th Special Forces Group Headquarters
Fort Campbell, Kentucky

Colonel John Mulholland was packing his personal gear when Major General Lambert returned from the isolation facility. He was even taller than the six-foot-three Lambert. He was letting his curly dark but graying hair grow out and sporting the beginnings of a "Tom Selleck" mustache.

Proudly reaching into one of his footlockers, Mulholland exclaimed, "I just received this from a seamstress downtown, sir!"

Mulholland displayed an American flag modified with broad white embroidered letters crossing the top, spelling out "5th Special Forces Group (Airborne)." It was exactly what many of the regiments had done during the American Civil War. Mulholland had studied the Irish regiments from New York and was extremely proud of them, given his own family's background.

Command Sergeant Major McIntyre poked his head into the room and proudly announced: "We'll fly it over the embassy after we liberate Kabul!" McIntyre was the top NCO in the 5th SF Group. He would be the hard-charging take-no-shit bulldog who would make stumbling blocks disappear and things happen in the months ahead.

Preparing the Wives and Families

When their partners are deployed, American Special Forces spouses are aided by an organization the U.S. Army calls the Family Readiness Group (FRG). General Lambert sat down with the FRG and asked if they had any concerns over the departure of their loved ones. Security and safety nets for the families seemed adequate after short discussion. One unique request surfaced and was immediately agreed to by all in the room, including the 5th Special Forces rear detachment commander. The wives asked that the word be passed that no one could approach a military dependent's house in the Class A uniform (dress greens with service ribbons) while the men were gone, unless the worst had happened. The wives knew that if their loved one perished the notification team would wear Class A's. They didn't want anyone to be needlessly alarmed.

One of the FRG leaders finally asked General Lambert the question the other military wives had been avoiding because they didn't want to seem unsupportive: "How long do you plan on keeping our husbands deployed?"

Lambert explained the complexities of giving an answer. It was a difficult question due to the ambiguity of the situation as well as the fact that this was a new global conflict and great sacrifices might be required for the next three to five years or even longer.

General Lambert offered his philosophy. "Spouses can tolerate six months without their loved ones before things start breaking. My goal is to have the 5th Special Forces Group home within this time frame. This is not a promise, but I will do my best."

He remembered his Syrian college roommate from many years before, relaying tales of the great Islamic empires. According to his roommate, hundreds of years earlier, as the Arab armies swept across Northern Africa and up into Spain, the Caliph had called a Muslim military wives' conference to air their problems. Thereafter, he created and used summer and winter armies to obtain the same yearlong operational tempo, yet prevent the hardship and stress of long deployments.

Send My Husband, Please . . .

Once the initial teams were in isolation and deployments were under way, it didn't take long before wives started lobbying another problem, one that is common in Special Forces: they wanted their stay-behind soldier-spouses to be sent into combat. The women could no longer bear their husbands' misery over being left behind. More than one senior officer had a wife tell him, "Take this son of a bitch to war—he's driving me crazy!"

Little had changed since the days of the Green Berets in Vietnam. I had been a close friend of their commander, General William Yarborough, during the sixties and early seventies. Green Berets and their wives would constantly deluge me with requests. They would beg me to use my influence with their commanders to get the soldiers deployed to Vietnam, and the more dangerous the assignment they were lobbying for, the more they pleaded for my help.

"Lord of the Rings"

Leaving the FRG meeting, General Lambert and Colonel Mulholland moved into the 5th Special Forces Group conference room. Lambert told the men that the Department of the Army had finally "opened the bank" for the unit in regards to equipment, cash, and priority. This was the best news yet— for once, Special Forces would not be the bastard child begging for a handout from the conventional military.

Pausing as he reached into the pocket of his camouflage BDUs, Lambert called for Command Sergeant Major McIntyre. In front of the unit's leadership, the general spoke from his heart.

"I want this Special Forces ring to be worn by the best man you have in the first element to deploy into Afghanistan," Lambert said. "Each time the Special Forces receives a new mission to engage in combat, this ring has been passed to a Special Forces soldier."

Lambert explained that the ring was originally crafted at Johnny Gems in Bangkok in 1964 for a now unknown Special Forces A-Team leader. The captain who had the ring made was wounded in action and later died. Before his death he gave the ring to another A-Team commander, who wore it for two years in Vietnam combat. Upon arriving home as a major in 1970, he partly attributed his safe return to some magical properties the ring possessed.

At Fort Bragg the major continued to wear his gold Special Forces ring, which held a large Burma star ruby. (This was an unusual gemstone for the Green Beret rings, traditionally implanted with the more common blue star sapphire, ruby, or tiger's eye. Josten's made the first ring with a star sapphire, and still makes a version to this day. Those rings, along with Rolex Submariner divers' watches, have been a trademark of Special Forces for almost forty years.) The major finally gave the ring to a young sergeant who went on to become a general after going through Officer Candidate School at Fort Benning, Georgia. He then returned to Special Forces.

The mustang captain (a former sergeant who becomes a career officer) rapidly progressed upward through the chain of command. He was an active participant in numerous special operations. Some are still classified top secret. Others, like OPERATION JUST CAUSE in Panama, were highly publicized. On each of six missions he loaned the ring out to a subordinate. In every case that Green Beret distinguished himself in combat and survived to return the ring.

"As the caretaker of the ring, I keep the private register of the men who have worn it. It has been on the hand of one man killed in action, yet it has always found its way home. *This* ring has not been passed to another man since the Congo in 1998," said Lambert.

The presentation of the ring, dormant for almost four years, emphasized the enormity of change wrought by the tragedy of September 11.

The general continued, "We are beginning a war against terrorism that may take years to win. We do not know where this war will lead us, or what our missions will be after we achieve victory. What we know for sure is that this is our destiny. . . ."

"One Ring to Bind Them"

Khoja-Bahaudeen, Northern Alliance Headquarters
Northern Afghanistan
September 21, 2001

In the third week of September, Master Sergeant John Bolduc stepped off the bird that had flown him into Afghanistan. He was the first Green Beret to link up with the Northern Alliance on their turf. The star ruby ring glinted crimson in the sun.

Bolduc's "pilot team" had the mission to determine what opportunities existed behind the lines in Afghanistan for unconventional warfare, and the feasibility of creating a cohesive ground force from among the willing Afghans. Bolduc would return to his team with the insights he had gleaned to enable them to conduct final preparations for the new Special Forces mission.

He was both dismayed and amazed. Bolduc discovered that the Northern Alliance had only a few vehicles, some infantry, artillery pieces, some horse cavalry, and an informal supply system. They were a ragtag, underequipped, undersupplied, underfed, underfunded mob of an army. But they had three resources that many armies lacked: they had the will to win and the heart to win, and they were looking for a fight. They also said they knew where bin Laden was, how they could get him, and who his leaders were. The Northern Alliance hated the Arab invaders. They blamed Osama bin Laden for the assassination of their leader only days before September 11, and, like the Green Berets, they wanted revenge. It was that common enemy that would bind them—that and the aura that surrounded the ring.

By the third day Bolduc was ready to provide some conclusions to his headquarters. He was certain that the Special Forces could energize the Northern Alliance and put Mullah Mohammed Omar, the leader of the Taliban, and Osama bin Laden's al-Qaida terrorists out of commission, if only logistics could be straightened out.

Standing in the desert night, surrounded by nothing but mud walls in an ancient city and a brilliant star-filled sky, Bolduc keyed his radio to the secure frequency he had preset earlier, and gave his report. The Northern Alliance was ready and willing for war.

By the time he finished transmitting, the rest of Bush's Jedi Knights were on the way.

CHAPTER 7

TASK FORCE DAGGER

"Our military action is . . . designed to clear the way for sustained, comprehensive, and relentless operations to drive them [bin Laden and his terrorists] out and bring them to justice."

—PRESIDENT GEORGE W. BUSH,
address to the nation,
October 7, 2001

Buildup and Deployment

Southern Uzbekistan
Mid-October 2001

Chaos ensues when operations erupt from nowhere. It is the sergeants who come to the fore and make everything happen in time-compressed situations. Innovation was the name of the game as American forces landed on an old piece of Soviet concrete in Uzbekistan, now known as K2. Support mechanisms for everything from fuel to chow were going to have to be created from scratch as the Green Berets built TASK FORCE DAGGER headquarters from the ground up.

TF DAGGER would operate as the JSOTF, or Joint Special Operations Task Force. It would encompass all U.S. Special Operations units that would conduct the elimination of the Taliban and al-Qaida, and, ultimately, the liberation of Afghanistan. The most important part of the mission would be the destruction of al-Qaida and the termination of Osama bin

Laden and his top men. TASK FORCE DAGGER would fight the war and TASK FORCE 11 would focus on bin Laden and all those on the "wanted list." JSOC, the supersecret Joint Special Operations Command hidden at Pope Air Force Base, next to Fort Bragg, would oversee all interservice activities, coordinating the Delta Force, Navy SEAL, DIA, TF 160, and CIA paramilitary forces operating in Afghanistan. TF DAGGER's logo would embody the spirit of the assault: a swooping eagle clutching an OSS dagger as it descends on a map of Afghanistan. Underneath would be the words of the day—STRENGTH and HONOR.

Colonel John Mulholland was given the task of destroying the Taliban through unconventional warfare only weeks after taking command. He had never taken his "boys" to the field to shake them out. He was not acquainted with his staff's strengths and weaknesses under stress, yet that staff would soon be overwhelmed, as Air Force and Army aviation units, base protection forces from the Army's 10th Mountain Division, logistical and communication units, and two service support and maintenance outfits arrived to join K2's population. In addition, thirteen hundred journalists in Uzbekistan and Tajikistan were trying to get across the Northern border of Afghanistan to get in on the war. K2, by necessity, was classified. Its existence had to remain as low profile as possible. If they learned of K2's existence, or location, it would be mayhem.

"At least a few hundred of the nosey little bastards would be camped outside on the doorstep trying to get a picture of a Green Beret so they could plaster it all over their front pages," a Special Forces analyst commented, "and the Taliban would have it posted on every shithouse wall in Afghanistan."

Mulholland had no joint manning document (JMD) designed before the war, as many units do because they are part of an operations or contingency plan. (Emergency JMDs work slowly, nothing like the title would suggest. In a perfect world, JMDs would be filled with combat-ready personnel in short order. However, over time, conventional commanders in chief had "poisoned the well" with their insatiable

appetites for soldiers and equipment. Since they have so frequently put excessive demands on special ops, USSOCOM
units now take their time and deliberately scrutinize JMDs
for exact rationale prior to filling the requested billets.) The
requirement to eliminate the Taliban regime in Afghanistan
with Special Forces was as much a surprise as the attack on
September 11.

Ahmad Shah Massoud

Early on, Colonel Mulholland flew into Khoja-Bahaudeen
for an important meeting. The two Blackhawks carried his
team across the border and worked their way down a windy
river's edge toward the dusty mud village. Touching down on
a hidden landing field beneath the headquarters of the Northern Alliance, they were met that night by a small group of the
Panshir's best bodyguards and soldiers. A Spectre gunship
loomed overhead and two more choppers stayed in the air
carrying a counterassault team of Delta Force operators as
Mulholland and his group jumped off their choppers. It was
his first sit-down with the leaders of the Northern Alliance.
More Delta Force commandos escorted him as the group was
taken to a guesthouse nearby.

Mulholland wisely spent his time listening, answering
only a few questions that arose during the meeting, mostly
about how Special Forces could help the alliance coordinate
ground operations throughout the country. Mulholland and
his team convinced the Northern Alliance they could win
with the Green Berets helping them.

"They are going to help us by providing the data to link up
more and more teams. General Franks wants us to pick up the
pace, and he's bonded with the Northern Alliance," Mulholland said. But special operators noted that Franks had pissed
off more than one Afghan commander with his attitude, when
he backed off from a customary Afghan embrace, and later

failed to listen to the commander's advice on bombing techniques and angles of attack.

Still, the Northern Alliance desperately needed to hear the
message. The U.S. had discreetly funded Ahmad Shah Massoud, the leader of the Northern Alliance, throughout the
1990s. Other international contributors like Russia and France
had also helped, which allowed the organization to hang on
to more than 10 percent of the land area of Afghanistan. But,
Massoud was never given enough resources to win, only
enough to ensure a stalemate. It was an error that helped
bring about bin Laden's ability to mount the 9/11 attacks.

Massoud was a force to be reckoned with. Bin Laden knew
that with Massoud heading the battle and with U.S. close air
support on hand, the Taliban could be overwhelmed. Bin
Laden needed Massoud out of the picture and the Northern
Alliance fragmented. Massoud's charisma had kept warring
tribal factions from splitting off the United Front coalition,
now known as the Northern Alliance, and the threat of his
powerful and professional Panshir army kept his tribal factions from killing each other for sport.

On September 9, Massoud was mortally wounded by AQ-
trained assassins from Belgium posing as journalists during a
filmed interview at his Khoja-Bahaudeen headquarters. The
bomb was concealed in a television camera, the same camera
the film crew had used to interview other Northern Alliance
officials, such as Dr. Abdullah Abdullah and Yunis Quanuni
over the preceding months. The assassination had been engineered months ahead of time by bin Laden, with the assassins gaining Massoud's trust each time they interviewed
one of his compatriots. During the interview at Massoud's
headquarters, they detonated the concealed explosive device,
killing one assassin and Commander Massoud, and wounding one assassin and Massoud's number-one man, Massoud
Khalili. The injured assassin was machine-gunned to death as
he fled the building. Then Massoud's bodyguards emptied
their weapons into the murderer's lifeless body as they cried
out for their beloved leader.

Massoud died in his MI-8 helicopter en route to a hospital in Dushanbe. Meanwhile Khalili, one of the most powerful and stabilizing forces in the Northern Alliance, was effectively taken out of the war while he underwent medical treatment for a lost eye and shredded arm. Khalili was a great leader, close to Massoud both in spirit and battle. It was a miracle he had survived the blast at all.

One possible choice to take over as defense minister was General Gada, but Gada was aging, almost in his sixties, ancient by Afghan standards. Khalili, Abdullah, and Quanuni decided to pass the reins to another who showed prowess in combat and absolute loyalty to Massoud.

The Northern Alliance was in danger of disintegrating until General Mohammed Qassim Fahim stepped up to take the helm and stabilize the organization. Fahim was loyal to Massoud, and loyal to the cause, and loyalty was a priceless commodity in Afghanistan.

The Agency

The biggest obstacle to progress in establishing relationships with potential resistance elements in Afghanistan was that the CIA had been gutted for so many decades. Human intelligence in Afghanistan was virtually nonexistent. That entire area of operations had been gravely overlooked during the Clinton administration, and now America was paying a hefty price for it. As ex–CIA operative Robert Baer explained in his book, *See No Evil,* the CIA was now "enamored of satellite technology and scared of its own shadow."

The nation, shocked by September 11, realized the shortfall and began investing heavily to correct the situation. The CIA's counterterrorism center increased rapidly in size, hiring hundreds of operatives. The effort was an absolute requirement for successful implementation of the global war against terrorism.

To help in Afghanistan, the Patriot Act was passed in Washington, D.C. The CIA was now authorized to use its

150-man covert paramilitary force, known as the Special Activities Division, or Special Purpose Force, to conduct sabotage missions, collect intelligence, and to help gather support from the Northern Alliance.

J. Cofer Black, director of the CIA's Counter-terrorism Center, was a huge hulk of a man, with short brushed-back hair, wire-rimmed glasses, and a constant scowl. While others called George Tenet "George," Cofer Black called him "Mr. Director." Black had served in the Sudan and had been involved in the 1994 capture of Carlos the Jackal. Although his budget and resources were virtually unlimited after September 11, Black complained he was shorthanded and underresourced. The highest levels of the CIA still didn't understand one thing—money could not compensate for lack of experience and lack of HUMINT skills, meaning human intelligence, in operators on the ground.

But at least he had a plan and he had a personal interest— in 1995 bin Laden's terrorists had tried to kill Black in Karthoum. The CIA sent teams into Afghanistan in late September and early October to make contact with the Northern Alliance and to set conditions for the arrival of the Green Berets. The most important task was to find key leaders who could bring followers and forces to bear against the Taliban. CIA agents were airdropped into northern Afghanistan. A four-man team set up a listening post to intercept al-Qaida communications and conducted training for Northern Alliance allies. But the brief training session was virtually worthless. "The briefing was conducted entirely in English," said Haroun Amin, the spokesman for the Northern Alliance in Washington.

The Agency's clandestine-services folks were not only shorthanded and overcommitted, they were totally unprepared for this new, unconventional war. The Agency found itself putting in operators fresh out of training and lacking in language skills. But the Agency did have a plan and a solution. The Green Berets jokingly referred to the Agency's "brilliant" tactical plan as OPERATION U.S. DOLLARS. They would correct zero planning and lack of operational understanding with hard cash. It was the American way. And there was no shortage of cash and no restrictions on how they spread it around. It worked well at first, but the rapidly escalating inflation was impacting the Special Forces teams on the ground. Coupled with the flurry of cash CNN, the BBC, and the major networks were paying out in northern Afghanistan, jeep rentals quickly went from $5 a day to $100 a day. United States Special Operations Forces and the CIA found themselves losing interpreters to news agencies that were paying more than $150 a day.

Special Forces always had a tenuous relationship with the CIA, but over the last few years that relationship had improved immeasurably. The task of keeping that relationship on track would fall to a single man known simply as "L."

Now on board at the Agency as special CIA advisor to the U.S. Army Special Operations Command, the former Green Beret colonel brought the two organizations together with hard work, honesty, and loyalty to both, and that would be a critical factor in winning the war. However, in spite of more money and people, the CIA's paramilitary forces would continue to fall short in Afghanistan. "L"'s Green Berets would not.

"The Natural Order of Things"

Mulholland recalled one of his mentors, a colonel in Panama back in 1989, discussing the "natural order of things." The colonel explained that the natural order of things was to have the Green Berets and the CIA work closely together to solve problems before they became large enough to cause the U.S. to deploy conventional forces. That strategy had been successful: the Agency and the Green Berets had extinguished almost a dozen Communist-inspired guerrilla wars in Latin America alone.

"The primary reason to keep the CIA and the Department of Defense's Special Operations capability separate, one with the responsibility for covert operations and the other with the 'punch' and a large military capability, should be clear to us all. We can always work together, but we need separate bosses."

The colonel had paused, then said, "We don't want a single agency to have both the covert mechanisms and a large military capability because, not now, but potentially at some dark moment in the future, such an organization could threaten the Constitution of the United States and our democratically elected leadership. It's all about positive friction, checks and balances."

The nation was beginning a new kind of war, and the powers of the CIA and the Green Berets would have to be combined for the War on Terror to be successful.

Mulholland walked into his Tactical Operations Center, which was growing by the day. He could see the natural order of things taking place. Yet getting teams into Afghanistan was becoming a major issue because of lack of intelligence and a shortage of Agency liaisons with the Northern Alliance. The CENTCOM staff was asking on a daily basis why the 5th Special Forces Group wasn't making more progress. The issue wasn't just intelligence. Enemy air defense, prohibitive weather, and dust storms were combining to create an environment unfavorable toward flying teams into a hostile area.

On the border regions of Afghanistan, where Special Forces could manage to link up with resistance forces, TASK FORCE DAGGER began to set up meetings with potential allies. One such meeting was particularly important. Captain Jason "Luke" Amerine and three other Green Berets flew in to hold a meeting with eight Afghan men who had their own troops and might be willing to join the fight. One of them was named Hamid Karzai. Karzai was suave, calm, cool, and collected. He looked like an aristocratic Afghan version of Jean-Luc Picard from *Star Trek: The Next Generation*. Karzai was bald but with a neatly trimmed beard. With his high-thread-count collarless Nehru-style shirts, he looked more like a fashion designer than a warlord. Unlike the other commanders, Hamid Karzai was a politician and a humanitarian first, a military officer

second. In some places *mujahadeen* followed their commanders out of fear or respect. The Pashtun people followed Karzai
out of love.

But things were still going slow. Bush and Rumsfeld
wanted action, and they wanted it now. Colonel Mulholland
decided to start taking greater risks by sending some teams in
virtually blind. Blind insertions meant that the Green Berets
going in would have scant information beyond the names of
Northern Alliance leaders they should seek out for discussion. The Green Berets were ecstatic—their leashes were
now completely off.

Freedom to Excel

General Doug Brown had given Colonel John Mulholland
something every Army officer dreams of: the freedom to command. As long as TASK FORCE DAGGER operated within
its charter, conducting unconventional warfare to overthrow
the Taliban, John could fight the battle as he wished. In the
Army, constraints on a commander's actions are called "left
and right limits," a borrowing of the military term for measures confining the field of fire on a firing range.

Mulholland's left and right limits were as broad as anyone
had ever seen. The staff of TASK FORCE DAGGER put together its plan and executed it in the manner they deemed appropriate. Later, as the theater became safer and more stable,
Franks would send in Lieutenant General Paul T. Mikolashek
to command as situations on the battlefield grew in complex-
ity. But initially, Mulholland had the operational control, and
the staff of TASK FORCE DAGGER embraced the moment.

The Task Force began inserting A-Teams deep into Afghanistan, playing a game of high-risk poker. They put one
team in with zero/zero visibility, which meant that the 160th
NightStalkers had to fly over the mountains and into steep valleys totally blind, using only their sophisticated radars and
thermal imagery to give them a virtual picture to fly by.

Who Dares Wins

Mulholland's JSOTF would also encompass the SAS operators working in Afghanistan, and their missions would be coordinated with JSOC as they would work closely with Delta Force and TF 160.

Captain David Stirling had formed the British Special Air Service Group in 1941, as a small World War II commando unit to operate in North Africa, Burma, and throughout the theaters. When he first went to pitch the idea to GHQ Cairo, he was turned away by the gate guards. Stirling, recovering from a parachute injury, and on crutches, circled around the compound, ditched his crutches, jumped the fence, and walked into Major General Neil Ritchie's office unannounced. The plan for a small raiding unit to attack German airfields in North Africa, to be known as Layforce, was accepted. The full name, "L Detachment Special Air Service," was by mere accident, invented by GHQ because it provided a deception of a far larger force in the British Order of Battle by virtue of its name.

By the end of World War II, the SAS, now a permanent regiment in the British Army, under the command of Colonel Sir David Stirling, DSO, CBE, OBE, had earned its place in history. The world would see their skills firsthand on May 5, 1980, as they staged their daring raid at 16 Princes Gate, rescuing hostages and killing the terrorists who had laid siege to the Iranian Embassy. Operation Nimrod had been an overwhelming success, but it was not their first, or their last. They would achieve legendary fame in places like Oman, and were particularly adept at desert warfare as they had proven in Desert Storm when SAS Sergeant Andy McNabb and his small team had decimated Iraqi opponents, although only five of McNabb's team survived. One even succeeded in escaping across enemy lines in spite of being chased by half the Iraqi Army.

The SAS was an incredibly small force, headquartered at Bradbury Lines in England, eventually renamed Stirling Lines after their legendary founder. They trained and trained hard in the Brecon Beacons, the harsh mountains in Wales.

As SAS hero Andy McNabb wrote in *Bravo Two Zero*, "you're turned loose on the Black Mountains dressed in Second World War battledress trousers and shirt, a greatcoat with no buttons and boots with no laces . . . you are subjected to intensive interrogation—stripped naked, hung up by your ankles . . ." and walking in miserable conditions for days on end.

The 22nd SAS is comprised of four operational squadrons and one reserve squadron, each with sixty men, plus a squadron commander (a major), an executive officer, a sergeant major, and the necessary quartermaster and administrative personnel. There are also two reserve groups, the 21st and 23rd, called Territorials—one headquartered at the Duke of York's Chelsea Barracks in London, the other at Birmingham. Colonel Charlie Beckwith had not only served with the SAS in Malaysia in the 1960s, he had actually attended the SAS selection course in 1962. He had come to admire them for their abilities to persevere in the most difficult situations, and their ability to think on their own without directive and in the absence of formal orders. More important, then-Captain Beckwith, had come to admire them because they didn't take everyone, hell, they almost didn't take anyone. Beckwith noted that it was not uncommon for the SAS to run a selection course and wash out the entire class. Back then you basically joined the U.S. Special Forces and were given your Green Beret, but Beckwith observed that you had to earn your way into the SAS, and you had to pass a selection course that was designed to fail you, before you were "badged" with the winged dagger, actually not a dagger, but the sword of Excalibur. Beckwith brought this concept back to Special Forces and it forever changed the way the Green Berets would recruit their men.

When Beckwith took over the Special Forces School in 1974, he immediately turned it into the course from Hell. When Beckwith formed Delta Force in 1978, he not only patterned Delta's near impossible selection course after the SAS selection course in Wales, but he also patterned their operational TO&E, Table of Organization and Equipment, after the

SAS. Relying on his old friend Sergeant Major Walt Shumate, Beckwith began building America's version of the SAS. Shumate had fashioned Beckwith's original Project Delta selection course in Vietnam around the British SAS selection course, and now, more than a decade later, Beckwith had brought Walt Shumate back to build an impossible and brutal selection course for his new Delta Force. An average-size man with a big handlebar mustache, Shumate was the kind of legend David Stirling would have been proud of. His battlefield exploits against the Viet Cong were still winning him medals in 1993, twenty-five years later, as missions were declassified. Beckwith even went so far as to set up Delta with Squadrons and Troops, which was virtually unheard of in the U.S. military prior to that, except in the air cavalry units.

Seventy-eight Britons had died in the World Trade Center attack, and British Defence Minister Geoff Hoon had gladly offered his lads to Generals Brown and Franks. Britain's MI6 would also come on board swiftly, working with the CIA and Special Operations Forces to collect, sort, and disseminate intelligence. The British Special Forces also had an advantage in that the DIS, MI5 and MI6 regularly exchanged and shared information, and came under the same command.

Less than one-tenth the size of the CIA, the Secret Intelligence Service had been in the espionage business long before the CIA. It was formed in 1909, under Sir Mansfield Cumming, who signed all documents and orders, as simply "C," which was to become a long-standing tradition. Since that time, all of his successors have been known only as "C" not "M," as portrayed in the Bond films. They were diffferent from the CIA in many ways, such as restraint—MI6 were immune to prosecution for crimes committed outside Great Britain, which gave them a level of operational flexibility that the CIA could only drool over. Another difference, which would be especially important in the new War on Terror, was the MI6 always had a direct line to SAS headquarters, and had a long history of joint operations with SAS operators specifically trained to undertake tasks too dangerous or too militarily specific for MI6. Known under the ultrasecret code word *Increment*, these dozen SAS operators would engage in the direct action strikes and assassination of AQ terrorists in a variety of countries. Although they didn't wear tuxedos, or drive Aston Martins, they really did have a license to kill.

Get Ready to Roll

The air component under the command of the U.S. Air Force's Lieutenant Colonel Frank Kinzer began contingency planning for tentative selection of landing zones in the respective areas of sympathetic Afghan leaders. Since each Northern Alliance leader had been given a brand-new Thuraya satellite cell phone at the end of the meeting, link-up plans were now within their capabilities. Unconfirmed reports stated that the leaders had also been paid more than $200,000 in cash each to pay and feed their troops, either by the State Department or the Agency, depending on the source of the information.

Problems persisted, however, including excessive enemy fire, horrible weather, and poor communications. In early November, the mountain weather was so bad that when one Green Beret fell desperately ill from altitude sickness, the Army aviators had to turn back even though the soldier was in serious trouble.

Colonel Mulholland ordered a USAF Special Operations helicopter to fly from another direction into the site. When the pilot pushed his chopper too far up the mountain, the rotors iced up, and the aircraft crashed. The crew had to climb down the mountain and be picked up at a lower altitude. Later, the 160th NightStalkers were able to pull the soldier out and medically evacuate him to Tajikistan, where he was stabilized, then on to Germany for further treatment.

The Army's point man on problems in Tajikistan was having a busy week. Major David Brigham was a tall, well-built, typically rock-hard Green Beret. His brother played professional football, and Brigham looked like he wasn't too bad at the "third and long" either. Officially Brigham was the defense attaché, or DAT, at the U.S. embassy in Dushanbe, Tajikistan. That meant dealing with everyday defense matters one might encounter in a post-Soviet regime, with more than 76,000 Russian troops still garrisoned in country, and with a violent civil war and border dispute with Uzbekistan in the not-too-distant past.

Unofficially, Brigham was a jack-of-all-trades. As the DAT, Brigham was, as he often put it, "busier than a one-armed paper hanger." Luckily for TASK FORCE DAGGER, he was an old-school, Special Forces–qualified officer. He was hard-core, smart, and relentless. When the teams on the ground needed help, Brigham was there, getting clearances for AC-130 Spectre gunships, housing aircrews and maintenance people, and, most important, greasing the wheels of cooperation with the Tajik government. His suave demeanor and low-key, likable style were his forte, and he kept supplies, aircraft, and people moving smoothly in and out of Tajikistan. When military, Agency, and civilian covert operators came in, Brigham was there to pave the way.

Brigham had already won Tajik hearts and minds; the pro-Russian Tajiks not only respected him, they genuinely liked him. Rather than using cash to gain their assistance, Brigham came up with a brilliant idea. He supplied Tajik officials with office equipment, copy machines, and leather recliners in return for their support, a strategy that had the collateral effect of nation building. During later meetings when additional landing permission or overflight clearances were needed, he simply had to smile and compliment their new offices. Brigham made the job of garnering cooperation from a government laden with multiple levels of Soviet-style bureaucracy look simple. He made solving impossible logistical problems look like magic. His skill paid off exponentially for TASK FORCE DAGGER and the American war effort.

Dave Brigham worked closely with Colonel Abdul Quadusy Wadood, the Senior Military Attaché for the United Front Military Forces (the Northern Alliance). Wadood, as his friends called him, was an exceptional Afghan soldier. He

had been a close friend of Commander Massoud, and had
been by his side many times in battle. Like the rest of the
Northern Alliance, Wadood was in a virtual state of depression since his beloved commander had been killed, but he
knew that now that America had turned its attention to
Afghanistan, there was hope for the Northern Alliance.
Wadood was a true friend of America, and became a friend of
Dave Brigham. Together they worked day and night to build
the American-Afghan coalition that would be needed to win
the war.

Not Panic, Concern

In the last few days of October, the temperature started to rise
in Washington, D.C. An insider in the Pentagon leaked that
there was "not yet panic, but growing concern that the unconventional warfare campaign was 'on its ass' and that more senior leaders might be needed to take over." The men at TASK
FORCE DAGGER knew the pressure was on to get the war
rolling when they heard that several generals were on their
way to take charge of the task force and other activities.

One of the majors in the Tactical Operations Center wondered aloud, "How in the fuck will putting generals in charge
make the goddamn weather improve?"

Smoke Bomb Hill

Fort Bragg, North Carolina

The anxiety in Washington worried Major General Lambert.
He was concerned that some wouldn't appreciate that the
Taliban were at the breaking point, vulnerable to cascading
effects and ready to fall like dominoes if only the Special
Forces could capture one or two major villages. Mulholland
and his Green Berets were so close to cranking it up and making good things happen.

All along, Lambert's command had contended that the two dramatic variables in the unconventional warfare campaign would be velocity and momentum. But Lambert also feared casualties. His boys would soon be in the thick of battle. He paced in his office at Fort Bragg; just a short distance away, on the other side of Smoke Bomb Hill, stood the statue of Colonel "Bull" Simons, inscribed with the Bull's answer to every dangerous mission: *Who will go? Send me.*

On October 17, Lambert received a letter from his hometown in Kansas, explaining that the congregation was going to have a special church service on the morning of Veterans Day.

CHAPTER 8

Northern Alliance— General Dostum

"I gave them fair warning."
> —PRESIDENT GEORGE W. BUSH,
> remarks to a small group
> of White House aides, October 8, 2001

"I asked for a few Americans. They brought with them the courage of a whole Army."
> —GENERAL ABDUL RASHID DOSTUM,
> late November 2001

Infiltration

Mazar-e-Sharif, Afghanistan
October 19, 2001

For several days, A-Team 595 had been trying to break out of isolation and get into the action. The aviators of the 160th SOAR had been breaking their backs to make it happen, but the weather, terrain, and enemy fire made for the worst combined conditions the veterans had ever seen. On October 19 after more intensive planning, the team tried yet again.

The MH-47, a modified twin-rotor U.S. Army Chinook CH-47, was equipped with millions of dollars' worth of equipment that allowed it to see at night, react to enemy fire, hover without using controls, and refuel in the air. With terrain-following radar, electronic countermeasures, and forward-looking infrared scanners, the MH-47 can carry twenty fully equipped special operations personnel. The MH-47s had performed exactly as expected. However, visibility and atmospheric conditions were so bad that the two MH-60 Blackhawk escorts had to turn back. The MH-47s, unprotected, continued on.

The twelve men of A-Team 595 came over the last range of mountains at almost twelve thousand feet, sliding down the back side, searching for enemy threats. Finally, in a steep valley, over a dry riverbed, the pilots' night-observation devices finally gave them the ability to pinpoint the landing zone. The problem was that it would disappear momentarily: as the helicopters broke forty feet above the ground, the swirling of fine dust that covered and permeated everything in Afghanistan caused a total blackout. The Afghan environment virtually ensured every single landing would be blind.

At 0200 hours (2 A.M.) there was a soft thump, and the men were out in seconds carrying their huge rucksacks. No longer A-Team 595, the men were now code-named TIGER 02. They were over fifty miles south of their strategic target of Mazar-e-Sharif in northern Afghanistan.

As the twin-engine MH-47s lifted off, the men waited for the rotor wash to subside before they got up from their prone positions. Their weapons were ready as they strained to see. Soon, there was no sound, only the night sky of Afghanistan. It reminded the Green Berets of the deep woods in the North Carolina mountains, where the beauty of the stars was undiminished by the lack of city lights.

The team's mission was to infiltrate and conduct the main attack in the effort to capture Mazar-e-Sharif. A victory would seize a key airfield, open a road to Uzbekistan, shake the very spine of the Taliban and al-Qaida, and hopefully have a cascading effect on the enemy in the north, causing a roll-up in subsequent battles.

Simplified, the mission was unlike any mission they had ever been on, or heard of before—"Find and support Dostum, stay with him and help. Go with him wherever he goes—if he wants to take over Kabul, go. If he wants to take over the whole fucking country, that's fine too. If he starts mass executions on the way, call HQ and advise, maybe exfil if you can't rein him in."

The members of TIGER 02 had listened well in isolation, even if it had been the shortest isolation of their career, only two days. They were going to operate on intent, and would find some way, somehow, to make it happen.

The dust had now cleared, and several Afghan men stood waiting in the distance. The Afghans began to walk carefully toward the team. Like a band of rebels from *Star Wars,* they were alien-looking. Their dress was ancient, but interspersed with various military uniform pieces: an odd top here, a different set of pants there. In one hand they held Russian assault rifles, in the other they held their turban on their head, or their scarf across their face, as the wind whipped it in the desert air. They began picking up their step as the second wave of dust settled from the MH-47's takeoff. There was little time for greetings or introductions; they had to move quickly off the dangerous LZ, landing zone. There was also little doubt they were linking up with the right guys, or else everyone would already be shooting at each other. TIGER 02 followed their escorts.

After traveling a few hours, the team reached a small village where they would stay the night. Like all the villages of northern Afghanistan, it was nothing more than a collection of mud huts and mud walls. The next morning a wave of more than sixty *muj* cavalry came thundering up and surrounded the guesthouse. The group's leader sat on his horse and yelled into his ten-dollar radio. Ten minutes later Dostum galloped into the middle of the first entourage wearing a blue turban and a big grin, surrounded by another sixty *muj* with their guns in the air. The first group had laid out Afghan carpets on the sand. Dostum shook their hands and motioned them toward the carpets for *chai* (tea) and a meeting.

The CIA had told them that Dostum spoke Arabic, and the team, most of them Arabic speakers, tried communicating with him. Neither Dostum, nor anyone else in his group, had a clue as to what they were trying to say. Luckily, the

Afghans were adept at conversing with hand gestures, eye contact, and innuendo. The A-Team's three Russian speakers asked if anyone spoke Russian, and used some common Russian military phrases. They figured that Dostum had fought the Russians and surely there must be "a goddamn Russian speaker" on his staff. Dostum did understand some Russian, although he never let on that he did. Dostum sent for several of his older men who knew Russian, and their language capability turned out to be adequate to start a dialogue with the Northern Alliance general.

Dostum had originally been trained by the Soviet Army and had led a special armored reaction unit that would be called into battle if the Soviets had problems with the Afghan locals. Dostum became disenchanted with the Soviets and distressed by the plight of his Uzbek brethren in the northern provinces of Afghanistan. He soon defected. It was a defection the Soviets would sorely regret.

From the moment the team had arrived and met Dostum, they realized they had gotten bad intelligence. This was no surprise: if you believed in ground truth from intelligence reports, you probably also believed in the tooth fairy.

According to the CIA's reports, General Dostum was eighty-three years old, had recently had a stroke, was missing one arm, and had a fierce hatred for Americans. When the team arrived, however, they noted that Dostum was only fifty-two or fifty-three years old, in fine physical shape, had all his arms and legs, and was waiting for the team with open arms and a big ear-to-ear grin.

So much for the CIA reports. . . .

General Dostum announced that they were leaving immediately to move to his headquarters. They had only six extra horses for their American allies, so TIGER 02 had to quickly split in half.

The team was given twenty minutes to prepare, and equipment was rapidly swapped around. The men negotiated for a mud hut for the remaining six team members and all of their gear. They immediately converted the hut to an aid station where the team's medics could look after wounded or ill *muj*.

The *mujahadeen* were irritated that the Americans always kept a man awake and on guard even though the *muj* had security well in hand. The Green Berets knew too well of past betrayals by guards in other Muslim countries who would switch allegiance for the highest bidder. They were taking no chances. TIGER 02 would have to find other ways to build trust and confidence with Dostum's troops; personal safety would not be one of them.

As TIGER 02 sent a small patrol to scout out the area and look for ways the Taliban would approach if they were to attack, the "docs" put poncho liners in the hut's shattered windows to help break the cold wind, and began to set up a guerrilla hospital. They would also guard the team's significant stash of U.S. dollars as well as the rest of their gear.

The role of the men left behind would be to work with General Dostum's supply officer to determine the needs of Dostum's forces. TIGER 02 would then survey drop zones for USAF cargo aircraft and request airdrops of equipment for their *muj* forces.

Captain Mark Nutsch was the only man on the team who was proficient at riding a horse. A biology major at Kansas State University, he had found time to ride in rodeos, his main event being calf roping. Nevertheless, he was terrified as they moved through the dark along the mountain trails. One slip would mean the horse and its rider would both fall to their deaths. He decided not to tell his team members how dangerous the trails were, letting ignorance be bliss for the novice riders.

Problems began after the first two hours. First of all, the brass stirrups were too small for most of the men's combat boots, so only their toes would fit, causing excessive jostling in the wooden saddles covered with carpet. The results were incredible soreness and discomfort.

The men had begun the trek with their load-bearing equipment, or "web gear," over their shoulders. The weight of all the gear and ammunition, bouncing up and down, compressed the back of one team member. He was in such excruciating pain he had to be physically lifted off his mount. The team medic gave him a muscle relaxer to allow him to continue, and the rest of the men tied down their web gear behind their saddles to take the pressure off their spines.

Finally, after six incredibly fatiguing hours, the team arrived at their destination, Dostum's headquarters, and bedded down. Every single bone and muscle in their bodies ached. They could barely sit down, let alone stand.

By morning, just a few hours away, the really hard work would begin.

Building Trust and Preparing for the Offensive

It became quite evident that Dostum considered TIGER 02 to be the crown jewels, his umbilical cord to gaining the wherewithal to fight. Dostum announced that he would rather lose five hundred of his cavalrymen before he would allow one American to be killed.

Working their way through the intricacies of Afghani planning, which always included cups of *chai* and small talk, the team slowly learned of the Northern Alliance cavalry's difficulties.

First of all, the "army" of General Dostum consisted of a few full-timers, who naturally expected to be paid. The real army was the militia, who showed up to fight at the last moment when called. Even so, Dostum could mass up to two thousand horse-mounted cavalry for short-duration skirmishes.

Second, Dostum had no trusted deputy commander, because having one meant that he would be extremely susceptible to being done in or sold out. Therefore, he deliberately kept all subordinates weak, so they had to rely on him alone for sustenance, recognition, and power.

Finally, although Dostum was glad to have TIGER 02 on board, he wasn't too keen on getting them into the fight. Dostum seemed to view the team more as bankers than warriors, and you have to keep your bankers alive. After several days the team finally convinced Dostum to take them near the frontlines, where they could observe the enemy.

When TIGER 02 was finally escorted to the front, they immediately called for some close air support assets. They were forced to use World War I and II techniques to bracket targets since they had yet to receive the airdrop of supplies from TASK FORCE DAGGER headquarters, which would include the team's laser markers and spotting scopes. These items would be necessary for calling in air strikes with laser-guided smart bombs.

Their first air strike easily destroyed an enemy bunker. The *muj* loved it, patting the Green Berets vigorously on their backs. The Northern Alliance had previously lost their faith in American air power because the early pounding had been solely against strategic targets and air defense systems. This was their first chance to see American firepower up close and personal. TIGER 02 complained to Dostum that they needed to get much closer to be really effective. However, General Dostum was still not ready to put them at risk, especially since General Fahim had repeatedly warned him not to let an American be killed, or even wounded, for fear of losing American support.

When they reluctantly returned to the rear, there was clearly a higher level of respect for the men of TIGER 02. The team and Dostum began to collaborate in earnest. The Green Berets requested saddles, feed, blankets, Soviet ammunition, food, and water airdrops to amass enough sustainment supplies to move into combat.

TIGER 02 quickly learned that the one absolute faux pas was to suggest to any of the *muj* that they needed training. It was the gravest insult. The *muj* had complete confidence that they were the finest warriors in the world; after all, they had beaten the Soviets. To suggest that they stand down from a fight for training first would be simply unacceptable.

The A-Team decided they needed to procure their own horses, and obtained several for $300 a head. Within a week, after the word spread, the price was up to $1,000 per horse for the Americans. It was the economy of war.

Master Sergeant Paul Evans was amazed. Everything was unfolding like the guerrilla warfare manuals stated, including the incredible inflation a small unconventional warfare effort could have on small-village economies. Little had changed from when the Special Forces' founder, Colonel Aaron Bank, after having worked with the French resistance and being supplied with free meals from a local restaurant, was handed an exorbitant bill immediately after the German surrender.

The Taliban still had antiaircraft capability, and the airdrops of supplies landed all over the map because of the high altitude necessary to ensure safe delivery. The advertised drop accuracy was supposedly within one hundred meters of the team's given grid coordinate. It proved to be more like one thousand meters. Many bundles were broken open, and sometimes the contents were destroyed after they bounced down rocky hillsides. The whole effort was extremely frustrating, but the force was slowly building and increasing in strength.

One night, TIGER 02 went out to receive a drop and was overjoyed that it had landed dead center of the given coordinates. The A-Team moved forward to inspect their bundles and immediately came under AK-47 fire. Hitting the ground, they returned fire with their M-4s, emptying several magazines, and watched as a cluster of a dozen or so men withdrew onto a hillside in the distance. The Taliban now appeared to be watching their drop zones.

The force finally built up to the point where their "motor pool," an Army term for the fleet of vehicles a unit has, consisted of over forty horses. One night, one of the A-Team's sergeants awoke to urinate. Stepping away from the bodies in sleeping bags and blankets, he moved toward where several of the horses were standing. In the bitter cold, the A-Team sergeant saw one of his newly befriended *muj* warriors sleeping fitfully on the ground, shaking, while his horse, nearby, had two brand-new U.S. Army blankets on its back. The *muj* was protecting his most valuable possession, and it left an indelible impression on the sergeant. Massoud's Northern Alliance soldiers were no strangers to personal sacrifice.

TIGER 02 was now ready to get into the action. They had finally obtained enough horses, and TF DAGGER had finally dropped their laser markers in to them. They now could advance from bracketing to precision laser targeting. The supply boys in Germany had also included another welcome addition to the airdrops: thousand-dollar saddles bought on the local German market, with stirrups big enough for their boots.

The Charge of the Light Brigade

> *"Forward, the Light Brigade!*
> *Charge for the guns!" he said.*
> *Into the valley of Death*
> *Rode the six hundred.*
> —From the poem
>   "The Charge of the Light Brigade"
>   by Alfred, Lord Tennyson

Dostum's cavalry liked to charge at a full gallop, firing its rifles on horseback. Ideally, they would close on the enemy so fast the enemy couldn't react, and the horsemen would mow them down with their AK-47s.

Over the next days, TIGER 02 would ride with the *muj,* and ride hard. They developed an effective method of warfare with Dostum's love of cavalry charges. One part of the team would stay on the ridges, lazing targets and sending in the bombs, and as soon as they detonated, the rest of the team would charge with Dostum, guns blazing. The Taliban and AQ would still have their heads down when Dostum and the boys overran the enemy positions jumping over AQ bodies and galloping through the bomb debris. At night the horses would literally drop from exhaustion and sleep on the ground. Some of the horses weren't broken in for the noise levels, and the team would frequently find themselves thrown off the startled horses onto the ground.

At one point as they were attacking the Taliban, a ZSU-23-4 Soviet antiaircraft gun was leveled at their cavalry. The ZSU was thumping as it sent rounds tearing through the horses and men. TIGER 02's CAS team was lazing targets as fast as they could, but fighters and bombers were off station.

"ZSU, ZSU, I need some fucking air support *now!*"

"We've got no one on station, pull back."

Ignoring the warning, the charge continued. ZSU bullets were raining down like a hailstorm on Dostum and Tiger 02. Dostum didn't flinch, he didn't pull back, and he didn't care how many men he lost. He was going to rout the terrorists once and for all now that he had started. TIGER 02 wasn't turning back either.

"Ride on, Regulators!" they screamed over the radio. "The Regulators" was the unofficial name of TIGER 02. The term was taken from the old cowboy days, when "Regulators" would be brought in by the wealthy cattle ranchers to shoot poachers with their Sharps .50-caliber long-range rifles. It was the Wild West, and they were on the wide-open ranges working with the ranchers and regulating the bad guys.

As the Regulators rode into the hail of bullets, they came to the base of the hill where the ZSU was. Dostum wasted no time waiting for air support or planning.

"The fucking lunatic is charging them!" The team was obviously growing fond of Dostum and couldn't help but admire his courage.

Dostum had grabbed an AK-47 from one of his men and charged up the hill on foot ahead of everyone else. Three TIGER 02 Green Berets were on his heels as Dostum took out the Taliban position. Such was the life of TIGER 02, riding with the *muj* cavalry and charging Taliban hills with Dostum and his band of rebels.

In their first major battle, TIGER 02 saw six hundred *muj* cavalrymen overrun a Taliban trench line, flushing the Taliban soldiers out and chasing them down like wild beasts. The team members' adrenaline peaked as they witnessed the scene. There was something instinctively stimulating about it. One team member said it was "deeper, almost genetic."

The Taliban had tricked them, however. They had pulled their tanks and personnel carriers off-line, hiding them on the reverse slope of the rolling ridgeline. The tanks were used to counterattack the vulnerable horsemen as they crested the ridge in pursuit of dismounted Taliban. Dostum's *muj* took heavy casualties, and after a day of fighting, the Taliban had retaken their original positions. The team couldn't see the reverse slope of the ridges held by the Taliban, which had limited their ability to levy effective firepower on the enemy.

Nonetheless, from four thousand meters away, the team had lazed a T-55 tank that the Taliban pulled into position on the ridgeline. A Marine F/A-18 pilot was overhead and dropped a smart bomb dead on top of the Russian tank, and the turret went spinning in the air. The reaction of the *muj* was unbelievable. The men cheered and clambered forward to embrace the team members.

From that point on Dostum was going to allow the Americans to get as close to the enemy as they wanted.

The First Publicized Field Report

The frustrations in Washington, D.C., over the seeming lack of progress with the Northern Alliance had impacted down to team level. On October 28, TIGER 02 sent the first the publicly released and most famous field report of the war. The report was printed in virtually every newspaper in America.

The complete, un-redacted message is below. The entire first paragraph was not released to the press for obvious reasons, and the rest is in the original form.

In regards to your questions about us and the Northern Alliance just sitting around and doing nothing let me explain some of the realities on the ground.

I am advising a man on how to best employ light infantry and horse cavalry in the attack against Taliban Russian T-55 tanks, Russian armored personnel carriers, BTRs, mortars, artillery, ZSU anti-aircraft guns and machine guns. I can't recall the U.S. fighting like this since the Gatling gun destroyed Pancho Villa's charges in the Mexican Civil War in the early 19th century.

We have done this every day since we hit the ground. The men attack with ten AK-47 bullets per man, with their machine gun (PK) gunners with less than 100 rounds, and with less than 5 rounds per RPG-7 (rocket launchers). They have little water and less food.

I observed a PK gunner who walked 10 miles to get into the fight who was proud to show his artificial right leg from the knee down, caused by a Talib round years ago.

We have witnessed the horse cavalry use bounding overwatch from spur to spur to carry wounded from Taliban strong points, under heavy mortar, ZSU, artillery, RPG, and PK fire.

There is little medical care for the injured, only a donkey-ride to the aid station, which is a mud hut.

We are doing amazingly well with what we have. We have killed over 125 Taliban and captured over 100 while losing 8 KIA [*mujahadeen*]. Frankly, I am surprised that we have not been slaughtered.

We will get better at working things out as we go. It is a challenge just to have food and water for a few days. These folks have nothing. I have ridden 15 miles a day since arriving, yet everywhere I go the civilians and the *"muj"* soldiers are always telling me they are glad the USA has come here with planes to kill the Taliban. They all speak of their hopes for a better Afghanistan once the Taliban are gone. We killed the bastards by the bushel-full today, and we'll get more tomorrow. The team sends its regards.

Dealing with the problem of being blind to the reverse slope of the rolling terrain was going to be the key to victory. Master Sergeant Evans decided to rectify the problem by splitting his A-Team into four groups of three men each. They would take up to twenty *muj* on horseback for protection, and would sneak behind enemy lines and set up on mountainous vantage points *beside* and *behind* the enemy, leapfrogging to maintain advantage while they called in vicious air strikes on the Taliban positions.

The A-Team was reunited once more, plans were made, and again the team split, hoping to see one another after the big push toward the city of Mazar-e-Sharif.

Air Support and the Angel of Death

One of the main problems with Navy fighters was that they usually only had around fifteen minutes of "loiter" time on an objective. If they couldn't be vectored onto a tank or other visible target quickly, they would divert to any Special Forces team that was trading blows with the enemy at that moment. USAF bombers, on the other hand, with their precision weapons mix, could hang around all day long. In fact, the difference was so striking that many of the A-Teams later recommended that investing in bomber and unmanned aerial vehicle (UAV) stocks would be a wise move over the next two decades. Fighters were rapidly becoming a third priority. Still, fighters would be important in Iraq and Iran when that day came.

The Joint Forces Air Component Command, or JFACC, managed the air campaign. TIGER 02 was initially not a popular customer. The first flare-up that occurred between TIGER 02 and the JFACC came over the initial wasting of bombs by bracketing. The Air Force officers in the JFACC were upset with the archaic means of adjusting fire and had to be educated by Special Forces Command that the A-Team didn't have the wherewithal to fight any other way at the moment. They had been forced to drop all of their heavy equipment to make the initial move through the mountains on horseback, and simply didn't yet have their laser markers, batteries, and other equipment needed to reach their full combat interdiction capacity.

The second "disagreement" between the Green Berets and the JFACC happened when a U.S. Marine Corps' F/A-18 Hornet came in hot and low and smoked the enemy with incredibly accurate fire for a ten-minute period. The Marine pilot was "switched on," with close air support down to an art, and it took seconds to talk him into action and turn him loose. The next day some Navy pilots flew overhead and were slow to pick up targets. TIGER 02 became impatient. The result was a JFACC call to TASK FORCE DAGGER's operations officer, Lieutenant Colonel Wes Rehorn. The JFACC officer was pissed.

Rehorn took the whipping over the phone. Apparently the TIGER 02 boys were frustrated that the Navy pilots couldn't vector in and verify what the team wanted to hit, so a team member had told one of the pilots to "get down below twenty-five thousand feet like the stud did yesterday and you might be able to see the fucking target!"

Rehorn scolded, "Captain Nutsch, if you want to be supported, don't berate the pilots. They'll stop showing up."

Nutsch, Evans, and the rest of their A-Team realized that being a little more congenial and professional was in their best interest. While they were Dostum's umbilical cord, precision weaponry was part of theirs.

For critical nighttime fire support, the team asked TASK FORCE DAGGER for an AC-130 Spectre gunship. The Spectre gunship flies only at night, blacked out, with no lights at all. The crew flies with the aid of sophisticated night-vision devices, and the AC-130's side-mounted cannons are equipped with thermal sensors that detect the heat from bodies and vehicles.

Like its Vietnam predecessor, "Puff the Magic Dragon," the Spectre is easily described by Special Forces troops on the ground as "raining death." With Chain guns, an auto-loading 105mm cannon, a 25mm Gatling gun and a Bofors 40mm cannon, the Spectre can cover a battlefield with more rounds per square foot than any other combat platform in the world, and the USAF Spectre crews live up to their motto: "Death Waits in the Dark."

The Spectre circles the battlefield in varying orbits to elude enemy antiaircraft fire. Spectre's crews quickly observed that enemy antiaircraft weapons were not a problem.

The Taliban and AQ did not have the night-vision devices needed to spot the elusive, low-flying weapons platform. "You could see the Taliban down below as we would fly over them," one of the Spectre's crew recalled, "but they would just shoot at the sounds of our engine, which makes a low droning sound that's hard to place. You could see through their body movements that they had no idea where the ammunition was coming from. When we would open up on them, they would just scatter like ants in every direction."

The Spectre's weapons release officer was a woman, a stunning USAF captain named Allison. "Ally" 's voice on the plane's intercom and over the radio, as she coordinated the deadly 105mm and 40mm explosive rounds, seemed to flow like poetry as the Taliban bodies stacked up, resulting in her being nicknamed "the Angel of Death."

Ally and the rest of her crew would watch the Taliban fighters on the ground through the Spectre's thermal optics, and after a bit of studying, they felt they could predict their movements. "The Taliban would be all grouped up in, say, the corner of a field, and we'd open fire, and they would scatter, only to group up again in another spot. So after a few minutes, we would just hold our fire and wait until they grouped up again. That saved on ammunition, and we wanted every shot to count," she recalled. Allison, originally from New York, was proud that she was able to "bring some justice" to the people who were responsible for striking out at the United States on September 11.

General Dostum was utterly amazed when he heard of Ally. He immediately called his Taliban foes on the appropriate frequency, and then asked for Allison to speak on the U.S. radio. Dostum first announced in Dari to the Taliban leader that "the United States has so little respect for you that they are using their *women* to fight you!" Then Dostum held his handset up and Allison would talk over the frequency, announcing that she had heard how badly the Taliban treated women, and she was here to give them a little payback. This was also translated to the enemy over their frequencies. The extreme gravity of the insult to an Islamic fundamentalist "holy warrior" cannot be translated.

The Spectre gunship also performed critical tasks aside from just providing fire support for the A-Teams. Special Forces A-Teams were officially called Operational Detachment Alphas, or ODAs. One such task was to provide aerial reconnaissance for the A-Teams on the ground. There is no hiding from thermal sensors, no matter how well concealed the Taliban may have been, and the information the Spectre provided to the ODAs gave them a sense of security that only "big eyes in the sky" could provide.

Working with the Spectre gunship, another variant of the aircraft, the Special Operations MC-130 Talon, performed midair refueling, often called "Texaco runs." The MC-130s provided fuel for Blackhawks, PaveLows, and other helicopters during mission-critical periods. The fuel-filled cargo planes would tell the helicopter crew to pick a time and point in space, and the two would meet at the designated location. Midair refueling enabled the helicopter pilots to work around the clock in support of Special Forces without having to return to an air base to fuel up.

The Medics

Even though their medical supplies were limited, the team would also treat the *muj*, and the Afghan soldiers and their commanders were incredibly grateful. The *muj* had never had such a luxury as quality medical support.

Special Forces medics are trained to a standard higher than any others in all the armed services. In fact, their training is so advanced that the Army Rangers, Navy SEALs, and U.S. Air Force Special Operations medics now attend a mini-version of the Special Forces training at Fort Bragg to upgrade their skills.

Green Beret medics are valued on the battlefield more than one can imagine. As combat medics, they fight alongside their teammates until someone is injured. In the field they do major surgery and other complex treatments well beyond their charter, and in the process save many lives. TIGER 02's docs were floating from mud hut to mud hut, and the guerrilla hospital was getting a thorough workout. They performed a variety of operations, including everything from treating abdominal wounds from rifle bullets to the amputation of legs and feet, the handling of land-mine-induced trauma, and the treatment of burn casualties.

TIGER 02's senior medic, Steve Kofron, treated Afghans for everything from limbs lost to land mines to bullet and shrapnel wounds. Many of the Afghans simply wanted painful teeth extracted. The A-Team docs were glad to assist, and the hospital's clientele grew and grew. One man treated by Kofron showed up weeks later in Mazar-e-Sharif, still taking his pills (called meds by the SF docs) and getting along with no signs of infection. Many *muj* came back to thank Kofron and the rest of the SF medics.

The rapport-building by Special Forces teams has always been the key to their effectiveness, and it has always been successful due to a combination of factors: language, cultural awareness, living under the same conditions, sharing common goals, war-fighting skills, and the fact that the teams care for their comrades, their families, villagers, and even captured enemy soldiers.

The Offensive

TIGER 02 had finally gained its battle rhythm. They were now familiar with Dostum's tactics, and could relay information to each other from all over the battlefield while continuously repositioning themselves so the Taliban couldn't hide.

They were also adapting well to the challenge of synchronizing cavalry charges with twenty-first-century fire support. Commander Lahl Mohammed, one of Dostum's cavalry commanders, had 250 men moving to an assault position, preparing to attack the enemy at full speed. The Taliban they were facing were fully dug in with interlocking machine-gun fire and scores of rocket-propelled grenades. While TIGER 02 was waiting for aircraft and bombers to arrive on station, Commander Mohammed was supposed to hold in place until ordered to attack. Mohammed jumped the gun and took off early without permission.

The cavalry was in full view of the enemy 1,500 meters away and closing fast. TIGER 02 radioed the close air support pilot that they had on a string to "step on the gas." They only had minutes before the 250-horse cavalry would hit the Taliban positions. As soon as CAS was over the target, TIGER 02 gave release authority. The bombs would take one minute to target impact.

It was almost dark and as the bombs closed, the Green Berets could see Taliban machine guns tearing into the formation as Dostum's horses began to fall. The TIGER 02 CAS team was certain that the cavalry charge was too close to the enemy trench line.

When Dostum's cavalry charged over the last outcropping just short of the Taliban trenches, adrenaline and anxiety were at a peak. Commander Mohammed and his men were only 250 meters from the enemy, riding at full tilt, with bombs in the air. TIGER 02 would either inflict serious damage on the Taliban or wipe out their allies—seconds more would tell.

Three bombs landed directly in front of the assaulting line and in the center of the enemy defense, stunning the Taliban. Al-Qaida and Taliban soldiers were sent flying in a dozen directions; the shock wave smashed into their skulls, bursting their eardrums and exploding the capillaries in their retinas. The cavalry flew into the disoriented enemy just seconds after they were hit by the shock from the concussion and blast, and annihilated the remaining Taliban with what they later named "U.S. Cavalry Close Quarter Combat."

"I can see our horses blasting through them in the dust clouds!" Sergeant Will Summers radioed back.

The horses were charging right through the clouds of dust and body parts thrown into the air by the bombs. The assault was an incredible success and demonstrated perfect, split-second timing. Lady luck, in this case, got the credit.

Dostum loved the Death Ray. He loved even more calling the Taliban commanders on their radios and talking to them.

"I have the Americans with me here today," Dostum would say in Dari.

"We don't believe you, send them in, we want to fight the Americans, we do not want to fight you," the Taliban would reply.

"Let me prove they are here." Dostum would hand the radio to Vince Makela, the senior commo chief, Pete Walther, Will Summers, Andy Marchal, or one of the other sergeants on the team. Pete was rough and ready, and rarely without his chewing tobacco, and Andy, one of the weapons sergeants, loved carrying his grenade launcher, mostly because it "carried more bang for the buck."

"Hey there, motherfucker, yep, I'm an American, apple pie, the Yankees, all that good shit, and you're real close to dying." Then they would hand the radio back to Dostum. The Taliban commander had no idea what the American was saying since he didn't speak English.

"I told you I had the Americans with me, and they have their Death Ray," Dostum would tell them.

"Send the Americans to fight us," the Taliban demanded.

"*Hoop,* I will send them to you now," Dostum would reply. *Hoop* meant "good," and Dostum was always happy when the Taliban accepted his invitation to meet the Americans and their Death Ray.

A short time later, Taliban bodies were flying through the air once again.

One day, to solve a particularly tough visibility problem, the team called in a Predator UAV to work a valley, designating "kill box" limits for the craft and asking it to vector in ordnance to kill any vehicles in its designated area.

The RQ-1 A/B Predator is a medium-altitude, long-endurance unmanned aerial vehicle (drone) used by the JFACC for reconnaissance, surveillance, and target acquisition over the battlefield. It is equipped with color daytime

cameras and infrared night vision, and can be outfitted with a
Hellfire missile targeted with its Multispectral Targeting System (MTS).

It has a wingspan of almost 50 feet and a range of over 450
miles, at a cruising speed of between 85 and 135 miles per
hour, powered by a Rotax four-cylinder engine producing
100+ horsepower. It has a ceiling of 25,000 feet and can be
controlled by a Ku-band satellite uplink when out of line of
sight. It is produced by General Atomics Aeronautical Systems, Inc., and the system cost is $40 million for four drones,
the Ground Control Station, and the satellite uplink.

The UAV was working well but couldn't find the exact
area. One team member told the UAV pilot to look out his
left window, a habit from working with fighter pilots. The
UAV pilot was sitting in front of a computer screen in Riyadh,
at the Combined Air Operations Center hidden inside the
Prince Sultan air base. He simply answered with a chuckle,
"That will be a bit too hard since I am well over a thousand
miles from there. Let's try cardinal direction or something."

One of TIGER 02's four elements lost their horses during
an attack. The horses had broken loose during the attack and
run away. The element stayed on their hilltop for six days,
calling in fire support with no resupply and very little to eat.
Finally, they had no choice but to reposition and rejoin the
rest of TIGER 02. Almost out of water, they "rucked up" and
walked across the battlefield, almost thirty miles, until they
found their four-legged partners huddled near the "motor
pool" in a valley by a stream.

One team saw al-Qaida indoctrination in practice. The
team was smoking a ridgeline, the Taliban control post was
gone, and the flanking unit's radios had gone dead, indicating
devastating hits. Taliban tanks and artillery pieces were being
pummeled. Suddenly, around twenty or so AQ fighters stood
up in their trench lines and went over the top of their trenches
like the doughboys of World War I.

The al-Qaida terrorists continued their mad assault, firing their AK-47s on automatic as they sprinted across the
open high desert.

"Whoa, baby, I feel like Grandpa in the Pacific during a Jap banzai charge," said one operator.

"Yeah, but Grandpa didn't have thousand-yard guns," his teammate replied as they focused in on the rushing mob. Firing madly as they ran, the running AQ were clearly not going to hit anyone with a shot except by accident. Meanwhile, TIGER 02's weapons sergeants were drilling holes straight through them as their arms flailed in the air, their feet came out from under them, and their lifeless bodies hit the sand. The terrorists continued their charge until every last one of them was slaughtered. The split element of the team watched the carnage in virtual silence. When it was over, the team's weapons man flexed his weary trigger finger and reflected on the event: "They are now exactly where they wanted to be."

Sergeants Chad Jacklet, Bill Bennett, Steve Bleigh, and Steve Kofron all agreed that it was also where they deserved to be, and hopefully Allah would have run out of virgins by now.

The *muj* told TIGER 02 that the Taliban and al-Qaida believed that no two bombs ever landed in the same place. Throughout the twentieth century, such a belief was valid, but precision-guided weapons had now changed everything.

The next day, the team watched the Talibs run to occupy a bomb crater after one of their positions was hit. For the next few days they bombed the trench lines and waited for the Taliban to regroup in the resulting crater. TIGER 02 would wait for the ignorant Taliban soldiers to climb into the fresh bomb crater for cover and then use their laser markers to put a second bomb right into their midst. It increased their kill ratio threefold.

At one point TIGER 02 was playing tag back and forth with a group of Taliban near the town of Shulgareh near the Tingi Pass, which the Green Berets had nicknamed the Gap of Doom. Dostum had called the team that night and needed their help. The enemy had reversed its withdrawal and was now trying to mount a counterassault against Dostum. The Taliban had deployed ZSU-23-4s and ZU-23-2s, antiaircraft guns, and armor to fire directly at Dostum's troops as they came up the pass. The team showed up before daybreak and gave the Taliban an 0600 (6 A.M.) wake-up from a B-52 bomber. The Taliban ducked and ran from one cover to the next as the plane passed overhead several times as the sun rose. When they didn't get bombed they just stayed there.

"Check out this asshole running back and forth getting ammo," Sergeant Walther said to his teammates as they looked through their spotting scopes.

"Laze the son of a bitch," came the response.

"I hate being irritated, especially when we could be sleeping right now," Walther said as he put the invisible infrared laser dot on the wall next to the terrorist's head.

BOOM! The bomb hit dead-on as body parts and turbans flew into the air. BOOM! More body parts and black turbans. BOOM!

"No more Taliban . . . ," Walther sneered.

Any Taliban that were left were beating feet to the safety of Mazar-e-Sharif, where they would amass once more.

BOXER Hits the Ground

On November 2, 2001, it was clear that the A-Teams converging on Mazar-e-Sharif would soon be face-to-face with the Taliban and al-Qaida terrorists. Dostum was having so much fun with TIGER 02 and the Death Ray that he asked, actually demanded, another A-Team. It was decided that inserting a Special Forces C-Team to command and control the effort would help coordinate the operations of the Northern Alliance and prevent conflicting movements as the varying Afghan militias drew closer and closer to each other.

Lieutenant Colonel Max Bowers was the man selected to command a composite group of operators from the 3rd Battalion, 5th Special Forces, to fill the requirement. The eight-man C-Team would now be known as BOXER. Bowers infiltrated the Darye Suf Valley in northern Afghanistan, near the Uzbek border, by chopper in the desert night, with two all-terrain vehicles to supplement TIGER 02's horses. TIGER 02 met them on the ground and helped them link up with General Dostum. Over the next weeks they would act in a variety of roles—with command, control, and coordination being the most important functions.

The Fall of Mazar-e-Sharif

Faced with extraordinary and mounting casualties, the Taliban's credo of "We will fight to the death" quickly fell by the wayside. As TF DAGGER and the Northern Alliance's forces closed on Mazar-e-Sharif, prisoners of war became a huge problem. In Taloqan and Kunduz alone, thousands of prisoners were later taken. The vast majority of the POWs were Taliban. Only a small percentage were AQ, and the rest of the AQ had either escaped or retreated south, and would have to be dealt with later.

TIGER 02 tried to help by teaching the basic "five *S*'s" to their Afghan comrades: *Search, Silence, Segregate, Safeguard,* and *Speed in Evacuation* (or *Speed to the Rear*). These ancient guidelines for the treatment of prisoners had withstood the test of time. The violation of these rules almost always led to disaster.

Search is pretty much self-explanatory, but it is always difficult to ensure that indigenous troops, especially those not used to taking prisoners, effect a comprehensive search, not just a cursory search. *Silence,* keeping the POWs quiet, keeps them from organizing any escape plans or collaborative resistance. *Segregate* means separating leaders from followers to prevent organization for resistance or escape, and restraining the prisoners so they can't hurt anyone or effect an escape. *Safeguard* means keeping angry soldiers or civilians on the battlefield from hurting the prisoners. *Speed in evacuation,* or *Speed to the rear,* means to remove the prisoners from the field of battle so military forces can go back to focusing on combat tasks. It also gets prisoners to a rear area, where escape becomes more difficult.

Special Forces knew that a prisoner of war's best chance of escape is just after capture. They had learned that lesson well in Colonel Nick Rowe's SERE School at Fort Bragg. Rowe, the legendary Green Beret and author of *Five Years to Freedom,* had escaped from the Viet Cong and come back to teach the Green Berets lessons the Northern Alliance would fail to assimilate.

The Afghani warriors had never been trained to search their prisoners. Jack, a Green Beret special advisor who lived alone with the *muj* for an extended time, observed that the Afghans didn't like to touch their enemies, especially the Arabs and Pakistani prisoners, whom they considered filthy animals. A cursory pat-down was all that was being done.

TIGER 02 was overwhelmed with the sheer numbers of prisoners. Along with security, the transport of so many prisoners at one time became increasingly difficult for the Green Berets on the ground in Taloqan, who numbered less than a dozen, and the loosely organized Northern Alliance working with them. Transportation finally *did* arrive, in the form of old flatbed trucks and tractor trailers, to move the growing mob to a nearby prison for collection and processing. The POWs were headed for Qala-i-Jangi, an ancient mud-walled fort right out of *Beau Geste,* complete with parapets and moats. It was located close to Mazar-e-Sharif, controlled by Dostum's forces, and was the largest fort in Afghanistan. (Herding the prisoners in like cattle, and prodding them with the barrels of their Kalashnikov assault rifles, the Northern Alliance troops would make a vital error in the search process, and the weapons missed in the chaos would come to bear two weeks later.)

The fall of Mazar-e-Sharif was ugly politics. It supposedly "fell" on November 9, 2001; yet there were seemingly endless negotiations for surrender, broken promises, and men attacked each other even when there was an agreement not to fight. At times, the battle, and the surrender, seemed to completely degenerate into Afghan tribal "business."

Amazingly, in the end, it all turned out quite well. On November 10, 2001, Dostum and TIGER 02 rode into Mazar-e-Sharif as conquering heroes. Dostum rode through the streets a virtual demigod to the people. The city was captured with minimal losses, and the Afghani Taliban fighters, imprisoned for a short time, would eventually receive amnesty. As Dostum rolled down the wide street into Mazar, he stood out of the sunroof of a captured 4×4, and TIGER 02 was right behind him. Dostum's vehicle headed straight toward the magnificent Blue Mosque. It was one of the great treasures of Afghanistan, and it was now Dostum's. He stopped the vehicles, got out, and walked toward the mosque. The crowds threw money for good luck, deluging him. The Blue Mosque held the tomb of Hazrat Ali, the son-in-law of the great prophet Mohammed. It was a staggering sight. Blue tile and marble topped by blue turrets and domes, surrounded by marble courtyards and mosaic inlays. Dostum gave thanks to Allah for his victory and then rejoined TIGER 02 for a celebration.

Just When You Thought It Was Over

After the capture of Mazar-e-Sharif, things were still in celebration mode when Dostum called TIGER 02 and told them that a large industrial building inside the city housed what might be eight hundred hard-core Taliban and AQ. Dostum's men relayed that the AQ were defending the complex and refused to give up. Something had failed in their withdrawal plans and they were trapped. Dostum's forces had arrived too swiftly and had bypassed the town, surrounding the building.

TIGER 02 sent three of its men ahead into the area to look at the problem. The industrial building turned out to be a *madrasah,* or Islamic school. It was a formidable piece of terrain taking up a whole city block. The terrorist fighters bottled up in the *madrasah* were mostly Pakistani Taliban. A large steel-and-concrete fence surrounded the two-story building, and the whitewashed walls were covered in al-Qaida and Taliban graffiti. Not only did the surrounded Taliban and al-Qaida refuse to negotiate, they shot and killed Dostum's emissaries who came to ask for their surrender. Even worse, they were sneaking patrols out into the surrounding neighborhoods, threatening to take innocent hostages. The team had to move quickly.

Everyone in TIGER 02 was tasked to his limit—on no sleep, with little time to eat or even sit down. The operators were on the verge of collapse. Their primary concern was quickly ascertaining the whereabouts of hidden al-Qaida leaders and, most important, bin Laden. It was certain from both NA intelligence and DIA intelligence that bin Laden was not in their AO, area of operations, but they hoped someone knew where he had been in the last few days. Surely someone had been in contact with bin Laden either immediately before or during the fall of the city—if only they could find that man. Any ground intelligence on Osama's location would be better than nothing. The CIA's paramilitary division had three operators working with TIGER 02 for the sole purpose of collecting intelligence about bin Laden and the AQ. TIGER 02 knew that the most important information to be gleaned from AQ prisoners was the location, modus operandi, and movements of bin Laden. All of this had to be put on hold for now—al-Qaida was still a viable threat in the city, and Dostum needed them.

Speaking with the Northern Alliance troops was now easier, since the team had found an elderly man who had been an English professor at an Afghan university in the early seventies, before the country had imploded. While TIGER 02 and their Afghan compatriots went from house to house asking people to pull back out of the neighborhood for a short period of time, they had the Northern Alliance give the AQ terrorists an ultimatum.

Staff Sergeant Will Summers told Dostum, "You've got hardened terrorists holed up in the middle of your town, and they are willing to die. If you don't mind, we'd like to oblige them."

Dostum agreed to let the team bring in their Death Rays.

The team took their Trimble Navigation Scout GPSs to the corners of the enemy compound to map it properly. That night Alliance soldiers helped to clear the area of civilians for the last time. Meanwhile, TIGER 02 set up on a rooftop about four hundred meters away from the *madrasah,* a distance close enough to exactly control the fires, but safe enough to preclude any friendly fire injuries.

Two birds came on station, but they had trouble picking up the team's laser. The air controller had to talk them onto the target and had the aircraft carefully describe what they were seeing. They had to be especially careful because of the civilian buildings nearby. Eventually the pilots had it. The first bomb was a direct hit in the center of the huge *madrasah.*

TIGER 02 called for more air strikes, but the first bird waved off with a hung bomb. The second aircraft picked up the blast and easily vectored in on the enemy target. As soon as the pilot picked up the laser, the next bomb went through the same hole in the school's roof and wreaked havoc inside.

Three bombs followed the first, and the team called a cease-fire. Dostum's forces then rushed the compound in the confusion while TIGER 02 snipers targeted the windows and roof positions.

Over 450 enemy dead were counted after the battle.

Chaos and Disaster

Everything seemed secure once again. Now that the airfield at Mazar was open, supplies could be air landed. More troops could also be brought in covertly. Within hours, two more four-man SAS teams landed to join BOXER and the Green

Berets. While the British Army carried the SA80 bullpup design rifle, the SAS preferred the American M-16, and were now using the shorter CAR-15, and older version of the M-4 in Afghanistan, along with Sig Sauer 9mm pistols. Several SAS operators were using the new H&K G36 assault rifle system. Working with TASK FORCE 11, their job would be solely to roam the countryside in the Land Rovers and hunt senior al-Qaida leaders. With the U.K. anti-terror mission codenamed Operation Veritas (truth), this would include installing small digital cameras on the sides of dirt roads and in areas where al-Qaida might pass or meet. The signals would be sent back to U.S. and British command centers, and a special TF 11 signals center at JSOC Headquarters.

CIA and DIA intelligence officers, supplemented by operators from Delta Force, were busy trying to deal with the hundreds of foreign Taliban and al-Qaida prisoners streaming into Dostum's makeshift POW camp at Qala-i-Jangi.

Qala-i-Jangi was chaos and ripe for disaster, a disaster that would be forthcoming. When the AQ rebellion at Qala-i-Jangi prison took place a few weeks later, TIGER 02 would be busy with Dostum's forces in the ancient city of Balkh. They were just about ready to annihilate another three thousand enemy forces, when Dostum walked into the city alone wearing a blue turban and negotiated a surrender. TIGER 02 was not happy with the diplomatic resolution—they wanted America's enemy dead.

As the Qala-i-Jangi prisoners revolted, TIGER 02 "was sitting on their asses" watching politics, the team leader would later recount, and the prison operation would primarily fall to Delta Force, special operators working with the CIA's covert action force, a few British Special Air Service commandos, and Max Bowers' command-and-control team from the 5th Group. TIGER 02 was desperate to return, but their superiors ordered them not to. In fact, TIGER 02 *begged* to return to help—they knew one of the CIA guys was MIA, and, unlike the CIA, they lived by their creed: Leave no man behind.

Dostum's forces never quite understood why they did not

return, and it plagued the team's conscience. As the revolt was in its last stages, TIGER 02 was finally allowed to return to help sort out the mess that was going to be left behind. That would not happen for several more weeks.

Meanwhile, the populace of Mazar-e-Sharif was no better off for food, medicine, and aid supplies than the Taliban prisoners. The Friendship Bridge that connected Afghanistan to Uzbekistan was the only reliable way to use ground transportation for aid that desperately needed to come into Afghanistan. The word *Friendship* no longer had anything to do with this bridge. The Uzbek government still feared the black-turbaned Taliban devils they thought were still lurking in the night. A dilapidated steel skeleton with silver peeling paint, the Friendship Bridge connected Termez in southern Uzbekistan to the northernmost part of Mazar-e-Sharif. In the center of the bridge stood steel I-beam "dragon's teeth" like the ones at the beaches of Normandy. They were used as an anti-vehicle barricade; even tanks couldn't roll over them.

Behind the sandbags and barbed wire, the ominous pro-Soviet Uzbek Border Police stood in their desert tan-and-lime-green pressed camouflage uniforms with their brand-new Russian machine guns glistening shiny black in the sun—a stark contrast to the ragtag, poverty-stricken Northern Alliance freedom fighters to the south. The Uzbek border post a few hundred yards beyond the bridge was immaculately maintained and fully staffed, even though it had not let a single vehicle cross the bridge in almost six years. The Uzbeks still wore the Soviet-era hammer and sickle on their uniform, and the last thing they wanted to do was open the border to Afghanistan in any direction. The political and diplomatic battle to open the bridge raged for months, forcing the U.S. to resort to airdrops in northern Afghanistan. Humanitarian aid organizations had little choice but to transport supplies across the Tajik border by barge and pay hefty bribes to the Russian border guards. In spite of the fact that the U.S. was paying what amounted to ransom and extortion money to the Uzbek government, the bridge was still closed. By December the Uzbeks were still not allowing the bridge to pass aid supplies from Termez to Mazar, and there appeared to be no end to the impasse in sight. It was making headlines across the world.

TIGER 02 considered it a great honor when General Dostum invited them to accompany him for a meal and a negotiating session on Friendship Bridge, now in the hands of the Northern Alliance, who had gladly opened their southern side. TIGER 02's fight with the Taliban was over; now diplomacy would reign.

Whatever happened next remains murky, but Green Berets and the Afghan ambassador to Uzbekistan, Hasham Sa'ad, eventually helped convince the Uzbeks to allow limited relief convoys to cross the bridge. (The Afghan side of the bridge now appears peaceful, decorated with flowers, manned by unarmed border guards, and with a repainted gate and reception center. The center of the bridge abruptly changes to barbed wire, steel I-beams, sandbags, and heavily armed Uzbek Spetsnaz soldiers. The bridge still remains closed to normal traffic—there is no indication the Uzbek government will ever relent on their policy.)

As reports flowed back to the United States, the team's reputation grew. Estimates of the havoc they had created varied: one summary included more than 2,500 enemy killed in action, over 50 enemy vehicles destroyed, and over 3,500 prisoners captured.

Such statistics really mean nothing: numbers of bodies, vehicles, or POWs can be irrelevant information, as they were in Vietnam. What was significant is that Master Sergeant Paul Evans, his XO Bob Pennington, and their men were sitting on Freedom Bridge, and Mazar-e-Sharif was free. TIGER 02 had accomplished its mission in just a few short weeks.

The unclassified summary of TIGER 02's role in the war was released in January 2002:

CPT Mark D. Nutsch and 595, after infiltration into Afghanistan, task organized into four separate teams. The teams moved to four different locations across 60 km of

mountainous terrain to support General Abdul Rashid
Dostum as he conducted combat operations against Taliban positions during the final Northern Alliance offensive
to seize the northern Afghanistan city of Mazar-e-Sharif.

The detachment, under the threat of fire, artillery and
mines, traveled primarily on horseback, 10–30 km a day
from mid-October to 10 November, meeting several Northern Alliance commanders and troops along the way, inspiring their confidence in U.S. forces while helping to
coordinate future attacks.

595 supported Gen. Dostum and his subordinate commanders in attacks throughout the Darye Suf and Balkh
valleys. Without their presence, the liberation of the six
Northern Provinces, including the key city of Mazar-e-
Sharif, could not have occurred. 595 was instrumental in
the liberation of over 50 towns and cities.

595 was responsible for the destruction of hundreds of
Taliban vehicles, bunkers and heavy equipment as well as
thousands of enemy soldiers killed, captured or surrendered.

When post-conflict operations began, this ODA immediately shifted from combat operations and began to assist in
humanitarian and civil matters in order to facilitate Afghanistan transition into a peaceful post-Taliban government.

On December 20, 2001, TIGER 02 presented General Dostum and his key leaders silver and blue U.S. Army Combat
Infantryman Badges as part of a farewell ceremony conducted in Russian. In celebration the day before, an unidentified Green Beret, wearing trademark Predator sunglasses,
long hair, beard, and a black-and-white *mujahadeen* scarf,
had been allowed to take part in a *buzkashi* match, a game
where warriors ride horses, struggling to capture a headless
goat or calf as the prize. It was a great honor bestowed on the
American Green Beret by his Afghan counterparts.

The Associated Press distributed a brilliant photo capturing the American horseman, the essence of the game, and the
essence of the Green Berets' bond with their indigenous
Afghan troops. A dead goat is placed in the center of a field

and surrounded by horsemen from two opposing teams. The object of the game is to get control of the carcass and move it to the scoring area. Teamwork and communication are the keys to success. These were exactly the same keys found by TIGER 02 that opened the door for defeat of the Taliban and the al-Qaida.

Dutch and Randy brought horsemanship skills honed in Wyoming to Afghanistan, where pack animals were crucial to the war effort. In the eighties Special Forces had the Ranchers, named as such for the location of their compound next to the stables at Fort Bragg, and their cowboy boot and blue jean attire. In El Salvador guys like Fred, Eddie, Stu, Bruce, and Jack wore guayabera shirts, cowboy boots, and twin Colt .45 pistols as they hunted the FMLN guerrillas in Chevy Suburbans. In Afghanistan the Ranchers were back again, only this time they had real horses, cavalry, and played *buzkashi,* the Afghani version of rodeo. Army skills that went out with Pershing's cavalry were also back, and as always, Special Forces adapted, just as the OSS had done in Burma, where Detachment 101 used pack animals to transport equipment and supplies during World War II.

For Special Forces, Afghanistan was the wild, wild West, and the new Ranchers reveled in it.

CHAPTER 9

Northern Alliance— General Fahim

"You accomplish an amazing feat each time a B-2 bomber lifts off from the plains of Missouri and crosses oceans and continents, undetected, to deliver justice from the skies above Afghanistan. The terrorists thought they could strike fear in the American heartland. Through you, the American heartland strikes back."

—DONALD RUMSFELD, remarks to the 509th Bomb Wing, Whiteman Air Force Base, Montana, October 19, 2001

The Triple Nickel

Kabul, Afghanistan

Dostum's TIGER 02 team was not the first A-Team into Afghanistan. Being first in was an honor coveted by every A-Team. The competition for it had been high. In the end, experience paid off for the "Triple Nickel." As the first team in, they also won the distinction of being code-named TIGER 01 when they hit the ground in Afghanistan.

The Nickel's (A-Team 555) team leader, Chief Warrant Officer David Diaz, was a thirty-eight-year-old veteran of numerous combat missions. Of the many missions he performed during his tenure with the Special Forces, one qualified him for the task more than any other. In 1987, Diaz had spent close to a year on CIA-sponsored black ops in Afghanistan along the Pakistani border, training *mujahadeen* resistance fighters for their *jihad* against the Soviets. (Black ops are missions so secret and so sensitive that the U.S. government completely denies their existence, and even disavows the men involved.) Diaz was involved in the top-secret mule program—a CIA/Special Forces clandestine operation to supply the Afghan resistance with mules, pack animals, supplies, and Stinger missiles to fight the Soviet Union. This alone made him one of the most qualified men the 5th Group had in their arsenal.

Almost everyone else on TIGER 01 was a combat vet, having operated in hot spots throughout the Middle East and Central Asia—Iraq, Somalia, Kuwait, Saudi Arabia, and places all over the Persian Gulf. TIGER 01 consisted of eleven Green Berets and one USAF special tactics airman to help direct close air support.

Although they were the first team to hit the ground, two CIA paramilitary agents had been deployed a short time before them to secure safehouses, link up with the Northern Alliance commanders, and set up drop zones for ammunition. "Hal" and "Phil" were the two spooks that were tasked to do this. Hal was an ex–Navy SEAL, a giant of a man, and part of the CIA's Special Activities Division, which worked quickly to build up a force of over seven hundred recruits in the days following 9/11. Phil was a more scholarly type, never without his beige vintage 1980s Members Only jacket. Like most CIA operatives in Afghanistan, Phil usually preferred to stay in the comfort of the safehouse unless it was absolutely necessary to venture out into "Indian country." Phil was part of the CIA's Analytical Branch.

On October 19, 2001, the Triple Nickel successfully infiltrated northern Afghanistan on their third attempt; the first two infiltrations had been scrubbed because of terrible weather.

It was a moonless night as the two MH-53 PaveLow helicopters touched down on opposite sides of a hill that divided the intended LZ. Each chopper carried half of the team, and as they ran off the ramp at the rear, the dozen men of 555 hunkered down in the darkness, waited for the rotor wash to settle after the birds once again lifted off, and switched on their night-vision goggles.

TIGER 01 and General Fahim

+ airfields
× start of infiltration
← captured city

TURKMENI

IRAN

BADGH
Qal'eh

+ Herat

HERAT

Shindand

FARAH
Farah

Las

HELM

Zaranj
NIMRUZ

IRAN

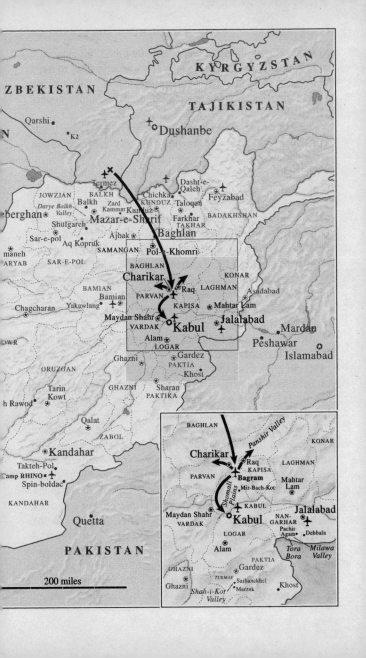

Diaz was with the six men on the side of the hill closest to the link-up site where the Agency rep was supposed to meet them, but he thought it was someone besides the CIA coming to greet them when he saw the bobbing of flashlights appear in the distance.

"Lock and load," Diaz whispered to his men. "These idiots with white lights can't be anyone with any common sense, and they sure as fuck can't be on our side."

The lights grew brighter, and some of the men had to look away, or switch off their goggles, because the intense white light was starting to flare out the delicate night-vision tubes. As the lights grew brighter their night-vision goggles would automatically black out to prevent the light-intensification tubes from frying. Diaz ripped his goggles off his head and let his eyes adjust to the darkness. As he leveled his weapon toward the bobbing light and took up the slack on his trigger finger, the beam of the Maglite swept over him.

"Hey, guys, I'm Hal," came a jovial voice. "Welcome to Afghanistan."

"Turn that fucking light off, you moron. You ever hear of OPSEC?" Diaz snapped.

Hal clicked off his four D-cell Maglite and replied, "Relax, you're in friendly territory. And yes, I know what operational security is, I was a goddamn SEAL." After a moment, Hal clicked the light back on. "Follow me."

Shaking their heads in disbelief, the split team followed Hal around a bend in the ridgeline, where they met up with the other half of the A-Team. Hal was big; he looked like a grizzly bear on its hind legs in the outline of the flashlight he fanned back and forth along the narrow trail in front of them.

After a short stretch, Hal and the Triple Nickel entered a safehouse in the tiny village of Astana. Astana was in the heart of the beautiful Panshir Valley, and close to the heart of "the Lion of Panshir," Ahmad Shah Massoud. This meant they were in the safest place in Afghanistan. That is, if you were on the side of the Northern Alliance. No enemy force had ever penetrated the Panshir. This was the Holy Land of

Massoud, and no enemy force *would* ever penetrate it as long as one single Panshiri still lived.

Inside the mud-walled house they were introduced to Phil, who acquainted himself with the team and gave them a run-down on the morning's events before the team bedded down for the night. Phil came off to the team like he had been in Afghanistan forever and had solid, long-term ties with the local leaders, even though he had been there only a few weeks.

The next day, Phil led the Triple Nickel down through the valley to another village called Taqhma and into another safe-house. Flanked by bodyguards in Panshir tiger stripes, an Afghan with a long beard and a crooked nose stepped forward to shake Phil's hand.

"Here are the American Special Forces warriors. I promised you they would come," Phil explained to the bearded Northern Alliance general.

Friendly, but somewhat reserved, General Bismullah Khan turned toward the team. "Okay then, show me what you can do."

"Just point us in the right direction," Diaz responded.

"Tomorrow we will travel south, toward the airfield. My commander, Babajan, is there with our troops," Bismullah Khan told the team. "Now, let us eat and have *chai,* and be thankful you have arrived in safety."

About midmorning, the men of TIGER 01 and Bismullah Khan arrived at Bagram airfield, an old military landing strip littered with Russian aircraft hulls, jet engines, abandoned vehicles, rubbled buildings, and the thick layer of dust that accompanied twenty years of neglect. Situated approximately thirty miles north of Kabul, the airfield was a key strategic objective because it could serve as the leaping-off point for any modern force seeking to seize the capital city of Kabul. It was second only to the airport in Mazar-e-Sharif for logistical capacity.

The airfield was split in half on the day that TIGER 01 arrived at the Shomali Plains. General Fahim's fighters, part of the Northern Alliance, controlled the northern half of the airfield and the Taliban controlled the southern half, which included the high ground to the southeast—rendering the airfield useless to either side in the conflict.

Chief Diaz sent a four-man element as far forward as they could penetrate, which meant they essentially sneaked through the carcasses of old wreckage and out toward the southern edge of the airfield. The team found a good position and began pulling out a spotting scope from one of their rucksacks.

"I don't think you're going to need that," one of the Green Berets said.

The others looked up, mouths hanging open. Directly in front of them was a massive Taliban formation, with at least fifty tanks, armored personnel carriers, and trucks with ZSU antiaircraft guns mounted on them. Taliban soldiers were dug in in fortified bunkers and trenches. "There have to be thousands of the black-turbaned devils," one Green Beret said, "and they are less than a kilometer away."

Meanwhile, back at the airfield, Babajan had arrived with a contingent of Panshir warriors. Babajan was a round, jovial man reminiscent of Santa Claus, but in the past he actually funded his troops by imposing road tolls and by capturing the vehicles of foreigners and charging them for their release. He led Diaz and the others to the burned-out control tower. Sneaking into the decrepit tower was no easy task. If the Taliban spotted them they would be eating rockets shortly thereafter. Getting to it was no cakewalk either. Every foot of ground was littered with unexploded ordnance and mines. Everywhere you looked, everywhere you stepped, you could be sure to just miss a rocket, a mortar shell, a mine, or some other explosive device that was just waiting to go postal on you. Stepping off the concrete was certain death to the unaware and inexperienced. Standing in the tower, you realized exactly how fucked up the place was. It was one big graveyard of Soviet mines and wrecked aircraft hulls.

Finally, after narrowly averting disaster a hundred times, they climbed to the top of the air traffic control tower, which sat low and squat on the top of a concrete-walled building that reminded one of the operators of the Alamo. Hopefully this battle wouldn't turn out that way, he thought.

The control tower offered the best vantage point they could imagine. With the naked eye they could see the huge entrenched force that lay on the other side of the airfield: over seven thousand Taliban terrorists and over fifty pieces of former Soviet armor.

Diaz hopped on the radio to the scout team, "Get over here *now,* and bring up the SOFLAM."

Commander Babajan gave the team a brief history lesson. "It has been a stalemate for three years now, but since *Amur Sahib* was killed, the terrorists have brought in three thousand more to fight me."

Amur Sahib meant "Big Boss" in Dari, and it was reserved for only one person: Ahmad Shah Massoud.

Soon, the whole team was up in the tower, and the team's Air Force combat controller was already on the satellite radio, trying to scramble anything in the air toward their position. The SOFLAM was set up, and everything was in position. Diaz scanned with the binoculars, and stopped right in the center of the Taliban frontline.

"Look there," Diaz said, as he handed the binos to Babajan. Babajan looked at a dug-in piece of artillery next to a command shack bristling with several antennas.

"That's our first target," Diaz said, a broad smile on his bearded face.

"We got an F/A-18 on deck!" the Air Force CAS specialist eagerly replied.

One of the Green Berets leaned forward and painted the control shack with the invisible laser beam.

"What happens next?" Babajan inquired.

"Just watch and see," Diaz responded.

Everyone in the control tower jumped as the bomb silently and unexpectedly found its mark. A giant explosion of brown dirt and streaking, white-hot sparks of molten metal shot a hundred feet in the air. For a moment it was silent, then BOOM! as the concussion reached them at the speed of sound.

Babajan and his men looked wide-eyed with disbelief for a moment or two, then cheers and screams of joy erupted from every direction. It was as if TIGER 01 had just kicked a field goal to win the Super Bowl in overtime.

As Babajan scribbled notes to the team about where to strike next, and the team called in bomb after bomb, the stunned and confused Taliban began to return fire—the problem was, they didn't know where the bombs were coming from, so they just started firing everywhere. Occasionally, a round would crack the cement in the control tower building, or throw up a puff of dirt from one of the thick mud walls next to the tower, but that was about it.

Over the next six hours, until just after dark, the men of TIGER 01 called in CAS on the Taliban frontlines. As the sun began to set, all they could see were the rising clouds of black smoke silhouetted by hundreds of fires amid the devastated wreckage that used to be the Taliban. Nothing moved on the Taliban frontlines, except when the occasional box of ammo or a vehicle gas tank ruptured, sending a Hollywood-style fireball into the air. Each time this happened, cheers erupted from the Panshir soldiers below—this was their kind of fireworks.

It didn't take long for the Triple Nickel to completely obliterate everything that stood between them and Kabul. And now that they had crossed that first obstacle, General Fahim was ready to meet them personally.

General Fahim was the successor to Massoud, the man that had formed and led the Northern Alliance. Massoud had been the critical link to keeping the Northern Alliance together and fighting against the Taliban. After Massoud's assassination by al-Qaida, the Northern Alliance was distraught, dysfunctional, and ready to break apart. Ironically, al-Qaida's September 11 attacks might have saved the movement. The U.S. offered hope, funding, resources, inspiration, and, most of all, air support. General Fahim would now be the critical link in the synchronized campaign to unseat the Taliban.

The team described General Fahim as an extremely intelligent operator. He seemed to be politically astute and was also able to obtain information from the rear of the Taliban better than any of the other Northern Alliance leaders. Fahim's forte was building an effective human intelligence network. He appeared to have had more agents in Kabul than the CIA had in the entire world. His bank of satellite phones rang continuously. The Taliban couldn't breathe without General Fahim's personal knowledge. Unbeknownst to American Special Forces, this vast intelligence net was run by "Engineer" Ali, loyal only to Massoud and his closest inner circle, which included Fahim. Ali had learned his skills from the KGB, and he put them to good use against the AQ and the Taliban. Over the months ahead, Ali would show a little-known side—a side that believed America was the key to a bright and peaceful future for his country. His network would make all the difference when it came time to attack. Engineer Ali and his intelligence network would make all the difference when it came time to attack.

First, however, TIGER 01 needed to assess the fighting force. The team was surprised to see that the thousands of soldiers supposedly under the direction of Fahim really numbered less than 1,500. This was not much of a force to dislodge the Taliban from Kabul. The issue was the on-call militia that would come when asked to fight, raising the numbers up into the thousands. These men, however, would not be able to participate in a fight for more than a few days because they would inevitably run out of food and ammunition.

Second, by now the Joint Forces Air Component Command was giving priority of air support to other locales, and General Fahim knew it. He was irate that he could only get a sortie now and then, but thanked TIGER 01 for the little support he was allocated. Using the burned-out control tower on Bagram airfield, the team could see deep into Taliban territory, and had the ability to exactly locate many of their command bunkers and observation posts.

Even though they were ready for the push to Kabul and air strikes were coming along nicely, the team was unable to get the supplies they needed for Fahim's forces. They couldn't even get enough ammo and food for Fahim's main body of Panshir soldiers. Luckily, the Panshir army was better equipped than the rest of the Afghan forces. They were, after all, Massoud's elite troops.

In early November, to help prepare for the final attack, a command-and-control element had been sent in to orchestrate and plan the assault. Lieutenant Colonel Chris Haas, one of the most respected officers in the 5th Special Forces Group, led them. He was hard-core, totally cool, and kickass, all in the same breath. His call sign was SHARK 85.

The attack on the city of Kabul would be a two-pronged affair. Basically, one assault would be on the desert floor tracking along the new highway from Bagram airfield straight into Kabul, while another would be along an old highway along the western wall of cliffs that bordered the rolling plain south of Bagram. It was the shortest route for Massoud's "Army of the Panshir" to make their push toward Kabul.

The terrain favored the defenders because of the hills and washes. The defenders could literally pick an attacking force apart with good positioning of tanks and artillery. The longer SHARK and TIGER 01 were on the ground, the longer they realized that their targets for victory wouldn't be troop formations. They would be tanks, armored personnel carriers, command-and-control bunkers, and field artillery pieces, in that order.

The team kept hustling about to find vantage points to direct effective fields of fire on the Taliban and al-Qaida. They finally found two locations of rising terrain that were almost as good as the tower had been. But air assets were sadly lacking. If the higher headquarters ever decided to stop starving Fahim with lack of air power, TIGER 01 could do some real damage.

A few days into November an out-of-the-ordinary exchange took place. A rear admiral and a U.S. government "representative" landed and discussed coordination of the upcoming offensive. General Fahim demanded to know when he would receive priority on air support so he could initiate his campaign to retake Kabul. They promised Fahim it would happen on the eighth of November.

SHARK and Fahim began planning in earnest, working the bugs out of their plan and estimating the terrain they could capture on each day of the campaign. They also created an impromptu fire support mission, visualizing the artillery and air support and how it could be orchestrated to complement the ground maneuvers of the Special Forces teams and their Northern Alliance compatriots.

TIGER 01 had the luxury of planning in more detail than most teams. The frontlines were fixed on TIGER 01's arrival; the team directly confronted the enemy. There were no significant intermediate objectives, and the human intelligence was high-quality. Finally, the terrain made the routes of attack obvious and straightforward.

Frustration and the Angel of Death

On the eighth of November, when no fire support came, General Fahim was furious. The rear admiral was gone, but the U.S. "representative," supposedly a member of the "OGA" (Office of Government Administration), but actually with the Agency, would bear the brunt of Fahim's anger even though he had a bag of cash to buy goods for the upcoming fight. OGA really stood for Other Government Agency, which was how the CIA was referred to in Afghanistan. Fahim called the spook into his headquarters and, in front of witnesses, berated him.

"You have lied. There is no close air support today. Therefore, you will not be able to accompany us in the attack. You will have to stay here, in the rear, until we call for you." The Afghan men in the room looked away in disgust.

The men of TIGER 01 were dismayed that the CIA agent didn't understand how deeply he had been insulted. The team tried to explain, but to no avail. To an Afghan warrior, in a culture where everything a man is or hopes to be is tied to his ability to fight, to be denied the honor of taking part in an attack is unbearable. It was the ultimate disgrace.

In the interim, awaiting the big fight, the SHARK element

was starting to have some fun. The Special Forces team found out that Taliban radio frequencies could easily be monitored. In fact, they were shocked to learn that both sides knew each other's frequencies. The team started having a *muj* translator listen to the radio with them. One day, a Taliban commander was telling his subordinates that the Americans had missed his position by overshooting it by several hundred meters. The air controller from TIGER 01 broke out laughing. He called on the radio, "Drop three hundred. Repeat."

The resultant explosion appeared on target, even though it was at extended range for effective observation, which also denied the team an exact bomb damage assessment. However, a few minutes later the lieutenants of the Taliban unit were calling on their radios, trying to gain contact with their leader. There was no answer, only dead air.

Dabbling in psychological operations, the team asked TASK FORCE DAGGER to give them an AC-130 Spectre gunship for a few nights. Once again, the weapons release officer was the efficient and attractive Air Force captain named Allison. When the bird came overhead, TIGER 01 would announce to the Taliban in Dari and Arabic that the "Angel of Death" had arrived and she had something to give them. Ally would then follow on the Taliban's command frequency, speaking with her soft, sensuous voice in English, calmly explaining to the enemy that she knew how they treated women, so it was only fair that she get an opportunity to repay their kindness. More than a few SF operators "got a woody" listening to her sultry description of the havoc that was about to be unleashed. Then, Ally's voice would abruptly disappear as the Spectre's 105mm cannons and mini-guns would let loose, wreaking death and destruction of biblical proportions on the Taliban's trench lines.

Small-town Prayers in the Heartland of America

As a small boy, Major General Lambert had learned the power of prayer from his mother. He recalled that prayers emanating from his hometown church in Kansas had been powerful in the past, so Lambert wrote a letter asking the Kansans to say a prayer for the Special Forces soldiers engaged against the forces of evil in Afghanistan.

On November 11, 2001, at a little after 11 A.M., Lambert sat down in the officer's mess at Fort Bragg with his family, closing his eyes for a moment in thought. He heard the bells pealing across the plains of Kansas. He saw the faithful walking up the church steps. He felt the A-Teams attacking with their Afghan compatriots on foot, horseback, and in decrepit Russian vehicles belching smoke as they clambered toward Kabul. By now the men had been fighting for days. Lambert felt the joy of his men surrounding the strategic target of Mazar-e-Sharif. He could visualize the team pushing toward Herat.

Bogged down in snow and zero visibility during World War II, General George S. Patton had asked his chaplain for a weather prayer to fight the Nazis. The Army chaplain had responded by noting Heaven may not look fondly upon a prayer to kill their fellow man. Patton had been blunt, reportedly answering, "Don't worry about Heaven. I'm in good with the Lord, just give me a goddamn prayer and we'll have good weather."

Over the next two days, Lambert sat in his office and read field reports from a string of resounding successes. Al-Qaida bodies were "stacking up like cordwood," said a sergeant major. The Taliban was falling, and Special Forces had not yet lost a man.

The Attack on Kabul

When the priority of fires was switched to the Taliban frontline positions at Bagram airfield on Veterans Day, November 11, General Fahim's motorized (read: anything that ran) "Toyota" infantry and the Green Berets of SHARK were poised to attack.

A private conversation had been held the evening before

between Fahim and the SHARK leadership. Fahim made Lieutenant Colonel Haas promise to have no preplanned targets to the east of Kabul. TIGER 01 reviewed their target lists to make sure there were none. Something was up. No forces were going to the east in any plan that had been discussed.

The close air support and smart bombs were devastating. On November 11, U.S. ordnance provided twenty-five air strikes. These strikes plus the earlier preparation of the battlefield resulted in bomb damage assessment from Fahim's sources of an estimated 2,200 enemy casualties, 29 tanks destroyed, 6 command bunkers destroyed via direct hit, and destruction of numerous vehicles, artillery pieces, and bunkers, "and even a few shithouse latrines."

Because of the effectiveness of the air strikes, Fahim could pick up momentum on the offensive. At the end of the day, the frontline was skewed because of tremendous progress along the Western Wall.

While General Fahim was handling his new duties as defense minister, the NA intelligence service commanders, both Engineer Ali and his boss, Engineer Araf, were tracking bin Laden as aggressively as the NSA, CIA, and DIA. But the Afghan intelligence operations weren't using satellites and radio intercepts—they were using human intelligence, and that indicated that bin Laden was on the move, heading east toward the border of Pakistan. His top leaders were already evacuating Kabul, the terrorist training camps on the Shomali Plains were deserted, and bin Laden was on the run. Ali and his spies were sure of it; bin Laden had made a run to Jalalabad on the eastern border of Afghanistan and Pakistan. If bin Laden made it into the mountains on the eastern border he would be virtually impossible to trap. He would also be close to Pakistan, which meant his friends in the Pakistani government would be able to help him.

Bin Laden was smart, and he knew where his most loyal core of supporters were. When bin Laden traveled to Afghanistan to fight the Soviets in the 1980's he brought with him money and aid for the Afghan *mujahadeen* and their families. Bin Laden became a hero through his family's money, setting up aid stations, orphanages, and homes for the widows of martyrs. He also brought in his family's heavy machinery and earth-moving equipment to dig trenches and bunkers for the *mujahadeen*. His hero status grew quickly, and bin Laden personally manned the bulldozers, on several occasions even being seen continuing to build defenses as Soviet air strikes were hitting all around his bulldozer. Osama bin Laden knew that the southeastern regions of Afghanistan were his best chance for refuge. It was here he had personally set up and funded *mujahadeen* training camps to build Afghanistan's fighting force against the Russian invaders. And it was here where he would flee to make his last stand.

The campaign in the north was moving so fast and furiously that the southern operation would not have time to seize enough ground to block the AQ hierarchy's escape into the east and southeast regions. Bin Laden and his top lieutenants would slip away again.

The next morning, TIGER 01 split in two and moved forward to hammer the dug-in tanks and artillery pieces along the highway to Kabul. They then saw Fahim's unspoken plan unfold. A large part of his force broke to the east and went straight toward the back side of Kabul. It was a classic single envelopment. The Taliban panicked. General Fahim's spies in Kabul relayed that they were fleeing with everything they owned. By November 13, 2001, it was over.

Fahim's troops swept across the Shomali Plains through the remaining defenders between Bagram and Kabul. Haas' SHARK and TIGER 01 had clobbered the Taliban and al-Qaida "into the fucking dirt," and the remaining enemy had been outflanked and outfought by General Fahim and his men.

Visiting the battlefield shortly after, Special Forces Command Sergeant Major Ames asked TIGER 01 why some bodies were left to rot while others were covered in stones or buried within twenty-four hours, in accordance with Muslim practice. The Triple Nickel's driver replied that the foreigners and AQ would be left to rot for a while as an insult. Fahim's warriors and fallen Afghani Taliban would be given a proper burial. However, the team couldn't explain the practice of putting Afghani currency into the dead enemies' wounds.

The attack across the Shomali Plains north of Kabul had been brutal, and rightfully so. The Taliban had decimated Shomali with their scorched-earth policies—cutting down orchards and grape vineyards and burning everything, including the roots of the trees, to punish the inhabitants for their resistance. The tide had turned and now the Taliban would be punished.

TIGER 01 went into the capital with the invading force and were the only American eyes and ears on the ground reporting the happenings there. Fahim's men had to eliminate only a few isolated pockets of resistance. The Taliban departed intact, leaving a small force and a few improvised sniper teams to cover their withdrawal.

As the city celebrated being free from the Taliban yoke, the team reported troop movements and gave hourly situation reports. It was a gentle takeover, however, and they saw little retribution, except for the occasional foreign al-Qaida terrorist who had either been too stupid or too hurt to escape—they were usually beaten to death in the street, or machine-gunned across the ground to a high volume of cheering.

It was a miracle. The entire Northern Alliance was victorious; the coordinated attacks had worked. The Taliban were mentally and physically beaten.

Apparently concerned with a possible counteroffensive or ambushes because the Taliban had left almost too easily, SHARK started weighing in contingency plans. Colonel Haas called for backup troops from the Army's 10th Mountain Division. Major General Franklin L. "Buster" Hagenbeck, the commander of the 10th, supplied Lieutenant Colonel Paul LaCamera, a Ranger accustomed to working closely with Special Forces. The 10th Mountain Division had been itching to do something, and up until now, "they'd been wiping their asses in Uzbekistan." He and one hundred of the infantrymen were on the ground north of Kabul in short order. Unlike the Marines, though, who would bring the entire press pool with them when they arrived later, the 10th was virtually unnoticed as it went about its business of force protection.

SHARK 85, aka Chris Haas, knew that southern Afghanistan could become a much tougher target. The Taliban would concentrate in Kandahar and make a stand. They had nowhere else to go.

Diplomats

SHARK and TIGER 01 then switched roles completely. Within a week they had settled into a swanky guesthouse in Kabul. TIGER 01 became the point men for the Department of State and anyone else that needed their help. As the only established American government presence, they became the conduits for information to the newly forming government in Kabul.

The team did the initial surveys of the U.S. embassy. Their demo men were busy for days removing booby traps. It was dangerous work, but it did have its payoffs. In the middle of clearing the booby traps, they found a complete CONEX shipping container, holding thousands of unopened bottles of Johnnie Walker Red Label scotch. It had been untouched since the U.S. evacuated years before. Johnnie Walker quickly became *the* bribe in Kabul—finding its way into the secret UN bar, various hotels, and a host of diplomatic offices.

TIGER 01 hosted the initial teams from the Department of State to determine how to get the embassy up and running. They sponsored and took care of the Marine guards for the embassy when they arrived, making sure they got off on the right foot. Of course, first the State Department insisted TIGER 01 made sure the embassy was safe; God forbid an embassy Marine were to get hurt on camera. All the while, the team improved and built better relationships with their Afghan compatriots, keeping the pulse, looking for abnormalities, advancing U.S. policy.

General Fahim became the defense minister in the new

government. He was loved and respected by the Afghan commanders and their armies. Eventually he would be elevated to field marshal and given control of all of Afghanistan's military forces. While the UN questioned Fahim's command, Jack and the other Green Berets knew the reality: Fahim had never changed sides, and he could care less about the UN—he wanted to be aligned with America.

Bagram was now totally secure by U.S. and coalition forces. Within days one complete squadron of the British Special Boat Service (SBS) had landed by C-130. The SBS had originally been part of the SAS in WWII, but had been split into its own regiment and developed into a Royal Marine version of the SAS. Officially the SBS was going to be used to ensure humanitarian aid would get through, but that cover story was weak at best; humanitarian aid would be slow in coming. The SBS's M Squadron, which specialized in anti-terrorism and was known as the "Black Group," would actually act as the advance party for General John McColl and ISAF, his security force that was preparing to enter Kabul one month later. They would need to photograph and assess bases that the security assistance force might be able to use, map out escape routes, set up communication transmitter sites, and procure safe houses for British intelligence agents. The SBS would also provide security for UN officials, such as the UN Special Counsel to Afghanistan. However, due to a lack of trust, the SBS would frequently fail to coordinate with Northern Alliance forces or include them in their planning. The SBS did not have the experience with the NA fighters that the Green Berets and SAS had, and often ran into problems because of it. The historical SBS mission was comprised of DA, or direct action missions, meaning they conducted Ranger-type raids, reconnaissance, ambushes, and sabotage missions, unlike the SAS and American Special Forces whose missions included UW, or unconventional warfare—working with partisans or guerilla fighters. The most classified mission of the SBS would be the protection of British nationals and diplomats, including MI6 and embassy personnel. If the chaos and violence that accompanied the last fall of Kabul in 1992 repeated itself, the SBS would be tasked with the evacuation of both British and UN personnel.

By mid-December SHARK thought they were through fighting. Haas' area of operations was rapidly becoming secure, and the UN-mandated International Security Assistance Force would soon move into Kabul.

Three months later, however, Colonel Mulholland would again call on SHARK 85, and throw him into the biggest military fight in Afghanistan. It would be code-named OPERATION ANACONDA.

CHAPTER 10

Northern Alliance— General Baryoli

"This isn't your war."

—AHMAD SHAH MASSOUD to John Rambo

"It is now."

—SYLVESTER STALLONE's answer
as John Rambo in the film
Rambo III, 1988

"One Ring to Rule Them All"

Kal-a-Khata, Afghanistan

The Triple Nickel (A-Team 555) was the first Green Beret team into Afghanistan, on October 19, 2001.

A-Team 595, the second team in, was close behind the Triple Nickel the following day, joining up with General Abdul Rashid Dostum to lead the Northern Alliance's offensive against Mazar-e-Sharif.

The third team selected to go into the box was 585.

A-Team 585 faced high winds and brutal freezing rain, all of it worsened by zero/zero-visibility conditions. After a five-day wait, on October 25, 2001, the weather cleared and TIGER 03's ten Special Forces sergeants finally reached their landing zone outside Dasht-e-Qaleh, a village in the upper northeast corner near the Tajikistan border.

Master Sergeant John Bolduc was the handpicked leader for A-Team 585, code-named TIGER 03 while on the battlefield.

He had already infiltrated into Afghanistan weeks before to survey the situation.

Usually a Special Forces A-Team was commanded by a captain, with a warrant officer as the XO, or executive officer and second in command. With two intelligence sergeants, two demolition specialists, two weapons experts, two communications specialists, and two highly trained medics, Bolduc's team had everything it needed. No officers had been currently assigned, so Bolduc took command as the senior NCO (sergeant).

Bolduc was a proven product, forged in battle in Panama and Desert Storm. He was a superb leader and physically imposing. Bolduc's men lovingly referred to him as "one of the toughest motherfuckers in the U.S. Army."

Unlike TIGER 04, John Bolduc was blessed with enough combat vets on the team to help carry the load. He would need them. TIGER 03 could anticipate a more difficult battle and more complicated set of problems than any other A-Team in the coming fight.

MSG Bolduc had something else going for him, and that was faith. John carried a pocket Bible on the battlefield. He also had a special talisman that the first Green Beret into each war had worn for thirty years—the magical, mystical ring. With the two of these sacred objects he would surely be invincible.

His focus on the mission was so intense that MSG Bolduc commented that what the enemy (Pakistani, Arab, Chechen AQ, and the Taliban) in TIGER 03's area of operations failed to realize was that TIGER 03 was prepared to fight to the death just like their rabid suicide killer opponents.

Northern Afghanistan

After infiltration that late October day, MSG Bolduc and his nine Green Beret sergeants operated in secret, with no direct support and little supervision. TASK FORCE DAGGER

TIGER 03 and General Baryoli

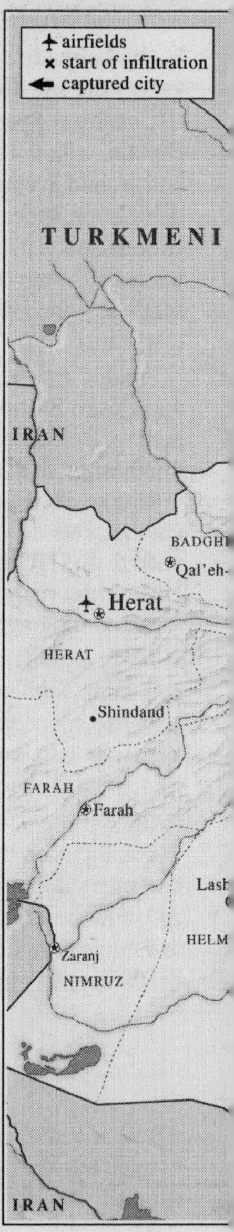

+ airfields
× start of infiltration
← captured city

TURKMENI

IRAN

BADGHI

Qal'eh-

✈ Herat

HERAT

Shindand

FARAH

Farah

Lash

HELM

Zaranj

NIMRUZ

IRAN

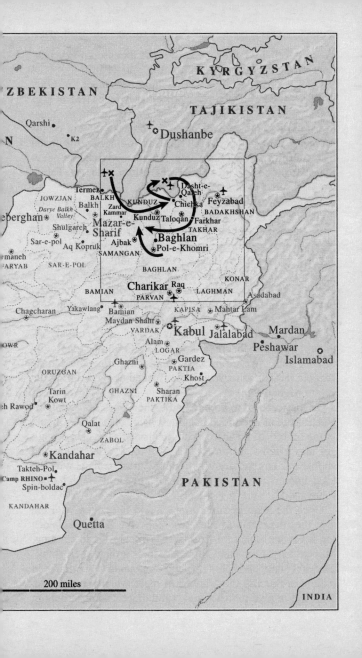

supported them, but by necessity was focused on key relationships with Generals Dostum, Atta, and Fahim.

TIGER 03's operation was without the links the other A-Teams supporting the Northern Alliance had. General Baryoli's force was important, but it was a sideline to the main thrust of the moment, which was the orchestration of events needed to bring about the fall of Mazar-e-Sharif. This meant that TIGER 03 would have great latitude and freedom of action. The "big fight" in support of Dostum, Atta, and Fahim would absorb TASK FORCE DAGGER.

Lieutenant Colonel Mark Rosengard, now the J3 (operations officer) at TF DAGGER headquarters in Uzbekistan, knew that MSG Bolduc could be turned loose and would let them know if anything was going seriously awry. Mark gave TIGER 03 free rein to "develop the situation."

The average age of John's A-Team was thirty-three. Years of training, and the judgment and intuition that came with repetitive Special Operations problem solving, gave them a definitive edge over al-Qaida and the Taliban.

"Our mission is not necessarily to outfight the enemy, although we can do that if we have to," MSG Bolduc repeatedly told his men. "We would rather outthink them." This phrase became famous as news agencies picked up on it during the war in Afghanistan.

As they readied to go into battle, the team's senior intelligence sergeant reminded his fellow sergeants, "We're alone, in the middle of nowhere, with no chance of exfil. Let's not get into a fair fight unless we have to, and let's pick and choose our targets carefully to do the most damage with the least amount of risk; we have to stay alive long enough to do some good."

Once the team became oriented and integrated with the *muj,* they did just that. They never gave the Taliban a chance for direct confrontation. They wore typical Afghan clothing, Massoud-style caps and Afghan scarves around their shoulders, long hair, and beards. Their compounds were hidden in remote areas, and they moved at night whenever possible. They hid in mud trenches and crumbling bunkers, calling in air strikes as they destroyed the Taliban. Narrowly missed by enemy mortars and rockets, they fought the terrorists. They used their long-range sniper rifles to kill them one by one when necessary.

By the end, one thing would be certain: the Taliban were neither trained nor proficient snipers, but Bolduc's men were.

Mission

TIGER 03's mission was to link up with the local Northern Alliance commander, General Baryoli, and assist his warfighting capability to the point where his force could go on the offense, seizing a series of villages with the ultimate objective of capturing the city of Kunduz, which held northern Afghanistan's largest concentration of Taliban soldiers. Captured al-Qaida terrorists would be turned over to TASK FORCE 11 and the CIA, as would any information or leads on the whereabouts of bin Laden or his senior staff.

Building Confidence

TIGER 03 was designated for Middle East operations. Their language, which was Arabic, didn't work with the Northern Alliance, who were all Dari speakers. Trying "pointee-talkee" in Arabic helped, but it wasn't going to do the job with the Dari speakers. The team finally found a basic translator, who, with the help of hand signals, could get new ideas across to the *muj* fighters.

General Baryoli, a young commander, but experienced, battle hardened, intelligent, and suave, was already heavily engaged in battle with the Taliban on the frontlines. He had little time for meetings. Eventually, they were taken to Baryoli's home, upon a heavily defended hill, where they would center their operations until the Northern Alliance offensive could be launched.

TIGER 03 was unable to find a reliable translator until two

weeks on the ground had passed. What they didn't know was
that CNN, BBC, and all the other major news networks had
plenty of interpreters just a short distance away in Khoja-
Bahaudeen. Like everything else, the media had escalated the
price of interpreters upward of $150 a day. Had Bolduc's
team known this, they could have sent a man to the press pool
at the makeshift Ministry of Foreign Affairs in Khoja to recruit one, as did a civilian military advisor to the Northern
Alliance.

The team tried to use sketches and other nonverbal means
of communication, but both sides were frustrated. Baryoli
found it hard to comprehend that the U.S. would send in military advisors without knowledge of the local language. But
Special Forces teams train for specific AOs, areas of operation, and are assigned language training based on where U.S.
intelligence agencies and policy dictate they may be needed
next; nobody had expected a war in Afghanistan.

Baryoli's *muj,* since they couldn't interact effectively with
TIGER 03, continued to be deeply skeptical about fighting
with U.S. troops. General Baryoli and his commanders feared
inaccuracies in bombing, especially because the Taliban and
NA trenches were so close to each other, and they thought the
U.S. bombs might hit their own men. They postponed taking
MSG Bolduc and his men to the frontlines.

To make matters worse, there were rumors that a U.S.
Navy fighter had dropped bombs on the wrong side of a river
in support of General Dostum, killing several civilians, and
Baryoli or his staff might have believed it. Baryoli had not
been impressed with the prior bombing behind the Taliban
frontlines, which was frequently inaccurate.

At meals, the Green Beret sergeants could see, but not
make out, animated debates by their *muj* associates over what
to do with their American guests. Even though the team
was itching to get to the frontlines and show the Northern
Alliance what they could do, they knew from many trips
to the Middle East that just standing by and drinking *chai*
was always the best course of action when there was nothing
else to do.

Several of the younger Green Berets were frustrated because they wanted to show the *muj* what the team could do. The team was beginning to develop the situation, but as one of the sergeants commented, "It sure wasn't with Polaroid technology." Almost another week had passed and TIGER 03 still wasn't close to being embraced or trusted by their Northern Alliance counterparts.

Then, to TIGER 03's surprise, they were moved forward with a *muj* detachment to see the frontlines at Kal-a-Khata and the Taliban's trenches. MSG Bolduc and his men were examining enemy positions with their binoculars when the team suddenly came under fire from enemy antiaircraft guns and dug-in tanks. They finally had a chance to show the NA what they could do. The team would send an "appropriate response" to the Taliban while gaining the confidence of Baryoli's troops.

On October 28 the team split, and half the men were driven in the back of a Russian KAMAZ truck to a hill overlooking Zard Kammar, which was now nothing more than a ghost town. The position proved to be perfect for observation of Taliban positions.

Taliban frontlines were about a mile away. TIGER 03 could see the wisdom of the Taliban placing their defenses where they were. The defensive lines dominated all approaches to a wide valley that led to Kunduz in the south. It was not only the largest mass of Taliban troops in northern Afghanistan, it was the Northern Alliance's ultimate objective for Baryoli's force.

Even though intelligence had indicated that bin Laden was not in the area, TIGER 03 had hoped for the remote possibility that he would come to the front. In the past, bin Laden had fought on the frontlines with the *mujahadeen* against the Soviets. As he grew more powerful and assumed more of a leadership role, he preferred to stay in the background, directing his men. But even then, bin Laden could be fairly close to the front, where he could speak directly to his lieutenants and commanders. In spite of the fact that the most recent intelligence showed that bin Laden was not in their area of operations, TIGER 03 did not completely discount the original CIA intelligence, which suggested that bin Laden would move to the north to direct his troops in battle. But bin Laden was probably not that foolish—surely he knew by now that U.S. Special Forces was inflicting unrestrained and deadly accurate fire upon his command posts and bunkers. Ironically, one reason that finding bin Laden was so difficult was the effectiveness of the few Special Forces troops now on the ground. If TASK FORCE DAGGER had encountered setbacks, delays, and extended battles, bin Laden might have come to the front. But the Green Berets were killing the bad guys so efficiently and effectively that bin Laden couldn't risk joining the AQ terrorists who were being slaughtered in the north.

The Green Beret sergeants were well within range of numerous Taliban weapons systems and were particularly vulnerable to enemy mortar fire. TIGER 03 moved to a Northern Alliance trench line that offered them protection, aware that the Taliban would reply to American firepower with their own.

The A-Team set up its equipment—SOFLAMs, long-range telescopes, INMARSAT radios, and LST-5 satellite communications—in a ditch on top of a hill. Now set up, the team wasted no time calling in air strikes.

TIGER 03 started with CAS available from the JFACC, which in the last days of October was plentiful since there were less than forty Green Berets on the ground placing demands on the system. Bolduc's team was well trained in conducting TGO (terminal guidance operations) and several of his men were graduates of a school for TGO run by the U.S. Army at Hurlburt Field, Florida. The training at Hurlburt had been excellent. Because the school was situated at the home of the U.S. Air Force Special Operations Command, the USAF pilots would actually incorporate Special Forces sergeants into their live-fire exercises.

TIGER 03 stood by to see what the JFACC could scramble for them. Fighter aircraft soon arrived loaded with dumb bombs. The first bombs missed the target. The team used basic forward observer techniques to eventually adjust the bomb runs onto the trench line. Once they were on target, they remained on.

Watching the Taliban activity, it was clear that TIGER 03 had gained the enemy's attention as Taliban soldiers dove for cover and ran up and down the trench line in a group panic.

JFACC called and let them know they were vectoring in the "big guns." A B-52 from Diego Garcia air base in the Indian Ocean was flying slow racetrack patterns in the sky. It was quickly dispatched to the SF team. The B-52 Stratofortress was loaded with two-thousand-pound iron bombs that had a new addition: on their noses were GPS guidance devices called JDAMs (Joint Direct Attack Munitions) that made them "smart." The JDAMs would prove to be the most important asset of the Special Forces teams in Afghanistan, even though they would continue to be in critically short supply throughout the war.

Receiving coordinates and targets from Bolduc's men, a load of JDAM bombs detonated directly on top of Taliban bunkers. The explosion tore off the top of the hill on impact and hurled Taliban and AQ terrorists out of their trenches and into the air, scattering their bodies down the front of the slope like toy soldiers being swept off a table.

TIGER 03's TGO training had obviously worked. When the dust cleared, the command-and-control bunkers no longer existed, and the NA militia could see piles of Taliban bodies littering the forward slope of the ridgeline.

The attitude of Baryoli's *muj* immediately changed in favor of the Americans. Mark, one of the team members, later told reporters, "After that [air strike], when we got back to the commander's house, people were lining up, clapping and slapping us on the back."

General Baryoli's attitude had changed, as had the attitude of his troops. MSG Bolduc was encouraged to go back the next day to continue engaging the enemy. Within a week Baryoli got the team a reliable translator. TIGER 03 was really in business. Team members jokingly commented that the more effective the day's bombing was (in terms of numbers of dead Taliban), the better the food was that night at General Baryoli's house.

Annihilating the Enemy

While some of Bolduc's team worked night and day to equip the ground troops for the upcoming offensive, the rest of TIGER 03 concentrated on producing "enemy attrition," making them suffer losses that would severely diminish their ability to fight when the offensive began.

For the next several weeks the team traveled to the frontlines each day. They would have to travel across the Kowkchach River in a rusty Russian UAZ-469 jeep and sneak by the scores of journalists. They paid $7,000 for the jeep—three times the going price. Their "problem set" continued to range far wider than any other team's in the war. Just ten sergeants were responsible, at one time, for 120 miles of battlefield border.

Eventually, TASK FORCE DAGGER assisted by flying in, via Special Operations MC-130 transport plane, eight Polaris all-terrain vehicles to give TIGER 03 the mobility it needed to cover its vast responsibilities. A USAF Special Operations crew flew their MC-130 Combat Talon into Northern Afghanistan and made a risky nighttime landing on a makeshift airfield to deliver the all-terrain vehicles, which had been contributed by the Army's 10th Mountain Division. TF DAGGER repaid the 10th when more ATVs arrived from the States.

Bolduc's team was in the "Wild West," as SF operators called it, and they realized they needed to find a way to get behind the Taliban so they could see what was happening on the reverse slope of its defenses—the back side of hills and ridgelines where Baryoli's observation and direct fires couldn't impact. To do this TIGER 03 knew they would have to leave Afghanistan, loop up through Tajikistan, and move to an observation post back inside Afghanistan. Knowing they were risking an international incident, the team decided it was worth taking the chance. They could cross where there were no marked borders, no signs, and no border guards. After all, international laws certainly weren't stopping the Taliban from doing what *they* needed to do.

One of the team members commented during the discussion, "At least we aren't going to permanently move the border twenty miles!" He was referring to Colonel "Bull" Simons permanently adjusting the Vietnam border for MACV-SOG operations in the 1960s so they could operate more effectively.

Infiltrating back in, TIGER 03 swarmed around the Taliban's positions like a pack of wolves. Covertly moving at night in long hair, beards, and civilian clothes, they decimated the enemy. Ripping, gouging, moving, probing, and slicing, they began to systematically disable Taliban and al-Qaida lines of communication, destroy trench lines, attack command bunkers, and clobber Taliban safe areas in the rear. No Taliban position was safe from TIGER 03. The team's deadly fires and tremendous casualty figures began to break the Taliban fighting spirit.

Air strikes began early in the morning and lasted until late in the afternoon. To keep the Taliban off guard, TASK FORCE DAGGER would unleash an AC-130 Spectre gunship, when it was available, for precision work at night. The Spectre was able to help keep the Taliban from reconstituting its defenses during the darkness.

Bolduc and the other men held to steadfast rules to ensure no fratricide from friendly ordnance occurred. One team member had to get a visual fix on the specific target before a strike could be called in, and a second team member had to check and confirm the target coordinates prior to transmission of target data to aircraft overhead. The safety measures worked well.

Sometimes specific targets were planned the night before or several days in advance for JFACC programming. Others were targets of opportunity, which the team would happen to spot. Since TIGER 03 was operating in a "target-rich environment," a euphemism for being surrounded, Navy aviators and USAF bombers started flocking to the area. Navy and USMC jet fighters only had the legs to stay in the AO about ten minutes, yet they kept coming, because there was always something to destroy. But the B-52 bombers, because of their ability to hang in the clouds for hours, were the team's obvious preference.

The Art of War

Smart munitions also allowed the Green Berets to fight with great cunning.

TIGER 03 noticed that Taliban and AQ fighters would come out of their trenches and bunkers to watch bombs falling on other ridgelines. The team started planning and choreographing bombing runs so that one USAF smart bomb would hit a ridge, then they would wait a few minutes. The Taliban would come out to inspect the damage, and then TIGER 03 would follow with more bombs, hitting key positions on the Taliban observer's ridge. The first test of the new tactic sent Taliban spectators flying through the air like bowling pins. "Smart munitions are science. We apply art" was the favorite phrase of TIGER 03's O & I sergeant.

According to Kevin, one of the special operators on the team, "If you know what you're doing it's easy. You drop bombs on hill #1 and they run to hill #2. Then you drop bombs on hill #2 and then on #1 again. Pretty soon they all bunch up in the same trenchline, concentrating the force. Then you just kill all the fuckers in one shot. Once that stops working you just invent something else."

But the Green Berets couldn't always rely on bombs, and many times they fought with their personal weapons: sniper rifles, assault rifles, and grenade launchers. A particular irritant to TIGER 03 was a Taliban machine-gun nest that started placing accurate fire on one of the team's best OPs.

The team grabbed a Mark-19 automatic grenade launcher and set the heavy weapon up on its tripod, overlooking the Taliban machine-gun position. The Mark-19 was an automatic version of the old single-shot M-79 grenade launcher in Vietnam. It was big, and it was heavy, but with its distinctive *thomp, thomp, thomp* sound it could reach out over two thousand meters and cover a large area with literally hundreds of grenades. The team mixed high-explosive (HE) rounds with armor-piercing (AP) rounds to do the most damage, and then they let loose. They shot "Forty Mike Mike" (40mm) rounds for hours until they ran out of ammo. That solved their problem: the Taliban machine-gun position was totally obliterated.

The enemy was losing fighters at a rapid rate. It was clear that the Northern Alliance would not face the same enemy that had existed only three weeks before.

TIGER 03's scorecard was posted at the Operations Center back at TASK FORCE DAGGER. Confirmed were 1,300 enemies KIA (killed in action); estimates went as high as more than ten thousand Taliban and al-Qaida either KIA or WIA (wounded in action). Fifty tanks and armored personnel carriers, antiaircraft artillery, and artillery pieces were destroyed. Countless numbers of command and observation posts were destroyed.

Collateral Damage

There were a lot of things going on around TIGER 03 that were impacting the battle, the team, and Baryoli's troops. Dr. Abdullah Abdullah, the foreign minister, was telling Baryoli to keep giving the press access to the battlefield. The Northern Alliance leaders had more than a thousand journalists in the north and they wanted them watching the war. Good press had been hard to find, and the destruction of the Taliban in Kal-a-Khata was one way to get it. It would also help get the word out about the Northern Alliance's desperate need for more support and supplies.

Baryoli's *muj* had nothing. Most were fighting in rubber

slippers or tattered loafers. Instead of uniforms most of them wore half uniforms or civilian clothes with a suit vest on top to carry some extra ammo, a rag, or a pack of Hi-Lite cigarettes. If the *mujahadeen* had extra magazines for their rifle, and most did not, they carried them in their pockets or in a cloth Viet Cong–style "chest pouch" made at the local market. Medical equipment was nonexistent. Weapons were also in short supply. Back behind the frontlines groups of *muj* gathered in a rear area the journalists would visit each day. They appeared to be lounging and waiting. They weren't lounging; they were waiting. Waiting for someone to come back wounded or killed, so they could take his gun and join in the fight.

The team tried to convince the *muj* to stop the press far behind the frontline area, but journalists were willing to pay whatever it took to see the action and do whatever it took to get a firsthand look at Americans fighting the Taliban.

On November 9, Gary Scurka, a journalist covering the collateral humanitarian aid effort, drove with his *National Geographic* film crew to the frontlines. He was with a Green Beret working on bringing in airdrops of food for the Northern Alliance and investigating rumors that the Taliban were poisoning the HDRs, Humanitarian Daily Rations, being dropped by USAF cargo planes. News reports back home were lauding the fact that the U.S. was dropping more food than bombs, and many Americans couldn't understand why the bombing was going well—better than well—while the food drops were not.

A critical situation was developing in northern Afghanistan. Anti-Taliban civilians were starving and Northern Alliance soldiers and their families weren't much better off. The HDRs were supposed to provide some relief and help keep the *muj* fighting. In late October the Pentagon broke the news that the Taliban appeared to be poisoning food they captured before sending it back to the Northern Alliance. The situation threatened to disrupt the still-delicate relationships SF operators on the ground were forming with their *muj* counterparts.

To complicate matters, most of the U.S. food drops were missing their targets and their intended recipients.

A civilian team of former Special Forces operators was already in-country trying to solve both problems. While retired Green Beret Lieutenant Colonel Gregg Long was working on humanitarian aid issues and helping assess critical needs, another "retired" Green Beret, Keith Idema, was briefing General Baryoli on a plan to organize *muj* drop-zone teams to secure the food. Idema was also covertly working on tracking down the source of the Taliban-poisoned food.

Long was an explosive mines expert who had run demining operations in Laos and Cambodia, skills that were desperately needed in Afghanistan. He had worked for DIA, the Defense Intelligence Agency, in the past. Long's partner and team leader, Idema, was a New Yorker who had plenty of experience in counterterrorism, and intelligence-gathering behind enemy lines. Like most of the active-duty special operators, Idema would later be known only by a single nickname. Their team's mission was strictly unofficial and unsanctioned, but they were Green Berets nonetheless.

Even though they had six DZs (drop zones) mapped and ready to receive food drops, the Air Force continued to drop the food packs blind, using what was referred to as the "flutter method," an untested procedure where the HDRs were simply dumped out of the back of cargo planes. Idema was not happy with the way food drops were being conducted and started firing off messages to his friends at Fort Benning, Fort Bragg, and the Pentagon. While he waited for a response he started collecting airdropped food packs. Recovering some from the mountains and desert floor, he paid the Afghans $5 each out of his own pocket so they could purchase rice instead. The Afghans had claimed the HDRs were making them ill. Once Idema had a selection of HDR samples from across northeastern Afghanistan, the investigation quickly took an unexpected turn.

The packs had desiccant in them, a drying agent and moisture retardant that was packaged in small paper pouches and looked just like Afghan medicine or the spice packets in Russian noodles. Afghans started eating the desiccant. Sick Afghans started eating even more, thinking the U.S. was kindly dropping medicine. Idema's civilian team fired off a report that Afghans were getting sick from desiccant. One village even claimed a man had died. (HDRs were printed in English, French, German, and Spanish, nonexistent languages in remote Afghan villages. Eventually the Air Force started dropping cartoon leaflets that explained how to eat the food.)

Colin Powell received a copy of the team's e-mail and wanted answers. Natick Labs in Massachusetts initially denied the report and told the Pentagon and Powell that there was no desiccant in the HDRs. Washington believed them. A message returned to Idema's team from "higher up" saying the team was wrong, their intel was bad, and they were basically out in left field and unreliable.

Pissed off, Idema went back to the drawing board. Twenty-four hours later he was e-mailing digital pictures of desiccant packs via INMARSAT. In the process he discovered something far worse.

The HDRs had been packed in Texas, Indiana, and South Carolina at low altitudes. They had been dropped at altitudes far exceeding ten thousand feet. The sealed packs expanded in the air, and then hit the ground at terminal velocity, exploding the sealed food inside and causing slight tears in the outer protective plastic wrapper. Exposed to the rugged Afghan terrain and harsh elements, the food inside rapidly spoiled and became contaminated. Digital pictures were transmitted through INMARSAT to Fort Benning's Battle Lab.

Idema got word that Donald Rumsfeld had demanded answers from Natick. The following day the team was ecstatic: a Natick official admitted the presence of desiccant and the more important contamination problem, stating that government contractors had violated DoD (Department of Defense) product specifications.

Back at Bragg, Special Forces Command moved quickly to solve the problem. Rice started coming in with airdrops to TASK FORCE DAGGER teams and within days USAID provided emergency funds to the UN's World Food Program to finance airdrops of rice, wheat, and cooking oil. WFP planes and Vietnam-vet crews had lots of experience dropping food in Africa, and it would pay off in northern Afghanistan.

The Army's Counter-Terrorist Task Force Office in New York City was also ecstatic. What might have been a disaster with the press had been curtailed by simple ground truth.

Another problem was about to develop, however. As Gary Scurka and his film team tried to get battlefield footage in Kal-a-Khata, TIGER 03 and the Taliban were slugging it out. Baryoli's *muj* were raining down mortar rounds on the Taliban trench lines with more than a fair amount of inaccuracy. Scurka was told not to leave his Green Beret escort's side under any circumstances. The frontline at Kal-a-Khata was treacherous; Taliban and Northern Alliance trenches were woven in and out of the hills and stretched across the countryside. With flat, barren desert only a short distance away, the Kal-a-Khata area was diverse in that some hills were desert sand and others were covered with vegetation, scrub brush, and tree lines.

Both sides had a variety of command posts on the tops of their hills, where the commanders would watch the action and call out orders to their troops over Radio Shack handheld radios, often repeating their call signs fifty times to get someone's attention.

Watching from the Northern Alliance hilltops was more of a spectator sport than watching from those of the Taliban. Exhilarated by the carnage, the NA observed TIGER 03 choreograph Taliban and AQ bodies into a macabre aerial ballet. TIGER 03's two-thousand-pound bomb hits were always met by arms waving in the air as the *muj* cheered "*Insh'allah,*" or "Thanks to God."

As Scurka's group was touring the frontlines, Idema spotted the NA mortar pit having problems targeting Taliban armor. He casually walked down to the *muj* and stood by for a minute, watching them adjust mortar fire by kicking the baseplate of the mortar to change windage and elevation. Asking the ragtag Afghan soldiers if he could try it, he adjusted the

T&E (traversing and elevation) mechanism and recommended they try it again. The *muj* graciously handed Idema a Russian mortar round to "hang in the tube."

Releasing the explosive round into the steel pipe, Idema sent a silent thought to the Taliban: *Welcome to New York. . . .* A few seconds later, Taliban bodies were in the air as a Taliban BMP armored vehicle was jolted off the ground in a smoking heap with a dead-center impact. Baryoli's Afghans on the hill above were waving and smiling. What the Afghans didn't know was the mortar had been adjusted to drop behind the Taliban armor to bracket it; it wasn't expected to hit it. What was simply a lucky mistake was probably seen by the *mujahadeen* as an act of God.

Now standing on the hilltop over the mortars, Idema was watching the trenches through binoculars and getting a GPS read on the observation post. Journalists were swarming over the Northern Alliance hills like bees around a hive. A CNN cameraman ran up to the observation post and frantically announced that Taliban rockets and artillery had just hit a journalist.

"Who was it, can you describe him?" Idema asked. The men couldn't, but he did have it on video. Looking through the television camera's eyepiece, it only took a second to realize it was Scurka who was bleeding.

Idema ran as fast as he could, sliding down the sandy hillside, hitting the dirt road, and running toward the nearby hill where Scurka was hit. His interpreter and several *muj* were close behind.

Drenched in blood from the waist down, Scurka was now standing up with the help of several people. Everyone was arguing about what to do. Tim Friend from *USA Today* and Kevin Sites from NBC News had wrapped Afghan scarves around Scurka's leg to stop the bleeding.

Idema didn't waste time yelling at his hardheaded friend: "You stupid bastard, I told you not to leave my side." Looking over at Lieutenant Colonel Gregg Long he observed a barely coherent, dazed, and blood-spattered man.

"Are you hit too?" he asked sharply. Long told him he didn't think so, it was Scurka's blood.

"Lay him down," Idema ordered. Several of the journalists began to argue that Scurka should be immediately put in a vehicle and driven to a hospital. Kevin Sites, the NBC producer, explained that Scurka was only hit in the leg and the bleeding wasn't that bad. A brief argument ensued. They were promptly asked how many bullet wounds they had seen and told to "shut the fuck up." Within seconds Idema was kneeling over Scurka and assessing the extent of the wounds. Scurka had holes through his right leg and thigh, and blood was pouring out of his upper thigh. "Looks like you've been shot in the ass too; how appropriate," Idema told him.

As Idema ripped off his black field jacket to start working on Scurka's wounds, cameras started to roll as the crowd saw an assault vest with an American flag on the breast pocket. NBC and *National Geographic* later agreed to cut Idema out of its tape.

Realizing that he had given virtually all of his combat medic field dressings to *muj* throughout the day, he asked his interpreter to go borrow some back. Within minutes Baryoli's *muj,* who had treasured the only medical supplies they had ever been given, were returning them . . . and Idema was bandaging Scurka's blood-spewing wounds. New York City cops and Dutchess County, N.Y., sheriffs had donated the medical dressings for the *muj.* The New York gift to the *muj* had now come full circle.

Scurka was in shock, and had lost a lot more blood than first suspected. He was quickly hit with controlled drugs, huge dosages of Ciproflaxin antibiotics and fluids. Putting him on a Northern Alliance truck, they forded the river back to the rear area. NBC correspondent Jim Maceda offered NBC's Toyota to the team.

"It's the fastest vehicle here, and will outrun that Russian junk heap of yours," Jim told them.

"It will be covered in blood, probably wrecked on the ride,

and left unattended at the LZ in Khoja-Bahaudeen. You might not ever see it again."

"I don't care, he's from New York," Maceda replied.

Once in the car Idema noticed the hand he had placed on Scurka's back was wet with blood and Scurka's breathing was hard. Scurka had also taken shrapnel in the right chest area, but it did not appear to have penetrated his lung. Idema also saw that Scurka's leg was still gushing blood through the bandage.

There was no way Scurka could be transported without further triage. Neil Barrett, *National Geographic*'s cameraman, put down his camera and started passing bandages out of Idema's M-5 medic bag. Idema cut off Scurka's blue jeans and examined the primary wound. It was a four-inch-long, three-inch-deep gaping wound. The muscle tissue was splayed open like a filleted trout, displaying the bright, pinkish-white bone in his leg. As Idema probed inside for ruptured arteries, Scurka finally began to complain. It took another ten minutes to stop the blood and dress the wound for transport.

Sites offered to follow the team in another vehicle. "What if your truck breaks down?"

"It's too dangerous and it will be dark before we get there," Idema told him.

"Matters not. I'll go in case you need me," Sites said. Kevin Sites had "bad ass" written all over him and was about as close to looking like a Green Beret as anyone Idema had ever seen. Only a few minutes before, Idema had found out it was Sites and Friend who had actually gotten Scurka out of the field of fire and Sites' levelheaded response that had kept things under control until Idema got there.

"Thanks, I'll take you up on it. One last thing: Thanks for getting him out of the impact area." Idema later made it clear that Sites was the hero that day—he had left no man behind.

"No problem," Sites said.

"Let's roll," Idema said as they drove off.

Calling from an INMARSAT as they raced across the desert in the dark of night, the team requested U.S. military intervention and air assets to medevac the wounded New Yorker. The answer was an unequivocal no, so the team implied that Scurka "wasn't really a journalist" and began negotiations for a chopper.

Understanding that this was probably going to be illegal, they called Massoud Khalili's nephew and asked for his help with General Baryoli and the NA. Abdul Khalili started contacting Dr. Abdullah and Baryoli.

Back at the Northern Alliance's secret landing zone near the Tajikistan border, they radioed the GPS coordinates for the medevac and then got the depressing word that a USAF chopper could exfil Scurka, but it was three hours off station. A few minutes later Khalili was informed by General Baryoli that he would make his personal MI-8 helicopter available for medevac. Khalili was an Afghan-American from Los Angeles who ran AfghanRelief.com and had been delivering more aid faster than anyone else to the Northern Alliance. Baryoli and the NA hierarchy wanted all Americans safe, not just the Green Berets helping the Northern Alliance. Gregg Long also had to be medevaced when it became evident that his medical condition, from the massive concussion caused by the Taliban artillery fire, was getting progressively worse. Meanwhile, Scurka was arguing that he wanted a blood transfusion and quick stitches so he could return to the battlefield. He was also obviously dazed.

"We're bringing him in on a Northern Alliance chopper; can you at least meet him and get him some help?" the team radioed in.

"Where's he from?" asked a senior SF officer, trying to figure out if Scurka was SPECAT, or Special Category, meaning CIA.

"New York" was the team's reply, an artful way to avoid lying.

"Can't let no more New Yorkers die," came the word back.

Even though they were specifically told not to render civilian assistance, Special Forces assets in Tajikistan met Scurka when he arrived in Dushanbe and wasted no time getting him American doctors. Major Dave Brigham was the military attaché in Tajikistan, and SF was moving that Bull Simons' borderline again in order to get the job done and save lives.

Back home, the news about Scurka was front-page, and he told the Fayetteville, North Carolina, *Observer* that his Green Beret friend had "whipped out some special medical dressings and saved his life."

As fate would have it, the first man down from Taliban fire would not be a Special Forces Green Beret, it would be a New York journalist, saved by a Green Beret from New York. Al-Qaida was still inflicting damage on the Big Apple, and New Yorkers were just beginning to fight back.

Three hours after Scurka and Long were hit, three more journalists went up on the hill overlooking Zard Kammar to observe. The Taliban started firing RPGs at the press, and they tried to get away on the back of a Northern Alliance armored vehicle. As the rockets hit around them, two fell off and the third jumped off.

The Taliban killed the German photographer, and dragged the two French journalists back into their trenches, where they were raped, machine-gunned, and mutilated. Surely inspired by American annihilation of Taliban on the hills and in the trenches, Baryoli's troops rallied a rescue attempt. Not knowing the women were already dead, they made a valiant charge into the Taliban trench. Almost all of them, roughly thirty, were cut down by PK and RPG fire as they hit the Taliban frontline. They were successful in recovering the journalists' bodies.

The Attack

After two weeks of eating air strikes and dying in the night clueless, the Taliban defense was falling apart. General Baryoli was prepared to mount an offensive. He discussed with MSG Bolduc and TIGER 03 what his spies were telling him: the Taliban believed what the United States and the international media, including that of the Muslim world, were saying:

that the struggle would be long and hard, and the ground offensive with the Northern Alliance would not begin until the spring.

The ground attack and the final Battle of Kal-a-Khata started midafternoon that very day.

The Northern Alliance militia was aggressive and broke the Taliban lines. Taliban positions were soon overwhelmed, making the retreating force easy prey for the *muj* infantry, especially since there was little cover to hide behind as they were flushed from their positions. In spite of desperate hand-to-hand fighting, the *muj* pressed on, clearly gaining decisive momentum, charging from ridgeline to ridgeline.

Baryoli's men were engaging the Taliban in the trenches, running down between the dugout dirt walls pumping AK rounds at point-blank range into the chests of the panicking Taliban opposition. Their biggest tactical problem was making sure they didn't trip over the AQ bodies piling up under their feet, or slip in slushy pools of bloody sand. The Taliban had to withdraw and reestablish its defensive lines if it were to survive.

After twenty-four hours into the attack, the Northern Alliance militia had pushed the Taliban back over twelve miles. Word quickly spread that the Taliban had retreated down the valley toward Kunduz, and they were regrouping in the town of Chichka, trying to restore some sort of coherent defense. Bolduc's TIGER 03 was in hot pursuit. They bounded forward to occupy new vantage points to pound the new defensive lines before the Taliban could effectively dig in.

The demoralized Taliban were no match for the emboldened infantry of the Northern Alliance, fortified by the Green Berets and U.S. airpower. Faced with the now-evident rapid pursuit of Baryoli's militia, the Taliban abandoned Chichka in short order, continuing to flee to the south, while the Northern Alliance paused to resupply, treat the wounded, and prepare for continued pursuit of the enemy. A short time later, TIGER 03 and their compatriots moved to the outskirts of Kunduz to prepare for a final attack on the Taliban's last remaining stronghold in the north. Kunduz, surrounded, was besieged for days, which once again offered U.S. air power the chance to inflict considerable harm.

Realizing the futility of their efforts, and the hopelessness of their defense, the Taliban eventually surrendered to the Northern Alliance.

USA Today interviewed Muhammed Shah, a Taliban leader who surrendered in Kunduz. Shah's rationale for surrender made sense: "They killed many people, [and] we are afraid to die."

MSG John Bolduc touched on the essence of the Green Berets in Afghanistan in an eloquent statement: "When we arrived, the area was crawling with Arabs, Pakistanis, Chechens, and the al-Qaida. We knew they would fight to the death rather than surrender. They did not expect that we would do so well. You see, we were also prepared to give *our* lives."

As the intensity of the fighting in the north began to subside, TIGER 03 started transitioning to reporting the humanitarian needs of the population, coordinating food drops, bringing in generators for electricity in small villages, and the like. The team also set up its own hospital, to treat children with wounds from land mines.

It wasn't long before they started running into aid workers in places like Dasht-e-Qaleh. TIGER 03 helped them as much as they could, sometimes protecting them without the aid workers knowing it, sometimes loaning them medical supplies, and sometimes just being a friendly face. In Dasht-e, as it was lovingly referred to, the humanitarian aid situation was critical. A few aid workers made it across the border, like "Dawn," an American nurse who quickly bonded with the Green Berets. Wanting to do her part after 9/11, she was one of the few American aid workers who ventured into northern Afghanistan as the war raged. Dawn was a thin, outdoorsy nurse from New England. Her good looks and daring relief work quickly endeared her to the Afghans, the Green Berets, and one of the Agency's operators—so much so that they taught the fiery redhead how to shoot when things got rough in the area. Faced with no medical supplies, lack of funding, and a dangerous environment, Dawn kept caring for children and improved the locals' rapport with Americans, which also meant the Green Berets.

More with Less

Colonel Mulholland, from TASK FORCE DAGGER, summed up A-Team 585's performance with a simple statement of fact: "TIGER 03 did more with less and had greater impact on the outcome of the war than anyone else."

In a war filled with heroes, if you had to pick one, the first one, it would be Master Sergeant John Bolduc.

Live Free or Die

Walking the streets of Kabul on the twenty-ninth of November, Green Beret Captain David Bolduc was upset that he couldn't find a way to see his older brother. He was proud of John, the master sergeant leading TIGER 03 in Kal-a-Khata, Kunduz, and Taloqan. The biggest killers on the battlefield, the men of A-Team 585 were the talk of the town at Fort Bragg's Special Warfare Center.

David also missed his other brother, a major, who had been put in the "box" with Chairman Karzai, who was then fighting north of Kandahar. Although they weren't physically together, they were standing together in spirit and action.

On February 8, 2002, the three brothers stood together again in the small town of Laconia, New Hampshire. This time, instead of acting as American avengers orchestrating the U.S. ground retaliation against AQ, they were overseeing the 73rd World Championship Dog Sled Derby. The Bolduc family, Laconia natives, had given their three sons to the 5th Special Forces Group, and the group had now returned them.

Three warriors, joyful to be among the cheering fans in small-town America: STRENGTH and HONOR—the words of a righteous war against cold-blooded murderers and oppressors.

But this was Laconia—Laconia, New Hampshire. And the words of the day were LIVE FREE OR DIE.

Alone and Out on a Limb

Scurka returned to New York, a virtual hero in the press as the first journalist wounded in action. Gregg Long recuperated and went back to demining operations in Cambodia. Rumsfeld announced on national television that wounded journalists would not be medevaced under any circumstances. The Northern Alliance turned over the bodies of the three dead journalists to the French government. Baryoli quickly brought peace to his region. The Green Berets took every major city in the north, east, and west within the next thirty days, and Idema, having assured himself that Scurka and Long were now safe, immediately returned to Afghanistan and joined the Northern Alliance, where he remained alone and unsupported for nine months fighting the Taliban and pursuing al-Qaida and bin Laden. In the Special Forces community it was known as going native, and Idema had clearly gone off the reservation.

CHAPTER 11

Northern Alliance—
General Atta

"I gave them ample opportunity to turn over al-Qaida. I made it very clear to them, in no uncertain terms, that, in order to avoid punishment, they should turn over the parasites that hide in their country. They obviously refused to do so. And now they're paying a price."

— PRESIDENT GEORGE W. BUSH,
White House press conference,
October 11, 2001

Link Up

Northwest Afghanistan

On November 2, 2001, the twelve men of TIGER 04, formerly ODA 534, along with their Air Force CAS asset piled into the vehicles parked in the mud outside their isolation-area wooden-floored tents. They were driven through the narrow roadway in the berm that separated the aviation section of K2 from the living quarters of the constantly growing secret HQ of TASK FORCE DAGGER. Their equipment was neatly stacked beside the MH-47 helicopter that was scheduled to deliver the team to the mysterious General Atta inside a Taliban-controlled area near Mazar-e-Sharif.

Little known, never seen, and heavily armed AH-60 Black Hawk attack helicopters from the 160th SOAR would ride shotgun for the team.

TURKMENIS

IRAN

BADGHIS
*Qal'eh-y

+ Herat

HERAT

Shindand

FARAH
*Farah

Lashk
G.

HELMA

*Zaranj
NIMRUZ

IRAN

TIGER 04 and General Atta

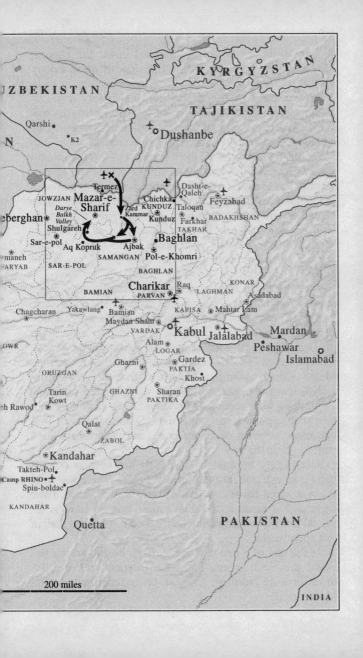

They would be would be cramped inside the chopper for hours before reaching their linkup with Atta's troops. TIGER 04 finally felt the Chinook setting down on the high-desert LZ, over eight miles inside Taliban territory. A *muj* reception party met them and they started off on a two-day trek across the rocky wasteland laden with the equipment they would need when they reached their destination.

TIGER 04 had prepared the fine points of this mission for weeks. "Drilling it" was the slang for rehearsing to perfection. The team had worked together during many missions in foreign lands. This assignment, carried out in secrecy deep behind enemy lines, would have gnawed upon the minds of lesser-trained and less hardened men. But as isolated as TIGER 04 was, the men were Green Berets trained to fight in situations where they could not know if they would live or die.

Their mission was quite simple—find the mysterious and elusive Commander Atta, train and supply his shoddy force, lead them against far superior forces, capture a dozen cities, destroy ten thousand Taliban and al-Qaida terrorists, learn the Dari language in a day or two, and then storm the largest, most protected Taliban stronghold in Northwest Afghanistan, Mazar-e-Sharif. After they finished all that, they were to establish law and order and rebuild the shattered province. While they were resting or between laying siege to cities, they were to guide laser bombs and U.S. aircraft against Taliban armor, vehicles, command posts, and whatever else happened to be in the way.

Surprisingly, no one on TIGER 04 had been in combat before, an extreme rarity in Special Forces. There was mild concern about the team's lack of combat experience. Their command assumed it would take more than six months for partial success in completing their mission. They did it all in just a few weeks.

At the end of a two-day trek through hostile enemy territory, they had already found and become trusted allies of an obscure Northern Alliance commander named Atta Mohammed.

A major complicating factor in their mission was that Atta and Dostum were in continual conflict. They were putting aside their own personal war only because they had a bigger, more powerful, and more despised enemy, the foreign al-Qaida. Their agreement to join together in the Northern Alliance to conduct coordinated attacks was tenuous at best, and then only as a result of pressure by Commander Massoud, who was now dead.

Atta greeted the team with open arms, hugs, kisses, and a smile that beamed with elation, respect, and relief. He was thirty-eight years old, with a Muslim full beard and piercing eyes. The former schoolteacher spoke not one word of English. The team's menu of languages failed to produce a common means of communication.

TIGER 04 had men that spoke English, French, Chinese, and several Arabic dialects—not one of them spoke a word of Dari. After trying to use the various Arabic dialects with no success, Captain Dean Newman, the team leader, tried Russian. One of Atta's *mujahadeen* responded in poor Russian, but Russian all the same. Newman now had a translator. Afghans reluctantly spoke, or even admitted that they could speak, Russian. The Russians were their sworn enemies, and no one wanted to acknowledge that they could converse in an enemy language, so that alone was a leap of faith in the Americans.

As the hours and days went by, the team realized that their many years of missions all over the Middle East and Central Asia, including three-week stints of living in the desert with no external resupply, had made them hard and agile. Their mix of communications, infantry, medical, engineering, intelligence, and tactical Special Forces skills made them a formidable bunch. Since they had considerable cross-training, the team could split into smaller groups or survive the loss of several members.

TIGER 04 was a group of men in their midthirties, and like the other Special Forces teams on the ground, most had college degrees, wives, and children. The team was going to be fighting with its own indigenous army, the ultimate test of

Green Beret skills. Their forefathers in the OSS had done this behind the lines in Europe. Then twenty-odd years later Green Berets in the Vietnam A-Camps had fought beside Cambodians, Laotians, Montagnards, Hmong, and Vietnamese. The advisors in El Salvador and Nicaragua had battled beside their native compadres. Now it was the turn of these new men, coming into another strange environment, to be judged against past teams of Green Berets as well as compared with current shadowy groups operating throughout Africa, South America, and the Middle East. These thoughts were running through the minds of the members of TIGER 04 as they joined General Atta in his collection of mud huts within the perimeters of Taliban control.

Building Rapport

After drinking *chai* and engaging in small talk, General Atta told the Americans of TIGER 04 that he had over two thousand troops in the Darye Balkh Valley, just south of Mazar-e-Sharif. Their first task, after some rest, was to move again to establish contact with the fighting force.

The next morning the men moved out by horse on tight, winding mountain trails flanked with minefields. They were told the trip would take more than a day. The trails were an ambush alley, so the team split up to ensure they wouldn't all be taken down in one fight. Six men stayed with Atta, while the other team scouted ahead from another direction. M203 grenade launchers and M249 SAW machine guns went to the front to break contact, and the team's snipers stayed with the rear element to eliminate potential ambushers from extended distances.

The men slowly made their way down the narrow trail. The Afghans had overloaded the horses so excessively that four of them buckled from sheer exhaustion during the trip. The horses were constantly on the verge of falling or becoming injured as they navigated the route. TIGER 04 tried to take it easy on the animals, but they were forced to keep up with Atta's men. Two other steeds eventually broke their legs on the rocky, uneven terrain. Nonetheless, the band persevered and finally reached Atta's army of Northern Alliance soldiers south of Mazar-e-Sharif.

Atta's men were in poor condition and needed a lot of help if they were going to get into the fight. TIGER 04 immediately called TASK FORCE DAGGER and requested airdrops of boots, uniforms, blankets, water, ammunition, and food. Atta's troops were in such bad shape that TIGER 04 had a hard time believing they could last even five seconds in a battle. Their guns were rusted, ammunition was in critically short supply, their boots nonexistent; the rags on their bodies were falling off, and some of the few men that were wearing socks had only one.

Airdrops of supplies were slow in coming; the Special Operations resupply boys in Germany were constantly running into problems with U.S. Air Force commanders there. Although their were dozens of containers pre-packed and ready to drop by parachute, the Air Force generals were afraid of the looming ground-to-air missile threat. Finally, TASK FORCE DAGGER convinced them that if airdrops didn't start coming quick, teams were going to start dying. Atta's *mujahadeen* decided they liked TIGER 04 after the first equipment drop even though it was still lacking many of the supplies an army needed to survive. Several men canvassed the warriors to determine their strength and most immediate needs. Atta's forces needed the basics before they could mount the offensive. It was a running battle to supply and equip Atta's men but they were still willing to fight, even without the support of TIGER 04's CAS and their dreaded smart bombs.

The Taliban, according to Atta, would not know of the American presence nor that his *muj* cavalry had been newly provisioned. American air power in concert with a newly energized ground assault would break the Taliban will to hold the town of Aq Kopruk. Atta's army would open the way for taking this key city on the road to conquering Mazar-e-Sharif.

The Fight for Aq Kopruk

TIGER 04, as was becoming common practice, split back into six-man elements to cover Atta's assaulting forces with adequate air support. One team concentrated on air strikes with dumb bombs, while the other moved closer with their SOFLAMs and lazed targets for Navy aviators. When split into two, the A-Team could cover both sides of the mountain, allowing the Taliban no escape route. At one point Atta looked through the team's spotting scope just in time to witness a Taliban command post receive a direct hit by a smart bomb. He observed the unfolding carnage in the Taliban defensive position with admiration, and smiled: the team had cut the mustard.

After that Atta didn't just want more laser, he wanted to look through the spotting scope himself and see the Taliban bodies exploding through the air. Because of the altitude of the aircraft, it would take about a minute or two for the bomb to impact. TIGER 04 would release the bomb and then let the Northern Alliance commanders watch through the laser target designator. Atta would hear the chirping noise from the laser, and then, BOOM, the enemy position explodes. The Death Ray was at it again. Atta was willing to take the team anywhere they wanted, as long as he could watch "Taliban TV." As far as Atta and his commanders were concerned, the Taliban might have had the anti-American al-Jazeera TV in Kabul, but Atta had the American-Afghan Armed Forces Laser Channel, and as the smart bombs vaporized his enemies it was playing his favorite show in the lens of the spotting scope.

The horse-mounted *muj* cavalry slaughtered the Taliban under the cover of U.S. close air support and smart bombs. First, the Taliban began to waver, then to withdraw altogether. Atta's maneuver broke the enemy's will, and late in the first day of battle, the remaining Taliban retreated. Aq Kopruk fell to the Death Ray.

TIGER 04 would have just one night in Aq Kopruk to consolidate and prepare for the next fight. They were on a roll and the last thing they wanted was for the Taliban and AQ to rearm, regroup, or counterassault. They knew what all the teams knew—once you have them on the run, you cut them down like rats as their backs are turned. The Green Berets ditched their horses and jumped into captured Taliban pickup trucks and an automobile, continuing north in hot pursuit toward Mazar with Atta and his men.

Onward to Mazar-e-Sharif

As they raced across the desert, the team continued to call in air strikes to destroy remaining pockets of resistance and Taliban artillery weapons on the high ground above the valleys. In one gorge, speckled with cave entrances, TIGER 04 saw the results of their handiwork. The gorge was strewn with Taliban bodies and burned-out vehicles.

Simultaneously, the armies of General Abdul Rashid Dostum and Mohahqeq Mohammed were progressing along two avenues of approach toward Mazar-e-Sharif. Although all the factions competed for power and influence, and in spite of the fact that Atta and Dostum were frequently at each other's throats, the linkup of the Northern Alliance forces, south of Mazar-e-Sharif, was an experience unique to most of them. It was an emotional moment for the A-Teams, too, as they all came together.

The simultaneous convergence of Northern Alliance infantry and cavalry outgunned the reeling enemy. Those who were left headed to the safety of Mazar-e-Sharif. It would not be long before they abandoned that stronghold too. Wedged among three converging forces, the Taliban again pulled out immediately, demoralized and in a panic. Atta's men charged through the villages south of Mazar-e-Sharif, doggedly pushing to the north to ensure everything was secure.

The swift capture of areas to the south elevated confidence that the final assaults on the strategic target, Mazar-e-Sharif, and its airfield, and the highway to Uzbekistan, would end favorably and quickly. As a result, the city fell without significant military activity, spurred by the granting of amnesty to large numbers of Afghan Taliban if they deserted and fought the AQ. The long, miserable winter war TIGER 04 had planned to fight with the Northern Alliance was now unlikely. The Taliban was collapsing and al-Qaida was on the run. Their defeat in the north would not have to wait until spring.

The population of Mazar-e-Sharif filled the streets with an emotional outpouring of thanks as the different Northern Alliance formations passed through. As for TIGER 04, crowds of men, women, and children ran crying and screaming to thank the American soldiers. One Special Forces sergeant said it was like being in a World War II movie, riding on top of a tank as they entered the liberated city, except that this time he was watching the experience in color instead of black and white.

While being interviewed by *Newsweek,* one of TIGER 04's men shared his feelings on how strange the scene became. "It was surreal," recalled Mike, TIGER 04's weapons specialist. "We didn't know what to expect. We were locked and loaded and didn't know whether or not there were any Taliban left in the city. I wondered whether it was the same feeling the Allies had when they liberated Paris."

After Mazar-e-Sharif fell, TIGER 04 turned to humanitarian relief as a main task. The team was asked to destroy more Taliban positions on several occasions, but when they checked the forces they found massed in the distance outside Mazar, quite frequently they proved to be General Dostum's men. The team had to be on its toes, however, to prevent a "green on green," which was the term for an Afghan-on-Afghan fratricide incident. The Afghan warlords were trying to gain superiority over each other by pitting the Special Forces against rival tribes.

The men became more and more native the longer they stayed in Afghanistan. Dari phrases became the norm in conversation. TIGER 04 soon became experts at participating in the mandatory fifteen minutes of greetings to show mutual respect, have *chai,* and then get down to business.

Eventually the friction between Atta and Dostum led to several armed incidents between the two Northern Alliance factions. Atta began pressing for more and more assistance. TASK FORCE DAGGER pulled the team from Atta as part of "reconfiguring Special Forces' presence in the area." But rumors abounded that Dostum had threatened retaliation if Special Forces remained with Atta and continued to intercede in their blood feud. Dostum had three men from the CIA's paramilitary-operations group with him, and the CIA favored Dostum with money and influence, probably because of his bigger-than-life style. The Agency viewed Dostum as a more powerful and valuable ally and had apparently worked hard to get TIGER 04 out of country so he could consolidate his power.

A few weeks prior to being pulled back to TASK FORCE DAGGER headquarters, TIGER 04 had been challenged by an unknown group of men. The team used their preplanned phrases to designate who would shoot who first. SOP (standard operating procedure) ensured that anyone who finished shooting his targets would start "double-tapping" the others, a term for quickly placing two additional bullets in the chest of your adversary. Captain Newman stared his *muj* opponents in the eyes. The men, who turned out to be from Dostum's force, withdrew, wishing to avoid a confrontation that they knew they would lose. The incident was just one more example of the chaos that would follow the twenty-three years of continuous war that had created a brutal warrior society.

TIGER 04 was deeply saddened to leave Atta, but their orders were clear. Unknown to TASK FORCE DAGGER and the U.S. Army Special Forces Command, Atta, and his deputy commander General S. Wasiqullah, remained loyal to America; they felt indebted for the help they had received, and continued to advance cooperation with the U.S. General Wasiqullah, a fighter since he was twelve years old, who had been trained as a protégé to Commander Massoud. Wasiq, as his close American friends called him, was tall, thin, handsome, and a man of infinite honor and bravery. Although he was highly religious, he was also well educated and an Islamic moderate. He had frequently warned the American forces of Dostum's disloyalty and tricks.

Atta and Dostum continued to slug it out in minor skirmishes in the many months ahead. Dostum turned out to be the wrong choice to back, as he started forging anti-American alliances with the Russians and Iranians.

In spite of losing his A-Team, Wasiq remained in close contact with the Northern Alliance's special advisor, Jack, and continued to help America behind the scenes. Wassiq's brother, whom Jack fondly nicknamed Alex, went to work for the Americans at AfghanRelief.com, helping his people rebuild and helping the families of American allies. Alex was later killed after leaving the American base at Bagram, a great loss for his brother, and for America.

CHAPTER 12

Northern Alliance—
Commander Khalili

"For all the fabled fighting qualities of the Afghans, they've never had to deal with a modern air campaign."
—unnamed U.S. official quoted in
the *Washington Post*, October 12, 2001

The Hazara

Bamian, Afghanistan
Halloween 2001

A-Team 553 became TIGER 07 and was inserted into Afghanistan on the last day of October 2001. TIGER 07 had a good blend of a dozen men. Some were from the Midwest and their horsemanship skills were especially welcomed in Bamian. Others were from the West Coast, and the rest from the East Coast. TIGER 07 faced a wide range of challenges working with Hazara forces.

The Hazara are one of several major ethnic groups in Afghanistan, representing approximately 20 percent of the total population. They live in the central mountainous region of the country, at the southern end of the Hindu Kush range. The Hazara historically have been the most oppressed ethnic group in Afghanistan. They have never been free to attend institutions of higher education, or to hold any positions of authority in the government or the military. The various factions who have controlled Afghanistan over the years have repeatedly slaughtered their race.

CHAPTER 7

Khutz, Khush—
Commander Khalili

TIGER 07 and Commander Khalili

TURKMENI

IRAN

BADGH

Qal'eh-ye-Now ⊛

✚ Herat

HERAT

• Shindand

FARAH

⊛ Farah

Las

HELM

✕ Zaranj

NIMRUZ

IRAN

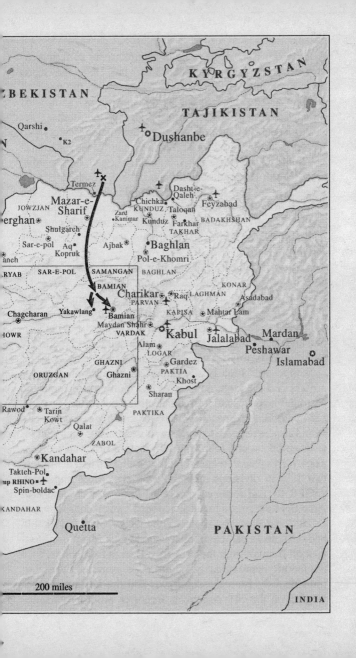

After the rise of the Taliban regime, their suffering increased dramatically. Between 1997 and 1998, thousands upon thousands of Hazara were massacred in the cities of Bamian and Mazar-e-Sharif by Taliban troops. Thousands more were marched off to various prisons to the south.

While the Taliban could control population centers and major roads, they could not effectively control the mountainous home of the Hazara. It was to this rugged, inhospitable area that the Hazara had withdrawn to build their resistance forces. The process had taken years, and in the meantime, the Taliban troops were free to destroy everything in areas they couldn't firmly control. Every village between Yakawlang and Bamian was burned to the ground, and their populations forcibly moved.

In one of TIGER 07's situation reports was a detailed description of the Hazara homeland. It told of burned-out hospitals, schools, and even mosques. The Green Berets of TIGER 07 were appalled at the devastation caused by the Taliban's scorched-earth campaign. Their outrage over the Taliban and AQ murder of Hazara women and children quickly manifested itself into a vicious pursuit of the enemy.

Bamian was strategically important because of its major airfield and the large number of AQ hiding throughout the surrounding province. It would be critical for follow-on combat operations if Special Forces became bogged down and would also be required to perform substantial humanitarian assistance operations following termination of combat operations. Intelligence, frequently faulty, indicated that there were two Taliban divisions defending the city. Most important, TIGER 07 had received reports of large concentrations of Arab fighters housed in the abandoned Iranian consulate.

The local Northern Alliance commander, Massoud Khalili, had designed a campaign plan to conduct a two-pronged attack on Bamian from the west. Two Hazara formations, each numbering approximately 1,500 troops, were to advance simultaneously from the southwest and the northwest, converging on the city. American firepower was sorely needed to soften the lines and also seal the enemy's escape routes to the east.

The End of the Stalemate

After a few days on the ground, the dozen or so men of TIGER 07 visited the front with Khalili well to the west of Bamian to examine his forces and their disposition, while gaining a chance to see the Taliban for the first time. The lines had been static for three years; no serious fighting had taken place during that time. Only occasional, brief skirmishes had occurred, with a few RPG-7 rounds and small arms fire being exchanged. The frontlines consisted of a series of widely dispersed observation posts on both sides. The Taliban and the Northern Alliance knew exactly where each other's positions were located.

Khalili had his frontlines organized into a northern half and a southern half. The overall frontline commander was a sixty-five-year-old man from Yakawlang. He seemed very capable and had been fighting for years, well grounded in his experiences against the Soviets during the 1980s.

On November 6, 2001, TIGER 07 moved out to view the northern positions. An escort of twenty to thirty *muj* accompanied the team. To reach the best vantage point they climbed an eleven-thousand-foot peak, and the Hazara escorts saved the men from exhaustion in the high altitude by supplying horses to carry their equipment.

When the team reached their final observation post, they were in plain sight of Taliban soldiers using Russian optics, yet they were well out of range of Taliban direct-fire weapons. The chance to show their new comrades what they could bring to the fight failed the first day; there was no close air support available. The JFACC was tasked to the limit with the few aircraft they had already heavily engaged in the north. The *muj* were disappointed, yet remained patient and supportive.

TIGER 07 was exposed. The Taliban and al-Qaida fighters could see them just as the team could peer at their positions in the valley. Special Operations usually use surprise as a combat multiplier, frequently attacking when no one expects it. This was different. The enemy forces watching them through their binoculars were ordered to hold their ground and kill the Americans only if they tried to dislodge them from their trench lines. But the Taliban and AQ knew that the Americans were here to kill them with their firepower and to assist in infantry charges on their positions, all in order to drive them from the field or kill them. Sooner or later, one side would move on the other. The three-year stalemate was about to end.

Word came back from the JFACC that no fire support would be available until the next air tasking order, which was the means of distributing joint firepower assets around the battlefield in a prioritized and fair-as-possible method. Pissed-off, the team decided to split and move half the men on horseback to observe the southern portion of the battlefield.

After climbing a mountain even higher than the one the previous day, the split team sent to the south reached its final vantage point late on November 7. They were overlooking the Foladi Canyon, an area infested with Taliban, yet no good targets were visible. Because of the terrain, they could not reach a position to effectively see and engage the enemy. It was frustrating, particularly when they heard the crackling of their radios as the rest of TIGER 07 began to light up the enemy.

The Fight Begins

The northern observation post had turned loose the close air support for their plentiful targets. The team had just been given air assets via TASK FORCE DAGGER's urgent request to the Joint Forces Air Component Command.

Having spotted the Green Berets on the mountain, the Taliban had moved a Russian ZSU-23-4 antiaircraft weapon into position in range of the mountaintop. As the Soviet antiaircraft system thumped away, putting heavy but ineffective fire on their position, TIGER 07 called for fire support.

F/A-18s answered the call, putting the pedal to the metal as they responded. After a few runs, the ZSU was instantly reduced to a smoking ruin. The team profusely thanked the pilot and then bore down to inflict some serious damage.

TIGER 07 proceeded to destroy Taliban observation posts, as well as other targets in the city, including the former Iranian consulate, which had been previously approved for destruction. When the aviators heard the area was hot they converged in the skies above TIGER 07. Most of the planes had ammunition left over from other missions, and they were eager to put it to good use. Nobody wanted to return to base with ammo and "look like a wimp."

The Green Berets of TIGER 07 took advantage of perfect weather and the bonanza of air platforms, working over the entire Taliban frontline and its rear positions until nighttime. Although bomb damage assessment was difficult, it was clear that the Taliban had taken significant heat. TIGER 07 knew that much of the leadership had been degraded by the series of hits on observation and command posts.

In the early morning hours, the team reunited in the town of Shaydon after traveling through the night. The dozen special operators had been split apart into four three-man close air support teams, and now back together, they could swap war stories and intelligence with each other.

Khalili's intelligence indicated that the team's assault on the Taliban had been truly disruptive. Encouraged, the team returned to the Northern Alliance headquarters and prepared for the planned assault with Khalili's forces. Khalili would be in overall charge and Commander Aliar would lead the battle.

TIGER 07 broke into three elements to advise their Afghan compatriots and to provide fire support. Two teams would go with each of Commander Aliar's major formations, while one team would act as a bounding team so that there would never be a gap in Green Beret observation of the fight.

While preparing for the offense, TIGER 07 never took its eyes off the Taliban. They left a two-man team in the field and ordnance continued to steadily rain down on the Taliban positions throughout the eighth and ninth of November. On

November 10, all was ready for the main offensive, and the troops gathered for final combat checks at Shaydon.

Veterans Day

The *muj* treated TIGER 07 with generous hospitality. The willingness of Americans to go into battle alongside them buoyed their spirits. Many were overwhelmed with emotion. Of Asian descent, the Hazara were more like the Montagnards than any of the other Afghan tribes. They were much easier for the Green Berets to bond with, and far more loyal than many of the other groups. In fact they were so loyal that they frequently came close to shooting anyone, including other Americans, and even journalists, that got too close to the Green Berets.

TIGER 07's team sergeant was large, like most Green Berets. Six feet tall and rough-looking, his appearance belied the fact that he had a laid-back way of running things—working more toward harmony than confrontation. He fit well with Commander Khalili, who was over six feet tall and an imposing presence himself. Khalili wore large glasses and had an aristocratic look; he was extremely intelligent and had a kind heart and love for his people.

On November 11, TIGER 07 waited for transportation to get into the fight. The first element mounted up and soon was directing air strikes on the Taliban defenses. The other two elements were upset and getting more and more pissed off. Russian and Toyota vehicles for the rapid assault were materializing far too late in the day. The plan was coming apart. However, TIGER 07 kept their focus, understanding the environment. This was not going to be as precise an operation as the U.S. Army practices at the National Training Center near Death Valley, California.

Finally, the remainder of Commander Aliar's forces and the last two elements of TIGER 07 were able to mount up on their horses and move out. They had just deployed when the SF lead element informed the rest of TIGER 07 that Khalili's troops, under the cover of American close air support, had already advanced to the outskirts of Bamian.

The assault timetable was now meaningless. The team passed the word to their compatriots and everyone hauled ass toward Bamian in fear of missing the fight.

Apparently the air strikes had intimidated the Taliban into withdrawing. The lead Special Forces element reported that there was only sporadic resistance. It appeared that another small force was left to harass them, as well as to keep them from trapping the Taliban as they withdrew. The team sergeant cautioned against overconfidence: "Be prepared for a counterattack, and stay sharp."

TIGER 07 raced into the city as the *muj* cleared the area of the remaining pockets of resistance and a few snipers. The forces swept through, moving well beyond the town to set up observation posts along the main roads and avenues of approach just in case the Taliban returned during the night. Bamian was now in the hands of Khalili, the Northern Alliance, and TIGER 07.

Late that afternoon, one of TIGER 07's team members called on his radio for the A-Team commander to come to his location. "Boss, you've got to see this from up close" was the invitation.

The sun was going down as the team leader linked up with the sergeant. The sergeant, cradling his M-4 assault rifle in the crook of his left arm, was smoking a cigarette and leaning against his Toyota. Two Hazara warriors were with him. He pointed up from the valley floor.

"You know, it doesn't quite hit you when you see them through binoculars; you kinda gotta get up close to realize the loss to the Hazara, to the whole damn world," the sergeant remarked.

The men observed large piles of formless rubble and shattered rock where once stood the world's two largest Buddha statues, one of which had been over 175 feet tall. The Buddhas had been carved into the mountainside in the third and fifth centuries, standing silently for over 1,500 years. In March 2001, the

Taliban had used direct artillery fire, Russian Katucha rockets, and demolitions to obliterate the ancient statues.

"If only we could have been here a little sooner," the sergeant said.

"Politics, my boy; we had to wait until bin Laden killed five thousand Americans before the politicians thought it was worth it to save these people," replied his team leader.

The Hazara could see how upset they were and told them how the Taliban had destroyed the two towering Buddhas that overlooked the city of Bamian because they were idols of men. It had been a great Taliban celebration, with posters of the rocket attack printed in Iran as mementos.

It was as though the Taliban had tried to enhance their spiritual status by reconstructing legends, miracles, and heroes of the early Islamic period. The Hazara told the Americans that by destroying the Buddhas, the Taliban were trying to imitate the Prophet Mohammed, who had destroyed the statues in Mecca.

The statues had been a major tourist attraction, and the Hazara had built a livelihood out of guiding tours to the site. But the Taliban had not only destroyed the historical treasures; they had destroyed and mined the remains at the base of the mountain to discourage any attempts to repair them.

"I hate politicians."

"I hate everyone, 'cept maybe these little brown guys."

"Ditto, boss. Now let's go find bin Laden and cut his fucking balls off," the sergeant said as he turned and walked away, looking back one last time at where the Great Buddhas of Bamian once stood.

In April 2002, Afghan sculptor Amanulah Haiderzad organized an effort to rebuild the site into a tribute to the American destruction of the cruel and inhuman Taliban regime.

Bamian had now fallen. Commander Khalili, a large, fatherly figure, was now governor of Bamian Province. The largest combat horse cavalry in the world was now resting and would hopefully soon return to farming. Special Forces and Delta Force, who had also played a large role in the liberation of

Bamian, would stay on to continue tracking, capturing, and killing the remaining enemy hiding throughout the province. Two teams of SAS operators from the mobility troop would join them. Charging across the Bamian desert in their Land Rovers without regard for danger, they would try and lure the AQ out of hiding and into firefights. Everyone soon found out that Osama bin Laden had not been in the region for years, but Bamian had been heavily controlled by the Taliban and al-Qaida, and some of his AQ continued to lurk in the remote areas.

Bamian would not be without continued threats and problems, including the dire need for humanitarian assistance and food. Equally a problem would be the Iranians. As they would in Herat, the Iranians would bring in guns to divide the new factions, finance Khalili to draw him away from the U.S., and secretly infiltrate Republican Guard officers to promote Iranian ties and continued destabilization and distance from the future interim government.

Still, TIGER 07 would be forever remembered in the hearts of the Hazara.

CHAPTER 13

Northern Alliance—
General Daoud

*"When you decide to surrender, approach United States forces
with your hands in the air. Sling your weapon across your
back, muzzle towards the ground. Remove your magazine and
expel any rounds. Doing this is your only chance of survival."*
— U.S. message to Taliban fighters,
early November 2001

Endless Isolation

Khanabad, Afghanistan

A-Team 586, code-named TEXAS 11, was alerted on October 5, 2001, to enter isolation to prepare for operations in Afghanistan.

The team members bid farewell to their families and entered the isolation facility in Fort Campbell, Kentucky. Going into isolation was a good thing. In fact, it was fantastic. They might have been leaving their families, but they were about to engage in their chief occupation, and this time it wasn't just training. It wasn't as if someone were ordering them to go. These men were "triple volunteers." They were volunteers for the all-volunteer Army first, volunteers for Airborne School second, and volunteers for Special Forces third. In many cases they had advanced skills, which required them to volunteer again. And with 9/11 firmly etched in their minds, virtually everyone in Special Forces hadn't just volunteered to go to Afghanistan: some had lobbied for the mission, some had pleaded to go, some had used friendships and contacts from as far back as twenty years to try to get assigned to the mission, and, finally, some had even begged.

They didn't all get to go, but TEXAS 11 did. The men prepared equipment, had medical classes, trained on communications gear, and did generic planning while waiting for a hard target to emerge.

Early on October 14, the team left Fort Campbell to begin the journey to its intermediate staging base, TASK FORCE DAGGER's K2. Thirty-two hours later, they arrived at their destination in Uzbekistan.

In isolation again, the team was pumped full of all available intelligence, and began planning to go into Afghanistan to fill whatever requirement Colonel Mulholland had for them. They had no single mission. Instead, they planned in sequence for six different missions, for three different areas of operation, and for linkup with several different Northern Alliance leaders, including Dostum, Atta, Fahim, and others.

Captain Patrick O'Hara, the team leader; Chief Warrant Officer 2 Rob Hart, the XO; and Master Sergeant Frank Nash, team sergeant, were all fit to be tied, fearing they would miss the war. Nash was pacing the floors. He was a doorkicker from way back, and he was definitely ready to do some shooting. Finally, a mission emerged that would stick: TEXAS 11 was assigned to be the combat advisors for General Daoud in Farkhar, Afghanistan. Infiltration was set for November 8, 2001, ending TEXAS 11's record of thirty-two straight days in isolation. It would stand as the TASK FORCE DAGGER record.

Infiltration

TEXAS 11's landing zone was code-named LZ Muddy. ODA 594 would ride in with them and split off for another highly classified mission. TIGER 03, already on the ground, would make contact with them once they had arrived. Their new

TEXAS 11 and General Daoud

+ airfields
× start of infiltration
← captured city

TURKMENIS

IRAN

BADGHI
⊛ Qal'eh-y

✛⊛ Herat

HERAT

•Shindand

FARAH
⊛Farah

Lash
C

HELMA

⊛Zaranj
NIMRUZ

IRAN

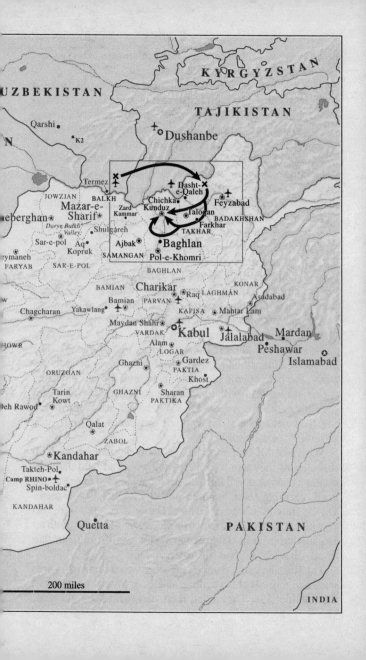

orders were to find means to move farther on to Farkhar and begin their work with General Daoud.

TEXAS 11's choices were limited: they could make a time-consuming move on horseback or risk taking a ride on an Afghan Northern Alliance helicopter, a rickety Russian MI-8 HIP left over from the Soviet invasion more than fifteen years earlier. They would be flying in from a secret Northern Alliance airfield in the south of neighboring Tajikistan.

Commander Amir John was the "general" in charge of Massoud's helicopters. Although they had almost a dozen choppers, only a few were barely safe. Amir John got a sat-phone call from Commander Abdul Wadood in Dushanbe to send Daoud's chopper for the team.

The MI-8 headed to LZ Muddy, where it would meet TIGER 03 and then take off for LZ Lovelace, near Farkhar. All the men knew they would be risking their lives. TF DAGGER command discussed the fact that there was virtually no maintenance program on the aircraft. But the real problem was even worse. There was always *daily* maintenance on the aircraft, because it literally took a crew engineer working full-time just to keep it from dropping out of the sky. The Northern Alliance had not received spare parts or tools for years, the helicopter's tires were bald, and the tail elevators were held together with baling wire and duct tape. The team jokingly called the rickety MI-8's SGLI Airlines, referring to the Servicemembers' Group Life Insurance program that covered American soldiers.

When the MI-8 first landed, the men shook their heads in disbelief as they removed the baling wire that held the helicopter's door shut. All thirteen personnel loaded onto the aircraft, carrying their hundred-pound rucksacks with them. On the front bulkhead of General Daoud's chopper were two significant items. The first was a picture of Massoud, with an English inscription. The second was a small American-flag decal—it said, "Afghan Air America, Jack."

The Russian camo paint on the sides was flaking off, wires were hanging out of the ceiling, and there were bullet holes in the outside skin. They piled their rucksacks, commo gear, and supplies into the center aisle of the aircraft and crammed into seats on the sides. Seeing the pilots for the first time elicited more than a few repressed snickers and laughs: they had no uniforms, no gear, and looked like a bunch of vagabonds. TEXAS 11 was about to find out that looks can be deceiving—the Northern Alliance pilots had more combat flight time than just about any pilots in the world. They might have been flying rattletraps, but they could fly into and out of just about anything, even without instruments. They did, however, avoid flying at night. With neither landing lights nor night-vision equipment, night operations were virtual suicide. The NA pilots looked nervously at the amount of equipment TEXAS 11 piled on the floor. Still, they flew. Weight became a significant concern when the MI-8 HIP kicked up dust and barely cleared some of the higher peaks of the breathtakingly beautiful Khvajeh Mohammad mountain range. TEXAS 11 peered out the hazy windows as the chopper rotors strained to make the mountains' crest. Everyone held their breath as they saw the rocks below them—the ground was close, dangerously close. With less than fifty feet between it and the crest of the mountain, the chopper cleared the crest and began its descent. After an hour of "Oh, shit" and "Oh, fuck," TEXAS 11 finally breathed a sigh of relief.

As they prepared to land, one of the sergeants joked as he checked his magazine and made sure a round was chambered that LZ Lovelace would hopefully not be as hot as Linda Lovelace, the star of *Deep Throat*.

With great relief, the men dismounted the aircraft at LZ Lovelace. Some of General Daoud's men were waiting and swiftly escorted TEXAS 11 to one of Daoud's guesthouses after ten minutes of Afghans hugging them. By the evening of November 10, Captain O'Hara and his A-Team were having dinner in Farkhar.

Daoud was a slim, soft-spoken man in his midthirties, and he could best be described as a quiet thinker. He had money, power, and intelligence. He was loyal to the Northern Alliance and to his dead commander, Massoud. General Daoud was an insider in the elite corps of the Northern Alliance commanders, who, like Baryoli, enjoyed the finer things in life, but he was also used to roughing it from his days as a *mujahadeen* in the great holy war against the Soviet invaders.

Attack on Taloqan

With the Veterans Day offensive under way, TEXAS 11 went straight into action. The team's first mission was to call in close air support for the attack on Taloqan. However, while the team was waiting for aircraft, General Daoud and his forces assaulted with such success that the team's close air support didn't arrive on station until after the battle.

The team called in its initial resupply bundles and packed up all personnel, equipment, and a dozen assigned Afghan security guards. MC-130 Combat Talons left from the U.S. air base in Incirlik, Turkey, and fourteen and a half hours later they arrived over the team in the dark of night. As the tailgate opened, the two-thousand-pound plywood containers parachuted out into the sky. They were filled with food, winter clothing, and ammunition. After weeks of empty promises by the Quartermaster Corps and the European command, the supply chain was finally starting to bring in enough gear to fight. Transportation for the A-Team was to be one small truck and an ancient, ratty Russian Army UAZ jeep.

TEXAS 11 was split into three CAS teams: Alpha, Bravo, and Charlie. On any given day, one CAS team would be on duty, the second would be resting from the previous day, and the third would be gearing up for the day to follow. Master Sergeant Tim Stamey, the Air Force CAS expert from the 720th Special Tactics Group, accompanied all three teams out on most of the days.

On the first day, Alpha team consisted of Captain O'Hara, Master Sergeant Frank Nash, CW2 Hart, and Sergeant First Class John Moore. Then, the CO, XO, and team sergeant split off to put one of them on each team.

Bravo team consisted of Sergeant First Class Don Thomas,

Sergeant First Class Leslie Lee, Staff Sergeant Sean Beebe, and Staff Sergeant Eric Russell.

Charlie team consisted of Sergeant First Class Tracy Broadbent, Sergeant First Class Pat Schorn, Staff Sergeant Marcus Branch, and Staff Sergeant Dan Grienke.

On the thirteenth of November, General Daoud was poised to continue the attack with the Taliban frontline just outside Taloqan. But after the earlier, easy victory, his troops had become overconfident. One of Daoud's subordinate commanders had attacked prematurely, triggering a heavy Taliban counterpunch from a nearby power plant. Pummeled by both direct heavy-weapons fire and indirect tank fire, Daoud's infantry reeled back, as the Taliban assault killed Daoud's junior commander and forty of his men.

The Afghan soldiers were in fear of the black-clad al-Qaida, and CW2 Hart observed, "It was like they thought the AQ were ninjas or something."

This time TEXAS 11 brought U.S. air power in on the Taliban and kept them from pursuing the Northern Alliance as they withdrew. At the end of the day, TEXAS 11 had destroyed three enemy command-and-control buildings and four enemy cargo trucks, and more than eighty-five Taliban terrorists were either killed in action or wounded. The rest had either surrendered or retreated to Kunduz.

Taloqan had fallen, not only to the Northern Alliance and TEXAS 11, but to total lawlessness. At one point a small group of al-Qaida prisoners had been taken and their toes tied, as was Afghan SOP. Tying their big toes together was cheaper then buying handcuffs, which the *muj* may have never heard of in the first place. When several of the terrorists tried to overpower their guards, the entire group was shot in the process. The NA then left them in the streets to rot, a warning to others who would resist or revolt.

The villagers were impossible to control—many of them were in a rage against the Taliban and the foreign al-Qaida who had been trapped when Taloqan fell. They frequently swarmed down on small groups of al-Qaida prisoners and beat them to death as the Northern Alliance soldiers offered token resistance. The Taliban and AQ's reign had been ruthless and devastating to the northern tribes of Afghanistan. There would be no pity for terrorists now.

Civilian casualties were also a problem, and TEXAS 11 had limited resources to help. Low on medical supplies and stretched for personnel, they did the best they could, frequently working on victims of Soviet mines, or yellow cluster bombs that had accidentally been detonated by the local populace. (The cluster bombs were almost the same color as the HDRs that had been dropped for food.)

Resetting the Defense

The Taliban's counterattack had sobered General Daoud, and he abandoned plans for a continued blitz toward Kunduz, deciding to hold tight on the frontlines and see if TEXAS 11 could use air strikes to soften up the enemy.

For the next ten days, starting on the fourteenth of November, Frank Nash and his boys called in smart bombs to pound Taliban and AQ positions in and around Khanabad and Kunduz. More MC-130 Combat Talons flew over. Matte black and with a fat, bulging "Jimmy Durante" nose cone, they navigated with their advanced terrain-following and terrain-avoidance systems into TEXAS 11's AO. Their fifteen-thousand-pound BLU-82 "daisy cutter" bombs decimated their targets. The Taliban forces facing General Daoud's frontline warriors were severely crippled by the damage TEXAS 11 inflicted.

TEXAS 11 found that the best place for them to fight was *in front* of friendly lines. Each day they would sneak forward and find the best-covered and -concealed position to apply their deadly skills. Each day the team would send back a daily log of their activities by satellite transmission to TF DAGGER headquarters at K2. While the reports were fairly extensive, these are just a few random samples:

14 November 2001
Significant Activities:
Taliban prepared to conduct another attack, CAS team received direct tank fire, moved to OP, called CAS to suppress tank, no attack occurred.
BDA (Bomb Damage Assessment):
3 × troop barracks, 1 × operations buildings, 90 KIA/WIA.

15 November 2001
Significant Activities:
Received small arms and heavy weapons fire, called emergency CAS to neutralize enemy fires, had to walk through mine fields to get to and from OP, received some inaccurate fire from Daoud's forces while returning from OP.

17 November 2001
Significant Activities:
Positioned 1–2 kilometers in front of Forward Line of Troops (FLOT)
BDA:
5 × tanks, 1 × BRDM, 1 × BTR-70, 4 × cargo trucks, 2 × troop barracks, several mortar/heavy weapons positions, 300 KIA/WIA.

20 November 2001
Significant Activities:
Positioned at FLOT, weather was socked in, but called CAS to demonstrate that weather was not a limiting factor.
BDA:
No confirmed BDA due to weather, but all ordinances were on target.

22 November 2001
Significant Activities:
Positioned ½ kilometer in front of FLOT, Daoud started his offensive toward Khanabad.

BDA:
9 × cargo trucks, 2 × buildings, 1 × bunker, many troops in the open, 335 KIA/WIA.

23 November 2001
Significant Activities:
General Daoud conducted major push west, positioned several kilometers in front of FLOT, enemy on all three sides, virgin targets, received sniper and machine-gun fire, called emergency CAS to suppress enemy fires.

In the end, TF DAGGER headquarters was able to summarize each team's destruction of the terrorist enemy. TEXAS 11 did not face the massive lines of Taliban as did other teams. They had to hunt their quarry with greater skill than the "shotgun mass destruction" that TIGER 02 and TIGER 03 were able to bring. Some teams dropped more bombs or were in the field longer, but according to the Air Force, TEXAS 11 destroyed as much equipment and as many enemy soldiers as any other team. TEXAS 11's efforts to bring death and destruction to America's enemies were reflected in the team's total log of damage inflicted and speaks for itself:

14–29 November 2001
BDA (Bomb Damage Assessment):
4 × ammo dumps, 12 × tanks, 5 × ZPU/ZSUs, 3 × BMP/BM-21s, 51 × trucks, 6 × HQ buildings, 44 × bunkers, 3 × BTR-70/BRDMs, 5 × troop barracks, 7 × mortars/heavy weapons, 2139 × enemy KIA/WIA.

Renewed Attacks

By November 22, more than five thousand Taliban and foreign al-Qaida terrorists buckled down in Kunduz for their defense of the north. It was their last stronghold in northern Afghanistan. TEXAS 11 was elated. Five thousand targets all in one place. Dostum was already approaching the city from the west, and the race was on to take Kunduz first. Daoud had to move fast.

"We will face many of the enemy in Kunduz," Daoud told TEXAS 11.

"We call that a target-rich environment where we come from," said the team's weapons sergeant, grinning.

Daoud smiled back. "Good, then let's begin."

On November 23, General Daoud assaulted to the west and captured Khanabad. The attack was made possible by the significant damage TEXAS 11 brought down on the Taliban. Daoud's troops had moved forward over fifty-four miles since the arrival of the A-Team, progress that amazed everyone, especially the conventional generals like Franks.

Six hundred terrorists surrendered as Captain O'Hara's team pushed toward Kunduz. A B-52 overhead continued to pummel the hills between Khanabad and Kunduz. Northern Alliance Minister of the Interior Yunis Quanuni called Daoud to congratulate him. They were now less than twelve miles from Kunduz. By the night of November 23, the city was completely encircled by the Northern Alliance.

As General Daoud's men and TEXAS 11 prepared to assault Kunduz, negotiations began for the city's surrender. Master Sergeant Frank Nash tried to convince Daoud that the Taliban were trying to buy time to build their defenses. The team had considerable air assets available, but the JFACC could provide only for a short window of opportunity, and the team wanted to attack immediately. The Northern Alliance continued to negotiate. Daoud wanted the thousands of Afghan Taliban to be given a chance to surrender, but the al-Qaida commanders, mostly Pakistani, Arabs, and Chechens, were in control and threatening to shoot those who did not resist the American infidels. Deals were changed constantly, cancelled, and renegotiated, so frustration among the men abounded.

More than five thousand Afghan Taliban were willing to lay down their arms, but their surrender was hampered by the two-thousand-plus foreign AQ terrorists who preferred martyrdom to giving up.

As the Afghan Taliban became more inclined to give up, the foreign al-Qaida troops were unrelenting, killing numerous Afghan Taliban who talked of surrender. Meanwhile, as negotiations for surrender stalled, Green Berets with Generals Dostum, Atta, and Daoud were ringing the city and preparing for a final bloodbath. Without surrender, most of the enemy would be killed. The foreign terrorists who survived would most surely suffer the fate of previous invaders captured by their Afghan opponents: they would be summarily executed and thrown into trenches to rot.

By midnight on November 23, the parties supposedly had a surrender deal, but there continued to be delays. In the meantime, two planes landed at the airfield in the enemy-controlled city under cover of darkness. The purpose of the planes, their mission, and their sponsor all remain unknown. What is known is that General Daoud would later state that the planes were flown in by the Pakistani ISI intelligence service for the purpose of removing top Pakistani intelligence aides to the Taliban and top al-Qaida officials who were caught in the siege with nowhere to run. Daoud and several other high-ranking NA generals charged that the U.S. had knowingly allowed this to happen.

"How else could these planes have penetrated the American air shield?" Daoud asked his American advisors. Secretly, the Green Berets discussed with General Daoud the possibility that there was some Pakistani/U.S. State Department deal to allow the escapes in return for Pakistani assistance against Taliban forces in southeastern Afghanistan and continued permission to use Pakistani air space. Still, more than fifteen hundred Pakistani al-Qaida terrorists remained behind, but once the top Pakistani ISI agents and officials were gone, the surrender negotiations seemed to be more in earnest.

In fact, if top AQ and ISI leaders had escaped, it meant that incredibly valuable intelligence had been lost. It was intelligence that could have helped find bin Laden, for surely, although bin Laden himself was not there, someone there would have known where he was. TEXAS 11 had captured

AQ and Taliban radios and sat phones; the CIA, TF 11, and TF DAGGER had developed a plan to contact bin Laden through one of the captured sat phones. They would have a prisoner pretend to be hiding from U.S. forces and ask for instructions. NSA would be able to track the sat phone signals and use reverse GPS locators to pinpoint bin Laden's location. The first problem they had was finding a high-ranking prisoner who would cooperate. It quickly became evident that most of the top guys had fled and that those who were left would rather die than cooperate. The second problem surfaced over the next few days. When the NSA and NRO finally did lock onto sat phones being used by bin Laden, they realized the plan would not work. Bin Laden spoke over a sat phone frequently, but pinpointing the satellite receiver would not pinpoint bin Laden. He had devised an ingenious failsafe to avoid having two dozen D-boys swoop down on his head and bring it back to Rumsfeld in a burlap bag: bin Laden would speak over a low-frequency VHF radio that would be transmitted to the satellite phone, which was in another location. In other words, NSA could pinpoint the satellite phone, but not the weak signal of the VHF radio relay and its remote transmitter over which bin Laden would be talking. U.S. intelligence might be able to capture and kill the relay operators, but bin Laden could be miles away in a cave with just a wire sticking out.

The Fall of Kunduz

After four days of continued sporadic fighting interlaced with negotiations, several hundred Afghan Taliban had laid down their arms and were taken into custody by the Northern Alliance. But thousands were still holding out.

Finally Daoud announced his decision. "We are ready to enter the city; those that resist will be killed."

TEXAS 11 prayed the al-Qaida terrorists would not give up. Sergeant First Class John Moore, the team's assistant ops sergeant, was thrilled. They had finally convinced Daoud to

let them assault Kunduz and wipe out the al-Qaida. Diplomats from around the world were complaining and pleading
with the Northern Alliance not to turn Kunduz into a slaugh-
terhouse. But Daoud's people had suffered for years—if the
foreign terrorists did not unconditionally surrender, he would
destroy them to the last man. Meanwhile, Dostum was on the
northwest side of Kunduz, and was conducting his own negotiations for surrender.

Dostum was negotiating back and forth, trying to get the
Taliban to give up. The Taliban radioed back that they would
march right into the camp and surrender, but they wanted to
keep their weapons.

"Put your guns down, take your jackets off, and march in
here or we'll turn the Americans on to you with their Death
Ray," Dostum finally demanded.

Instantly, you could see the Taliban bending over, putting
their weapons on the ground, and taking off their shawls.
Then they marched single file right into the middle of the
perimeter. They knew it was all over if the Americans pulled
out the Death Ray.

There was still another group of Taliban on the other side
facing Daoud. As an AC-130 Spectre gunship flew overhead,
Dostum heard Ally talking to TEXAS 11. He brought over
Mohammed Fazal, the Taliban chief of staff. Fazal was desperately trying to delay the surrender while his forces attempted to recapture Mazar-e-Sharif. Dostum held up the
radio for Fazal and let him listen in to Ally's voice for a short
time. He then explained to the Taliban leader that not only did
he possess the Death Ray, he now had the Angel of Death
overhead.

"If you do not surrender immediately, the Americans will
ensure the Taliban will all burn in Hell," Dostum growled.

Shaking with fear, Fazal immediately jumped on the radio
and his forces were giving up within minutes.

As the first Americans into Kunduz, TEXAS 11 moved
quickly to the airport and surveyed the facility, reporting the
situation to TASK FORCE DAGGER.

Like some of the other teams, TEXAS 11 had to deal with

vast amounts of prisoners. The next weeks would be hectic and dangerous. Taliban and al-Qaida remnants would be hiding throughout the area, and the team would work to ferret out and clean up the remaining enemy. Nightly raids on enemy safehouses would also continue.

Meanwhile, the NA needed a way to transport the prisoners west to Sheberghan prison near Dasht-e-Leili. They commandeered everything from Russian KAMAZ military trucks to flatbeds and commercial container trucks. The sheer logistics of transporting this many prisoners was a nightmare. Several hundreds would die during transport in container trucks. Nine months later, on August 26, 2002, *Newsweek* would print a story questioning whether or not the U.S. forces had the responsibility for the deaths, and whether or not they were present. The facts contradicted *Newsweek*'s story. First, although several hundred prisoners had died en route to Sheberghan prison, many were wounded, malnourished, diseased, and in poor condition before transport. The conditions had been hard, as was often the case in the long history of Afghan war. The prisoners inside the container trucks were brutal terrorists who had murdered civilians on a daily basis, cut the hands off children, and raped and dismembered women. They were not to be treated like traffic offenders in the suburbs of Iowa. Second, the Northern Alliance did not have enough food and medical supplies for their own people, much less for the enemy. Third, with less than a handful of Special Forces medics on the ground, it would have been impossible to treat thousands upon thousands of prisoners. Fourth, and most important, the few dozen Green Berets in northern Afghanistan were still faced with a considerable number of enemy combatants who had escaped, were hiding, or were still fighting in other areas. TIGER 02 and TEXAS 11 were already moving against other enemy forces that were still fighting viciously as the prisoners were being prepared for transport.

The world jumped on the *Newsweek* container death story as a new revelation. But the media had already published the story in early December 2001, with articles in the *Dallas Morning News, The Guardian,* the *Hindustan Times,* and other newspapers. General Jurabek had even held a formal press conference in early December 2001, in Sheberghan, at which he stated that prisoners had died during transport, and it was clear to the press that no Special Forces personnel had been present—dozens of reporters had followed the prisoner convoys, taking pictures along the way, and not one American soldier had been with them. The Green Berets were too busy continuing to fight America's enemies.

On November 27 a Swedish journalist would be killed during a robbery, reportedly by Northern Alliance soldiers, but intelligence sources would later show that the killing was the work of the AQ, an attempt to gain cash and satellite phones to make their escape to Pakistan. Ulf Stroemberg was sharing a house with several other Swedish journalists. (Kunduz had thirty times more journalists occupying the city than TF DAGGER had Green Berets.) The AQ were everywhere, many of them hiding in houses where they held the occupants at gunpoint. Late that night, several men climbed over the wall of Stroemberg's guesthouse. They knocked on the door and demanded it be opened. When the response from inside came, they opened fire—Stroemberg was hit and died seconds later. The attackers stole exactly what they needed to escape—computers, money, and satellite phones—before fleeing.

Stroemberg was the eighth journalist killed in less than a month. Within hours of the murder, journalists were fleeing Kunduz back to the safety of the Tajikistan Hotel in Dushanbe and TEXAS 11 was hunting the killers. Over the next few weeks TEXAS 11 and Daoud's *mujahadeen* would ferret out hundreds of al-Qaida terrorists hiding in Kunduz and the surrounding areas.

Kunduz was a disaster area; the Taliban and AQ had destroyed the city with their failed defense. They had taken the local populace's food, money, and livestock to feed their troops; starvation and disease were rampant.

In Vietnam, Special Forces had learned the value of humanitarian aid efforts and care for the indigenous populations they so relied on in their shadow wars. It was the same type of operation Special Forces conducted in the poverty-stricken areas of America during peacetime. Officially, this program had been called SPARTAN, Special Proficiency at Rugged Training and Nation-Building, and it was a lost concept for more than a quarter century. But Special Forces still understood the value of winning hearts and minds, and in Afghanistan SPARTAN was back.

The SF teams not only trained and advised their counterparts, they were helping put the country back on track. By building and staffing hospitals and repairing schools and infrastructure like generators and water systems, they were giving the *muj* the ability to concentrate on the fight and see day-to-day benefits of an American alliance. Bringing food in and distributing aid only served to further separate the American Green Beret freedom fighters from the former Soviet oppressors and conquerors. When the fight was on, collateral programs were hard to devote much time to, but when the fight slowed, TIGER 11 shifted quickly and efficiently into caring for the Afghan people.

Left Behind

The Special Forces men on the ground needed equipment and supplies, and needed them badly. The war was moving so quickly that it was stretching the Special Forces' supply lines to the breaking point. Lieutenant Colonel Frank Hudson stayed behind to run the 5th Special Forces Group rear detachment, which pushed the Green Berets out by air, procured and shipped their equipment and supplies, and recovered and reconstituted battle-scarred A-Teams as they returned from operations in Afghanistan.

Hudson never complained. He was the 5th Group "fireman," putting out potential brushfires before they adversely affected the teams on the ground. He also worked with the team members' wives to try to solve their problems. Hudson slaved away seven days a week, never taking a break, on call twenty-four hours a day. No problem was too trivial for him to make it a priority. Everyone in the Special Forces community, including the families, knew that Frank Hudson would take care of them.

His deputy was not so helpful. Chief Warrant Officer Rob Way had a reputation among the wives for dismissing their concerns too easily. Apparently Way had told several wives that he was too busy to confirm or deny whether or not their husbands had been killed when CNN reported three casualties in their husbands' team's area of operation. Way told them they could wait for a telegram and allegedly refused to handle their problems at a unit level, instead referring them to the Pentagon. This was definitely not the way the tightly knit Special Forces community usually worked. More than one spouse expressed the opinion that Chief Warrant Officer Way "treated the wives like shit." A short, heavyset fellow, several wives stated he didn't deploy because he wanted to stay in school. In their view, he gladly stayed behind and continued to annoy the wives. The teams were happy about that—nobody wanted him anyway.

But Hudson was a warrior, and Frank Hudson's heart was broken, like the hearts of all the other Green Berets who didn't make it on the "first wave in," yet he never let it show. A Desert Storm veteran, he knew it would probably be his last chance to go into combat before he retired from the Army.

As the first teams were hitting the ground, a Special Forces general spoke to a small group of wives: "Frank is the ultimate Special Forces soldier. He has sublimated his personal desires for the good of the men doing the fighting. He has placed duty first; he is selfless and loves his fellow soldiers and his families. In this war, *he* is *my* personal hero."

As the next weeks passed, there would be no shortage of heroes in America's War on Terrorism.

CHAPTER 14

Northern Alliance— Ismail Khan

"We're not running out of [fixed] targets. Afghanistan is."
—DONALD RUMSFELD,
Department of Defense briefing,
October 9, 2001

Western Afghanistan

Herat, Afghanistan

Special Forces A-Team 554 was code-named TIGER 08, and inserted into an area Northeast of Herat on the night of November 11th, 2001, to link up with their Northern Alliance allies. A twelve-man A-Team, with one Combat Controller on board for calling in close air support, TIGER 08 was to be the only team to operate in the politically charged province in western Afghanistan.

Herat is economically critical to Afghanistan. Strategically located near the Iranian border, it is the key city for Iranian imports and land routes to the capital. While Kabul is the seat of government, and Kandahar is the Afghan "Vatican," Herat is the center of Afghan capitalism.

Herat's geographical situation places it in a position to control the major lines of communication and commerce to all of northern Afghanistan. The economy of Herat is completely dominated by Iran. Candies, foodstuffs, clothing, carpets, building materials, and medicines are all Iranian exports. The close proximity of the open Iranian border also allows for

TIGER 08 and Ismail Khan

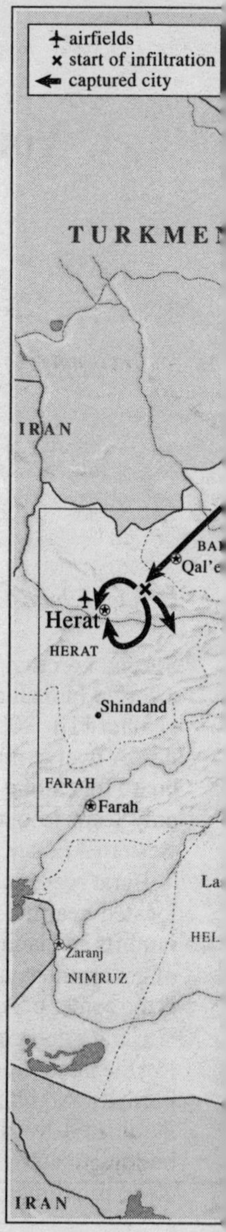

- ✈ airfields
- ✗ start of infiltration
- ← captured city

TURKMEN

IRAN

BA

Qal'e

Herat

HERAT

Shindand

FARAH

Farah

La

HEL

Zaranj

NIMRUZ

IRAN

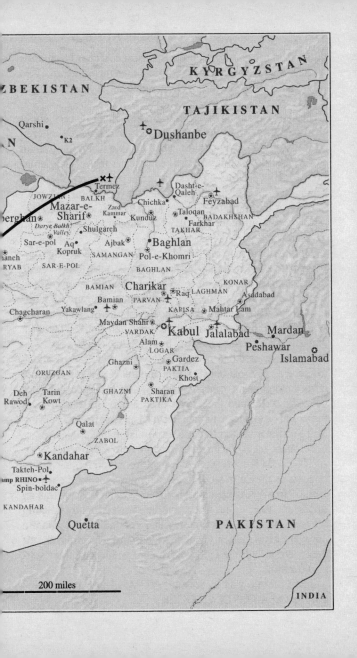

significant mischief by Iranian-sponsored Afghani elements. TIGER 08 was aware of the political intrigue in the area and anticipated problems from the tangled alliances that might come into play.

In fact, Ismail Khan had more opponents to worry about than just the Taliban and al-Qaida. Rivals who were sheltered in Iran could be expected to cause trouble when the Iranian government sensed it was time to unleash them. Their chief concern was Gulbuddin Hekmatyar, a psychotic killer who maintained an office in Tehran under the protection and sponsorship of the Iranians. Closely aligned with al-Qaida, Hekmatyar was intimately involved in supporting terrorism in Afghanistan.

During initial meetings with the CIA, Commander Khan appeared to have a healthy distrust of U.S. intentions; yet he clearly understood that the team he was about to receive would be his lifeline to weapons, ammunition, recognition, and funding. All of which meant the ultimate capture of the prize, the city of Herat. It was also reported that Khan disliked the West and was considered by many to be an Islamic fundamentalist.

It was expected that Ismail Khan would try to keep as much distance as possible between him and the U.S. team. But, like other commanders, when he finally met his Special Forces team, he welcomed them with open arms. He wanted them there, and he took care of them well. Khan was, in fact, a devout Sufi Muslim and therefore more spiritual in his religious practices, but he was not a threat to freedom or to the Americans.

TIGER 08 quickly gained respect from their Afghan counterparts as they moved through the mountains on the way to Herat. Ismail Khan quickly realized that TIGER 08 was an important asset to his force, and he showed this by keeping the team near him. Like many other commanders, Khan did not want his American friends killed, and was afraid that if they were killed, the U.S. government would pull their support for him.

Team morale was increasing. A CIA advisor sent a message to TASK FORCE DAGGER:

I need tags. Where are the hip-pocket UAVs we've heard about for five years? Gotta have GPS-identifying lasers and pointers in greater numbers. Last load crashed in when airdropped. I know we have no airfields, keep the stuff coming, and just pack it better. We've got to get this down to an art form before winter closes. Can't believe I am doing this. Surrounded by the enemy, cut off from any resupply except aircraft flying through enemy fire. I'm livin' large. Wish Granddad was alive. Buttons would pop off his pinks. Thanks for the Dari dictionary. Pointee-talkee is getting better everyday. Gotta run.

TIGER 08 was fortunate that the battles in and around Mazar-e-Sharif had gone well. The willingness of the Taliban to fight was weakening as they approached Herat from the northeast. Taliban commanders were actually starting to change sides. A Taliban commander became the lead driver for TIGER 08's convoy, and the team started picking up other former Taliban commanders who now wanted to fight with Khan. The entire scenario was incredibly strange to the team, and especially to Don, the team's intel sergeant. Watching the enemy join forces with Khan and be welcomed into the fight was literally freaking them out. When word of the capture of Kabul became common knowledge, Taliban resistance completely collapsed. After a few small skirmishes, the team simply ran out of targets. TIGER 08, led by "Carl," "Jimmy," and "Mike," the team leader, XO, and team sergeant, respectively, entered the city of herat on November 15, 2001. It was easier than expected.

The Iranians

Once in Herat, the A-Team was about to have other concerns. There were unidentified aircraft landing at the Herat airport. It took about two seconds for the team to identify the planes as Iranian. Some of Ismail Khan's men were extremely nervous and did their best to keep TIGER 08 from observing happenings at the airfield.

CIA operators reported secretive meetings, partial truths, and limits on where Americans could move. But TIGER 08 was allowed to move anywhere, with only the simple caveat that they brought one or two of Khan's men with them. That made sense, because having one of Khan's men ensured there were no "problems" with the locals. TIGER 08's commander examined how they could be of value, now that they were no longer needed to fight alongside their *muj* counterparts. The A-Team decided to get to work on post-combat tasks to prove their worth.

TIGER 08, now self-converting from Special Forces warriors to ambassadors without portfolios, were the only American presence in Herat. The team summarized their activities as follows in a report:

> We work closely with the *muj*, advising them on military, security, and humanitarian assistance matters. We directly negotiate with local commanders for the placement of multinational humanitarian assistance teams to be stationed at Herat airfield. We are instrumental in assessing the population and the situation both inside the city of Herat and in the surrounding towns to the south and east. Without our presence and perseverance, Ismail Khan and his followers would not be as supportive of the interim government as they currently are.

Their work paid off. TIGER 08 was allowed to stay in the area and continue to improve relations. It put them in a position to see the Iranian threat to stability in Afghanistan firsthand. The war in Herat was barely over when Iran sent in five hundred Iranian-made Heckler & Koch MP-5 submachine guns for the Herat police. By mid-January of 2002, Iranian military officers were working in Nimruz, Farah, and Helmand provinces trying to lure away local warlords from backing the new central government, now led by Hamid Karzai in Kabul. TIGER 08 reported that Iranian generals were in the region offering cash and arms for those who would withdraw support for the new government.

TASK FORCE DAGGER was surprised when Iran began funneling money and weapons deep into Afghanistan. General Dostum, who now dominated Mazar-e-Sharif in a power-sharing agreement with Atta, was reported to have been provided with cars, trucks, firearms, ammunition, and cash for his soldiers. The credibility of the reports was reinforced by comments from two senior intelligence officials in Afghanistan's newly formed central government. Khalili, now the governor of Bamian, also began receiving support from the Iranians, including cases and cases of brand-new Iranian AKS-74 assault rifles.

The new government in Kabul as well as the U.S. military began to weigh in on the situation. Hamid Karzai publicly warned in January 2002 that Iran should not meddle in the internal affairs of the country. Another government spokesman, Mohammed Yusef Pushtoon, charged that "Iran had broken some basic international norms by sending high-ranking military officers into the country without our permission and without informing the central government. Cooperation between the Herat administration and Iran is beyond all logical involvement."

Iran, of course, denied any involvement in western or northern Afghanistan. President George W. Bush nonetheless put Iran on notice during his State of the Union address in January 2002 with the depiction of a new "axis of evil," namely Iran, Iraq, and North Korea.

Bush followed with his budget proposal, asking for greater funding of the military for the long-term struggle against terrorism. Secretary of State Colin Powell supported Karzai on February 6, and accused Iran of trying to destabilize the fragile post-Taliban government. Other American officials piled on criticisms of Iran for giving refuge to antigovernment figures and their supporters in Afghanistan.

On Monday, February 11, 2002, the Iranians deported the psychotic Gulbuddin Hekmatyar to Pakistan and supposedly closed his offices in Tehran and Mashhad. The deportation may not have affected matters much. In fact, it may have been carefully planned with Hekmatyar to cover his movements and conceal his motives in Pakistan and eastern Afghanistan.

In January an American advisor started uncovering threats by
Hizb-e-Islami, Hekmatyar's former political party, to the new
interim government. In early April 2002, Engineer Ali's intelligence service conducted a massive sweep, arresting more
than two hundred suspected members of the Hizb-e-Islami,
Gulbuddin Hekmatyar's former political party, now under operational control of former Finance Minister Wahidullah Sah-
bauan. The Afghan government announced that the movement
had been forming networks to engage in terror, sabotage, and
assassination against the current leaders of the government.

Iranian President Mohammad Khatami was reported to
have said, "We should all be worried that the President of the
United States has put forward the [largest] military budget [in
the world]. We should be thinking about a coalition for peace,
not war."

Iran, however, apparently wasn't intimidated enough to
cease its attempts to destabilize Afghanistan. On March 13,
2002, it was revealed that Special Forces teams in Kandahar
had captured eleven men suspected of being Afghan infiltra-
tors that had emigrated to Iran years earlier.

Their partner, supposedly a general from Iran's Revolutionary Guards who claimed to be an Afghan, had been
turned in by some of his compatriots. Apparently his "compatriots" were actually spies for the Afghan Foreign Intelligence Chief, Engineer Ali.

Iran continued to offer enticements to Commander Ismail
Khan. One was a plan to fund for the Afghan government a
$560-million aid package to include paving the road system
from Herat to Iran and opening another border crossing in the
south. At work was simple Iranian strategic common sense;
Iran was going to do all it could to prevent any permanent
American bases or military presence in an adjoining country
such as Afghanistan.

As governor of the entire Herat province, with a population
of over 120,000, Iran's influence became evident in Ismail
Khan's administration. While the other governors struggle, he
has over 50,000 men under arms, and a large police force.
Khan remained firmly opposed to the creation of a national

army because it would erode his power. Although Ismail Khan reopened the religious police, the Office to Promote Virtue and Prevent Vice, it was a supposedly kinder and gentler version, without a jail and beatings. Khan did explain to TIGER 08 that he wanted to give his people freedom, but it had to be done in moderation and over time, he couldn't just open the floodgates to those that had been oppressed for so long.

TIGER 08's greatest contribution, after lengthy isolation, a tough infiltration, and a struggle to be accepted by its Afghan partners, may have been the simple reporting of the true situation and their observations to TASK FORCE DAGGER, who relayed the information daily to the CINC.

TIGER 08's replacement A-Team, from the 19th Special Forces Group, continued the Special Forces' work in Herat. In the spring of 2002 the team was meeting with Ismail Khan once or twice a week, and continued to coordinate humanitarian aid. Occasionally invited to go riding with the governor, they proved the value of sustaining open communication with a critical player in the reshaping of Afghanistan, and with a leader that the United States still needed to court.

After TIGER 08 was exfiltrated, the United States argued to keep Taliban and al-Qaida prisoners under lock and key until they could be sorted out. Unfortunately, someone was already releasing the most important prisoners and ferrying them out of Afghanistan and into Iran. There was strong evidence that Tehran was paying for the release of America's enemies, and giving them sanctuary inside Iran. The CIA soon learned that Iranian intelligence intended to fund their excursions back into Afghanistan to fight the western soldiers that would remain to rebuild Afghanistan.

One person not getting sanctuary in Iran was Osama bin Laden. The intel was pretty clear that bin Laden's run had been to the east, not the west. The AQ did not have a great deal of support in the Herat region and bin Laden would have been taking a greater risk seeking refuge there. Like TIGER 08, their replacement team spent their time in more of a classic Special Forces role, rather than a counter-terrorist role.

CHAPTER 15

The Qala-i-Jangi
Uprising

"America must know that the storm of airplanes will not stop, and there are thousands of young people who look forward to death like the Americans look forward to life."
—al-Qaida "spokesman" SULAIMAN ABU GHAITH
on al-Jazeera television, October 10, 2001

Mud Walls and Bullets

Qala-i-Jangi, Afghanistan

After the fall of Mazar, the thousands of prisoners from Kunduz and Taloqan were now being moved just outside the city. Just thirty days after the Green Berets hit the ground, the war in the north was effectively over.

On November 25, 2001, CIA operative John Micheal Spann (Mike) and his partner, David Tyson (Dave), were filtering through hundreds of captured prisoners at the Qala-i-Jangi "Fortress of War," or "House of War," which was the literal translation.

The two CIA officers were inside the fortress questioning prisoners and attempting to segregate those who were considered strategically important. They were both from the CIA's covert operations side, a paramilitary branch of the Agency. They hoped the prisoners at Qala-i-Jangi would be a gold mine for intelligence exploitation. One thing was for sure—the Pakistani, Iraqi, Iranian, Saudi, Chechen, Somali, and other foreign soldiers were clearly AQ. It was easy for the

Afghans to tell the difference between the foreign al-Qaida and the Afghan Taliban, and the Northern Alliance had done an excellent job of screening out anyone suspected of being AQ from the rest.

The fortress could have been a huge castle and its defenses transplanted from central Europe. It was over three football fields across, surrounded by mud-brick walls up to ten meters thick, and the design included moats, ramparts, and walls almost twenty feet high with parapets across the top. One half of the fortress had been turned into a prison. The other half was used by the Northern Alliance to store materiel, weapons, and to house their headquarters and personnel.

The prisoners, who had supposedly been searched and bound, were standing or kneeling on the small parade ground inside the fortress' walls. Mike and Dave took digital pictures of each of the prisoners while they interviewed them in an effort to assess their importance. Most refused to cooperate.

As Mike and Dave interviewed the captured al-Qaida terrorists, it seemed obvious to everyone that the two men were CIA operatives. They wore blue jeans and carried Russian AK-47s. Mike was young, fair-skinned, and clean-shaven. Dave was older, not in the greatest shape, with a graying beard covering his pockmarked face, and an Afghan smock hiding his potbelly.

"The problem is, he needs to decide if he wants to live or die, and die here," Dave said as he interviewed a suspected terrorist. "I mean if he don't wanna die here . . . he's gonna die here. 'Cause this is where we're just gonna leave him. . . . He's gonna sit in prison the rest of his fucking short life, it's his decision." Mike knelt in front of the suspected terrorist as Dave talked.

"We can only help those guys that want to talk to us. We can only get the Red Cross to help so many guys," Dave said.

"You know, you know the people that you're working with are terrorists?" Mike asked the prisoner. "They killed other Muslims. There were several hundred other Muslims killed in the bombing in New York City," Mike said as he tried to convince the prisoner to cooperate. "Are you going to talk to us?"

"This guy got his chance," Dave complained loudly. "He got his chance."

The al-Qaida terrorist who was being interviewed would later be identified as an American, John Walker Lindh.

Accounts are conflicting as to exactly what happened after that and in what order. One thing is certain—Mike and Dave were acting fairly officious and open, and the AQ chose them as their target.

Revolt and Rebellion

Because of an unwritten Afghan custom that when a warrior surrendered, he simply stated he was through, and then negotiations followed, the prison rebellion took the Northern Alliance guards by complete surprise. The Afghans gave their POWs a level of trust and a degree of latitude completely foreign to Western culture.

What the Northern Alliance failed to fully take into account was that most of the POWs inside the "Fortress of War" were the AQ, and the AQ had a separate set of homicidal, even suicidal, ethics and values.

The revolt supposedly started when a detainee hurled a rock at a guard, knocking him down, allowing a compatriot to seize a rifle. But the AQ prisoners also had hidden grenades, which had been missed during the search process. Explosions went off, and within minutes the prisoners had overpowered and killed a half dozen of Dostum's guards as gunfire spread throughout the fortress.

The enemy fighters, who were supposed to be prisoners of war, were now enemy fighters again, using the weapons they had concealed during their capture to rejoin the fight.

The prisoners made their way to a weapons cache and began to arm themselves with rifles and mortars. The likelihood of a complete breakout was feared, and quite possibly imminent, and the prison guards were forced to pull back to the large mud walls surrounding the fortress. It was as if the interior of a medieval castle had been taken over by rebels while loyalist forces still held the castle walls and the surrounding fields. It had now turned into a classic castle siege, except the walls held the enemy combatants in, not out.

Some reported that Mike was beaten and shot, but according to Dostum's ethnic Uzbek soldiers, a Taliban prisoner who was either wired with explosives or clutching a hand grenade ran over to the CIA operative and embraced him, killing both in a compressed explosion. Other witnesses claimed that Mike fought bravely with his AK-47, pinned by bodies to the ground, peppering the rushing mob with his pistol until he ran out of ammunition, going down fighting with his bare hands.

Leave NO Man Behind

The CIA lauded the bravery of their other operative, Dave, stating that he killed "many" terrorists while trying to defend Mike Spann. According to official accounts, Dave continued to fire shots from his pistol while fleeing from the al-Qaida. Eventually he ran out of ammunition and was forced to break contact with hand-to-hand combat, before running to another part of the prison for shelter. From his temporarily safe location, Dave used his radio to call in a situation report to his headquarters. He did not know what had happened to his partner.

The facts appear somewhat different. Dave had run, and run quickly. He was captured on video as he sprinted toward a building, holding his pistol by the barrel instead of the grip. If an al-Qaida terrorist had jumped out at him, there would have been no way he could have even returned fire. Seeking cover inside a building where journalists were hiding, Dave gasped for breath, and he seemed confused. He repeatedly fumbled while trying to put his 9mm pistol back in his belt, even forgetting to put the safety on although the hammer was back. He had probably gotten a couple of rounds off. He used a CNN journalist's satellite phone to call the embassy in Tashkent where his SITREP (situation report) was unclear. Dave wasn't sure what had happened—he certainly didn't know what had happened to his partner.

Over one-half of the prison was already in AQ hands, and things were spiraling out of control. John Walker Lindh escaped in the confusion with his cohorts.

"We have SPECAT down! Repeat, two SPECAT personnel are down!" came the Green Beret's voice over the radio. SF knew what that meant, and they were moving into action at lightning speed. They may not have always gotten along with the CIA, but damned if any of them were going to be left behind on *their* watch.

By the afternoon of November 25, Lieutenant Colonel Max Bowers' BOXER element had received information that Dostum's fortress had been taken over by the AQ. His command post had to consider the real possibility that six hundred AQ and Taliban occupants might succeed in breaking out. The initial report also relayed the news that two U.S. CIA officers were trapped and required immediate assistance.

The initial intelligence from Dostum's soldiers turned out to be true and indicated that the incident began with prisoners igniting an explosive device, overpowering the guards, and then successfully seizing control of a cache of small arms and mortars.

BOXER immediately responded by organizing a team of U.S. and British Special Forces and D-boys. They were backed up by a platoon from the U.S. Army's 10th Mountain Division, along with all available interpreters and intelligence officers. Their mission was going to be tough. If Mike and Dave were trapped inside, and still alive, the rescue team would have to infiltrate the prison held by the suicidal AQ to find them, rescue them, and then fight their way out.

Major Mark Mitchell

Major Mark Mitchell, the ground force commander from BOXER, would take overall command of the combined force. Upon arrival at the fortress, Mitchell quickly deployed his team around the edges of the facility's walls, taking small-arms fire as they assessed the situation.

From Northern Alliance commanders at the fort, Mitchell determined there was a strong possibility that although one of the CIA officers had been killed, another was possibly alive, and still trapped inside. Unknown to him at the time, Dave had escaped and found his way to another makeshift headquarters inside a nearby school. Mike was assuredly lost, but through some miracle might still be alive. They needed to be found, and found quickly.

A short time later Dave showed up outside the prison walls after sliding down the dirt embankment near the building he and the journalists had been hiding in. Once Major Mitchell had Dave back, they sent a message to the al-Qaida terrorists that they wanted Mike back and would negotiate for his release. The AQ quickly refused. Throughout the night, Mitchell used a USAF AC-130 Spectre gunship to pound the al-Qaida revolters inside the prison walls. An ammunition warehouse was hit, and the explosion shook the area as ordnance flew through the air. Journalists on the scene remarked that it was like a "giant fireworks display." The fire burned through the night.

On the morning of November 26, 2001, Mitchell's teams began to ring the tops of the prison walls, dodging small-arms fire as they positioned themselves in the parapets. Mitchell established a casualty collection point that he would almost assuredly need. He also established an observation point that looked down into the fortress' huge open yards and buildings so they could effectively call in fire support and precision-guided weapons.

As Mitchell and his U.S./U.K. team tried to determine the best way to assault down off the walls and into the center of the prison, the volume of enemy fire increased immensely.

Dozens of AQ RPG rocket rounds started impacting dangerously close to their positions.

As the AQ charged one wall, three Green Berets leaned over the parapets, oblivious to the enemy small-arms fire that was cracking by their heads and shoulders. "Focus, squeeze, focus, squeeze," they recited quietly. Each time, a 5.56mm boat-tailed bullet exploded through the brain of an al-Qaida terrorist; the lifeless body would snap back through the desert air and drop onto the sandy courtyard.

Still, the enemy appeared to be impervious to the teams' small-arms fire. In spite of the fact that the Green Berets were on the parapets drilling the enemy in their foreheads as fast as they could, they just kept coming, even though the prison courtyard was littered with bodies. The momentum was swinging definitively toward the Taliban as they seized the armory and started to rearm.

Faced with a breakout and overwhelming odds, the team's only recourse was to put heavier ordnance inside the walls to disrupt the enemy and regain control. This was going to be risky; the bombs would land within "danger close" distances to the Special Forces troops and Northern Alliance *muj* manning the outer walls.

As the battle raged on throughout the day, the team exchanged fire with the terrorists and used their laser markers to aim smart bombs inside the prison walls. Many landed within 150 meters of friendly forces, well within the "danger close" margins. Finally, as the day ended, the enemy seemed to be partially subdued.

On the third day of the uprising, Major Mitchell and five other operators entered the prison. They knew there was a good chance they could die in the process, but if Mike was still alive, they had to get him out. Dave would remain in the safety of the Special Forces command post that had been set up.

They approached the AQ-held, southern half of the fortress from the northern half, which was now back in Northern Alliance hands. Heading into the unknown with a contingent of Dostum's soldiers, Mitchell now had more firepower—two

Soviet-era tanks brought in by Dostum. Using the limited cover and concealment available to move across the fortress' interior, the major and his small party fought their way into several of the mud-caked hallways searching for Mike. The team realized that the al-Qaida would have a tremendous advantage inside the buildings, since they themselves were not familiar with any of the interior layouts. It would be close quarter battle (CQB), with room-to-room combat. That would increase the chance of friendly casualties.

Mitchell picked one group of assaulters to go with him. Luckily almost all of the special operators there had considerable CQB experience and were graduates of what used to be known as the Special Forces SOT course, which specialized in building assaults and CQB. A British team also volunteered to take on the other buildings opposite from where they thought Spann was. They also had extensive experience in CQB, both in the killing houses at Hereford, and their secret training base in Pontralis.

As the Northern Alliance and Mitchell's team worked its way through the area, sporadic fire continued as one firefight after another raged in the southern-fortress complex.

As the inside team fought up close and personal, Mitchell's headquarters, now relocated to the northern part of the fortress, was notified that Mike was dead and a Northern Alliance squad carrying Mike's body would soon be at their location. His body had been booby-trapped with a grenade, but the team disarmed it. BOXER called in a helicopter to transport the agent's body to K2, where it would be taken home later by fixed-wing aircraft via Germany. Once Mike's body was out of the fortress, the British and American commandos conducted an impromptu and emotional ceremony near the helicopter before it lifted off.

Johnny Micheal Spann was a thirty-two-year-old former Marine officer from Alabama who was on his first combat assignment for the CIA after completion of his training at the Farm, the CIA's camp in Virginia where covert agents are trained in clandestine activities and operations. He was officially part of the CIA's Directorate of Operations, Special

Activities Division, also referred to as the Special Operations Group.

Spann's body would bear out the worst of the rumors—he had been captured alive and tortured by the AQ. Both of his legs had been broken below the knees in a typical al-Qaida torture method. What was not reported was that he had been alive for quite some time after. Two bullets had been placed in the small of his back, on either side of his spine. A final bullet, which killed him, had been inflicted some time later, in the back of his neck, probably as he knelt down with his hands tied behind his back.

Blue on Blue

Spann's body was recovered, but the fight was still raging on, and a tragic "blue on blue" (friendly fire) incident was about to occur. BOXER's men had moved up to the battle and were coordinating fire support and special ops troops from the various units. With total chaos in every direction, fast movers were called in, and just as things were starting to look better, a Hellfire missile went astray.

A U.S. Air Force combat controller called in the target's coordinates, danger-close and just inside the prison walls, as two Green Berets carefully peered over the parapets.

First Sergeant David B. Betz leaned over to Captain Kevin Leahy and spoke hesitantly, "Sir, this one is damn close, I sure hope it hits the target." *Damn close* was worse than *danger close;* they were only a very short distance away.

He sighted his weapon on where he thought the impact might flush out the enemy, and where the missile was supposed to hit. The round hit exactly where it was programmed, but not where Betz wanted it.

The Air Force pilot above had apparently punched in the coordinates of the observers, not their target.

Leahy was thrown completely into the air as the thick mud walls of the fortress came apart under his men. SFC Paul Beck was thrown up in the air and slammed into the dirt, barely conscious. The explosive concussion was devastating. Leahy landed unconscious and was covered under the rubble, lost as the other members of Mitchell's team tried to regain control of the situation and their wits.

Betz and the other Green Berets struggled to put things together; the medics went into action as the soldiers that could still move tried to pull the victims to safety for treatment on the spot, and then move them to the casualty collection point.

Captain Paul R. Syverson was thrown into the air, spinning and dazed, but without losing consciousness. Flying through the air, he hit the ground so hard that he temporarily lost all feeling in his legs. Everything seemed in ultra-slow motion, totally surreal.

Impact, Syverson later said, made everything "go brown." The men who dragged him to the collection point said his sole concern was the status of his lower body, since he feared his legs were "completely gone."

All of the men's eardrums were ruptured, rendering them totally deaf, so the use of a radio was impossible. Other American commandos rushed to their side to provide protection as they were moved to the casualty collection point.

Leahy was the most severely injured—his hip was shattered. By some miracle, all of the other injuries were less serious. It would take a week for the men to regain their hearing as the ruptured membranes healed. Everyone had black eyes from the concussion, and most had lacerations from flying shrapnel.

Under fire, the infantry from Lieutenant Bradley Maroyka's rifle platoon of the Army's 10th Mountain Division ran forward to help drag the fallen Green Berets and their Afghan counterparts to safety. TASK FORCE DAGGER immediately deployed Special Operations helicopters from K2 to evacuate the wounded, which were later taken to Germany after the K2 base-camp medics had stabilized them.

Back at K2, CIA case officers arrived at the Army's morgue to see Spann's body. The military mortuary team had cut off Spann's combat boots and removed his blue jeans and shirt. It was obvious that Spann's death had been long and painful.

The Agency men ordered all existing medical records and autopsy reports destroyed and cautioned the Army staff not to make any new records or take photographs of Spann. His body would be placed in a sealed metal casket and sent back to the United States for a hero's burial. Although the intricate details of his death would be concealed and remain highly classified, the CIA would break, for the first time in history, its long-standing rule of not acknowledging the identity, background, and circumstances of a covert-action agent killed in the line of duty. While many old-time CIA case officers objected, like Paul Payne, a Green Beret and retired CIA officer from Fort Bragg, many believed the Agency had done the right thing. President Bush decided that Americans needed to know who Mike really was, and that he had died in the service of his country.

Apparently they did not need to know the brutality of his death—maybe because CIA officials worried that Americans would react the way they had when tortured American soldiers were dragged through the streets in Somalia. That imagery caused an immediate U.S. withdrawal. The truth of the matter seemed to elude U.S. officials: Americans were ready for brutal casualties, Americans wanted the AQ stopped, and Americans were ready to meet violence with violence to protect their homeland.

To the Green Berets and clandestine operators in Afghanistan, Johnny Spann's brutalized body only reemphasized the fact that, like al-Qaida's suicide terrorists, they also must fight to the death and never be captured.

The CIA dispatched a five-man "grief team" to inform Mike's wife, Shannon Spann, of her husband's death. Shannon was better prepared than most women to deal with the tragedy; she wasn't just his wife, she was also a fellow operative. Mike and Shannon had met in the summer of 1999 while they were going through the CIA's Clandestine Services Course. Mike had children from his first marriage, while he was in the Marine Corps, and a new child from his marriage to Shannon.

K2 was not without its own losses during this time. One young 10th Mountain Division soldier was on guard duty the night he received a "Dear John" letter from his girlfriend. He fired a single round from his M-16 through the roof of his mouth, ending his tour of duty. It was a vivid reminder that the battlefield would not be the only place for American casualties.

American *Taliban* or American *al-Qaida*?

The Taliban revolt had been met with VOA, Violence of Action, the special ops term for a violent, unrelenting response to opposition. As the revolt subsided, mostly through "enemy attrition," the few left alive retreated underground into a dungeon. More than four hundred enemy corpses lay strewn across the prison courtyard. If AQ ever wanted to really fight to the death, they had come to the right place.

John Walker Lindh was one of the eighty-plus hard-core al-Qaida still barricaded in the dungeon. Walker and the others had refused to give up, even after the riot was finally quelled.

Colonel General Jurabek, the Northern Alliance prison commander, started flooding ice-cold water into the basements where the last AQ radicals were now hiding. When that didn't work, they poured in diesel fuel and tried to burn them out. Dostum sent troops to find gasoline, jet fuel, or anything else that could be used to finish off the remaining terrorists. One thing was for sure—the enemy had given up their POW status voluntarily and taken up arms, and if they didn't surrender now they were going to die, every last one of them.

It was the last straw for the hungry, wounded, and freezing al-Qaida zealots. When the last former prisoners finally gave up, they had been entrenched underground for three days. They were suffering from hypothermia, concussions, and shrapnel wounds and looking ghastly.

In the confusion of the surrender, Walker made his way to a mud-hut hospital. TIGER 02 had now arrived back at Qala-i-Jangi.

As he sat there shaking, a reporter from *Newsweek,* looking much like a CIA officer, walked up to him. Wearing a sage-green U.S. military parka, blue jeans, and similar in age and build to the real intelligence agents there, the *Newsweek* reporter started to question Walker. No one seemed to notice. John Walker Lindh answered the reporter in English as he sat with his teeth chattering. He said his name was Suleyman al-Faris.

Walker was terribly thin and severely hypothermic. He had minor shrapnel wounds in the right upper thigh, minor cuts from grenade shrapnel in his back, and part of his second toe on his left foot had been shot away. He had on a dark blue "wooly pully" sweater, its V-neck and shoulder and elbow pads exposing its Pakistani Army roots. A white rope, à la Jethro Bodine, held up Walker's ragged pants. The olive-drab three-button shirt under his Pakistani Army sweater was a familiar piece of gear for the AQ terrorists.

Black charcoal stains wrapped across the right side of Walker's face and nose, and his eyes were black and deep-set. He bore the telltale marks of a man who had lived with an AK-47 in his hands.

Newsweek's reporter told him he had two choices: talk or die. He told him that if he didn't start telling someone who cared about him who he was, the military was going to let him die right there. *Newsweek*'s man assured him that some publicity and the fact that he was an American would guarantee him medical treatment and evacuation. Lindh gave his interview to *Newsweek. Newsweek*'s lucky stringer showed up on Larry King a few months later and was quickly promoted to bureau chief for counterterrorism.

Walker talked freely to *Newsweek* in the hospital. He had studied Arabic in Yemen, went first to Bamian in Afghanistan and then enrolled in a *madrasah* in northern Pakistan. His heart had gone out to the Taliban, and he entered Afghanistan to join an Arabic-speaking element in Osama bin Laden's network. Walker had seen Osama many times in the training camps and up on the frontlines. To *Newsweek* and the press, Walker played down his implicit role in terrorism and his hatred for the United States. His true feelings were not so well hidden when he spoke to the American soldiers.

Walker's catalyst had apparently been *The Autobiography of Malcolm X.* He supported the bombing of the USS *Cole,* believed America was evil, and that the attacks on 9/11 were well deserved. He admitted knowing about the attacks in advance, even as far back as June 2001, when he was informed that Osama bin Laden had sent people to the U.S. on suicide missions. Walker said bin Laden was his true leader, and Americans must die to "cleanse the world of the infidel."

Initially, Walker had been assigned to fight in Takhar Province, but American bombing had decimated al-Qaida forces in that region. Walker and his compatriots fled on foot nearly a hundred miles west to Kunduz. All, of course, for nothing, since the Veterans Day offensive would trap him. Walker freely admitted that the Taliban hadn't wanted him because he spoke only Arabic, and he was sent to work for al-Qaida, under the direct command of Osama bin Laden. Even worse, Walker admitted that his goal was to be martyred, dying in the act of killing Americans. John Walker was not the "American Taliban," as he was portrayed by the press, but a foreign AQ member of the most extreme sort—one who claimed he was willing to die for his beliefs, even after capture and imprisonment. John Walker Lindh was a traitor of the worst sort.

While *Newsweek* was interviewing Walker, an Afghan reporter who had discovered Walker the previous day found TIGER 02 and told them that a wounded man was speaking English in a mud-hut hospital nearby. The team moved quickly to the hospital, took a digital photo with their Sony still camera, and "bursted" it by satellite to TASK FORCE DAGGER headquarters. The man's name was John Walker Lindh. He had last been seen shortly before the prison rebellion. Lindh was now in U.S. hands, but as a formality TIGER 02 asked the Northern Alliance to put him in U.S.

custody "so he could receive professional medical care." The Northern Alliance quickly consented.

The AQ and foreign Taliban, on the other hand, had no such luxury. The Afghanis, down to the last man, hated those who had so damaged their country.

Walker had no problem bragging that he had met bin Laden, "who thanked me personally for taking part in *jihad.*" Once in the custody of TIGER 02, Walker, lying on a stretcher, also spoke to CNN reporter Robert Young Pelton, who was with TIGER 02. "The people have a great love for the Taliban," Walker claimed. He obviously had not seen the Afghan people dancing and cheering in the streets of Kabul, and virtually every other liberated city, as the Taliban fell from power.

Some special operators suggested that Walker's professional medical care should have been administered in the same way Spann's had been, with a bullet to the back of the neck; at least that would save taxpayer dollars. But reporters had not only interviewed Walker, he had been photographed, and, unfortunately, that pretty much assured him safe passage to a cozy American prison cell.

As Walker lay in the makeshift hospital, TIGER 02's team medic asked him, "Is this what you thought it would be?"

"Exactly what I thought it would be," Walker responded.

The more they questioned Walker, the more disgusted the Green Berets became. Walker had no right to live, one special advisor told Dostum in an effort to seal Walker's fate, in spite of the press knowing an American al-Qaida member was alive.

Although Walker would later come off as just a young, misguided youth, the fact remains that the AQ, their hierarchy, and bin Laden himself trusted him. For the AQ to trust an American and give him access to bin Laden and their leadership meant that Walker must have proven himself to their hierarchy. How exactly may never be established, but the al-Qaida is known to initiate non-Muslim-born converts by watching them perform acts of violence, including murder and the torture of captured victims.

Walker admitted that he had attended the al-Farooq al-Qaida terrorist training camp just west of Kandahar, but did not acknowledge any other training. Walker had, in fact, also visited the premier al-Qaida terrorist-training camp in Mir-Bach-Kot, north of Kabul. There he had helped other terrorists learn English, and learn the nuances of dealing with English-speaking hostages. According to Jack, a special advisor to the Northern Alliance who captured the now famous *8mm VideoX* al-Qaida terrorist training tapes from the Mir-Bach-Kot camp, several AQ prisoners admitted that Walker, "the American," as they referred to him, had helped train "sleepers" to infiltrate the United States by explaining American customs and thinking. Walker was also suspected of hiding hand grenades on his body that were later used in the prison uprising.

According to the American commandos on the ground in Afghanistan, John Walker Lindh was no misguided youth. He was a dangerous and trusted operative for bin Laden who was complicit in the deaths of thousands of innocent Americans on September 11, 2001.

Be that as it may, of the six hundred al-Qaida fighters who started the revolt, eighty-six were still alive and John Walker Lindh was one of them.

At the beginning of John Walker's trial, Tonya Spann Ingram, Spann's sister, had two questions for Walker: She wanted to know why he wouldn't speak to her brother during his interrogation. She also wanted to know if Walker knew of the hidden weapons and planned rebellion that cost her brother his life. She never got an answer.

"John Loves America"

In July 2002, the U.S. Attorney for the Eastern District of Virginia announced a deal had been reached prior to Walker's trial proceedings. The now cleaned-up and shaved John Walker Lindh would plead guilty to "aiding the Taliban" and "carrying explosives." All charges directly relating to terrorism, including a charge of conspiracy to murder U.S. nationals, would be dismissed.

"It is a tough sentence and a great victory in the war on terrorism," the U.S. Attorney announced.

But some Green Berets say the reality is far different. Walker will be out of jail before he reaches age thirty-seven. He will serve about seventeen years, less than a Detroit gangbanger caught with three rocks of crack cocaine would receive; less than someone caught with a few ounces of heroin would receive; less time than some people received in the savings and loan scandals of the 1980s; and only about twice as long as Congressman James Traficant's sentence for bribery a week later.

"John loves America," said his father, Frank Lindh, a lawyer for Pacific Gas & Electric, in August 2002.

Several al-Qaida prisoners claimed that Walker was present when Spann was tortured and killed, and that the AQ used Walker to interpret conversations between Spann and his partner while they were interviewing the prisoners. They also admitted that Walker interpreted AQ conversations with Spann later during his torture. Spann's father believes that Walker was directly involved in planning the revolt. "Information provided to me shows that my son's death occurred immediately after attempting interrogation of John Walker Lindh," Spann said. "[It] also shows that the defendant was actively involved in this conspiracy of prisoners that planned the uprising."

"Walker may have been taken off the street for twenty years, but Johnny Spann was taken away forever," said a fellow CIA operator.

The Red Cross came in to examine and clean up the hundreds of bodies at the prison. They had tried to recover bodies earlier, and the psychotic al-Qaida had rewarded them by shooting at the rescue workers, killing one and wounding two others. Amnesty International, flinging unfounded accusations, charged that the prison revolt had been a massacre.

Normally keen to jump on such accusations, the world press chose to ignore them. The Taliban and al-Qaida had killed and wounded and raped journalists all over the country. They had chosen to go from prisoners to armed combatants— and they had sealed their own fate on the world's front pages.

The Purple Heart

Weeks later, wounded soldiers from the fortress and several other combat actions in Afghanistan received Purple Hearts from the chief of staff of the Army. The chief of staff talked about where men like Major Mitchell and the others can be found.

"When I was asked, in an allusion to the last presidential election, whether U.S. Army Special Forces come mostly from red [rural] or blue [coastal/urban] America, the answer was simple," he said. "These great Army soldiers come from one singular, beautiful place: red, white, and blue America."

Great they were . . . Major Mark Mitchell would later be awarded the Distinguished Service Cross for heroism at the Qala-i-Jangi fortress. While attempting to recover Mike Spann, Mitchell's actions inside the prison, and his bravery under fire, was a "mark of distinction" for the Green Berets in Afghanistan. It would be the first time the Distinguished Service Cross, the nation's second highest award, second only to the Medal of Honor, would be awarded in America's war on terrorism. President Bush would personally present the award to Mitchell.

"And the Truth Shall Set Ye Free"

Walking through the doors of the CIA's headquarters in Langley, Virginia, you cannot help staring down at the beautiful marble crest inlaid at your feet, nor can you miss the words so perfectly carved in the stone. But it is not the words "And the Truth Shall Set Ye Free" that remain in your mind when you leave. It is the white marble wall of gold intelligence stars, seventy-nine of them, each one for a member of the Central

Intelligence Agency who was lost in the service of their country. Most of them are anonymous. Americans everywhere can now place another name to one of those shining stars, and that name is John Micheal Spann.

CHAPTER 16

Northern Alliance— General Naderi

"We're so conditioned as a people to think that a military campaign has to be cruise missiles and television images of airplanes dropping bombs, and that's just false. This is a totally different war. We need a new vocabulary. We need to get rid of old thinking and start thinking about this thing the way it really is."

—DONALD RUMSFELD on the
CBS Evening News, October 9, 2001

COBRA and the Hell's Angel

Pol-e-Khomri, Afghanistan

On November 26, A-Team 532, code-named COBRA 22, consisting of eleven men and an Air Force sergeant, commanded by Captain Michael Rezabeck, left their post north of the newly taken capital of Kabul. With the Triple Nickel (ODA 555) fully in command of the streets of the capital of Afghanistan, it was time for the Green Berets to complete the takeover of the northern sector of the country.

COBRA 22 was told to proceed north from Kabul through the mountains and settle in the northern village of Kayan. It was here that COBRA 22, operating in the Northern Alliance–contested area near Mazar-e-Sharif, pursued their mission to conduct unconventional warfare under the command of General Said Jaffar Naderi.

Even though the lavish mansions acquired by the Taliban

Legend:
+ airfields
✕ start of infiltration
← captured city

TURKMENI

IRAN

BADGHIS

⊛ Qal'eh-y

+ Herat

HERAT

• Shindand

FARAH

⊛ Farah

Lashk
G

HELMA

✕ Zaranj

NIMRUZ

IRAN

Cobra 22 and General Naderi

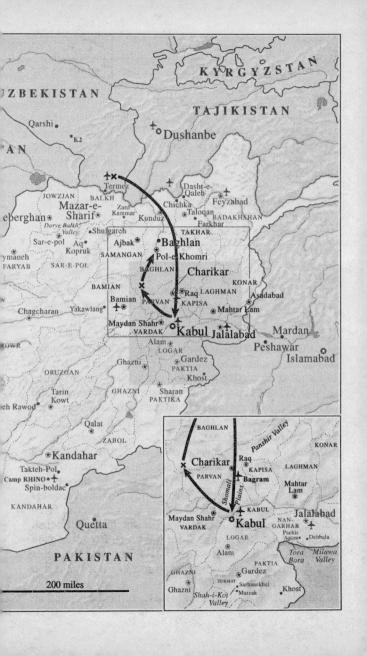

leader Mullah Omar, in Kabul and Kandahar, boasted every modern convenience and luxury accessory known to the richest men of today, the Taliban leaders had severely disparaged all the conveniences of modern living and ordered their minions to tear apart water pipes and electrical amenities in villages and towns occupied or even briefly visited by Taliban soldiers. All of life's conveniences based on any mechanical or scientific discoveries occurring since the lifetime of the Prophet Mohammed were ordered destroyed.

However, electric power was something even the Taliban found necessary in order to maintain an urban existence. Pol-e-Khomri was therefore a strategic gold mine. Unknown to TF DAGGER at the time, the area was an important hydroelectric power source, and the center of electric power dissemination to the northern part of Kabul; it could command a heavy ransom for its electrical power passage station. As a result the warlord who controlled the area after the war would enjoy a commanding position in the new government and a substantial price tag for transmission of the electricity.

Captain Rezabeck was charged with bringing his split team of six Green Berets, along with an Air Force CAS expert and more than two hundred *mujahadeen,* from their camp north of Kabul up through a mountain pass toward Kayan, where they would meet up with the Northern Alliance commander General Said Jaffar Naderi. In concert with General Fahim, they would destroy the Taliban and take over the strategic city of Pol-e-Khomri.

All that the team sergeant knew of Naderi was derived from a *National Geographic* documentary he had watched at home with his wife before the war. It told the story of the young son of a prominent Afghan family who had been sent at an early age to the U.S. to live with his mother in Pittsburgh, Pennsylvania. Naderi soon became fluent in English and joined the Hell's Angels. He was an outlaw biker-gang member when the Soviets attacked Afghanistan. His father sent for his then nineteen-year-old son to come home and fight the invaders.

Said Jaffar Naderi, now in his late thirties, compiled an

outstanding record against the Russians and was soon, at an extraordinarily young age, the leader of his family's *mujahadeen*. The American Green Berets would be assisting an Americanized young warlord, Captain Rezabeck thought as the convoy proceeded north from Shomali.

The trip through the mountains with their original group of 250 Ismaili *mujahadeen* was harrowing, to say the least. For two weeks COBRA 22 fed and supplied a growing number of Northern Alliance soldiers. Cold-weather clothing had been distributed, although not enough for every Afghan had been issued. The *muj* shared the kits, two and three to each packet. One took the parka, another the bottoms, and a third wore the boots. The black-knit watch caps were divided up among them. Long johns became outerwear. The Afghans didn't like the white fuzzy collars on the cold-weather parkas because they made the men stand out, so they cut them off and later gave the strips of fur to their appreciative wives.

It was a crazy formation winding through the mountain trails to meet with Naderi. The area around their meeting place, at the small village of Kayan, was a black hole on the maps and charts of Afghanistan. In the cold before daylight the string of vehicles and pack animals worked north through the mountains along thin slits of roadway called the "Muj Trail," carved out of the rocky side of the terrain. Each truck held forty to fifty Ismaili fighters, Afghanistan's lowest clan in terms of prestige and respect. But the fighters were on their way to a major battle and that kept their morale up.

By 7:30 A.M. on November 27, daylight was just beginning to seep into the darkness of the mountainous region. Then as the sunlight suddenly illuminated the ravines through which the procession was passing, a cold wave of fear swept through the Americans. There was barely a foot of clearance between the outside of the trucks' wheelbases and the edge of the cut falling down the side of the mountain they were ascending. The forward vehicle stopped and Captain Rezabeck surveyed their position. His word was passed down the convoy: "Be careful . . . go slow."

So they proceeded along the narrow trail until the wheels

of the largest truck in the procession directly in the middle of the convoy began to spin out in the muddy trail. The men behind and in front of the truck could only watch in disbelief as the rear outside wheel slid over the edge of the precipice. A few of the Ismaili *muj* managed to jump off the truck as it slid over the edge. It was an excruciating horror show as the truck tumbled down the side of the gorge, men falling off or jumping as the vehicle began to roll over, descending faster each time it flipped.

Finally the truck came to rest at the bottom of the gorge. The team sergeant stared down the side of the hill, littered with AK-47 assault rifles, cold-weather gear, sprawled bodies, and some men attempting to climb back up the steep incline. The injuries grew worse as the team made their way down the hillside to the crushed bodies under the truck itself, a rear wheel spinning above a smashed head.

As rocks rolled down the steep hillside, they defined the dead and the living. When they hit the bodies, the dead remained immobile, while the living groaned and made some gesture of protection with an arm or hand.

The most moving sight the team's weapons sergeant recalled was of a wiry *mujahadeen,* a pack still on his back, thrusting his head and shoulders between the legs of a sprawled and broken *muj* and literally head-butting him, moaning in pain, back up the side of the steep ravine to the road, where others were waiting to assist.

"I was a volunteer fireman for several years and I saw a lot of shit, but never anything like that," the weapons sergeant concluded. Then sighing at the memory of that assignment he added, "It was only the beginning of a thirty-six-hour day."

The six men of the team, all of them cross-trained or fully certified as Special Forces medics, worked hard to save lives and limbs, but they only had two hours, since they had to link up with Naderi and start their attack on the Taliban guarding Pol-e-Khomri.

Calling in medevacs to come and save as many of the Ismaili *muj* as possible, COBRA 22 resumed the uphill climb. The Americans and their *muj* contingent, now numbering fewer than two hundred after the disastrous spill, headed northwest for the meeting with Naderi.

Finally arriving at their village rendezvous, the Berets found a decimated population. The Taliban had been there a few months before and massacred more than four hundred men, women, and children; raped women and young girls at random; ripped the roofs off houses; and destroyed the hospital and school. A nine-year-old girl was executed for having a calculator. Grave mounds were everywhere.

Finally, Captain Rezabeck met up with Naderi, who was waiting for him in what remained of the center of the razed village of Kayan. This would be a moment to remember and write about. Having seen Naderi on the *National Geographic* documentary, he wondered if he would ever run into the "American Afghan" when his team had finally arrived on the ground in Afghanistan.

Naderi was everything the Green Beret captain expected. He was bronze of face and heavyset with a neatly trimmed black beard, and he looked aristocratic in his finely pressed Afghan dress and long-tailed shirt. He wore a slightly crooked smile that was accented by a trimmed mustache.

His English was a little on the rough side, still reflecting his years with the outlaw biker gang. "So you're the Green Beret that's going to call in the bombs on the Taliban for me?"

The captain nodded, happy to be able to converse directly in English. "We had a terrible time getting up here, and we lost about fifty men on the way."

For a moment the Northern Alliance warlord allowed a worried or concerned look to cross his face. "Any Americans?"

"No. All Ismaili *mujahadeen*."

A smile of relief twitched his lips and the mustache. "I have told my men that each American is worth a hundred of them if we are going to win the war and wipe out the Taliban. They will all protect you and stay in front of you if we get into a close battle."

This worried Rezabeck. The thought of fifty *muj* getting in the way of one or two of his men in a close firefight was not good—COBRA 22 hadn't been on the ground long enough to be able to tell the difference between the good guys and the bad guys, and everyone might get blasted. The team leader said nothing for the time being. Instead he asked how soon it would be before they hit the enemy.

Naderi simply answered, "We will all stay here in Kayan until the time is right to take Pol-e-Khomri."

Rezabeck's look brought a knowing smile to the NA general. Naderi assumed he was worried about the accommodations.

"Not to worry. I have already picked the least damaged house in town for you and your guys," Naderi told him.

"When do we start killing the AQ and the Taliban? The other teams have already taken Mazar-e-Sharif and Kunduz and we're camped up here doing nothing," Rezabeck complained.

"Don't worry yourself. You'll be calling in air strikes on the enemy as soon as we pick out the motherfuckers." Naderi grinned at his use of the American Army's favorite word.

"What do we do with the two hundred *muj*?" the captain asked. "What do we do about feeding them? They didn't bring any food with them."

"They've got their weapons and ammo. That's all they need. They'll find food. The people here in Kayan will see that they eat. What about you Americans?"

"We've got enough MREs in the trucks to keep us going."

"Like C rations?" Naderi asked.

Rezabeck chuckled at the question. "That was the old stuff. Meals ready to eat give you a hot lunch or dinner."

The winter evening was setting in as Rezabeck and the Americanized NA general discussed his plan of action, which seemed to center on taking Pol-e-Khomri and then no further action, no push through to the fighting around Mazar-e-Sharif to help secure the city.

COBRA 22 spent a week with General Naderi in Kayan, and each man on the team pulled guard duty two hours per night. They had tens of thousands of dollars in cash besides all their equipment, commo gear, and night-vision goggles. Like the other teams, they paid no attention to the guards posted by General Naderi.

Finally after a week, Naderi sent the Green Berets out to

recon Pol-e-Khomri. Naderi was now ready for battle and dressed in American camouflage BDUs. He had also requested that all of his troops be outfitted with U.S. uniforms as well—something that COBRA 22 requested, but like everywhere, supplies were slow in coming. Rezabeck and his men advanced toward the city in Naderi's dark green Toyota Hilux pickup trucks, aware through their own communications with TF DAGGER back at K2 that General Daoud and his forces were also moving to attack the Taliban and occupy Pol-e-Khomri.

Naderi had long nursed a rivalry with General Daoud, and both generals were planning to attack each other and take over Pol-e-Khomri when the Taliban were defeated. The warlord who controlled the hydroelectric power source to the areas north of Kabul, and the midpoint between Kabul and Mazar, would be a powerful force in the nation.

Naderi asked Rezabeck to call in air strikes against what appeared to be Taliban opposing their entry into the city on December 12. It turned out to be General Daoud's men who had already forced the Taliban to flee from the city and south to fight another day. Daoud's forces started firing 12.7mm DSHK (pronounced *Dishka* by the Afghans) heavy machine guns at Naderi's troops and COBRA 22. The .51-caliber Soviet bullets were cracking over their heads as COBRA 22 tried to alert both sides that it was friendly fire. COBRA 22 had to consider the fact that if it was just overhead warning fire, it was inaccurate enough that it might hit one of them.

"Goddammit, the stupid motherfuckers are supposed to be on our side," yelled the team sergeant.

Just then, the machine-gun fire hit two of Naderi's men, and COBRA 22 got on their CAS channel. Five minutes later, ordnance started to hit Daoud's forces.

"Okay, asshole, now will you stop shooting at us?" one of the sergeants said as the bombs hit just in front of Daoud's men, eighty of whom were injured by the blasts.

Daoud's force fired a few more rounds and COBRA 22 was about to call in more strikes when they were told over the radio that they were engaging General Daoud and were about to inflict heavy casualties on an allied NA force.

"We'll stop dropping bombs as soon as they stop shooting at us," the team's radio operator said.

The team had no choice in what they did—Daoud's men had clearly been the aggressors. Now Naderi wanted them destroyed. COBRA 22 refused.

General Fahim, the overall commander of the NA forces in the north, sent the word to Daoud to withdraw before the air strikes resumed and leave the city to Naderi. It was too late, however. Daoud had already taken Pol-e-Khomri, and Naderi was pushed back to Kayan, where he then aligned with General Dostum's forces to the north.

Naderi stuck to his Hell's Angels roots, riding a Harley-Davidson in Afghanistan and making his own rules. One such rule was a new custom Naderi instituted in Kayan. He claimed it was a special kind of Muslim observance, which made the town of Kayan different from any other in Afghanistan. Similar to the "right of the lord" (*droit du seigneur*) in France during the fourteenth and fifteenth centuries, it said that all new brides in Kayan must first be presented to Naderi before their new husbands could even touch them. As lord of the town, Naderi maintains the right to deflower the town's newlyweds. New Kayan brides are lined up on his doorstep on a regular basis. The Special Forces withdrew all support.

CHAPTER 17

Attack in the South— Karzai

"This is not war as you have ever known it before. This is vengeance for the women and children they murdered on 9/11. Our responsibility is to implement that vengeance. Fight as though your own families were killed in New York. You are America's avenging angels. Your goal is justice and you are authorized to use all means necessary towards that end."
> —unidentified U.S. Special Forces officer
> during a classified briefing, October 2001

On Again, Off Again

K2, Uzbekistan

For weeks, A-Team 574, code-named TEXAS 12, had been anxious to hit the ground. Things were frustrating, to say the least. It appeared they were going nowhere fast.

Meanwhile, Hamid Karzai had called the U.S. embassy in Rome, and then Islamabad on a borrowed satellite phone, and said, "Look, I need some help. I'm willing to fight the Taliban, but I need equipment and supplies."

Two days later Karzai's men lit four fires in four corners of a remote mountain area. U.S. intelligence satellites locked on to the signal. The NRO (National Reconnaissance Office) plotted the grid coordinates and sent the DZ imagery to TF DAGGER. The next night Special Operations C-130s started dropping containers of gear.

After weeks in isolation it finally seemed time to move.

CHALLENGE 12

Attack in the South—
Kunduz

TEXAS 12 and Hamid Karzai

airfields
start of infiltration
captured city

TURKMEN

IRAN

BADGHI
Qal'eh-

Herat

HERAT

Shindand

FARAH
Farah

Las

HELM

Zaranj
NIMRUZ

IRAN

First it was six hours to infiltration, then eight, then one, then four, then one again. The only sure thing was that there was no sure thing, and no one knew if they would really leave K2 at midnight, which was the last word. Finally it was off completely. The entire team was in a state of depression.

Then TEXAS 12 got the word: The team sergeant and team leader would be leaving to meet Karzai in a secret location, close to the Pakistan border, where Karzai was also meeting with the CIA and was ready to immediately meet with TEXAS 12.

TEXAS 12's team leader, Captain Jason Amerine, left K2 to meet with Hamid Karzai the next day and soon realized that they had a long list of problems. TEXAS 12 was going in through the south, into the heart of Taliban territory, where Pashtun tribes had strong cultural links to Pakistan and the Taliban.

Taliban officials and forces had collapsed into the Kandahar region from the north and west of Afghanistan, and there was nowhere else to go that would permit their survival as a government. With their backs to the wall, the cornered terrorists would be much more tenacious than they had been in the northern battles. Once again the enemy announced this would be their last stand. This time it might be true.

The situation was far different from the earlier one in the north. Karzai was still attempting to recruit a force, which at the time numbered as few as 25 men, at most 250. TASK FORCE DAGGER didn't want to send in a full team and create the "big ground signature" a dozen Green Berets would result in until Karzai had at least a thousand men. TEXAS 12 was going to have to help convince others through word and deed to join Karzai's movement.

The Green Berets were also going to be wanted men. The first Pashtun leader that tried to develop a resistance movement in the south had been tracked by the Taliban, ambushed as he moved on horseback in the mountains, and subsequently hanged in the streets of Kandahar.

In other words, instead of defending, as the Taliban had

done in the north, the Taliban in the south would be hunting—hunting TEXAS 12 and Karzai.

Murphy's Laws of Combat

At a secret location in Pakistan, CIA agents and the TEXAS 12 team sergeant had given classes to *muj* fighters on how to use IR (infrared) chemlights to mark the landing zones; their glow could be seen only with the aid of night-vision devices. They had also taught them basic LZ setup procedures and how to use GPS to identify their position, and INMARSAT radios to contact the A-Team. The different guerrilla chiefs had each been given a bag of equipment, including satellite cell phones, and sent back into the Kandahar area.

On November 14, four Blackhawks came across the border carrying in the Special Forces A-Team designated as TEXAS 12, one Air Force combat controller, two operators from Special Forces Operational Detachment-Delta, and six agents from the CIA's paramilitary forces. Two TEXAS 12 team members had to be left behind because the choppers were overloaded. The A-Team would fight the Taliban with Karzai, while the D-boys and TASK FORCE 11 would hunt for Mullah Omar. The Hawks were flanked overhead by heavily armed AH-60 Attack Hawks and fast movers for firepower. The LZ would be covered by two AC-130 Spectre gunships and watched by Predator drones. It was exceptional firepower and highly unusual for an A-Team infiltration.

As the entourage crossed the Pakistani border into the Oruzgan Province of Afghanistan, almost everything that could go wrong went wrong. Murphy's Laws of Combat—which said that all perfect military plans would completely go afoul as the operation unfolded—were alive and well.

Over Afghanistan, Karzai called to make sure the LZ was marked, and it was. Problem was that when the choppers got overhead, the *muj* once again had huge bonfires blazing and the choppers couldn't land—not only due to security, but their night-vision equipment would flare out. It was bad enough that the sand would cause a brownout when they landed, but bonfires were a total disaster.

The *muj* were supposed to use the IR chemlights, to mark their exact location, and the NRO imagery would be used by the 160th's GPS navigation systems to locate the area.

The team diverted to their secondary LZ, but they couldn't find that, and there was no CLZ, or contingency landing zone, because staff officers in the rear had decided it wasn't needed. Finally they found a place to land, but they could only get three choppers in, and they had to put on their white lights to see: a risky proposition at best. The other helicopter stayed in the air while they looked for a fourth place to land.

No sooner had the team dismounted than they saw movement to their front. The team's weapons sergeant spoke Farsi, and hopefully that would be enough to establish a linkup with friendly forces. If they weren't friendly, the difference between Farsi and Pashto "wouldn't mean shit," the initial conversation would be conducted with bullets, and then everyone would be speaking the same language.

It didn't take long to learn they were friendly; Karzai's *muj* had seen the white lights when the team landed. TEXAS 12's team checked their GPS on the ground. They were only two miles from the primary LZ.

Commo was down. They couldn't talk to the other half of the team, which had just landed. The *muj* didn't expect them and the mules weren't there to move their stacks of equipment and their 140-plus-pound rucksacks. They switched to the alternate plan to link up the next morning. No one wanted to have a friendly fire incident bumping into each other in the middle of the night, permanently destroying any chance of building a bond before they even got started.

But the other SF guys knew where they were too, and sent their *muj* down to link up with them. The Afghans were amused as TEXAS 12 tried to load their seemingly excessive supplies, almost two hundred pounds per man, on the few mules they did have. It was decided to leave the *muj* guarding the gear and move toward Karzai while the Afghans found more pack animals.

They arrived at the safehouse first, and the mules showed up later. One rucksack had been stolen, but there was no sense in making a big deal about it. Everything had been cross-loaded, which meant spread out, so if they lost one bag, or even a few, they still had enough gear to complete their mission. This was SOP in SF, and learned early in the qualification course. Shortly thereafter, the special operators linked up with Hamid Karzai. Karzai's fluent English eliminated the communication obstacles encountered by many of Captain Amerine's peers.

To survive, Karzai and TEXAS 12 needed to move into the rough terrain of the mountains, so without pause they set off into the darkness, advancing in columns throughout the night, finally reaching a small mud-hut village of three hundred to five hundred people at daybreak. Moving into a designated mud hut, the A-Team was ever vigilant, and, like the other teams, kept some of its men on guard. This continued to be a practice the *muj* didn't understand. Some SF teams explained it was to assist the *muj*. Others explained it was to monitor the radio. TEXAS 12 explained that it was simply the way the Americans did business. Nobody explained the real reason—in a guerrilla warfare environment, you could trust no one until after the first battles, and even then it was subject to change.

Building the Force

Over the next weeks the team worked around the clock arranging for airdrops of supplies and ammunition, while trying to build rapport and confidence with Karzai's followers and striking the Taliban.

SFC David Kennedy organized his medical gear and made sure everyone on the team had compression bandages in case of bullet wounds. His prior combat-medic experience told him injuries were inevitable. SFC Gil Magallanes, SSG Wes McGirr, SFC Vaughn Berntson, and young SSG Brad Fowers organized their supplies and checked everything from radios to night vision—there would be no time later.

Like all the teams, TEXAS 12 became experts at drinking tea and sitting through lengthy debates between factional leaders at night. They learned that Karzai was a wise team-builder who would listen patiently, then interject with a solution based on consensus.

TEXAS 12's team sergeant had also been a good listener. In spite of the fact that he was known as a rough, tough, hell-raising Harley rider, Master Sergeant Jefferson Davis had a gentle heart and a caring nature. Back at Fort Campbell, much of his time was spent mentoring his men and making sure their personal lives were squared away. Davis would frequently give his boys time off if they needed to handle family affairs, and when an officer questioned him, his response was straightforward: "These guys work day and night and they will be called upon by the country, and by me, to do extraordinary deeds. I can't have them worrying about family problems when the bullets start flying." His wife would always figure out their family budget and give him what was left over each month to spend on himself. Instead, J. D. would take the money and buy his team breakfast, or take them all out to lunch.

The night after they first landed, a weapons drop came in and TEXAS 12 started distributing guns and ammo, the main resource Karzai was critically lacking. Karzai's men were the most loyal, but they weren't soldiers, they were shopkeepers, farmers, and friends. As recruits increased, Karzai discussed his plans with the Green Berets of TEXAS 12. He wanted to capture the city of Tarin Kowt, seventy miles north of Kandahar in the Oruzgan Province.

Karzai believed that the capture of this provincial capital, situated in a valley at a major intersection of two main highways, would cause the Taliban to collapse throughout the entire province. Karzai also philosophized that public discontent in Tarin Kowt was so great that the *muj* could practically walk into the town and take it.

The Offensive Begins

TEXAS 12 believed Karzai to be correct. In a coordinated uprising, Karzai used his auxiliary and his supporters within Tarin Kowt's population to riot against the Taliban the day before he occupied the city with his forces. Just one day before Ramadan, the occupants of Tarin Kowt rebelled and succeeded in expelling the small group of Taliban administrators.

The minute Karzai heard about the success over his satellite cell phone, he announced that it was time to strike. His men and TEXAS 12 packed all they had on commandeered pickups, flatbeds, and even a few former UN vehicles and headed into town, loaded down to the axles with soldiers and ammunition.

On the night of November 17, Karzai and the A-Team occupied the Taliban governor's mansion and held a tribal council.

During the three short days TEXAS 12 had been working with Karzai to build his force, the Taliban had been searching for Karzai day and night. The Taliban hierarchy had quickly spread word to the domestic population about what lay ahead for those who dared to challenge the Taliban in the south.

Karzai was a fixed target. He had to die before he could build more support. The Taliban was going to come on like gangbusters and strike with a vengeance like never before.

The Battle of Tarin Kowt

The next day villagers reported to Karzai that the Taliban was about to launch a massive counterattack from Kandahar to punish the city of Tarin Kowt, seventy miles to the north, for its insolence. The rumor was that every man, woman, and child in the city would be murdered in retaliation for the

previous day's uprising. Karzai's intel assets called and confirmed that a Taliban convoy of eighty to one hundred trucks
would soon be traveling toward Tarin Kowt with more than
five hundred fighters.

In spite of growing anxiety, Karzai ate a leisurely meal
with his followers, even though TEXAS 12 desperately wanted
to take advantage of every second available to prepare defensive positions. Later the team would conclude that Karzai did
so to ensure that all present could see he was fully in charge
and not panicking. Karzai was a calm, cool, and collected
character. Even so, after the feast of stew, rice with almonds
and raisins, and bread, most of the *muj* had decided to pull
out, not telling Karzai or Captain Amerine of their intent.

Once Captain Amerine digested the gravity of the situation, he stood, shook hands with all present, and said, "Well,
it was nice meeting all of you, but I think we better get organized and prepare to defend this place." The Pashtun leaders
insisted he stay and have some more tea. Ten minutes later
Amerine finally convinced the group he had to leave.

The Green Berets rapidly moved forward to set up a defense. They saw the *muj* on their flanks starting to withdraw,
and sent part of the team back to inform Karzai. Karzai personally took charge of an attempt to rally his subordinates but
convinced only a few to stay and fight. Karzai was in trouble,
deep trouble. Observing his difficulties, TEXAS 12 realized
that success or failure was up to them, and they came up with
an audacious plan of action.

The first thing the team did was get aircraft and Spectre
in the sky to confirm the number of approaching vehicles.
Sergeant "Yoshi" Yoshita got on the horn and gave the aircraft a heads-up that they might need them, lots of them. The
weapons sergeants started analyzing maps and laying out a
tactical plan for the ambush. The commo sergeants starting
sending messages to TF DAGGER, letting them know they
were about to make contact with a superior enemy force.
Master Sergeant Jefferson Donald Davis kept everything organized and on track. About four hours later they knew for

sure that the Taliban was coming toward them, and in large numbers.

TEXAS 12 and its few remaining Afghan partners hustled down to a small southern mountain pass toward the Taliban convoy. The Navy F/A-18 fighters spotted the first ten Taliban vehicles heading toward TEXAS 12. Captain Amerine and his team sergeant, Davis, quickly moved their A-Team to key observation points and to hilly terrain surrounding narrow passes. They started planning how Taliban convoys could be ambushed and killed before they reached Tarin Kowt. As soon as TEXAS 12 got there, they saw the Taliban vehicles coming through the pass. They were now less than three miles away. It was 0700 hours on the morning of November 18.

TEXAS 12 knew they were about to fire the first shots in the war for their team. Amerine had them all together and started to formulate his words; he wanted them to be eloquent.

"Well"—he paused—"smoke 'em, boys." The team smiled as Amerine made his four-word speech. It wasn't eloquent, but it was the right thing to say.

Over the horizon came the Taliban with more than eighty vehicles and at least five hundred men, odds of almost fifty to one over the eleven-man A-Team and its small band of Karzai's *mujahadeen*. Most of the *muj* had already retreated to the safety of Karzai's headquarters, but Master Sergeant Davis' men stood fast and faced the superior force without flinching. TF DAGGER headquarters told them to disengage and withdraw. Davis thought about his wife Mi and his kids. He also thought about the families of his teammates. He knew there was a pretty good chance that they would all die over next few hours. He asked his boys what they wanted to do, and the response was no more, and no less, than what J. D. expected. If they ran, the entire population of Tarin Kowt would be annihilated by the Taliban. TEXAS 12 would make the stand to the very last man, and if necessary, use their weapons as clubs when they ran out of bullets.

The team's USAF combat controller, Sergeant "Yoshi" Yoshita, was an unusual airman—he lived and breathed special ops. He sent the enemy's coordinates back to the Joint Forces Air Component Command, and he already had more air support in line, and up in the clouds, than the team thought possible.

"It's showtime, boys," Davis said.

"Roger that" came the response over the radio as the pilots locked onto the team's lasers.

The first bomb missed. But the second bomb hit the lead Taliban vehicle dead-on. The Toyota flipped over twice and sailed through the crisp desert air. After that they were all hitting dead-on. Shit was starting to hit the fan and TEXAS 12 hoped the flyboys had enough bombs and ammo on their wings. Coordinates started pumping back to the air assets, and Taliban trucks kept flipping through the air. The enemy column was only a few miles ahead but it was already smoking.

The surviving lead elements of the Taliban closed in, not knowing that many of their mounted compatriots were turning tail behind them or already dead. The close air support had broken the back of the main assault. Still, the waves kept coming. As one truck would explode, the ones behind it would floor the vehicle around and through the wreckage and keep moving toward TEXAS 12.

By 1100 hours, three Taliban vehicles had made it completely through the hail of fire and ordnance. Rocking, swaying, and jolting on the bumps and ruts in the terrain, they came blazing up the hill and directly into one of the team's positions. Some jumped out still shooting as they tried to envelop the defensive positions from a flank. The defense of Karzai's men and Amerine's team was so effective that of the more than five hundred attacking enemy soldiers, only ten or twelve men made it to Karzai's position alive.

They were cut down in short order at extremely close range.

Throughout the morning, Sergeant First Class Ronnie L.

Raikes watched secondary explosions as fuel tanks and ammunition went up at varying intervals across the desert floor. Peering through his binoculars, he saw rocket-propelled grenades impacting all around his teammates, hitting in every direction. Another wave was charging. Raikes couldn't see all the action from his position, but he could hear the fireworks.

TEXAS 12 didn't have their own trucks yet, and had to rely on the Afghans, who usually cut and run at the first sign of Taliban. As the column got closer, the friendly Afghan *muj* were running up the hill screaming, "Taliban are coming, Taliban are coming!" The *muj* were freaking out. Here were a dozen Americans, and a handful of Afghans, defending a stupid rock and facing a huge convoy of Taliban vehicles and five hundred enemy forces. The *muj* clearly didn't get it. Most had driven away, leaving TEXAS 12 behind.

"Remind me to take the fucking keys next time," Amerine told his men as the *muj* trucks drove away. They had to grab the last vehicles leaving so they wouldn't get completely left behind.

Amerine and some of his teammates raced back to Tarin Kowt, where they skidded up to Karzai's headquarters and explained the situation. He needed the vehicles, and they had to stop the Taliban in the pass, now, or lose the whole town.

"Go, go," Karzai yelled, "I'll send more men behind you."

Amerine turned to one of the Green Berets with him and yelled, "Do you want to fucking drive?"

"Hell yes, boss!"

They jumped in the car and sped back to the mountain pass.

The team prepared to make their final stand against the vehicles that were making it through. If they didn't stop them here, the town was lost; they couldn't call CAS in on the village once the Taliban occupied it. They'd have to send some of the team to grab Karzai and make a run for it. They could not allow Karzai to be captured or killed.

TEXAS 12 was dropping ordnance as fast as they could designate targets and sending the Taliban to meet Allah at a high rate of speed. As the battle finally turned in favor of the Green Berets, the *muj* were now coming back in droves to watch the carnage, and carnage it was. The air strikes and shooting went on all day. First they bombed the front and then they bombed the rear. The middle would be annihilated over the next six hours.

Dan Petithory of Massachusetts was the team's communications sergeant. He had a knack for directing air strikes and dealing with pilots to vector them onto their targets. He loved adjusting mortars, artillery, and close air support. He loved his job. He loved his team. He loved all of it. "Dan-o," as they called him, was still cracking jokes as ordnance was exploding all around him.

With common sense and knowledge of ground combat in the trenches, Petithory took the tools of the trade—radios, maps, terrain knowledge, laser markers, and range estimation—and created magical effects.

"Dan-o," one of the team members yelled over the radio, "it's like fucking Disneyland on a Saturday night!"

The entire pass looked like one big Fourth of July celebration.

"Go Yankees!" came Dan-o's response, even though he constantly wore a Red Sox hat. The Green Berets had set aside their sports team loyalties; all of them were New York fans since 9/11.

RPG rockets streaked over his head and bullets cracked all around him as Petithory used his laser range finder and GPS to target the Taliban 4×4s.

Dust rose on the horizon as the remaining Taliban picked up the pace. Master Sergeant Davis had already nailed the lead portions of the Taliban columns, creating chaos as the Taliban tried to deploy its forces over the sides to surround the village. As the Taliban was finally stalled, with its lead echelon burning and dozens of wounded terrorists writhing in pain and covered in blood, Sergeant First Class Petithory went to work eating up those who paused in the open.

This was a target-rich environment, which meant they would have no problem using lots of ammo and making it

The Hunters

They came by car, by truck, by van, by helicopter, by ATV, by foot, even by horse—whatever it took. The hunters came to bring justice, and revenge . . . and they brought the ring with them.

The mountains of the Hindu Kush were a formidable opponent and taxed U.S. choppers and soldiers to their limits.

When rare daylight insertions had to be made, Green Berets borrowed low-profile, indigenous MI-8 choppers.

One of the Special Forces teams hunting Osama bin Laden.

The Hunted

On September 11, 2001, Osama bin Laden's al-Qaida network murdered thousands of American civilians. Less than forty-eight hours later, the Green Berets were receiving deployment orders. Within weeks, they began hunting bin Laden, Mullah Omar, and every single member of their terrorist network.

Osama bin Laden.

Mullah Omar.

Al-Qaida remains on the run, and the necessity of George W. Bush's campaign is underscored by the terrifying visions and tactics revealed in the *8mm VideoX* tapes captured by Jack, an American advisor. The tapes exposed al-Qaida's faces—and future plans.

RIGHT: Scenes from the *8mm VideoX* tapes show al-Qaida practicing assassinations at the Shomali camp, training to take hostages, and practicing to kill world leaders at a golf tournament.

The Command

Lieutenant General Doug Brown started out as a private in 1967 and served as a sergeant on a Special Forces A-Team. He would rise to command all the Green Berets in the world, and to orchestrate the Special Operations war behind the scenes.

Colonel Aaron Bank with Major Kathleen Culp in June 2002. Bank started the Green Berets fifty years ago and turned one hundred as this book was being published. Culp, a civil affairs officer, lost a cousin in the World Trade Center.

Special Forces Colonel John Mulholland formed and deployed TASK FORCE DAGGER, unleashing hell on the Taliban and al-Qaida just five short weeks after 9/11.

A rare picture of General William Yarborough winning approval of the Green Beret from President John F. Kennedy in 1963.

Major Dave Brigham, operating out of Tajikistan, worked day and night with Tajik officials to move men and materiel through an uncooperative former Soviet satellite.

The Northern Alliance

On September 8, 2001, the Taliban and al-Qaida, with help from Pakistani intelligence, assassinated Commander Ahmad Shah Massoud. It was a devastating blow to the Alliance.

Massoud in the early days of the *mujahadeen.* Most Northern Alliance commanders carried this picture in their pockets . . . a gift to them from Jack.

Massoud's closest commanders pay tribute to their beloved fallen leader in May 2002.

Zabi, an interpreter for a Northern Alliance advisor, prays at Massoud's grave in the Panshir Valley.

Northern Afghanistan—the Hunt Begins

TASK FORCE DAGGER's ultrasecret Special Forces staging base in Uzbekistan, known as K2. America's avengers would launch their hunt from here.

TF DAGGER started the hunt on horses. Here are two Green Berets with a *muj* on the right wearing a U.S. parka as willing sniper bait. Note the M-4 rifle hidden under the Green Beret's Afghan shawl.

Massoud's Panshir Army had been staging a desperate last stand in Khoja-Bahaudeen when the Green Berets arrived. They described the city as "the dawn of Christ with SUVs and machine guns." One SF team sergeant called it "the fucking moon." The Panshiri were America's most loyal allies in the war.

Shomali Plains—with General Fahim

Special Operations MH-47s carried the heavy loads of troops and supplies into places like the Shomali Plains, shown here.

Colonel John Mulholland and his boys with the first flag that flew over a liberated Kabul.

The Bagram control tower from which Master Sergeant Diaz's TIGER 01 called in devastating CAS (close air support).

Green Berets "bagging and tagging" al-Qaida prisoners in December 2001. Some of these terrorists were Iranians.

Mazar-e-Sharif—with General Dostum

Using their lasers, the Green Berets brought down a torrent of deadly USAF JDAM bombs upon the Taliban. This one killed dozens of the terrorists.

Robin Moore interviews the TIGER 02 team back at K2. Most of the pictures taken at K2 were reduced to low-resolution thumbnails by public affairs officers for "security reasons."

When the Green Berets weren't killing terrorists or bombing the Taliban, they were passing out humanitarian aid and operating on wounded soldiers. SF medics are the best-trained combat medical personnel in the world.

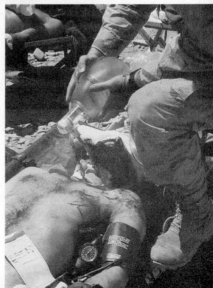

Kal-a-Khata—with General Baryoli

Gary Scurka, a *National Geographic* producer, shows his bloody passport and press card while waiting for an NA medevac. Green Berets helped save him after al-Qaida attacked a hilltop. He was the only wounded journalist to survive an AQ attack during the war.

In October 2001, the Afghan people were starving and on the run from Taliban forces. The Green Berets would not only kill their terrorist enemies, they would feed the Afghan women and children.

TF SABER uncovered the real source of "Taliban food poisoning" and U.S. Special Forces were quickly able to avert a potential disaster.

Baryoli's *muj* in Kal-a-Khata. Out of ammo and food, they waited behind the frontlines for a comrade to be wounded or killed so they could take his gun and join the fight. A Green Beret is on the right with sunglasses.

Bamian—with Commander Khalili

High ground and lookout towers over makeshift outposts gave TASK FORCE 11 additional security between "hunting trips."

A Zeus antiaircraft gun captured from the Taliban at Bamian. The Taliban had already destroyed the ancient Bamian Buddhas.

A Special Forces A-Team with their *mujahadeen* allies.

Mazar-e-Sharif—with General Atta

A Northern Alliance *muj* keeps lookout over a compound.

"The Angel of Death."
A New Yorker, "Ally" rained death from her AC-130 Spectre gunship on those responsible for 9/11.

Ally's Spectre 105mm howitzer shells were saved, decorated with the TF DAGGER logo, and used as containers to bury pieces of the World Trade Center in cities liberated by the Green Berets.

Green Berets brought in the coin of the realm, and lots of it. U.S. dollars greased the wheels when policy failed, which was often the case.

General Wasiq, *left,* one of the youngest of all the NA generals and a protégé of the great Commander Massoud, with Abdul Khalili of the Los Angeles–based Afghanistan Relief Organization.

Kandahar—with Commander Sharzai

LEFT: Green Berets inspect an al-Qaida truck after a point-blank hit destroyed the vehicle and its occupants. RIGHT: "JDAM the dog" in Kandahar with Sergeant First Class Jeff Bright. JDAM deserted the SEAL camp and headed over to hang out with the Berets. As in Vietnam, the Green Berets found mascots wherever they fought.

A Special Forces A-Team with their *muj* counterparts and allies. By January and February 2002, American uniforms and equipment had finally started coming in to the Green Berets' allies. The Afghan troops are wearing U.S. cold-weather parkas and U.S. Army polypropylene-insulated underwear.

Kandahar—with Commander Karzai

Hamid Karzai leaves the May 2002 *mujahadeen* celebration parade in Kabul. His bond with the Green Berets would be deep and lasting.

Dan-o's mates stand with their newly constructed latrine, named after Sergeant First Class Dan Petithory and inspired by the movie *The Green Berets. Left to right:* Staff Sergeant Jeff Thompson, Sergeant First Class Jeff Bright, Sergeant First Class "Cubby" Wojciehowski.

The boys assault the Mir Wais hospital. The terrorists inside would not survive the hailstorm of bullets.

Shortly before Master Sergeant Jefferson Davis' team was decimated, Lieutenant Colonel Dave Fox and TEXAS 12 posed for this picture with Hamid Karzai.

Tora Bora—with General Hazrat Ali

New York's Police Department and Fire Department were on the mind of every Green Beret in Afghanistan, and they let that be known to the Taliban and AQ terrorists.

A special operator recovers an AQ computer in Tora Bora. It was hoped that it would yield clues to bin Laden's network and whereabouts.

Hazrat Ali and his security chief give a press briefing on the whereabouts of bin Laden.

Green Berets find AQ mines left to stop their advance into Tora Bora caves and enemy arms caches.

Inside an al-Qaida cave in the Tora Bora Mountains.

Gardez—with Commander Gul Haider

A Green Beret operator stands with his *mujahadeen* counterpart outside their safehouse in Gardez. American 5.56mm M-4 assault rifles had no problem laying out the Taliban and AQ.

A Special Forces team poses with the American flag in southern Afghanistan. Notice the three stars on the hat in the middle—some generals were not afraid to ride into the hellstorm.

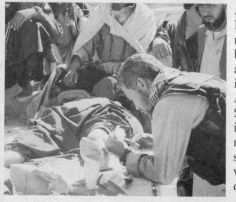

An advisor to the Northern Alliance removes an al-Qaida bullet from the leg of an NA soldier wounded in OPERATION ANACONDA. TF SABER operated alone in the middle of nowhere with no support and with only what they could carry on their backs.

OPERATION ANACONDA

COBRA 72 meeting with the Australian SAS moments before they started their attack on the Shah-i-Kot Valley on March 1, 2002. TF DAGGER would be severely hindered by conventional generals.

Taking a break after securing the village. For Lieutenant Colonel Chris Haas' Green Berets in Shah-i-Kot, victory was overshadowed by the loss of their teammate Stanley Harriman to friendly fire from a USAF AC-130 Spectre gunship.

Mulholland's boys went in "locked and loaded" and destroyed everything that stood in their way as they routed the al-Qaida terrorists.

TF 160 stands in front of an MH-47. They would lose choppers and more men in the days ahead, as would TASK FORCE 11 and the Rangers.

"When the last Angel has fallen and evil has had its day, you will find the gates of Heaven guarded by one lone Green Beret."

"Back at home a young wife waits, her Green Beret has met his fate . . ."

The Green Berets have buried more comrades since 9/11 than in any other conflict since Vietnam. Still, they keep volunteering again and again for dangerous missions.

Shannon Spann, *top*, follows as an honor guard buries her husband at Arlington National Cemetery. CIA officer Mike Spann was the first American killed in Afghanistan.

Shawna Prosser at her husband's funeral.

Before TF DAGGER left Afghanistan, they buried pieces of the World Trade Center with members of the NYPD and FDNY.

count. SFC Mike McElhiney, the team's weapons sergeant, looked over at Yoshita and his buddies and smiled. He stared back at the burning Taliban column and, in his Dirty Harry voice, said through clenched teeth, "How do you like New York now, motherfuckers?"

Taking advantage of the short lull in the fighting, Davis took charge, realizing that the battle was no sure thing. He needed to deploy TEXAS 12 where it could make a last stand to hold the village. The Taliban were sure to have sent reinforcements around the sides. He ordered his men to mount any vehicle they could find and move to key vantage points on the edge of the village, where TEXAS 12 could call in final protective fires yet would still have enough visibility to fight at greater ranges. Davis also had the team position their machine guns and sniper weapons in case the Taliban broke through and assaulted their positions.

The men deployed to four key points to make their stand, laying in the guns and getting the ammunition arranged to hold their ground or lose everything, including their lives. Meanwhile, Yoshi and Petithory rocked the airways, filling the sky with deadly and accurate ordnance.

"Is that a BRDM?" McElhiney asked.

"Damn, it looks like a BRDM," Davis replied, surprised to see al-Qaida using Soviet armored personnel carriers for the attack.

"Hey, that is a BRDM," McElhiney said again.

"Yep, that's a BRDM sure as I've got a Harley," Davis answered.

"Do these idiots actually think that thing will make it through?" Petithory asked.

"Yep, let's blow that motherfucker up and teach 'em a lesson."

One minute later a laser-guided bomb was in the air heading toward the target almost two miles away. They were thrilled to be blowing up Soviet armor.

"Aw shit, that's a fucking flatbed with a ZSU," McElhiney told Davis. "We just wasted a two-thousand-pounder on an old truck."

"Fuck 'em . . . ," Dan Petithory chimed in.

The al-Qaida truck with the ZSU antiaircraft gun was engulfed in a blast of brilliant orange, and as the brilliance passed, they could see the ZSU flipping through the air, burning.

"OK you little pricks, that makes up for one hinge on the World Trade Center; we still got fifty thousand more hinges to even up on before we move to windows and doors," McElhiney said. He had just started the official TEXAS 12 scorecard.

The other split-team element was at their vehicle overlooking the pass and calling in airstrikes. They had SOFLAMs on their hood. If the Taliban got that close they could deal with them too. As TEXAS 12 repulsed wave after wave, more and more friendly *mujahadeen* began to return from the hills to join the fight.

"Let's go, boys, I've got six JDAMs on this bird and I'm itching to drop 'em," cracked the pilot's voice over the radio.

The pilots were having a field day "mauling the enemy," as TEXAS 12 vectored them in. Once the carnage began, TEXAS 12 didn't have a shortage of aircraft; they had a shortage of vehicles to kill.

"We're running out of targets here, dude. I'm having to sort through the wreckage," responded the operator on the ground.

"Look, I'm not gonna be the one to head back with something left, so let's keep this party going for a while," the pilot countered. The pilots overhead were clearly disappointed that they were running out of "really good moving targets."

As some of the Taliban and al-Qaida were fleeing, TEXAS 12 kept lazing targets, and Taliban forces kept careening through the air as the fighter jocks lit them up.

"That makes 49,923 New York door hinges to go, asshole," McElhiney said as another Taliban vehicle flipped through the air.

Sergeant First Class Ronnie L. Raikes, in the hospital from wounds later in the war, described how the daylong battle resulted in twenty-seven enemy vehicles destroyed that he could personally verify.

The entire team would later be awarded the Bronze Star medal for heroism, and almost all would receive the Purple Heart for wounds.

Davis and his boys were leading by example, an example that would be remembered forever by friend and foe.

Victory

The Special Forces soldiers and a small group of *mujahadeen* had fought the Taliban and al-Qaida for more than seven straight hours. Together, they had held, and held strong. Those seven hours would be their bond in the days ahead. Those few *muj* would also be the Green Berets' most trusted soldiers from there on out.

As the chaos of the valley floor settled down in the pass below, part of the team moved in with *muj* to find survivors, take prisoners, and care for the wounded. It took great effort to organize the *muj,* and eventually it just couldn't be done. The team went in with only a few of their Afghans. As soon as they got there, TEXAS 12 took more enemy fire from RPG rockets. The AQ neither surrendered nor accepted medical assistance, so the team immediately pulled back and continued the destruction of the convoy's remnants.

Of the estimated eighty vehicles full of troops, between thirty-five and forty-eight vehicles were reduced to smoking hulls and completely destroyed. The number of enemy killed in action was estimated to be more than three hundred, a number later verified to the press by the Taliban commander of the assault. TF DAGGER radioed back to confirm the name of the Taliban commander for their report.

"His name matters not, the Taliban are merely nameless minions of Osama, and they will all be vanquished" came the reply.

The team quickly moved back to the town and set up a tight

perimeter overlooking the valley. Their plan was to keep Spectre in the air to protect the village. Escaping Taliban and al-Qaida had gone up into the mountains, and could be expected to come back to exact their vengeance on Tarin Kowt. Only days before two hundred Taliban had come into the town and threatened to kill every man, woman, and child if they helped Karzai or the Americans. (One of the few prisoners taken alive admitted that the Taliban's mission was to enter the town and kill the villagers in order to make them an example to other would-be "rebels.")

SF wasn't going to allow that on their watch. The Taliban soon learned that TEXAS 12 was waiting to "dish out a little more justice." Each time the Taliban came out of the mountains and attacked Tarin Kowt over the next few days, they were viciously repulsed and driven back. Realizing that TEXAS 12 was not going to be beaten, the Islamic radicals finally gave up and retreated for good. The townspeople were grateful, and the word spread throughout the Pashtun tribes. The Green Berets had saved the men, the women, the children, and the mullahs from slaughter, and SF had now won their hearts and minds.

The next day TEXAS 12 went in and did BDA, bomb damage assessment. There were more than forty fresh graves on the side of the road with the soldiers' AK-47 chest pouches hanging on sticks above. In accordance with Muslim practice, the Afghans had buried their dead that next day, while the AQ were usually taken away and thrown in a ditch or left to rot in the sun on a hill.

Taliban authority in the area was shattered.

According to Karzai, Tarin Kowt was an important city in the psyche of the Taliban. The Taliban's leader, Mullah Mohammed Omar, came from the village of Deh Rawod, about twenty-five miles east of Tarin Kowt, and it had now been proven that he couldn't even hold his home province. The warlords would now start looking for other options to replace their allegiance to the Taliban.

Karzai and his followers, now proven in combat, had seized the initiative and had gained momentum. TEXAS 12 paused after the battle to refit the Afghan troops and plan their strategy to continue the fight toward their ultimate strategic target, the final stronghold of the Taliban government and site of Mullah Mohammed Omar's official residence, Kandahar.

A Turning Point in the South

Washington, D.C.

On the nineteenth of November, a bespectacled Special Forces intelligence analyst looked up at his supervisor in the Pentagon and commented: "Sir, in my opinion the battle at Tarin Kowt will be recognized as the turning point of the war in southern Afghanistan, the equivalent of the fall of Mazar-e-Sharif in the north."

The Taliban had received a decisive defeat. They were no longer invincible in the southern Pashtun part of Afghanistan. The Taliban's leader, Mullah Mohammed Omar, would find it difficult to coerce ethnic groups to remain loyal. The warrior culture's respect had begun to migrate to Hamid Karzai and his bands fighting alongside the Green Berets.

The same day, a former commander of the 3rd Special Forces Group called the U.S. Army Special Forces Command with a virtually identical analysis.

CHAPTER 18

Attack in the South— Sharzai

"Get Mullah Omar, and Osama won't be able to operate. He'll be on the run. You must take out the center of gravity. That's what I would do if I were running this campaign."
— PRESIDENT PERVEZ MUSHARRAF,
remarks to CBS Radio and *USA Today*,
quoted in London's *Daily Telegraph*,
October 16, 2001

Hunting Omar

Takteh-Pol, Afghanistan

TASK FORCE DAGGER needed to put more pressure on Mullah Mohammed Omar to make him realize he was out of options. If they could grab or kill Omar, they might get closer to bin Laden. (Both men continued to occupy the top two positions on the Most Wanted list.) Colonel Mulholland searched for a way to open another front in the south that would further isolate Omar and convince him that he was being outmaneuvered militarily.

Two months before, Colonel Joe Votel had led the Rangers and D-boys into OBJECTIVE RHINO, destroyed and captured everything they could, and left. The airfield would now need to be taken permanently.

Commander Sharzai

Miles away from RHINO, Colonel Mulholland found exactly what he needed. Mulholland's operations officer, Lieutenant Colonel Mark Rosengard, had launched A-Team 583 into a location near the border of Pakistan, southeast of Kandahar. The operations sergeant in the "ops shop" called it the Taliban's "soft underbelly."

As soon as Hamid Karzai and TEXAS 12 had taken Tarin Kowt, six men from A-Team 583, now called TEXAS 17, commanded by the Vietnamese-born Captain Smith, were on their way into the southern Kandahar region. They infiltrated the Shin Narai Valley in the southeastern corner of Afghanistan on the night of November 19. CIA operators accompanied them with their most critical asset—bags of money. They were to meet another Pashtun warlord who was vehemently anti-Taliban, and could work with Karzai. Commander Sharzai had, like most of the anti-Taliban commanders, fought the Soviets first, and then the Taliban. He was big, robust, and missing a few teeth, but his happy smile was always present. The Agency had already promised him an A-Team. After initial contact at the landing zone, the team settled in to explain how they could help. Commander Sharzai told them what he needed first and foremost: weapons, ammunitions, food, and medicine, and, of course, money. Money was no problem; TEXAS 17 and the Agency had plenty of that with them.

TEXAS 17 surveyed the force and was pleasantly surprised. Sharzai had over six hundred loyal *muj,* and hundreds of part-time reinforcements who were on call if needed.

TEXAS 17 and Commander Sharzai's mission was to sever the mail, weapons, and goods supply route between Kandahar and eastern Spin-boldac by cutting off Highway 4. Spin-boldac sat between Pakistan and Kandahar, and was a route the Taliban used with impunity. A successful operation would virtually isolate Kandahar from Pakistan. The psychological objective was to convince the Taliban leadership that

TEXAS 17 and Sharzai

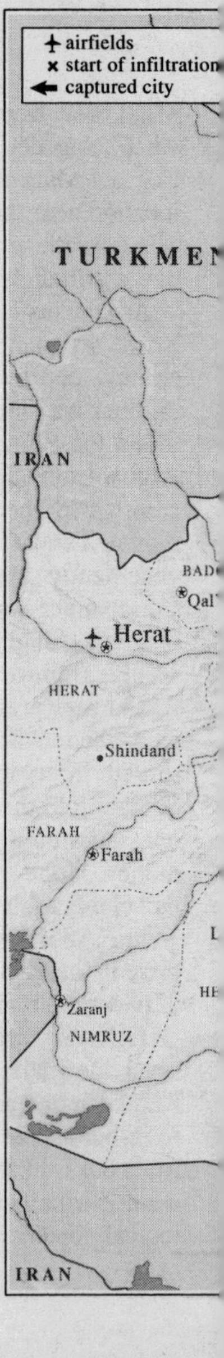

+ airfields
x start of infiltration
← captured city

TURKMEN

IRAN

BAD
Qal

✈ Herat

HERAT

Shindand

FARAH

Farah

Zaranj
NIMRUZ

L

HE

IRAN

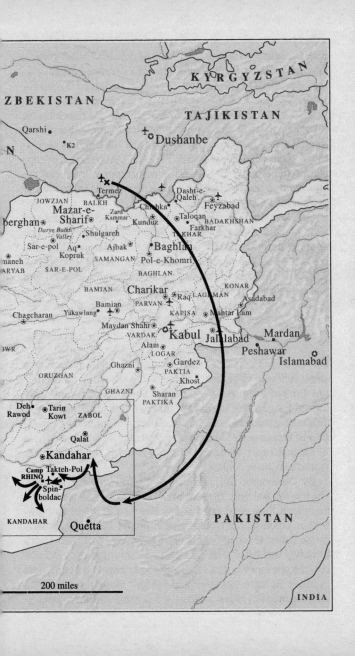

resistance in the Pashtun region of Afghanistan was growing and not limited to only that of Hamid Karzai and his followers. The strategic target for everyone remained Kandahar itself.

TEXAS 17 and Sharzai rapidly built a solid relationship. Sharzai wanted to quickly move into battle, and the team did as well. They developed their "want list" of supplies and radioed their needs into TASK FORCE DAGGER. Airdrops started to come in, and the force was equipped with enough ammunition and food to allow them to proceed into battle and conduct sustained operations.

On November 22, the remainder of TEXAS 17's team and a USAF combat controller were brought in by helicopter. The combined force moved out of the Shin Narai Valley and pushed their way toward a small town named Takteh-Pol. Takteh-Pol was ideal terrain, situated on defensible ground and straddling Highway 4 into Pakistan.

Into the Fight

On November 23, the *muj* and TEXAS 17 stealthily secured a small foothold in Takteh-Pol and in the process took numerous Taliban prisoners. Commander Sharzai's men cautiously moved through the small city slowly eliminating pockets of Taliban resistance. In the process they reassured the population of their safety. Commander Sharzai also informed them of the new order of things, whereby Sharzai, not the Taliban, would now be in control.

By November 25, Takteh-Pol was completely secured. During the fighting, the *muj* and TEXAS 17 had captured a vehicle, killing what appeared to be an Arab driver and passenger. Upon searching the vehicle, one of the team members immediately reached for his radio to make a call. The Arab's truckbed was filled with surface-to-air missiles, the kind that could knock down U.S. helicopters, transport aircraft, and even jet fighters. Stingers and SAM-7 shoulder-fired anti-aircraft missiles were a terrorist's dream, and their possession by al-Qaida was an American nightmare. Intercepting the traffic on Highway 4 had paid off in spades, and it may have even saved civilian aircraft from future attacks.

After seizing the city, Sharzai went about setting up his defenses, while TEXAS 17 moved farther to the north and the south to get their "big eyes" (long-range optics) into play. This would allow them to continue their interdiction mission and guarantee their survival by being able to spot any Taliban counterattacks the moment that they assumed a combat formation.

Part of TEXAS 17 moved north to establish an excellent observation point near the Agbestan River. The terrain allowed long-range observation all the way to the Kandahar airfield. TEXAS 17 manned the remote observation point along with the *mujahadeen* so they could provide enough muscle to hold if attacked by a small force. Another observation post was established to the south to cover Takteh-Pol from the opposite flank.

Rock and Roll

The news media in and around Kandahar referred to the Special Forces troops there as "the cowboys." Wearing their low-slung pistol holsters, loose-fitting shirts, wraparound sunglasses, and scruffy beards, and dismounting from their 4×4s, they conjured visions of *The Good, the Bad, and the Ugly*. Kandahar was a modern-day spaghetti Western, except the bad guys had AKs and the good guys had gunships.

TEXAS 17 was ready to rock and roll, and rock and roll they did. They basically just drove around in their 4×4s blowing things up. For five straight days they inflicted terrific damage on the Taliban. The first day they destroyed five convoys, and the next day they reached all the way to Kandahar airport to smoke a Taliban truck loaded with fuel. It was an impressive display as it exploded several kilometers away in a tremendous fireball illuminating the high-desert floor.

No counterattacks came, but the Taliban still remained

crafty. Somehow they knew that American rules of engagement precluded the bombing of bridges, because it would
limit friendly mobility and increase the cost of reconstruc-
tion after victory. When bombs started dropping the Taliban
would often speed up their vehicles, get to a bridge, and run
underneath it for personal protection.

TEXAS 17 called TASK FORCE DAGGER and pleaded
for a change in the rules of engagement, but finally realized
none would come. Instead, they played a game of chess
with the Taliban. Once the Taliban were under the bridge,
TEXAS 17 would tell all fighter-type aircraft to leave the
area, and punch in coordinates for smart bombs from the virtually unnoticed USAF bombers high overhead. When the
Taliban would finally uncover, the team would try to synchro-
nize the smart bombs' impact with convoy movements. On
several occasions they used their laser markers to "skip"
smart bombs onto those who were hiding underneath the
bridge.

Local *mujahadeen* were starting to change sides, for love
and money—they loved being on the winning side, and they
wanted the hundreds of dollars a month the U.S. was willing
to pay them to fight.

Mullah Mohammed Omar, the Taliban head of government now hiding in Kandahar, was caught in a vise from
the north and the south. He now clearly understood that his
own population was armed and closing in. So were TASK
FORCE 11 and TASK FORCE DAGGER.

Beating the Clock

While TF DAGGER and the TEXAS teams were busy recruiting and leading Afghan ATF, anti-Taliban forces, against
the large formations of enemy, TF 11 tasked the SAS to hit a
mountain hideout just southeast of Kandahar. It was believed
to hold a group of senior Taliban and al-Qaida officials,
which were too close to the Pakistani border for comfort.

Satellite photos and ground intelligence had confirmed

several mountain hideouts in mud-walled compounds and cave bunkers. The operation was planned and coordinated between JSOTF, JSOC, and the British Permanent Joint Headquarters at Northwood, Middlesex. They would also hit an al-Qaida training and headquarters compound in the same region. It would be one of the largest SAS operations in thirty years. The U.S. JFACC would provide the air support with fast movers, helicopters, and an AC-130 Spectre gunship.

NSA and NRO had positive intercepts of satellite transmissions from the Hada mountain region southeast of Kandahar. The limited U.S. Special Forces presence in the region was consumed with the battles in support of Karzai and Sharzai. Delta was chasing Omar, and the escaping Taliban government. The SAS was preparing to move to Tora Bora to support the Green Beret teams arriving there. That placed the SAS in a position to have a large force unengaged and ready to move.

It would be a textbook search-and-destroy mission, aimed at hitting the enemy complexes fast, killing everyone that resisted, killing the ones that hesitated, and taking prisoner whomever remained alive at the end.

The assaulters/operators were known as Sabre teams. Divided into the standard four-man bricks, the teams poured over satellite photos and Soviet maps as they developed their plan and actions on the objective. Four possible entrances were identified, and the four-man teams were composed in groups of two, with two additional twelve-man elements providing cover fire, support, and rescue firepower for the entry teams. With a quick plan developed and code-names issued, signalers set up the communications link to provide commo with TASK FORCE 160, TF 11 headquarters, and the GCHQ in England. Everything would be heard by JSOC and the British Joint Headquarters.

Carrying their standard M-16s, belt-fed machine guns, thigh-mounted pistols, and fragmentation grenades, team members made sure that each of them had a Morphine syrette and battlefield dressings. Although the walk in would be a good ten miles through arduous terrain, they maxed-out their

armor, with both front and back ceramic plates, and their ammunition loads.

Remembering it was easier to fight downhill than it was to
fight uphill, TF 160 Black Hawks delivered the bulk of the
force on the crest of a ridgeline adjoining the ridge behind the
complex. MD-500 Littlebirds, super quiet, agile and stealthy,
took in twelve troopers six miles closer to the target. They
would be the advance party, reconnoitering the area, and
monitoring AQ movement. It would also allow them to arrive
at the target far ahead of the main force, so they could monitor the cave entrances and mountain paths in the event that
somehow the main party's advance was discovered and al-
Qaida deployed their forces in an offensive posture. The advance party also carried MP-5 SD3 suppressed submachine
guns to eliminate threats without alerting the primary enemy
force. They would come in handy in just a few hours.

Reaching the complex first, the advance party used their
night-vision goggles to identify the entrances, sentries, communication antennas, and look for ventilation shafts. Two
satellite antennas and one VHF antennae were spotted, one
ventilation shaft identified, and five, not four, possible cave
entrances were located. In addition, it appeared that there
were at least five dug-in fighting positions in the side of the
hills, which were most likely shallow fighting positions for
guards and defensive forces.

The entire force was in place and ready for the assault for
more than two hours prior to the scheduled attack time. The
assault would begin prior to sunrise, allowing the Sabre
teams to take advantage of their night-vision capability, and
the AC-130 Spectre gunship that the JFACC had not only
promised would be in the air, but had promised to divert if
needed, unless another team was already engaged in the Kandahar or Deh Rawod area.

With everyone in position, the troop sergeant major keyed
his radio and gave a ten-minute warning. Each team reported
in and ready. Four snipers laid their crosshairs on four
guards, all of whom appeared to be sleeping. Seconds before

initiation, the snipers would turn on their IR illuminators, which would light up the area of their scope in a brilliant green visual display of the area, as opposed to the now dark green view. Assuming that someone on the opposing side might have Soviet night-vision capability, they would use only their ambient light night-vision capability until the shooting started.

The advance team hiding just twenty meters south of the primary cave entrance was shocked to see an AQ fighter stumble to within a few meters of them, squat down facing a rock, and piss. Finishing his task, he stood, tied his belt, and looked over toward the four hidden commandos. Lowering his head and hunching his shoulders, he squinted again. Maybe he saw them and maybe he didn't. This was no time for playing the odds. Twenty odd 9mm rounds impacted his chest from two different shooters, sending only the dull sound of the bullets whacking his sternum across the slope.

"Contact, repeat, contact," an advance team member whispered across his radio. No one seemed to hear anything, and no one moved. But the sound of the H&K bolts cycling, and the bullets impacting, had definitely been heard by their teammates in the thin mountain air.

"One minute lads, hold steady," the mission commander transmitted.

Twenty-nine seconds later, sniper team Alpha One Zero's shooter held his breath and pressed his trigger to the rear, as another AQ sentry stood up and looked around. The AQ guard's head exploded in a beautiful mist of liquid red. Through the night scope the shooter only saw his body snap back and fall from the view of his scope. For better or for worse, the op was now on.

In less than a second after the first sniper's 7.62 bullet cracked through the night, every other sniper had killed his target, and was acquiring a second target.

The assault teams were hitting the cave entrances at a full dead run, and at one entrance, where two AQ terrorists had charged out of blindly firing their AK-47s the enemy fighters were driven into the rocks by the 5.56mm bullets that were lacing them up from head to toe. As the teams made their way inside the complex entrances, one SAS trooper was wounded, hit in the side just below his armor, and in the left shoulder.

Moving swiftly through the caves, the four-man bricks found themselves stumbling over all sorts of paraphernalia and equipment, it was like running into a crack house in Belfast; there was garbage and shit everywhere. One team ran straight into a wall as they discovered that the cave they were assaulting was only ten meters deep, and consisted of nothing more than twenty terrorists sleeping together side-by-side on rug mats.

Watching from the side of an outcropping on the hill, an SAS Troop commander saw another large group of AQ and Taliban pouring out of a bunker that had not been seen. Radioing the security element he pointed toward them to the three men with him. 7.62 machine gun bullets started pouring into the enemy group.

Meanwhile, the entry team that hit the third entrance gave "all clear" for their target, but reported a second wounded soldier. Dragging him out close to the entrance and starting first aid, they radioed for a medic from the support element. Signaling with an IR Light, they marked their position. Two men, one a medic, headed for the downed trooper's position. Still fifty meters away, a barrage of enemy fire opened up pinning them down and cutting them off from good cover in either direction. The Taliban and AQ were now all over the opposite hillside, and the first RPG rounds started to arc through the air like Chinese bottle rockets. It was beginning to look like a Hong Kong slum on New Year's Day.

A troop sergeant major wasted no time in crossing the barren hillside through a hail of AK-47 and RPG rocket fire to reach his mate. SAS belt-fed machine guns ripped rounds into the AQ positions to provide covering fire. SOP was to fire short bursts to allow the barrel to cool in between. Fuck the manual, the triggers stayed back and barrels glowed red-hot—"kit" meant shit when a mate's life was on the line.

Another man was wounded when an RPG exploded on the rocks over his head. Both he and his teammate were dazed by the explosion, and two more teammates rushed over to their position. Minutes later enemy fighters charged the position, expecting to overrun and kill them. The AQ assaulters were sadly surprised to see two GPMG come up over the rocks and light up the mountainside with the brilliant muzzle flashes of a belt-fed machine gun.

Two hours later, the sun had risen. Four SAS personnel were wounded, twenty-two terrorists were killed, seventeen were captured, and half of them were wounded. Six of them had already been flex-cuffed inside one of the bunkers during the initial phase of the assault. Five more had surrendered as soon as the shooting started, and had been left laying face-down on the dirt, with their hands and feet cuffed as their captors ran back out onto the hill to help their comrades under fire. The rest had finally given up because those that weren't dying from automatic weapons fire, were being killed by single sniper rounds—even though the task of sniping had been rendered far more difficult by the volume of muzzle flashes that were limiting the snipers' night-vision capability. Ordering the last holdouts to kneel down, the commandos flex-cuffed each of the survivors and placed bags over their heads, then laid them all facedown in a line.

Squadron medics had already stabilized the four wounded commandos and medevac choppers were already on the way. The medics were now tending to the wounded enemy soldiers as two teams climbed the ridges to reinforce the lookouts watching for AQ or Taliban reinforcements, and the others scoured the area for additional enemy holdouts or survivors in hiding. The assault element commander radioed back to TF 160 for choppers to airlift the rest of the force out, and transport the prisoners.

The four wounded soldiers were taken by helicopter to a support ship in the Arabian Sea, where they were treated before transferred to Centre for Defence Medicine at The Queen Elizabeth Hospital in Birmingham.

More than 160 SAS soldiers have died while serving with

the SAS since 1950; hundreds more died in World War II. They are remembered on the Memorial Clock Tower at SAS Headquarters at Stirling Lines. In May 1999, Stirling Lines was moved from the Regiment's beloved Hereford location to the abandoned RAF Base at Credenhill, just northwest of Hereford, but still in Herfordshire. The Clock Tower had been moved to the barracks memorial garden in front of the Regimental church. As a matter of tradition, the SAS still refers to their relocated Stirling Lines base as Hereford. Like the Green Beret Statue at Fort Bragg, North Carolina, where the name of every fallen U.S. Special operator is inscribed on a series of bronze plaques, the SAS Clock Tower has a special significance for British commandos. If you are killed in action your name is inscribed on the base of the Clock Tower. To survive a mission is to "beat the clock."

Quiet, Make That *Silent,* Professionals

TEXAS 17 and Commander Sharzai had bonded fast and were working extremely well as a team. After fighting for sixteen days, Kandahar airport fell into Sharzai's hands.

Special ops had again taken the airfield and now controlled what would be later called Camp RHINO. This effectively cut off the main highway that ran into Kandahar. Small teams executed intimidation operations by stopping convoys, burning fuel trucks, and then allowing the drivers to go free. Most of the vehicular traffic was from Pakistan. They spread the message that there was an American presence lurking in the dark. . . .

The Special Forces soldiers are touted as the "silent professionals." Officially that description was changed long ago to the "quiet professionals" by a past general. It was a general officer initiative to tone down their Rambo/SnakeEater image and bring them more into the fold of the conventional Army. But most of the men of Special Forces despised this designation and continue to privately call themselves the silent professionals. There are times when even quiet, make that *silent,* men have to make a statement.

After the fall of Kandahar, General Franks was going to move the Marines forward by having them drive up the road from RHINO to occupy the "now vacant" Kandahar airfield. TF DAGGER notified TEXAS 17 that the Navy SEALs were sending in SEAL Team 3, Echo platoon, to do strategic reconnaissance on the airfield. TEXAS 17 knew the media information campaign would explode, and the Marines would be billed as the first liberators of the airfield the Green Berets already secretly occupied.

TEXAS Fanfare

Before the Navy or the Marines' arrival, two TEXAS 17 sergeants entered their mud hut late in the afternoon covered with paint. The team leader and team sergeant asked what the men had been doing.

"Well, boss, why don't you and the team mount up and follow us," one of the sergeants suggested.

"Yeah, you might like this new addition to the airfield," the other sergeant added.

The team piled into their Toyotas and followed the two sergeants across the bombed-out airfield, circled the airport control tower, and turned the vehicles, coming to a stop. The team dismounted and looked up. On the control tower of Kandahar's airport were huge, newly painted letters and numbers.

One of the paint-covered special operators smiled and commented: "My grandchildren are going to know who really took this son of a bitch."

It would be in the background of press photos and television footage of the Marines for weeks. No one would ever know what it meant until now.

The letters proudly read: TEXAS 17.

CHAPTER 19

Attack in the South—
Kandahar Falls

"Destroy bin Laden's infrastructure. Destroy his terrorist apparatus. Destroy his camps. Destroy his command element from the bottom up. Kill them as they eat, sleep, and pray. Kill everything bin Laden holds dear. I want him running so hard and fast that he can't stop to puke. And finally, when he has lost everything, kill him."

—Special Mission Unit commander
to his men immediately prior
to infiltration, October 2001

Rice Krispies Treats

Kandahar, Afghanistan

For the Green Berets and D-boys fighting in Afghanistan, mail from home was a rare commodity. The typical letter or CARE package found its way to the military APO address and then was flown to Europe, placed on military aircraft, and delivered to K2.

From there, TASK FORCE DAGGER would send the A-Team's mail on the next combat mission in support of the team, usually by helicopter, sometimes by parachute. The headquarters staff was getting mail on a regular basis, but it took months for the first mail to finally get into the hands of the soldiers on the ground. But that was okay, they never really expected it; they were busy fighting a war.

In early November Mrs. Jefferson Donald Davis mailed a

package to her husband from Fort Campbell, Kentucky. It contained his favorite snack—Rice Krispies Treats.

Attack on Sayed Alam-a-Kalay

The triumph at Tarin Kowt brought more and more forces into the Karzai camp. TASK FORCE DAGGER decided that it was time to move a greater command-and-control capability into the region to direct the assault on Kandahar. When Kandahar fell, they felt it would be better to have a field-grade officer on the ground; that meant a major or above. The battalion commander chosen for the honor was a sturdy former college football player named Lieutenant Colonel Dave Fox. He would take command of TEXAS 12, TEXAS 17, and the additional forces he brought with him, including a major. Having a colonel on the ground would also serve as clout for the SF sergeants if problems arose with the rank-heavy Marine troops coming into Camp RHINO. They infiltrated in to meet TEXAS 12. Fox's code name: RAMBO.

Karzai and his Special Forces comrades pressed south toward Kandahar. Their strength had now grown to approximately seven hundred *mujahadeen* warriors. They had only been there a few weeks. In terms of what the Warren Zevon song asks for, they had plenty of money and guns, and they didn't need lawyers. The Taliban were weakening. The force occupied the villages of Petawec and Damana with minimal resistance.

The next objective, Sayed Alam-a-Kalay, was the seat of another small, provincial Taliban government office. The town was captured by occupying the area "with force projection": the sheer number of Karzai's men storming into the village simply forced the Taliban to flee. Another ten to fifteen remaining Taliban soldiers were driven off in a quick gun battle, and offered only meager resistance. Lead elements saw the Taliban fall back across a river to regroup with other

PYTHON 33 and 36

TURKMEN

IRAN

BADG
*Qal'e

+ Herat

HERAT

•Shindand

FARAH

*Farah

Las

HELI

Zaranj
NIMRUZ

IRAN

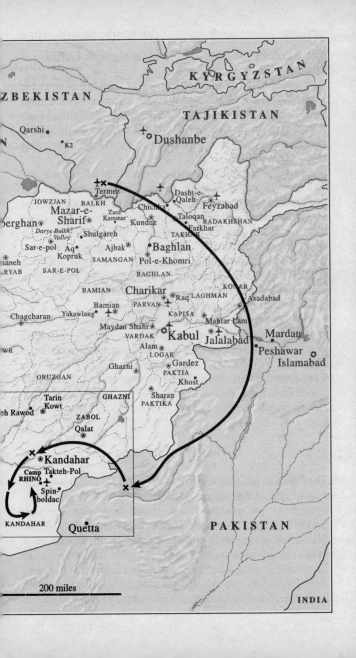

forces in defensive positions facing the new frontline now occupied by RAMBO and Karzai.

Situated between the two forces was a bridge of strategic significance, because it was the only way to cross the river and continue the march toward Kandahar. The Taliban realized it had an opportunity to stop Karzai at the bridge, a "choke point" well worth defending. The Taliban were going to make a stand.

On the other side of the river, hundreds of Taliban and AQ terrorists tried to delay Karzai's advance with harassing fire and probes throughout the night of December 3. The Green Berets targeted the probing enemy forces with close air support and smart bombs while the Taliban tried to gain a foothold on Karzai's side of the bridge. Sergeants Petithory and Yoshita were at it again, calling in air strike after air strike as they targeted the Taliban armor and vehicles. Facing several hundred enemy troops, MSG Davis was leading the Afghans in a head-on ground assault.

The *muj* troops and the Green Berets reached out with their M-4s and Kalashnikovs using small-arms fire, SAW machine guns, and RPG rockets to drive the enemy back in disarray. American 5.56 bullets tore into the attacking Taliban with three-round bursts from the M-4s and seven-to-ten-round bursts from the SAWs as the *muj* wildly sprayed Soviet 7.62 rounds into the horde.

Taking the Bridge

They fought most of the day. As night fell, TEXAS 12 defended against the Taliban attacks while RAMBO was developing a scheme of maneuver to secure the bridge. The plan for the next day was simple: Half of the twelve-man A-Team would man observation posts and focus on the Taliban lines to kill any advance assaults and to keep the Taliban in check. Their covering fire would assist the other half of the A-Team, which would position itself near a ridgeline overlooking the bridge and conduct a reconnaissance of the best way to assault the bridge along a relatively protected route that offered a good assault path. Simultaneously, they would move with about one hundred *muj* to occupy the mud ruins above the bridge. The men would then pour small-arms fire down on the bridge in great volume, thus covering any eventual assault that might result from the enemy's reconnaissance. Finally, a third *muj* element of two hundred men led by two of the Green Berets was readied in a secure attack position to launch at a moment's notice. Like the Mike Forces in Vietnam, they would be the quick-reaction force, just in case anything went wrong.

After final coordination the following day, the Afghan force and the three teams departed in Toyota pickups stuffed with *muj* soldiers and loaded with equipment. They were a motley crew, dressed in ragged half-uniforms, turbans, blankets, and sandals, and loaded with RPGs, AK-47s, and American M-4 carbines.

Things progressed smoothly until the hundred or so over-watching *muj* and part of an A-Team occupied the dominant terrain. The Taliban realized that Karzai and RAMBO had outmaneuvered them, putting them at a significant disadvantage. The Taliban immediately opened up with small-arms fire and a flurry of rockets from approximately fifteen men, trying to target the force in the mud ruins.

The Green Berets and their troops began to get the upper hand with their assault rifles and close air support. Too close for heavy air support, the battle was one of the most pronounced uses of U.S. small arms in broad daylight. The bravery of the enemy Taliban defending the bridge was notable, convincing RAMBO and TEXAS 12 that many of them were hardened AQ fighters.

Green Berets spit down streams of M-4 5.56-caliber fire into the AQ and Taliban from their overwatch position. Sergeant Mike McElhiney was firing 40mm HE grenades out of his 203 grenade launcher as fast as he could load them. Both sides could see each other clearly in the broad daylight as they slugged it out, toe to toe.

In the middle of the firefight, and totally oblivious to the battle frenzy around it, a yellow Afghan taxi pulled right into the line of fire, just short of the bridge. In a highly unusual move, both sides did the gentlemanly thing: they ceased fire until the confused driver could reorient himself and drive out of the kill zone. According to one team member, "It was totally surreal."

As the Taliban started to flank RAMBO with a superior force, Karzai's *mujahadeen* base camp commander ran up to Fox's position, pointing to the flank and frantically screaming, "Taliban, Taliban!"

The quick-reaction force launched immediately, leaving one Green Beret and a small number of troops to protect the base camp and vehicles. The maneuver worked: they countered the Taliban flanking movement, and destroyed the Taliban force trying to cross the dry riverbed. More close air support came into play as the JFACC spread the word that an A-Team was in heavy contact.

SFC Magallanes and Captain Amerine moved up the middle, as SFC Kennedy, SSG McGirr, and McElhiney went up the side to cover the bridge. Magallanes and Amerine were taking fire from the flank. There were ruins on the eastern side of the bridge; on the western side were guerrillas. Magallanes and Amerine were quickly pinned down. Kennedy and his group had to pull back and go for more ammo and a Russian 82mm mortar. Mortar rounds would start upping the stakes for the al-Qaida that had Amerine and Magallanes trapped.

As McGirr, Kennedy, and McElhiney attempted to rescue Amerine and Magallanes, an enemy 7.62mm round hit McGirr, momentarily knocking him off balance. SSG Wes McGirr was the junior commo man on the team. The terrorist's bullet ripped through soft tissue, spraying blood out of his back as it exited his shoulder.

Struggling to get back on his feet, McGirr screamed out, "I'm hit, I'm hit!" and kept shooting until the medics got there. The SF medics quickly arrived and got started working on McGirr, and the team called for a medevac. McGirr refused to leave; he wanted to stay in the battle. Everyone agreed it was too dangerous to move him out for medical treatment. He would remain in the fight until the next day.

Three times the Taliban tried to flank the dominant terrain, and three times they were rejected with heavy losses. Finally, night fell and so did the volume of enemy fire. The Taliban were running out of steam, and their counterattacks had repeatedly failed. Smart bombs were now pounding the enemy's forward and rear positions, and they had almost certainly lost the battle. Still, the AQ could launch an offensive at night. Hamid Karzai and Dave Fox decided to give up their gains of the day and get better prepared to assault across the bridge in the morning. The team pulled back to "the Alamo," the name for their rear camp. They had lost two miles of ground, but they would take it back the following day.

One thing was clear about Captain Amerine's actions on the night of December 3: "He *led* that night, out front, under fire. He's the real thing . . . ," said one team member. And that was the way it always was with TEXAS 12—they were always up front, and their team leader was always with them.

The next day's thrust across the bridge was uneventful; the Taliban and AQ had not even tried to occupy the bridge during the night. Unknown to RAMBO, the Taliban was through. Harassing fire had continued through the night, but it was merely to cover the majority of the enemy forces' withdrawal. The Taliban and their AQ cohorts had decided to run and were thinning their lines accordingly. The door to Kandahar was now wide open.

Blue-on-Blue Snafu

Karzai's forces and those of Sharzai from the south began to press closer and closer to Kandahar. Fox's men and Karzai were in static positions about twenty miles short of the city. They had set up a command-and-control area to plan the Kandahar assault.

TEXAS 12 was still sending in air strikes on Taliban positions about one thousand meters to their front. They weren't under attack and they weren't under fire. But they were close to the targets.

The resupply choppers arrived during the early morning darkness. They also brought the mail for the team with them. The team members, who had gone to sleep at 0400 (4 A.M.), were up now, at 0700 (7 A.M.). MSG Davis had found his box of Rice Krispies Treats waiting for him.

As the sun rose that morning, TEXAS 12 had a better chance of seeing the cave entrance positions of the enemy forces. At one point they could see four Taliban soldiers entering a cave opening in the side of a hill. They confirmed they were enemy troops with the team's *mujahadeen* "sergeant major," Madi Ghul, and called in CAS.

The Air Force tactical air control officer on Fox's staff had just arrived in-country with Major Don Bolduc and a headquarters element. They had come in by chopper less than a week before. He called for a smart munition to hit a location around a thousand meters to the command post's front. The B-52 bombardier above asked for re-verification of the grid coordinates. That should have been a wake-up call for the Air Force controller and the officer with him.

TEXAS 12 had gotten their new GPS and sat phones when they were in isolation. But some teams didn't get them until they were already in battle. It was a major screw-up, and it meant that some Green Berets were going to be calling in air strikes without ever having used the equipment before. As SFC Mike McElhiney pointed out, "They tried to practice as much as possible," but there was one problem. If you went from your "lat long," latitude longitude, readout for the target, then to your elevation, it reset the first readout to your location, not the enemies'. When you went back to "lat long," you were reading your own position, not the enemies'. You had almost a dozen steps to go from a grid coordinate to elevation. TEXAS 12 had theirs down pat, but the new guys would have a problem, and these were the most important pieces of gear they had.

"Hey, you guys just called that grid coordinate in twenty minutes ago as friendly, you sure you want it there?" the Air Force bomber asked the new combat controller.

"We've got Taliban close, just drop it" came the word back.

As the GB-31 two-thousand-pound high-explosive bomb fell through the air, Master Sergeant Jefferson Donald "J. D." Davis, the thirty-nine-year-old team sergeant who had led their valiant stand at Tarin Kowt, was at ground zero. He and SSG Brad Fowers had just loaded their trucks with the resupplies, and he was passing out Rice Krispies Treats as the air strikes were hitting. He told his wife, Mi, before leaving the States: "I have waited my whole life for this. If I die in the fight, it will have been worth it."

Close by was thirty-two-year-old Sergeant First Class Dan Petithory, the team's most jovial member, famous for having once been seen wearing a coconut bra, grass skirt, and flowers in his hair during a kayak race. "Dan-o" had laid the Taliban out like cordwood at the battle of Tarin Kowt. Next to him was Staff Sergeant Brian "Cody" Prosser, from California, a twenty-eight-year-old regular Mr. Fix-it with a garage full of tools for every imaginable purpose. A signal-intelligence specialist, Prosser had been listening in on the Taliban frequencies and reporting his findings to Fox.

Fox was only a short distance from where the satellite-guided bomb would impact. As it arced toward its target, he bent over to reach down to his rucksack. He was facing toward the impact point. On a small foundation of concrete, directly in front of him, sat three *muj* warriors. Their bodies were an extension of the concrete wall that would save his life.

As the bomb closed, Hamid Karzai, already secretly acknowledged as the best hope to be the chairman of an interim government for a new Afghanistan, unknowingly sat down into what would be the bomb's busting radius. He was meeting tribal leaders, and had just been joined by "Greg," a CIA special operator nicknamed "Bush" by the Afghans, because they thought he looked like President Bush. Karzai was mapping out his plan to assault Kandahar and discussing the possibility of surrender with several of his aides, the Green Berets, and Hajji Abdul Rahim, a Karzai ally.

The huge bomb plummeted toward impact as the men at ground zero went about planning assaults and counter-assaults. Captain Amerine, Sergeant First Class Ronnie Raikes, Sergeant First Class McElhiney, and Staff Sergeant Fowers had no idea of the devastation that was about to befall them.

The bomb was incorrectly programmed with Fox's position.

McElhiney first saw the two-thousand-pound bomb flash about ten feet off the ground. He didn't have time to look for cover. He didn't have time for anything. He remembered nothing else after he was thrown through the air and knocked out by the concussion of the blast. The bottom of his right arm was torn half off as he was smashed into the desert sand. His left arm was mangled.

Karzai's three *mujahadeen* in front of Fox were literally blown apart. Fox was thrown backward, instantly knocked out from concussion. He would awaken with half of a man's body lying on top of him.

Men were bleeding from the eyes and ears. Body parts were strewn everywhere, and no one knew how many were dead yet. Somebody's voice came over the radio, screaming for medics and medevacs: "We've got a fucking disaster here!" That pretty much summed it up.

Jefferson Davis was gone—that was known almost immediately.

"Bush" had instinctively jumped onto Karzai and tried to shield him with his body. This was one CIA operator who knew what it meant to risk one's life for another.

As the dust and debris settled, Karzai was moved outside immediately in case it was an al-Qaida attack and they knew where he was. Green Berets quickly pulled up a vehicle to stand by to evacuate Karzai. Five minutes later, standing in a sea of blood and destruction, Karzai got a call on his sat phone. His good friend Lyse Doucet from the BBC wanted to tell him that the BBC had just gotten news that he had been chosen as chairman of the new Afghan government in Kabul. Five minutes after that, Taliban Commander Mullah Naqub called him to say they were ready to deliver the surrender of Kandahar.

Karzai listened quietly to the phone calls, surprised by the news, but shocked by the devastation and bodies surrounding him: they were his *muj,* his American friends, and his supporters. Traumatized, Karzai still maintained his composure.

At TASK FORCE DAGGER headquarters in K2, Colonel Mulholland rushed to take the handset in the communications center. The voice on the other end was heavy, reporting the facts as best they could be determined during the chaos on the ground.

Word spread quickly at K2. Colonel Mulholland looked across the interior of the tent and saw his entire staff awaiting instructions. The screams in the background of the radio transmissions made calm discussion mandatory to reassure the men on the ground.

Mulholland sent back his simple reply, "Roger, help is on the way," as he turned to give instructions to his staff.

TF DAGGER worked from all angles to amass medical assistance and to arrange helicopter medevacs for the injured. At the same time, they never lost sight of tactical necessity. With more than half the team on the ground dead or injured, they immediately launched more Green Berets to assume effective combat command and to continue the fight toward Kandahar.

A deputy for Lieutenant General P. T. Mikolashek called TASK FORCE DAGGER in the middle of the medevac. "I realize you are up to your necks in working out the ground truth and taking care of your men, but we need not lose sight of continuing the mission," the deputy explained. The battle was still ongoing.

TASK FORCE DAGGER thanked the deputy for the advice, and informed him that a replacement B-Team, 570 (Company Headquarters), and a replacement A-Team, 573, had already been mobilized virtually without notice and put on the medevac birds. Now called PYTHON 33 and PYTHON 36, the two new A-Teams were en route to pick up the fight where the wounded had left off.

TASK FORCE DAGGER initially called the closest air

assets, the Marine helicopters just south of Kandahar. The USMC refused to put birds in the air to help. It would take more than five hours before help began to arrive. Some of the wounded would lie on the ground for over six hours as they waited to be extracted.

Since the first report was that RAMBO was under enemy attack (a logical conclusion since the enemy had Soviet-era artillery), the Marines reportedly didn't want to risk their aircraft without confirmed reports of the situation on the ground. Journalists immediately started calling Fort Bragg in hot pursuit of the story, but were told not to move quickly because hard facts in such cases were difficult to ascertain.

A hard-charging Special Forces command sergeant major boarded a chopper back at the FOB and told them to fly. Nobody wanted to jump off half cocked, but they headed to Kandahar airfield anyway. Nobody was going to say no to a pissed off Green Beret command sergeant major. When they landed at Kandahar Airfield they again asked the Marines to fly in with them and medevac the wounded Green Berets. The USMC pilots were willing. "Hell, the pilots were already in their seats ready to go," one witness recalls. However, the Marine Corps' commandant on the airfield ordered them to stand down.

Some people claim the USMC's failure to respond was because they didn't have any aircraft on strip alert, ready to launch at a moment's notice, even though they were in a combat zone. The real reason was probably that the commandant wasn't going to risk losing Marine choppers in a daylight rescue into enemy territory in the middle of a firefight.

The reason didn't matter to TASK FORCE DAGGER. The answer was a negative. And that was not acceptable. TF DAGGER had wounded men and someone had to get there. The call was immediately switched to a group of 160th SOAR MH-53J Special Operations helicopters in Pakistan.

Lieutenant Colonel Steve Hadley had once been a member of the NightStalkers, before deciding to go to medical school to become a doctor. Rejoining the Army, Hadley had been headed for a specialty he didn't warm to, so he branch-transferred to the U.S. Air Force, where he could treat troops, which was his passion. Hadley grabbed his medic bag as the MH-53Js took off; his old Army mates needed his help. In fact, Hadley knew most of the guys on the team prior to their insertion. He knew he was going to be in a lot of "trouble with the staff pukes" for going, but go he did. Along with him were the two Special Forces PYTHON teams abruptly charged to take over the fighting.

The special ops "53s" launched immediately. Flying in broad daylight, they totally ignored the risk of being exposed to ground fire and air defense weapons. Special operators were down and all rules were off.

The word had gone out that TEXAS 12 was hit hard and Green Berets were dead and wounded. Delta Force hauled operators' ass to the location. Even though there weren't many of them, D-boys were coming in from every direction, abandoning missions and plans, because their brothers were hit.

As Delta medics swarmed the scene, they started barking instructions to their teammates. In crisis, SF medics are trained to take charge, ignoring rank and any other impediments to treatment for the fallen. The operators that weren't medic qualified fell in like new recruits, administering IVs and applying tourniquets and pressure dressings. Many of the men, even the otherwise uninjured, were either deaf or had severely impaired hearing from the concussion. They were screaming at the top of their lungs to try and pass instructions to each other. That first hour, called the "golden hour," was the most important; in those critical sixty minutes the medics had to stabilize and triage the wounded to reduce permanent injuries and fatalities.

SAS operators assigned to TF 11 immediately headed for scene. They set up perimeter reaction points in case of a Taliban attack on the area, and sent in several medics to assist.

Petithory and Prosser were already dead, but Special Forces and Delta medics saved many lives and limbs that day.

The most critically injured survivors were Sergeant First Class Magallanes with severe trauma to the head, and Sergeant First Class McElhiney, who had suffered the traumatic loss of one arm and severe injuries to his other.

As the 160th choppers set down, Hadley hit the ground and ran toward the men, taking command of the entire area. He was the most qualified of all those on the ground. Randy, one of the medics from PYTHON 33, was already doing whatever he could to help get the situation under control. Hadley ran from medic to medic, analyzing their decision making, and personally treating those who needed his attention. The most severely injured were triaged and loaded on the birds first.

Hamid Karzai was slightly wounded in the face by shrapnel. Calls flowed in from the United States laden with concern. Repetitive reports on his condition assuaged rumors that the United States had lost a key ally. They had not. Karzai was, and would remain, a great admirer of the U.S. Special Forces, and a great friend to America.

The tragedy was that Prosser, Davis, and Petithory were KIA, only forty-eight hours before they would have seen the fall of Kandahar.

Major Don Bolduc and a headquarters element had come in six days before. Major Bolduc, slightly wounded, would have been standing next to Fox had it not been for some reason still unknown. What *was* known was that while the headquarters personnel had used their day trip to qualify for CIBs and medals, someone had later recommended downgrading TEXAS 12's Silver Star decorations for heroism to Bronze Stars—a recommendation that was apparently approved by a general officer. Even worse, while Green Beret sergeants in the thick of battle, dying or wounded, were getting their medals downgraded to Bronze Stars, conventional Army officers from the 10th Mountain Division were getting Silver Stars without ever getting shot at.

The End of the Taliban

The vise formed around Kandahar, by Karzai on the north side and Sharzai on the south side, had squeezed Mullah Mohammed Omar to the breaking point. It was only a matter of time before he lost his terrorist empire. Scouts penetrated the city and reported that the Taliban were pulling out. His terrorist government had completely collapsed by December 9, 2001, leaving the city open for occupation by Karzai's and Sharzai's forces.

Sharzai invited TEXAS 17 to enter the city with his troops. Karzai's and RAMBO's troops entered from the north. Deliriously happy crowds welcomed the liberators.

Shortly before the complete takeover, Mullah Mohammed Omar fled on a motorcycle disguised as a common man. Northern Alliance intelligence also told their special advisor that between December 6 and December 9, thousands of al-Qaida and Taliban had escaped into the mountains and across the border. Omar had escaped, but the Taliban were through. And Special Forces would continue to hunt him and bin Laden.

Kandahar was still teeming with al-Qaida and Taliban terrorists, but by now it was clear from radio intercepts and satellite reconnaissance that bin Laden had not been with Omar. Bin Laden had clearly run to the east, not to the southern region of Kandahar, but toward Tora Bora in the north. As regions of Afghanistan were liberated by TF DAGGER and occupied by the Northern Alliance, the result was a severe reduction in geographical hiding places for bin Laden and his top aides. TASK FORCE 11 operators in Kandahar would focus on Omar and TF 11 would move additional assets up to Jalalabad to meet the TF DAGGER teams there and focus on pinpointing bin Laden. The AQ's sanctuary was severely narrowing: they were running out of places to hide and the places that were left were rugged, inhospitable, and dangerous. The task was becoming more focused, but more complicated.

Petithory's Privy

Busy as they were, the Green Berets near Kandahar did not forget their lost comrades. Like all Special Forces soldiers, Sergeant First Class Daniel Petithory had been a fan of John Wayne and the movie *The Green Berets,* especially loving the scene where a field latrine was named for a fallen Special Forces' soldier. Petithory, who wore Elvis-style glasses when he made parachute jumps, could quote every single line from the John Wayne movie.

In the 1960s, Sergeant Provo was killed during enemy action in a particularly heated battle with the Viet Cong. Before he died, Provo had told his teammates his last request. He had seen the names of fallen SF soldiers on the roads and buildings at Fort Bragg, and it always impressed him. Provo wanted something named after him where everyone would have to go, and he wanted it to have a ring to it.

Provo got his wish. His team erected a beautiful latrine at the 5th Group headquarters in Vietnam and named it "Provo's Privy."

About forty years later, Dan Petithory was killed in Afghanistan. His team erected a wooden latrine at Kandahar airfield, and covered it for privacy with a captured Taliban parachute of Russian origin. Like many of the events in Afghanistan, life imitated art, and Afghanistan often imitated Vietnam.

It was named "Petithory's Privy."

"Peace"

On December 13, 2001, church bells rang out over the town of Cheshire, Massachusetts.

Hundreds who had known the Petithory family attended the funeral. Also present were the bishop of Springfield, Senators Ted Kennedy and John Kerry, Governor Jane Swift, Major General Geoff Lambert, Lieutenant General Doug Brown, and a sea of Green Berets from across the nation.

Senator Kerry had been in Vietnam before becoming a key leader of Vietnam Veterans Against the War. The senator began speaking:

It is my extraordinary privilege to share a few words with you about Sergeant Petithory. . . .

We will never forget: Dan was a warrior on our behalf. Twice he went to war so we can live our lives in security and freedom. When the terrorists brought the frontlines here to America, Sergeant Petithory took the battle back to them in Afghanistan—just as he had taken it to Saddam Hussein in the Gulf War a decade ago. . . .

For his ultimate sacrifice in the performance of duty, Sergeant Petithory is to be awarded the Silver Star and the Purple Heart—badges of distinction from a grateful nation. But following his courageous example, the duty is now left to us to spare no sacrifice to finish the mission for which Dan earned our eternal respect, gratitude—and awe.

His unit commander, Captain Jason Amerine, who was wounded at the same time, said we should remember not how Dan and his brothers in arms died, but what they did beforehand. What an extraordinary story of courage, initiative, and resolve: a member of an eleven-man team, the elite of the American fighting forces, dropped into a valley deep inside enemy territory in Central Afghanistan, a part of the world they said looked like the "back side of the moon."

In the darkness in those initial tense moments, they came face-to-face with Hamid Karzai, then the leader of a committed band of freedom fighters taking on the Taliban, and now—thanks to Dan and his fellow soldiers—about to become the leader of a free Afghanistan. Together they became one, a fighting force with a common mission. For six weeks the men in this small band of brothers depended on each other for life and death—calling in air strikes, repelling Taliban counterattacks, organizing the opposition—carrying on their shoulders the hopes of all who were outraged by the acts of September 11. And in that far off place, where danger was everywhere, Dan excelled on behalf of this nation—proving as his fellow soldiers said of him, that he was among the best America had to offer. On several occasions Dan directed the air attacks that turned the tide of battle. Captain Amerine said of him: "It's an art. And the guy I had was the best I've ever seen. . . ."

President Harry Truman . . . fifty years ago honored the Greatest Generation and said of America: "We are not a warlike nation. We do not go to war for gain or for territory; we go to war for principles, and we produce young men like these."

Once again, our peaceful nation is at war. We did not seek this war, but we will win it for a principle that is timeless and values that shall forever define the greatness of yet another generation of citizen soldiers. And even in our grief, we can say with pride, and conviction, this is America—the nation we love because it produces and keeps faith with men like Dan Petithory. God bless you, Dan, and I think he would want us to say, "God bless the United States of America."

Near the end of the Mass, Senator Ted Kennedy turned and robustly shook the generals' hands, saying, "Peace."

The Green Berets appreciated Kerry's speech, but they didn't appreciate his recent stand against their Montagnard allies from Vietnam. They silently wondered if the senator would someday turn on their new Northern Alliance allies.

The solemn procession left the church and headed for Cheshire's beautiful cemetery, nested in the rolling western Massachusetts hills. The grade-school children in the town lined the streets holding American flags. Some had their hands on their hearts, while others saluted.

In the procession, Chief Warrant Officer 5 Larry Plesser, with over thirty years of service, shed tears. Plesser had lived a hard-knock life, and understood the pain of the Afghans. He recalled the days of his youth, when he would collect Coke bottles on the roadsides, turning them in to a neighborhood woman who gave him slices of boiled ham in return for the empties. Still, he had persevered, and eventually became the highest-ranking warrant officer in the history of Special Forces.

After the presentation of Petithory's Silver Star and Purple Heart, those assembled departed. Crowds of mourners had covered the hills in small groups, including members of American Veterans, the Veterans of Foreign Wars, the American Legion, the Special Forces Association, and the Order of the Purple Heart. Proudly present were numerous NYPD officers and a contingent of New York firefighters, many of whom were survivors of Ground Zero.

Thirty minutes after the ceremony, Danny's A-Team and Danny's father, Louis, and brother, Michael, were all that remained. They opened a bottle of Wild Turkey 101, Danny's favorite. Shot glasses were passed around. They downed the whisky in the bitter wind, as the Green Berets told Dan's father how much they would miss his son, how brave he was, and how much they loved him.

One of the soldiers toasted him with a stanza from "In Flanders Fields" by Lieutenant Colonel John McCrae of the Canadian Army, written during World War I:

> *We are the Dead. Short days ago*
> *We lived, felt dawn, saw sunset glow,*
> *Loved, and were loved, and now we lie*
> *In Flanders Fields . . .*

The A-Team put the remainder of the whisky bottle on Petithory's casket, and set his shot glass beside it. A 5th Special Forces Group coin was placed alongside. Each of the men took a handful of dirt and covered the casket as a final farewell.

Together, they slowly turned and walked away.

Elizabethton, Tennessee

Master Sergeant Jefferson Donald Davis was buried in Eliza-
bethton, Tennessee. The day after his death, his daughter
Cristina sent a letter via e-mail to her friend, the daughter of
Sergeant First Class Randall Leblanc:

December 6, 2001
10:40 PM

On December 5th my father, Master Sgt. Jefferson Donald Davis, died in Afghanistan along with 2 other men, Sgt.
1st Class Daniel Henry Petithory, 32, of Massachusetts,
and Staff Sgt. Brian Cody Prosser, 28, of California. He died
doing something he was proud of and loved doing. While
all of his men were together a 2,000-pound satellite-guided
bomb from a US B-52 missed its target north of Kandahar,
killing 3 men and wounding 20 other U.S. soldiers.

My father was a great man, and I love and am proud of
what he did. He died defending the U.S. He died defending
YOU. I went to school one morning with a mother, father,
and a brother, but when I came home, I didn't have a father.
There are NO words to express how I feel right now. Sadness and anger mostly fill my mind but I am also the proud-
est daughter in the world. . . . God could have never given
me a better father. When you read this go to your mom and
dad . . . give them a hug . . . tell them you love them because you don't know the next time you will see them. I
just want everyone to know how proud of my dad I am.

Master Sgt. Jefferson Donald Davis
October 22, 1962–December 5, 2001

Sincerely,
Cristina Davis

Hundreds of Elizabethton citizens attended the funeral
at Master Sergeant Davis' high school. Shortly before, the
funeral director spotted a large group of Green Berets clus-
tered together in the cafeteria of the high school. The funeral

director went back to see if something was wrong. The men were standing around a small Vietnam memorial wall. A map of Vietnam was highlighted where each of Elizabethton's finest had fallen, with a picture of each alumnus killed in the war.

There was nothing amiss; the men had simply never seen such a thing.

Arlington National Cemetery

"Cody" Prosser was being buried at Arlington National Cemetery, just where he would have wanted. His beautiful wife, Shawna, was seated near the "old guard" Army chaplain, from the 3rd Infantry, who was presiding over the ceremony.

Prosser was from a small town in the mountains of Los Padres National Park in California. The family had already held a memorial service there. With a population of 8,400, the entire community of Fraizer Park had been affected.

To friends who knew him in high school, it was inevitable that Cody would grow up to be a war hero. Now, he was being buried as one, with the vice chief of staff of the Army, General John Keane, in attendance. Keane oversaw the shadowy U.S. Army Counter-Terrorism Task Force in New York City. He was a broad-shouldered, towering soldier who believed in unconventional warfare and Special Forces soldiers quite possibly more than any other general on active duty. Keane made it a point to personally attend the funerals of every Green Beret killed, if possible. He constantly promoted the guerrilla warfare strategy of the Green Berets in Afghanistan, and directed his PAOs (public affairs officers) like Major Kirk Harrington in New York City, to bring the story of the Green Berets to the American people and to help them understand both combat and humanitarian aspects of their missions. Unlike the PAOs at Fort Bragg, Harrington's office had a unique SOP; it was called, always tell the truth, don't play petty politics, and understand that the Americans might not have a right to know the classified details of secret missions, but they do have a right to know something.

Old warhorses were there too, and hidden among them were men in civilian suits. The Agency, invisible, but there in strength, was present to pay its respects as well.

As the burial was taking place, one of the Green Berets told Command Sergeant Major Ames to "look up." Cody was being buried directly in line with and in full view of the Pentagon. Ames shook his head and smiled. Straight ahead was the exact point where the terrorists had hit the building. For eternity, Cody would be standing vigil over where it all began on September 11, 2001.

In the cold, several men were quietly observing from the edge of the street, a few yards away. They were wrapped in white blankets. Saying good-bye were McElhiney, Yoshi, and Raikes; their wheelchairs were being pushed by Judy McElhiney and the nurses of Walter Reed Army Medical Center.

CHAPTER 20

Tora Bora

"I don't get up in the morning and ask myself where he is. I am interested in the problem of terrorists and terrorist networks and countries that harbor them all across the globe. And if he were gone tomorrow, the al-Qaida network would continue functioning essentially as it does today. He is certainly a problem; he is not the problem."

—DONALD RUMSFELD,
Department of Defense briefing,
October 11, 2001

"What is my program? You mean my goal? I want bin Laden's head in a burlap bag on Rumsfeld's desk. If I can't have that, then I'll settle for every al-Qaida terrorist dead."

—American advisor to the director
of the Afghan CIA, December 2001

The Chase

Tora Bora, Afghanistan

At the same time Kandahar was encircled and about to fall, things were heating up just north in Tora Bora. While TEXAS 12 were burying their three fallen men, the Green Berets were burying al-Qaida in the caves of Tora Bora.

Special Operations Forces were hot to catch fleeing AQ and Taliban leaders. Osama bin Laden was, of course, at the top of the list. Armed with their pre-prepared black (highest priority) and gray (secondary priority) kill lists, the "shooters" were

PYTHON/COBRA and Hazrat Ali

airfields
start of infiltration
captured city

TURKMENI

IRAN

BAD
Qal

Herat

HERAT

Shindand

FARAH

Farah

L

HE

Zaranj

NIMRUZ

IRAN

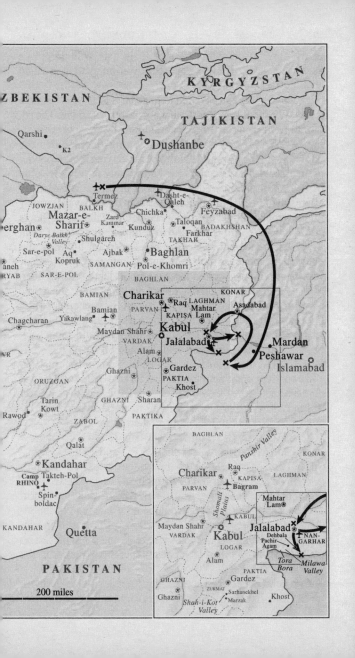

ready. Special operators carried their lists with large X's across the faces of key leaders already eliminated or in allied custody.

Originally, operators could engage targets at will. At some point after the fall of Kabul, this apparently changed. The regional command staff and General Franks were now attempting to exercise more control and trying to micromanage operators on the ground, and this was delaying and impeding their success. The Green Berets had already proven the value of being left unhindered and without directive: it had, after all, resulted in the fall of Kabul less than thirty days after they hit the ground. Some operators claimed that the staff officers at K2 and at Central Command in Tampa feared a lone Green Beret buck sergeant whacking bin Laden on his own and denying the top brass their moment of shining glory. The conventional military wanted the capture or death of bin Laden to be a "team effort," and that meant the "big team": the Army, Navy, Air Force, and Marines. It meant that generals sitting thousands of miles away had to be part of the act. Anything less would be unacceptable. This mentality would come back to haunt America, just as it had doomed OPERATION EAGLE CLAW, the Delta Force rescue mission in Iran in 1980 and countless other operations. To TF DAGGER and TF 11 it mattered not—they would drive on in their relentless pursuit of bin Laden and al-Qaida, hoping to work around their increasing restraints and accomplish their mission.

The U.S. Army's Counter-Terrorism Task Force in New York City had arranged for the NYPD and FDNY to give Special Forces troops in Afghanistan their department shoulder patches, five thousand of them, many of which were embroidered with the name of a fallen American at the World Trade Center. The patches would send a message to the al-Qaida. As in Vietnam, they were left as calling cards in suspected al-Qaida hideouts and safe areas, and often placed on the bodies of AQ killed by Special Operations Forces in the middle of the night.

Everyone expected a spectacular hunt as al-Qaida dug in for the long haul. Unfortunately, the rapid roll-up and retreat of the Taliban had created such chaotic conditions that no clear intelligence picture was developing. The men of Special Forces were doing all they could to run down leads, but several realities were emerging. First of all, the AQ and Taliban had emptied the national treasury on the way out, and now had millions of U.S. dollars and Afghanis (the local currency) to spread around. SF was still dealing with a tough enemy, bankrolled with the money of bin Laden, and operating in ragtag territory with a now virtually unlimited budget.

The local populace was making less than $10 per month, and the terrorists were willing to pay them a hundred dollars a day to cooperate with refuge, food, and silence. It was difficult for American soldiers to win their hearts and minds. In the chaos, the highest bidder could easily buy the opposition commanders and clans, purchasing their loyalty or silence, which allowed the al-Qaida and Taliban to move freely in the region.

Second, the AQ and Taliban were fleeing and moving across their own turf, within their established networks, especially in the southeast, where they had always been strong. Human intelligence (HUMINT) from prisoners, turncoats, and walk-ins, while valuable, was slow in coming, and unlikely to help in the immediate pursuit. The lack of HUMINT was the single critical factor in the way. Northern Alliance Afghans knew that the AQ and Taliban could not be trusted, and everything had a price on it, even the smallest detail of information. More important, HUMINT could only be developed by small teams, or even one man, on the ground and deep inside the Afghan community, and the U.S. was not prepared to risk lives that boldly, nor was it ready to allow a single man to wade into such incredible danger. What was needed were individual men, or a man, with the Northern Alliance twenty-four hours a day. There was one such Green Beret operator, and his name was Jack. But he wasn't working for Rumsfeld or Tenet, although he was helping them as much as he could behind the scenes. The CIA was still relying more on Predator UAVs and satellites than people on the ground.

The Tora Bora showdown was escalating faster and with a wider scope than anyone initially expected. In the last days of November, intelligence from all sources indicated a massing of Taliban and AQ in the Tora Bora cave complex near Pakistan's border, approximately twenty-five miles southwest of Jalalabad. Unreliable human intelligence from many sources indicated that Osama bin Laden might be present, and there were "eyewitness reports" of a man well over six feet tall, and "in command." Another report stated that there was a "tall man in charge, with subordinates showing deference to him." These reports were somewhat backed up by National Security Agency (NSA) intelligence, gleaned from satellites and radio transmission intercepts.

When it finally looked as if bin Laden *was* in Tora Bora, indicated by additional NSA intelligence and ISA HUMINT, operations were too disjointed to react quickly enough. Everyone at the higher levels expected bin Laden would surface in Kandahar with Mullah Omar, and that's where the effort had been concentrated. Now it seemed the elusive quarry was in the impenetrable mountains of Tora Bora.

In Panama, Special Operations Forces had found how difficult it was to locate a single man. General Manuel Noriega, a cocaine addict and cruel egomaniac, was so incompetent that he had failed to build an effective evasion plan even though he knew the United States would eventually come after him. Even though Panama was openly transparent and a virtual U.S. intelligence playground, the Special Operations troops were lucky to have captured him. Noriega had made the critical mistake of holing up in the Vatican headquarters, and American forces already had that area encircled.

Everyone involved in the Panamanian operation sent a clear message to all forums: the President of the United States, the State Department, and the Department of Defense should never tout that the United States was going to mount a military operation against a single man. After the 1991 failure to kill Saddam Hussein in Iraq and capture Mohamed Farrah Aidid in Somalia in 1993, it was obvious that killing or capturing a single man was an almost impossible task for special ops. Over time, that message had taken hold in Washington, or at least everyone in Special Operations thought it had.

After September 11, President Bush repeatedly relayed to the American public that the War on Terror was an attack on organizations, on funding, on leaders, and on the worldwide terrorist network's capability to attack America. Even so, bin Laden had caused such damage to the U.S., killed so many Americans, become such a figurehead of evil, that the administration could not resist the temptation to focus the gunfight on that single man in particular.

In spite of the fact that U.S. Special Operations Forces, down to the last man, were repeatedly told that the war was bigger than bin Laden, it was Osama himself who remained their primary target. And every single special operator wanted Osama bin Laden's head. Most of them wanted it mounted on a stick. Going into hot pursuit was the only logical course of action. The U.S., with luck, might catch key leaders, lots of intelligence materiel, or both. Any one of those things could lead to bin Laden.

The VOA, Violence of Action, against bin Laden that swelled in every operator as they reflected on the image of the Twin Towers collapsing was a powerful motivator. If caught, bin Laden would not survive. They would almost assuredly kill him even if the command said no.

Unannounced, teams were slamming into villages on their Special Operations MO-500 series Little Bird black helicopters, "turning over rocks," as the teams called it. It was dangerous work, but hopefully under one of the rocks would lay the "golden nugget," as one Special Forces sergeant commented. Intelligence nets were manned 24/7 and had "triggers" established to broadcast hot leads. In January a team from a Special Mission Unit swooped down on a village six miles west of Khost, executing a lightning-fast helicopter raid to snatch four men suspected of having close ties with Taliban Frontier Affairs Minister Jalaluddin Haqqani.

Tora Bora

Tangai, the mountains of Afghanistan. They cover vast regions of the country, and their rugged terrain and narrow passes have made parts of the country impenetrable by foreign invaders. The mountains that separate Afghanistan from Pakistan have also given safe haven to tribal bandits and nomadic smugglers for hundreds of years. Rising up into the sky, they are often capped with snow throughout the scorching summer. The narrow roads cut into the sides of Afghanistan's mountains for a thousand years under the hooves of pack animals are dangerous to even a camel train, much less a Toyota 4×4. Tora Bora is no different.

Used as a refugee camp for the *mujahadeen* during their *jihad* against the Soviets, Tora Bora is an expansive complex of caves that were used to hide equipment and people. Intelligence reports said that the caves were a veritable labyrinth, an underground fortress on par with Hitler's World War II underground complexes. Fox News and other networks gave extensive airtime to experts with drawings and diagrams predicting what American commandos might expect. They outlined elaborate sleeping quarters, mess halls ammunition dumps, state-of-the-art communications complexes, command-and-control quarters, ventilation and generator facilities, and fighting positions. The Russian and British experts all said it would be a monumental effort to penetrate the caves and rout their defenders. The Russians had not done it, and now bin Laden would flaunt his staying power at the American empire.

Intelligence reports flowed in as the foreign AQ and Taliban dug in for yet another "last stand." There were thousands of them, and the caves were thought to contain enough food, ammo, fuel, and supplies to make it through several winters.

Green Berets were sent to the site to scope out the situation. There were three separate anti-Taliban Afghan forces that had to be dealt with, aligned with, satisfied, and organized. Tora Bora could not be taken down without a strong alliance with at least one of them. In the back of all three groups' minds was the fact that they would be competing for the funding they hoped the American SF teams would bring to outfit their *muj*.

The groups were led by Commander Mohammed Zaman Ghun Shareef, Commander Hajji Zahir, and Commander Hazrat Ali. Each of their forces roamed freely in the Jalalabad area, and carved out their own power bases and areas of operations. Hazrat Ali was the warlord of choice. He was a moderate, and loyal to the Northern Alliance, and the Northern Alliance had made him the de facto chief of security in the area. He had fought the Taliban for years, and he seemed to be, and would prove to be, the most loyal of the bunch. When the others had left the country years before, Ali had stayed and fought alongside Massoud.

Special Forces agreed to outfit the groups for their mission, and to cut off escape routes from the caves and to help in the assault itself. The incredibly tough terrain and the hidden passes in the Tora Bora area meant that escape was likely. The peaks above the Milawa Valley held hidden trails for a seventeen-hour walk to Pakistan, where radical Muslim groups of all stripes would offer refuge and support.

There was another "commander" also to be dealt with, Hajji Qadir, who became the governor of Jalalabad as soon as the city fell. Without many soldiers, Qadir still had political savvy and the ear of the Pashtun populace.

A campaign was going to be difficult to put together. However, the U.S. Special Operations Command decided they had to go ahead based on what little information they had to develop potentially hot leads that might prove invaluable. The fight began in earnest with the heavy bombing of some of the more than thirty known caves on November 30, 2001.

All of the factions wanted to be part of the battle, and all would compete for power, territory, and victory. The assembled tribal elements mounted a three-pronged attack. They were supported by virtually unlimited fire support, which included "cave penetrator" USAF smart bombs, and laser-guided bombs that could fly into cave openings, killing or wounding anyone hiding deep inside with the concussion.

The bombs used included the U.S. Air Force's BLU-82, a fifteen-thousand-pound "daisy cutter" from the Vietnam era so powerful it could instantly make a landing zone for a helicopter in triple-canopy jungle. The concussion from the BLU-82 was so momentous that it could kill people over a hundred meters away, inside an underground maze teeming with twists and turns.

From behind, Special Forces operators and a local warlord named Musa inserted via helicopter and attempted to seal the multitude of egress routes, backed by the Pakistan Army as it deployed to protect its border from escaping AQ terrorists. The Pakistanis had assured that they would help seal the border. They did not, not in the beginning, and certainly not in the end. The snow that fell on the mountain passes in mid-December did more to stop and slow down the enemy that chose to escape than the Pakistanis ever would. According to the NA's American special advisor, the Pakistani ISI (Inter-Service Intelligence agency) wanted, and needed, to keep Afghanistan off balance and in turmoil.

Meanwhile, tribal forces faced a determined al-Qaida that was running out of options. If the AQ were ever were going to make a last stand, this might be the best place for it. By December 10, a ridgeline was under control as well as a small valley near the village of Milawa, where some storage caves were located. Special ops snipers in the area also killed four AQ fighters.

The same day, rumors swirled that Osama bin Laden had escaped. In fact, an intermediary long on al-Qaida's payroll, named Mirajuddin, was secretly negotiating with the *muj* to turn in bin Laden. He was paid five thousand U.S. dollars to provide the necessary information; then he ran off with the cash. In subsequent fighting against the coalition forces, twenty members of his extended family were killed in the bombing of Pachir Agam.

Although this was an unfortunate coincidence, it had a side

effect now in the minds of would-be ripoff artists: they now knew it didn't pay to double-cross the Green Berets.

Progress on taking the tough terrain was slow, but was made nevertheless. Early estimates of dead AQ were up to six hundred, later cut in half. Bomb damage assessment on collapsed caves was difficult and pure speculation on actual numbers killed, but firm numbers could be derived by confirmed sniper kills. Finally, on the night of the eleventh, there was an attempt to surrender, delivered over the radio, from the AQ. Mohammed Zaman Ghun Shareef, supposedly speaking for the Northern Alliance, negotiated a cease-fire for 8 A.M. on December 12.

However, there were conditions. The AQ and Taliban surrender would be to UN personnel. The other NA commanders knew conditional surrenders were not what the Americans, who were footing the bill, wanted. At the same time, the AQ were pleading with the Northern Alliance to withdraw and let them fight the Americans. They told the NA that they did not want to fight and kill other Muslims, and continually announced that their war was not with the Afghans, it was with the American infidel.

The U.S. promptly announced no surrender would be considered. Hazrat Ali and the Northern Alliance immediately announced that they would not be accepting any surrender either, and privately said that foreign terrorists could have their original wish, to visit with Allah personally. Hazrat Ali also insisted that his personal condition of any surrender would be the capture of Osama bin Laden alive. Ali and the NA wanted no doubt that they were aligned with the U.S.

The Agency rep met with Ali and explained America's desperation to find bin Laden. Was bin Laden there? Did Ali have any spies inside al-Qaida, and did he have any prisoners who might cooperate? All of these were pressing questions. All of the answers were typical Afghan. "All things are possible if Allah wishes" was the response. Rob called his superiors at Langley and asked for clarification on the $25 million reward for bin Laden—could it be given to an Afghan commander? He was quickly advised of the obvious: it could be given to a chimpanzee if he caught or killed bin Laden. The reward money had already become a factor: Each of the three main Afghan commanders was vying for the good graces of TF DAGGER and the Agency, all of the subcommanders were looking for ways to collect without their commanders knowing, and all of the soldiers knew that even if they had bin Laden in the back of their Toyota tied up in barbed wire, it would not matter—they would never see one dime of the money because it would all go to big commanders and politicians. In one way it was even worse: Afghans had virtually no understanding of what $25 million meant. Exactly how many donkeys, camels, or Toyota Land Cruisers did that add up to? That was the way Afghans counted wealth and power—by livestock, Land Cruisers, and the number of soldiers you could feed. Jack tried to explain to the Agency that they should offer to outfit a commander's army, or permanently feed and clothe his troops—it took only $15,000 per month to feed a thousand soldiers. Rice meant more than pie-in-the-sky promises of $25 million.

Immediately after 8 A.M. the American forces responded with more B-52 smart bombs at the mouths of the remaining caves occupied by the al-Qaida faithful. The Green Berets continued to call in fire and shift from vantage point to vantage point as the Afghani lines slowly progressed up the valley. Around 10 A.M. another fifteen-thousand-pound BLU-82 was dropped near the mouth of several more cave entrances in close proximity. A huge cloud of dust and smoke covered the valley.

The AQ were now pulling out, retreating and leaving their areas littered with equipment, including clothes, bedrolls, ammunition, documents, and even computers. Fleeing toward the frozen mountaintops, they could carry only the gear necessary for survival. They found themselves running straight into the 22 SAS Regiment's four-man SR teams and Delta operators placed on the eastern slopes facing Pakistan.

By December 13, there were more than fifty special operators in the area, and many had begun the task of searching the caves for bodies, ammunition, heavy weapons, and intelligence materiel.

Commander Hazrat Ali was forty-five years old; his wavy thick hair sported a tan Massoud cap cocked to one side. His traditional black robe and off-white linen shirt were neat and always pressed, even in battle. He was a kind and gentle-speaking man, loved by his men, as evidenced by the hundreds of pictures of him that adorned their tanks, armored personnel carriers, and Toyotas. He boasted of having eight-thousand-plus troops, and although his force only numbered a little more than a few thousand, they were seasoned fighters, and had fought with him for many years.

During the Tora Bora campaign Ali lived on a small mountaintop between Tora Bora and Jalalabad. No one was allowed to visit, especially the press. Ali preferred to give his press interviews and briefings from the SpinGar Hotel in Jalalabad, where the hotel security staff was completely made up of his soldiers.

During the battle, Hazrat Ali never gave private interviews, with one exception, at the request of his American special advisor. He spoke eloquently, and made no bones about the fact that he wanted bin Laden dead or alive, preferably dead. All three local commanders agreed on that issue, and all three had been given a rather lucrative incentive by the U.S.: they had been offered a $25 million reward for bin Laden.

The U.S. tried a classic encirclement operation and frontal assault by Ali's forces. It would not be the first time that military planners forgot the lessons of Vietnam, World War II, and history.

General George S. Patton once stood on the plains of North Africa and told his aides that there was no such thing as a new tactic in war. Everything had already been done, tested by the Roman Legions, the Spartans, the Huns, or others. One should examine closely the history of a battle and make his plans accordingly. Old special operators argued that a "hammer and anvil" approach should be used, a classic counterguerrilla maneuver, which had been proven time and again by Hitler's forces during their operations against the Yugoslavian resistance in World War II.

But that was not to happen, and although there were successes at Tora Bora, the bulk of the al-Qaida would escape.

Some of the successes included the capture of prisoners in the top level of the AQ's fighting battalions. Even though they were more ground commanders than international-terrorist types, they knew much about al-Qaida. The problem would be getting them to talk. That problem would be compounded when the U.S. decided to take them out of NA custody and into U.S. custody. In the hands of the Northern Alliance they faced torture, brutality, life imprisonment, or violent death at the whim of the NA commanders. In U.S. custody they knew they were going to enter into a "civilized" imprisonment, with civil rights, food, and medical care that ensured their resistance would not be futile.

Night operations in Tora Bora became the order of the day. Unlike Vietnam, where the Viet Cong owned the night, this was the age of advanced technology, and as many foes had learned in the last two decades of conflict, the U.S. now owned the night, and the Special Forces basked in it. With long-range sniper rifles capable of reaching out eight hundred to one thousand yards, Barrett Light 50 sniper rifles sending their deadly .50-caliber projectiles even farther, and Litton night-vision scopes targeting anything that moved, the operators on the ground had open season when the sun fell.

More than sixty additional members of the British SAS had arrived in Tora Bora. Tony Blair, who had adamantly supported President Bush in the aftermath of the 9/11 attacks, was putting his money where his mouth was.

David Stirling had formed the British Special Air Service in World War II as a commando unit to operate in North Africa, Burma, and throughout the theaters.

Now the SAS was in Tora Bora, and they would work with the D-boys and the other Green Berets to eliminate the remaining AQ terrorists holed up in the mountains and caves.

SAS forces in Tora Bora now exceeded 110 men; they would work with the D-boys and the other Green Berets to eliminate the remaining AQ terrorists holed up in the mountains and caves. With two squadrons engaged, it was clearly the largest group of SAS commandos to ever engage in a single battle, since the 1971 assaults on the *adoo* in Dhofar, code-named OPERATION JAGUAR.

Delta and the SAS would work on surgical strikes and the assault of cave complexes, using their CQB (close quarter battle) skills to engage in room-to-room combat, only this time it would be cave to cave. They were also trained to engage terrorists at long ranges during hostage rescue operations, or CRW (counterrevolutionary warfare) ops, as the Brits referred to them. At night their snipers would engage the enemy in the high mountain passes, killing everything that walked or moved. Their primary target remained the violent interdiction of Osama bin Laden.

At least once the SAS were sure they had their sights on bin Laden. They believed they had him trapped in a small valley of Tora Bora. The plan was to hunt as they would hunt game animals in Africa. They would be in two groups; one would go in and push al-Qaida and bin Laden into a run. As if beating their drums in the Serengeti plains of Kenya, they would use their personal weapons and grenade launchers to flush the terrorists out. The second group would be the shooters at "the edge of the high grass." They would wait in the trap and kill everything that crossed their path.

Ready to work with their brothers in Delta Force, and delighted to have U.S. air support, they believed the plan would work, and they were ready to implement it. They knew there would be casualties, and that was an accepted risk. It would not be the first time that the SAS and the D-boys went into a hot location knowing they would likely die.

The SAS apparently never got the chance. The U.S. commanders in the rear were not ready to risk such casualties, nor were they prepared to release aircraft below twelve thousand feet. The dramatic rises and narrow valleys of the

Tora Bora mountains made high-altitude close air support difficult because of the steep angles of attack that would result. The last thing the command wanted was a downed fighter jet, and it was clear that al-Qaida had shoulder-fired surface-to-air missiles in Tora Bora. There were no attack helicopters or close air support planes like the A-10 Warthog in-country yet.

According to several U.S. and British special operators, while generals fretted about body bags and downed aircraft, bin Laden was escaping. There were three mottos at play: *Who Dares Wins,* the words of the winged dagger of the SAS; *Strength and Honor,* the credo by which TF DAGGER would operate; and *Speed, Surprise, and Violence of Action,* the modus operandi of Delta Force. All three mottos would be ignored by the generals, who were still emasculated by visions of Vietnam. It would not be the last time the men on the ground, prepared to win or die, were told to stand down.

This was completely alien to the Special Air Service. David Stirling had set up a unique command system from the very beginning, which had not only survived the sixty-year history of the SAS, but had prospered and improved. The Commander, SAS Group, which encompasses all three regiments, deals direct with cabinet ministers, and even the Prime Minister when necessary. The SAS carried a big stick with colonial thinking military officers; if a bureaucrat wanted to stand in the way, he had to consider the real possibility that the SAS command was going to ring up #10 Downing Street—American generals never had to worry about U.S. Special Forces calling the White House to intercede. To have an operation stall or bog down in bureaucracy, and lose momentum or the opportunity of success, was not only confusing, it was simply unacceptable to the Regiment.

One of the few things that did go right, at least most nights, was the practice of taking all anti-Taliban Afghan troops off the mountain prior to sunset. While the press rode on the fact that the Afghans only fought from nine to five, the SF, SAS, and Delta snipers in the Tora Bora Mountains had a "free kill zone." If it moved at night, they could kill it with impunity. The strategy worked well, and each morning the proof of the pudding was in the bodies of dead or wounded AQ terrorists thrown in the back of pickup trucks by the Northern Alliance and brought back to Jalalabad for identification and "disposal."

As Special Operations troops closed in, one thing became clear: the "elaborate cave complexes" everyone had been talking about just didn't exist. Most of the caves were no more than improved fighting positions, capable of holding only a few men, and those that were larger were crude at best, simply crevices dug into the side of the mountain where ammunition and supplies could be stored.

Going into the caves, they found none of the technology everyone had expected. The small tunnels curved in a few dozen yards, and often opened up into a moderate inner chamber where supplies were haphazardly stacked. A few of them had crude ventilation shafts, and almost all had sleeping mats strewn on the dirt floors. Some intelligence was gleaned from laptop computers and documents left behind, and the lot numbers of Russian, Chinese, and U.S. ammunition. As with the ammunition found in the Shomali terrorist training camps, there was ample evidence that the Pakistanis had been sending U.S. ammunition, bought from U.S. manufacturers with U.S. money, to the Taliban and AQ.

As the Tora Bora battle raged on, special operators again thought they had located Osama bin Laden. Two days later, at approximately 2 A.M., the STU-III phones at NSA, NRO, ISA, and USSOCOM lit up. Bin Laden had been positively identified talking on a radio and the conversation had been completely recorded and transcribed. He was still in Tora Bora. He was still leading the strategic focus of the fight, and it appeared he was about to leave. It was going to be a windfall—or a potential disaster: TF DAGGER finally had him trapped, but the mountains were beyond anything imaginable; they were miles and miles of dynamic peaks and valleys. Al-Qaida had been pushed so far into the mountains that it was now a six-hour walk to the edge of the frontlines. Two-man sniper teams from TF DAGGER and TF 11 were immediately forward-deployed into AQ-held ground, where they would dig into crevices and empty caves and wait. Each team was armed with 5.56 M-4 long-barrel sniper rifles for the spotter and 7.62 sniper rifles equipped with laser designators, Leupold 40× scopes, and night-vision scopes for the shooter. The teams would sit and wait for as long as needed. Sooner or later bin Laden might appear, and when he did, it was party time.

They didn't have to wait long. Less than thirty-six hours later, one of the Green Berets radioed in that they had a positive identification on bin Laden, and confirmed the grid coordinate with the satellite fix. They could have the entire team there in thirty minutes or less. The operator's team leader refused to allow the mission without the approval of higher headquarters. Even though the small group was prepared to risk it alone, go without support, and die in the process if need be, it was deemed that the attempt would be too risky and might be a trap, and that more forces were needed. They were ordered to stand down until more support could be brought in. Bin Laden had been lost again.

Every available surveillance plane, unmanned aerial vehicle, and satellite was tasked over Tora Bora in an attempt to find bin Laden or AQ groups. As soon as satellite imagery, thermal imagery, or real-time video indicated where someone was, teams were dispatched. At one point close to forty-five terrorists were seen moving into a cave region that had been previously empty, and was now thought to contain the AQ's Tora Bora command-and-control center. The U.S. Space Command notified TF DAGGER and TF 11. That many enemy troops, moving that tight, and at one time, meant that it could be bin Laden. A 22 SAS squadron got the call.

"Paddy, get the lads together, we got a positive ID on a large force of AQ in Zone 4. The task force is transmitting maps and pictures to the signals squadron now."

"How many men are we talking?"

"All of them."

They would be going in as the classic four-man SAS squads, but working together in highly unusual groups of twelve to twenty-four. As they waited for coordinates and intel information, the teams rushed to ready their kit, forming small groups and jumping up and down. They weren't jumping for joy, although they were elated to have a hard target, they were jumping for sound. It was the best way to determine if something loose would make noise as they quietly entered the AO. Like their Green Beret partners, they carried 5.56mm M-16 version assault rifles, and low-slung 9mm pistols strapped to their legs. Since they knew they would be clearing caves with hard rock walls, they exchanged their ball ammo for ceramic ammunition that would fragment on the cave walls instead of ricocheting. They wouldn't be using the standard non-lethal stun grenades; in Afghanistan high explosive fragmentation grenades were the order of the day.

Two D-boys would be going along as liaisons to coordinate with TF 160, JSOC, and Mulholland's JSOTF. The cave assaults would start at first glimmer of light. Infiltration would be several miles away from the targets, which would require a lengthy and difficult trek through the darkness to the tunnel entrances. The teams would use GPS to locate and identify the specific targets for each group.

As the first ray of light clipped over the Tora Bora peaks, the teams double-checked their safeties to make sure they were off, checked their chambers, and placed their thumbs over the switches for their weapons lights. As soon as they entered the caves, their torches would come on and the room clearing and noise would begin. All four areas went basically the same—one or two four-man teams went in, depending on the size of the entrance and tunnel area, and the other teams stayed outside to cover their backs and come in if a man went down and needed exfil.

Although the caves were relatively small, basically hide-outs and bunkers built into the ravines and crevices of the mountain slope, the battle was not to be a short one. The first team made contact as soon as their lights came on. Two AQ were sleeping and died as soon as they awoke and grabbed for their weapons; a third terrorist didn't have much chance either. Once bullets started flying, every single terrorist on the mountain was awakened to the adrenaline rush alarm of automatic weapons fire—and there turned out to be quite a few more AQ than anyone expected—as was often the case with intelligence reports.

Battling from cave to cave the entry teams engaged the AQ, while the security teams posted on the mountain slopes engaged al-Qaida fighters that were hidden or sleeping in other areas. A second team took the first SAS casualty, and dragged him out of the entrance to the security team, only to come under heavy fire from terrorists on another close ridge. As a second SAS assaulter was hit in the leg and hip, the team leader called to put CAS on standby—but that was quickly abandoned when the AQ moved closer, putting friendly and enemy forces in the same bursting radius. The AQ were so close that 500-pound bombs wouldn't have impacted *danger close*; they would have impacted directly on top of the SAS assaulters. The battle would have to be fought with small arms for now.

Two hours later, at least six of the four-man teams were running critically low on ammunition. MD-500 Little Birds brought in twenty-four more reinforcements loaded with 7.62 GPMGs, belt-fed General Purpose Machine Guns, and landed them on a mountain crest nearby. It was the only place close enough not under fire, and that put them more than two miles away, which was a four-plus-mile trek, considering the steep inclines that would have to be traversed.

Two more Little Birds came through a narrow ravine, so low, and so close to the ground that their rotors were ripping rocks and debris off the slopes as they passed. Banking left and leveling out, they did not need direction or ground control; the pilots could clearly see the enemy with their long black scraggly hair and beards. In fact, the pilots could also smell them.

"I've got sights on targets, everyone down there needs to duck. . . ." The 7.62 mini-gun solenoids clicked on as the triggers were depressed, and didn't stop firing until the guns were empty. With mini-guns spinning empty, the Little Bird started releasing rockets, oblivious to small-arms fire and RPG rounds flying past its rotors.

"Out of ammo boys, but I think that chewed a few up," the pilot said as he banked hard and pulled up out of the ravine.

"Fuckin' a mate, I'll buy you a pint if you ever get to London," the troop sergeant major radioed back.

"Say again." The pilot had no idea of what he was saying.

"Fuckin' a mate, I'll buy you a pint if you ever get to London!"

"Say again." The pilot still couldn't understand him.

"A beeer, a beeeer, I'll buy you a fu-ckin' beer," he responded slowly and methodically.

"You'll buy me two beers for that one, I've got holes all over this bird."

"Bring back more ammo and I'll get you laid in South London," he replied with a White Chapel accent.

"Get me laid in Belgravia, I've been to South London." And then the Little Birds were gone. They had done everything they could; the next hours would continue to be a slugfest on the ground.

For four and a half hours the firefights had raged. When all was said and done, the SAS had performed admirably. More than admirably. The SAS troops had fought a battle that was comparable to the eight-man stand at Mirbat on 19 July 1972, when the SAS held off more than 250 rebels. Captain Mike Kealy received the Distinguished Service Order for his actions there. And, like A Squadron's Djebel Ashqab firefight in April 1964, in which Corporal Paddy Baker won the Military Medal. Baker later became a close friend of Charlie Beckwith, and of Jack's, fifteen years later, by which time he had attained the rank of Colonel. The boys were back again, and new legends were being born in the mountains of Tora Bora.

Two SAS troops were wounded, more than ten had enemy rounds embedded in their armor chest plates, the AQ body count was thirty-eight, more than ten were wounded—mostly Chechen, Arab, and a few Pakistanis. Twenty-one prisoners were captured and flex-cuffed awaiting transport to Hazrat Ali's prison in Jalalabad.

The wounded troops were medevac'd back to the U.K. and treated at the Centre for Defence Medicine, where the best possible treatment was available.

Like all operations there were lessons learned and lessons reinforced. First, bad intel causes casualties. Second, never underestimate the enemy, or his willingness to die. Third, never leave your teammate. Fourth, train hard, fight easy.

And most important, a lesson for the world, as so eloquently put by David Stirling so many years before, "The regiment is the Man, and the man is the Regiment."

There was no doubt that the SAS had garnered a significant amount of hard intelligence with their raid, and captured some good prisoners, but at what cost? CENTCOM preferred sending precision-guided munitions into operational cave openings, the caves were out of commission, the AQ died, and friendly casualties were reduced. Even with that practice, the snipers were still wounding a significant number of terrorists, which allowed them to be taken prisoner.

Although there was now decent intelligence coming out of Tora Bora, the fact remained that U.S. bombing had sealed many caves. The impossibility of excavating the caves, especially at such high altitudes, would limit the chance to uncover their buried intelligence, or identify the bodies inside—and the question would always remain as to whether or not bin Laden was one of those buried bodies.

By the eighteenth of December the search was expanding in two other directions: Helmand Province, where Mohammed Omar was said to be protected by about five hundred Taliban, according to Jaji Gullalai, the Afghan government's local intelligence chief in Kandahar; and south of Tora Bora to the Zhawar Kili al-Badr cave complex and the area around the towns of Khost and Gardez in eastern Afghanistan's Paktia Province.

The Zhawar Kili complex, in the Sodyaki Ghar mountains, was the most advanced in Afghanistan. That complex had eleven large tunnels carved into the earth and included crude but effective facilities to support the *mujahadeen* during the Soviet occupation.

On the nineteenth of December, Hazrat Ali called his private press conference with ABC Australia, *The New Yorker, Newsweek,* and CBS. He explained that al-Qaida was still a force to be reckoned with, and implored the American military to continue their operations in Tora Bora. A Green Beret advisor flanked him, just out of the camera's view.

Privately, Hazrat Ali complained to the advisor that he was unhappy with the Special Forces team's rapport with his troops. They had not bonded well with the *muj* in Tora Bora, nor had they attempted to operate with them. Instead of including Hazrat Ali's *mujahadeen* in their planning, and operating with them as partners and allies in the battle, the team had chosen to use them as gophers, guards, and bouncers.

That whole relationship created problems. Unlikely virtually every other SF team on the ground throughout Afghanistan, the team in Tora Bora seemed to be alienating their *muj* counterparts instead of aligning with them. The team chose to live in a safehouse in Jalalabad instead of up in the mountains, and they wouldn't eat with the *muj*, even going so far as to laugh at what the Afghans ate, never engaging in the sampling of their food. For medical reasons it was important not to eat everything the Afghan soldiers ate; for loyalty reasons it was important to eat at least some of what the Afghans ate and share their meals with them. It was a lesson that would have serious ramifications later on, and counter to the lessons they had learned in training.

On January 9, the U.S. was still bombing suspected hideouts in the region. South of Tora Bora in another cave "complex," two senior AQ members along with twelve others were captured near their underground hideout.

By the end of January 2002, Tora Bora, which had previously been inundated with press and U.S. military forces, was now a ghost town.

On February 5, Jack, the American advisor working with the Northern Alliance, targeted Osama bin Laden just south of Tora Bora in the Dehbala region. He had been working with secret intelligence assets in the mountains for two months to locate bin Laden. The group in hiding was positively confirmed to be extremely high-ranking AQ commanders. There was also a very good chance bin Laden himself was with them, and receiving constant medical care for his kidney problems, and a shrapnel wound Jack knew bin Laden received in Tora Bora. On February 6, just as Jack was organizing his force to attack, a CIA Predator UAV flew high over the mountain area. The remote operator zoomed in the camera and locked on to the small group of men. He quickly spotted what Jack already knew: there was a tall man in the group who was surrounded by bodyguards.

Banking to the right, the Predator came over the barren terrain and fired its single Hellfire missile at part of the suspected group. The Hellfire rocket sliced through the thin air and impacted within meters of the running men. Most escaped death—the terrorists scattered and ran before the American advisor and his *muj* troops could assemble and close in on them.

The few terrorists hit by the Hellfire were completely decimated beyond recognition. The CIA sent in a team to recover DNA samples from the remains. The operations, both Jack's and the Agency's, would be clouded in secrecy and questions would always remain as to the identity of the men on that mountaintop.

The Hammer Misses the Anvil

The results of the Tora Bora operations were muddied and unclear. Thousands of al-Qaida terrorists had escaped in what should have been their final demise. Still, the final scorecard read: U.S. 450, AQ 0. The Army of Pakistan captured 150 al-Qaida fighters as they tried to cross the border, although some charged that the Pakistanis had simply grabbed a small group in a token effort to appease the U.S. government.

Even by conservative estimates, three hundred AQ terrorists were killed in the Tora Bora caves. More important, the intelligence gathered could only be gathered from the caves. Perhaps some of the human remains would someday be proven as bin Laden's or other leaders'. Only time will tell.

The breaking of an al-Qaida Singapore/Malaysia network, actively developing advanced plans to kill U.S. Navy personnel and American citizens, was the result of the hard work after target take-downs in Tora Bora and other regions of Afghanistan. It was specifically that captured intelligence that thwarted a variety of attacks about to occur in the United States and England.

The press focused on the Tora Bora operation because it was the most visible at the time. The media could set up on a high hill behind Northern Alliance lines and look out over the mountains filming the American bombs as they impacted into the sides of the caves. There were also plenty of sound bytes from Afghan forces driving back and forth, and the hill became a swarm of news crews and a sea of satellite dishes. The press continued to report that Tora Bora was being "carpet bombed," but that was complete fiction. Not a single piece of ordnance was released from the air without a special operator on the ground, spotting a target and guiding the bomb in with a laser designator.

Tora Bora was important, and bin Laden was believed to be there, but there were many more important, clandestine and covert actions going on all around Afghanistan. Those remained quiet successes.

The media frenzy caused by the caves of Tora Bora was fed by Geraldo Rivera and others, and resulted in heavy second-guessing in Washington when no "big fish" were caught, and many Americans had been misled into believing that the capture of Osama bin Laden was imminent. Rivera was a constant thorn in everyone's side. He had hired his own private army of *muj* and was making the same mistakes Special Forces had already learned earlier—paying big bucks for intelligence from locals rarely resulted in accurate information. According to press reports and other journalists, it seemed as though Rivera was more interested in headlines than truth, and he was reportedly paying *muj* for information on where the Green Berets were. All of this was continuing to create problems for the soldiers on the ground.

In a widely covered story, Rivera reported from Tora Bora about a friendly fire incident in Kandahar that took the lives of Green Beret sergeants Jefferson Donald "J. D." Davis, Daniel "Dan-O" Petithory, and Brian "Cody" Prosser. On the air, Rivera appeared choked up and emotional while claiming to have "recited the Lord's Prayer" over the "hallowed ground" where "friendly fire took so many, many of our men and *mujahadeen* yesterday." He was, in fact, more than three hundred miles away. Rivera was supposedly disoriented in the "fog of war," claiming to have confused the incident at Kandahar with a "similar" friendly fire incident in Tora Bora that killed several *muj*. The problem with that excuse, which Fox News so readily backed, was that the Tora Bora friendly fire incident didn't happen until three days after Rivera made his report, on December 9. His credibility would be shattered over the next few weeks, and ethics articles about Rivera would make headlines around the country.

Things really got heated when Geraldo offered to let some Green Berets he cornered say hello to their wives and families on national TV if they would only give him an interview. Geraldo apparently thought it was cute. He did not know that several Green Berets were on the verge of drawing straws as to who would "knock him the fuck out."

The Fox News Channel was having myriad problems, first with Rivera, then with their "military expert and senior consultant," retired Green Beret Lieutenant Colonel Joseph A. Cafasso. Cafasso was interacting with the Pentagon and Green Beret operators on the ground so that Fox could bring real-time combat reporting to the American public. The problem was that "Colonel" Cafasso was a fraud. He was neither a Green Beret nor a colonel, having spent just forty-four days in the military before being discharged. In fact, Cafasso was using Fox News to provide misinformation to the public, and using his phony credentials to gain access to confidential Special Operations information.

Apparently, Cafasso and Fox News were upset that CBS's *60 Minutes II* had obtained captured al-Qaida training footage from an American special advisor that Cafasso and Fox News had wanted first. Cafasso seemed willing to go to any lengths to get exclusive Fox coverage.

Green Berets began a covert investigation into Cafasso and leaked his phony credentials. The *New York Times* published a story a short time later, called "At Fox News, the Colonel Who Wasn't."

Meanwhile, while Tora Bora was suffering setbacks, more setbacks were hitting in Kandahar. Mullah Mohammed Omar, who apparently fled after being surrounded in Kandahar, was supposedly ready to surrender. Special Forces troops from Kandahar, with Marine infantrymen used for security, were sent into the area to help encircle the enemy's top leaders. It had been another huge waste of resources and time: No key Taliban personnel were there when the Green Berets arrived.

Pentagon officials said there would be a subtle policy shift in the manhunt "to quit chasing shadows and create a total intelligence mosaic to pinpoint all of the AQ and Taliban pockets," and devoting less effort trying to pinpoint various individuals.

Others demanded that the U.S. work less with the problematic Afghan warlords and start conducting more unilateral operations. The danger of not fighting with the Afghans would prove to be allegations, after every action, that innocents were harmed.

A simple fact existed: any sizable operation would have to have an Afghan force to ensure that friend and foe could be clearly identified for the U.S. troops, and to ensure that the

Afghan population and the rest of the world would see Muslims fighting Muslims.

After the Monday-morning quarterbacking of the fight at Tora Bora, the Green Beret operators thought that perhaps the best course of action was just to leave them alone to do their job. After all, TF DAGGER had been shackled because the CIA had been starved for so long. In fact, the root cause of military mistakes and the elusiveness of Osama bin Laden and Mohammed Omar was the lack of qualified CIA intelligence officers and the CIA's lack of ability to plan detailed military operations. It had been a problem in Qala-i-Jangi, and was continuing to be a problem everywhere.

The entire thing was one big fuckup. Lessons learned hard in Iran twenty years earlier, and in other "joint" operations, were still being ignored. Although several of the Special Forces teams in Tora Bora had performed poorly, in general the Special Forces functioned best alone, unleashed, and in the wilderness, answering to no one. These were not eighteen-year-old infantry troops; these were extremely intelligent, incredibly resourceful, highly experienced, and completely motivated commandos. They were much like the JDAM precision-guided bombs they sent against the Taliban and al-Qaida: they only needed to be pointed in the right direction and they would handle the rest. Layers of bureaucracy only impeded their chances of success. If America wanted bin Laden, then Special Forces had to be let loose as they had been in the first sixty days of war.

After Tora Bora, General Franks issued a summation, and acknowledged USASOC's work so far: "I am pleased with the progress that has been made over the past ninety days, but I would also say that much more very dangerous work remains to be done." Franks said one thing the Green Berets appreciated for its lucid intent: "Osama bin Laden is dead or he is alive. He is in Afghanistan or he is not."

On February 28, 2002, Democratic Senator Tom Daschle stated that bin Laden and other terrorist leaders must be caught "or we will have failed." Most soldiers thought that the best measure of the war's effectiveness would be the absence of more attacks on American citizens.

According to the Special Forces commander, the senator's logic meant that the Department of Defense could wipe out sixty countries' worth of infrastructure, eliminate terrorist recruitment and training, and put the AQ and its associates completely out of business—without being a success.

CHAPTER 21

Flags over the Embassy

"To say these [U.S.] attacks are in any way against Afghanistan or the Afghan people is flat wrong. We support the Afghan people against the al-Qaida, a foreign presence on their land, and against the Taliban regime that supports them."
— DONALD RUMSFELD,
Department of Defense briefing,
October 7, 2001

"The calculations of the crusade coalition were very mistaken when it thought it could wage a war on Afghanistan, achieving victory swiftly."
— MOHAMMED ATEF,
al-Qaida's military commander,
to Reuters, October 19, 2001

The Official Flag-Raising

Kabul, Afghanistan

The American embassy's national colors last flew over the Afghan capital on January 30, 1989. The Department of State had closed the embassy after the Afghans' defeat of the Soviet Union. The chaos following the collapse of the Soviet's surrogate Afghan government had been overwhelming.

For more than twelve years, the State Department held the flag in storage, hoping one day to return it to Kabul. On December 16, 2001, the U.S. Marine guards, as part of the embassy reopening ceremony, would once again raise the flag.

Ambassador James Dobbins and a skeleton staff had arrived a few days prior to the ceremony. Dobbins presided over a short, formal program attended by Chairman-elect Hamid Karzai and the cabinet of the interim government of a free Afghanistan.

In the background, as the VIPs were being seated, were the 5th Special Forces Group colors. Attached were twenty-seven multicolored streamers from Army campaigns it and its predecessor, the 1st Special Service Force, had participated in since 1942. Colonel Mulholland embraced General Fahim in the customary Afghan tradition. General Fahim, the commander of the Northern Alliance, had been named the nation's minister of defense.

In November, the Green Berets had been tasked to conduct an initial reconnaissance of the long-abandoned embassy to determine the degree of destruction to the facilities and to check it for booby traps or other dangers. They accomplished the task with the assistance of an explosive ordnance detachment from the Army's 10th Mountain Division.

One of the sergeants returned to give a summary of the team's findings, ending with: "They murdered our ambassador, Adolph Dubbs, on Valentine's Day 1979. They defaced his memorial on the embassy grounds, and on September 26 of this year they torched part of the embassy and ripped the Department of State seal off the building as part of a staged propaganda event. Yet, through the years of war, without tending, the embassy roses survived; some were still blooming, even in November."

The Unauthorized Scarf

Near the end of the ceremony, Colonel John Mulholland stood up to speak as the senior U.S. military officer present. Around his neck Mulholland was wearing a black-and-white scarf, not part of any U.S. military uniform, an act that would surely be questioned by some in the continental United States.

The scarf had tremendous significance early in the war

when the 5th Special Forces Group was given the task to
work with the Northern Alliance's opposition groups that opposed the Taliban and the AQ.

Ahmad Shah Massoud, the charismatic, college-educated,
French-speaking engineer, had been the combat-proven
leader of the Northern Alliance. Osama bin Laden's minions
had murdered Massoud three days before the attacks of September 11. Massoud had worn a scarf similar to the one being
worn by Mulholland. Common among Afghani warriors, a
scarf can identify specific allegiance. All who wore Massoud's scarf were considered not only to affiliate themselves
with him, but also with the struggle he led against the Taliban
regime and their terrorist brothers, the al-Qaida.

In the dark days of October, after Massoud's murder, the
Special Forces had arrived, offering hope. Many Green
Berets adopted the scarf as a symbol of their solidarity with
the *mujahadeen* warriors and their absolute dedication and
willingness to give all to achieve victory.

Mulholland spoke for a short time, saying, "It was an
honor to serve with our Afghan brothers in a common endeavor. . . . Massoud and brave 5th Special Forces Legion-
naires gave their lives. Strength and Honor."

"The Star-spangled Banner" was played as the Marine
embassy guards raised the flag. The U.S. embassy in Afghanistan was officially open for business.

The Unofficial Ceremonies

The flag raised in the official ceremony was not the first to
fly above the American embassy after September 11. On the
eighth of December 2001, at approximately 6:40 in the morning, a group of Special Forces soldiers gathered on the
grounds of the U.S. embassy in Afghanistan.

The 5th Special Forces' modified version of the Stars and
Stripes, similar to those of the Army's regiments in the Civil
War, was raised. The men stood at attention and saluted. In a
short ceremony, fragments of twisted, burned metal from the

World Trade Center were buried at the base of the flagpole. A moment of silence followed. The flag was then lowered, and properly folded into a triangle. The ceremony took eleven minutes.

Colonel Mulholland conveyed the feelings of the Green Berets as he made the following statement:

> The attack on September 11 changed all of our lives and the burial of a few pieces of the World Trade Center in Afghan soil, where Taliban and AQ fighters who brought pain and suffering to our great nation were defeated, is meant as a symbol to our brave citizens that we will defeat those who dare attack what we love and who we love. The symbolism of bringing debris from New York to this country is powerful.

Special Forces A-Teams were holding similar ceremonies all over Afghanistan. SF commanders planned to later present a map of all the burial sites to New York's police and fire departments and other city officials.

A TASK FORCE DAGGER helicopter had delivered TIGER 03's piece of debris on New Year's Day, 2002. In the icy wind of northern Afghanistan, Master Sergeant John Bolduc and the Green Berets of TIGER 03 read a passage from the Bible.

"Yea, though I walk through the valley of the shadow of death . . . ," Bolduc recited, as they buried a twisted shard of steel left from the destruction of the Twin Towers. They were standing in the compound that they had used as a base camp since their arrival on the ground in Afghanistan.

Bolduc's team chose not to leave a marker—they did not want anyone digging it up, ever. Bolduc wanted to ensure that a piece of American suffering would remain in the sands of Afghanistan throughout eternity, linking the two nations together as one against the forces of evil: "We want the American people to know that the victims didn't die in vain, that they have been remembered . . . and that something good can come of this."

CHAPTER 22

Occupation and Pursuit

"The truth of the matter is, in order to fully defend America, we must defeat the evildoers where they hide. We must round them up and we must bring them to justice. And that's exactly what we're doing in Afghanistan."
— PRESIDENT GEORGE W. BUSH,
White House press conference,
October 11, 2001

Transition into Defense and Interdiction

Kabul, Afghanistan

Just a week after the ceremony at the U.S. embassy, the British embassy conducted their own ceremony. SAS commandos and MI6 operators had already taken over the embassy and started setting up security systems and defensive procedures. Secure satellite links, communications equipment, and evacuation plans were being put in place. The entire scenario, a liberated Kabul in just weeks, seemed too good to be true.

On December 21, 2001, additional forces, including the SBS, had come into Bagram airfield, and proceeded via a fast and tight convoy south to Kabul. Their SAS guides would take them down the back streets of Kabul and straight into the British embassy. The Northern Alliance, very concerned with a large British military presence back in Afghanistan, sent Jack and some of his *muj* to scope out their arrival. The British embassy still had the bronze placard on the front gates, and the compound was one of the most secure places in the city.

Kandahar, Afghanistan

After the demise of the Taliban in Kandahar, Hamid Karzai was flown by Task Force 160 to Kabul and assumed his new role as the interim leader of Afghanistan on December 22, 2001.

Washington, D.C.

One month later Chairman Karzai attended President George W. Bush's January State of the Union address. Karzai was leaving with the first lady when he noticed several Green Berets in the crowd. They didn't look familiar at first, without their beards, then the new leader immediately recognized the soldiers. He abruptly left the first lady's side and the rest of the entourage and walked straight toward them. Karzai embraced them, and with tears in his eyes thanked them for their heroism and their sacrifice. He took SFC Mike McElhiney in his arms and hugged and kissed him. Karzai looked at McElhiney's wife, Judy, and said, "Look what he has given for my country, look what he has sacrificed." Karzai grabbed one of McElhiney's wounded arms and dragged him over to his new friend President Bush. "Look what these men have sacrificed for my country's freedom." Then he asked the president, "How can we ever repay your Green Berets for their courage?"

Army Special Operations Deputy Commander General David Burford looked on and smiled. To defeat the Taliban, the Special Forces had created a significant force structure. Chairman Karzai was now presiding over a collection of warlords who needed funding, craved power, and were clandestinely posturing with foreign sponsors and each other to gain comparative advantage over their competitors.

Kandahar, Afghanistan

Chaos after victory is a normal phenomenon, not unlike Germany after World War II. Special Forces would need to stay in Afghanistan for a long time to ensure chaos did not permanently return. In Panama, for example, Special Forces stayed in the provinces of the country for almost a year after the conventional military forces had held their welcome-home parades. The A-Teams lived in Panama's *cuartels,* or military facilities, with the defeated Panamanian Defense Forces (converted to National Police) to make sure that the local mayors and politicos were left alone to bring democracy and stability to the countryside. Their work terminated only when the American ambassador declared that enough progress had been made to guarantee the survival of Panamanian democracy under the new president.

In Afghanistan, an unspoken consensus offered some hope for the transition period. Most of the warlords were in general agreement to tolerate Karzai's interim central government while they jockeyed for advantage in the *loya jirga,* which would consist of representatives from throughout Afghanistan. The task of the *loya jirga,* set to meet six months after Chairman Karzai's selection as an interim leader, would be to design a new national government.

Vectoring In on the AQ

Colonel Mulholland and TASK FORCE DAGGER set out in multiple directions. From a single focus, the overthrow of the Taliban, Special Forces would now coordinate a long list of new mission objectives. They would include humanitarian assistance, pursuing intelligence leads, and doing everything from searching caves and rifling through Mullah Omar's archives to building the AQ intelligence data banks by conducting reconnaissance and raids to capture or destroy nests of al-Qaida and Taliban hard-liners. They would also work with either conventional forces from the U.S. Army or Fahim's continuing Northern Alliance Coalition on larger operations such as the upcoming OPERATION ANACONDA.

Special Forces would begin counterinsurgency operations in the eastern provinces of Afghanistan to counter Taliban and AQ attempts to reassert themselves along the border with Pakistan. All of this activity helped complement the ongoing and relentless pursuit and destruction of Osama bin Laden and the al-Qaida by "opening as many doors as possible to find out who is hiding inside."

Colonel Mulholland and TASK FORCE DAGGER were well situated to help in transition. Lieutenant Colonel Bowers was in Mazar-e-Sharif, Lieutenant Colonel Haas was in Kabul, and Lieutenant Colonel Fox, recovered from his wounds, was back in Kandahar.

Fixed Targets

With RAMBO as his outfit's continued code name in Kandahar, Lieutenant Colonel Fox faced a myriad of tasks that were passed off on Special Forces units as soon as the Taliban collapsed. The most radical change was that now many of the Special Forces units would be quartered in fixed locations. Stopping and building a fixed location would be dangerous, and most of the Green Berets on the ground were against it. The AQ and hard-core Taliban would now be able to find them.

On the same day that Colonel Mulholland gave his short speech at the ceremony reopening the embassy in Kabul, RAMBO's troops moved into the abandoned residence of the Taliban's leader, Mohammed Omar.

As soon as the transfer of power from President Rabbani to Hamid Karzai took place, Karzai gave RAMBO's men wide range and latitude to act, due to the personal rapport and friendship developed between them during their fight against the Taliban.

TASK FORCE DAGGER allowed RAMBO's TEXAS and PYTHON teams to develop their own task list. They had a better appreciation for the situation in newly liberated Kandahar, and Karzai was their Afghan "big stick."

Security was the first issue. The Green Berets set up security in the compound, moving into the bombed-out facility for shelter and a base of operations.

A "commo shop" was the second priority, since reliable communication was the key to survival in an emergency. Third, immediate-action drills in case of attack were rehearsed and rehearsed again. Last, the men began laying out their gear for sleeping and maintenance, while the team's medics took a look at water and sanitation.

Fox had his men move throughout Kandahar to gain "atmospherics" and "ground truth," by observing the population, commerce, and the like, looking for signs of danger. They continued to dress in Afghan clothing to limit long-range recognition, knowing that in a close engagement they would still be recognized as foreigners. The use of beards and Afghan hats while riding in vehicles also helped shorten recognition time for evildoers that might want to engage the Green Berets.

Loitering on every corner in Kandahar were men carrying Kalashnikovs and RPGs. Initial rough estimates derived from multiple intelligence sources indicated that approximately 5 percent of the population were highly displeased that the Americans were in town. The rest had varying degrees of tolerance. The real fact was "Most Pashtun in the Kandahar area hate Americans and love psycho Islamic fundamentalists in turbans," said one Green Beret sergeant. But still, the Green Berets had made many friends with the Pashtun tribes after saving so many of them from the Taliban and al-Qaida oppression.

As the men drove through Kandahar, signs of change were evident, the same as in Kabul only days after liberation. Balloon sellers appeared on their bicycles. Music could be heard. A few women, still fully covered by their pale blue *burkas,* were out and about without their husbands, a practice not permitted under the old regime.

The grounds of Omar's residence were opened for the public to help the word spread that in one of the nation's poorest countries, Omar had lived in incredible comfort, with beautiful murals and gold chandeliers, water and electricity, both scarce resources, in unlimited quantity. The populace had not expected Mullah Mohammed Omar to live in such splendor.

The Taliban's behavior reminded the Green Berets of Sandinista behavior in Nicaragua. After the Communists had defeated Somosa in 1978, they immediately occupied all the houses of the elite and promptly began wearing three-hundred-dollar sunglasses they had mail-ordered from Rodeo Drive.

Senior Military Advisor to the Governor

Chairman Karzai appointed Gul Agha Sharzai, befriended in combat by TEXAS 17, as the interim governor of Kandahar province. Sharzai loved the Green Berets, and he wanted them with him forever. Lieutenant Colonel Fox became Sharzai's senior military advisor. The new Kandahar government was ready to get under way.

RAMBO and its A-Teams did a 360-degree inspection of the buildings where the new government would first be meeting. Their advance security details operated much like the U.S. Secret Service at home. They scouted areas prior to important events or high-level meetings. In the process, they discovered an incredibly huge, interlocking booby trap embedded in the roof of one of the buildings.

Over fifty separate Russian 122mm artillery rounds and dozens of Soviet antitank mines were all wired together in a chain and ready to be detonated. Fox's demo men disarmed the system. If the booby trap had been initiated during the meeting of the new government of Kandahar, the entire organization, along with most of RAMBO, would have surely been killed in a gigantic explosion.

Governor Sharzai stated that law and order would be the first priority, a tall order indeed. The Special Forces responded by establishing a small police force. After obtaining some uniforms, boots, and other light infantry gear, RAMBO went to work. In short order they had a basic law enforcement team up and running under the control of a Northern Alliance commander named Mamack.

RAMBO also picked up responsibility for coordinating with nongovernmental relief organizations, rendering reports and acting as an extension of the American embassy in Kabul. Potable water, plumbing, and other public services were significant concerns. As in Vietnam and El Salvador, nation building continued to be an important task. Even though the highest levels of the military command passed it off, the SF teams in Afghanistan did it on their own.

Fox's beard was an unlikely key to his success as the military advisor to the appointed governor. Graying, his beard took on a unique shade that matched that of the dominant clan in Kandahar. It measurably increased his respect and acceptance among the locals. Special Forces' cultural awareness and ability to bond led to other revelations as well, and they discovered more and more cultural nuances as time went by. For instance, beards were more than a way to simply tell where a man was from or his social standing; they were also a sign of manhood. Clean-shaven men were called "girly boys" and were considered to have homosexual tendencies.

"Girly Boys"

Culturally, Afghanistan seems to share some of the traits of the ancient Greeks. According to one Afghani soldier, "Women are for babies, and men are for pleasure." This placed American, British, and Australian special operators in a unique and precarious predicament in how to deal with southern Afghanistan's flagrantly homosexual community, which appeared to be quite extensive, especially in the isolated mountainous regions of Afghanistan.

"Well, with this new development . . . the SF Qualification Course developers at Fort Bragg are now going to have to incorporate a new lesson: how to deal with gays in an unconventional warfare environment," said one of the Green Berets.

British Marines also had their share of interactions with the "girly boys." According to Scottish journalist Chris Stephen, British Marines had sent patrols into the mountains near the town of Khost, hoping to catch up with AQ suspects who the week before had fought a four-hour gun battle with soldiers of the Australian SAS. When they came out of the mountains, they claim they were swarmed by local farmers, who stroked their hair, offered to paint their toenails, and propositioned them for sex.

"They were more terrifying than the al-Qaida. One bloke who had painted toenails was offering to paint ours," recalled Marine James Fletcher.

"It was hell," added British Marine Corporal Paul Richard. "Every village we went into, we got a group of men wearing makeup coming up, stroking our hair and cheeks and making kissing noises. Some of the guys turned tail and fled. It was hideous."

"I think a lot of the problem is that they don't have the women around a lot," recounted another British Marine. "We only saw about two women in the whole six days. It was very disconcerting."

Taliban leader Mullah Mohammed Omar was reported to have actually gained fame and a following when he led a military campaign against two local warlords who were fighting over which one of them was going to get to sodomize twelve-year-old twin boys who lived in his village.

Searching for Clues

Although TEXAS 12 was decimated by the misguided smart bomb, PYTHON 33 and PYTHON 36 were continuing their mission. The teams were issued orders to search ex-Taliban and al-Qaida hangouts. If, in their searches, they found intelligence material, unexploded ordnance, or weapons caches, so much the better.

Each morning they clarified their task list with RAMBO after conducting mission preparation the evening before. They would "chalk-talk" any contingencies or emergencies they might encounter during the day en route to, at, or on the way back from their targets. With weapons locked and loaded, wearing Afghani clothing and beards for "signature reduction," PYTHON teams left the compound in civilian pickups, along with a new addition to RAMBO. 10th Mountain Division explosive ordnance detachments were brought in to help handle and destroy enemy ammunition and weapons.

A small force of loyal Pashtun fighters would usually accompany PYTHON to meet Sharzai. The Green Berets labeled them Afghan Mobile Forces. Similar groups would be trained and held close by Special Forces teams throughout Afghanistan as their best bet for enhanced legitimacy and personal protection. They especially needed the Afghan *muj* with them in the southern areas or the locals would just regard them as foreign invaders.

PYTHON's men had become quite expert at searching through caves. They once lowered a man into a two-hundred-foot-deep man-made hole to search connecting caves with a flashlight and pistol. "Tunnel rats" were supposed to have been a historical footnote in books about Vietnam. However, Afghanistan had its own version of the VC tunnels of Cu Chi. In the caves and crevasses of one valley, PYTHON teams collected an estimated sixteen thousand artillery rounds, eight thousand boxes of heavy-machine-gun ammunition, and assorted mortar shells, tank rounds, and rockets.

Each night, PYTHON's elements would bring back anything they found of intelligence value and send back detailed reports on their findings to TF DAGGER. The Green Beret's HUMINT activity was important: they were now the point men for the various intel agencies at work against worldwide terror.

Lieutenant General Robert Noonan, Jr., the highest-ranking intelligence officer in the U.S. Army, said that in April of 2001, 85,000 pages of captured documents were in American hands and these records clearly indicated that the AQ was working inside the United States, England, Germany, the Netherlands, Spain, Canada, and South America.

Some of the "intelligence" collected was not sent back, like the ring of keys to Taliban leader Mullah Omar's bombed-out palace. The men of PYTHON 33 each brought one of the keys home to Fort Campbell as a memento.

Day after day, the Green Berets had to stay on their toes. Afghanistan clearly remained a dangerous place. In the late spring, a Special Forces soldier and three Army EOD personnel died when working with captured enemy mines and artillery shells at a site near Kandahar. Although the powerful explosion eliminated most of the evidence on the scene, it is believed to have been booby-trapped.

The huge stockpiles of Chinese and Soviet ammunition reminded the teams of the caches they found in Bosnia after the war. In Bosnia, NATO forces destroyed them in large demolition pits. In Afghanistan, recovered ammunition was turned over to the new government for use against the terrorists.

Special Operations Forces weren't the only ones to uncover valuable clues, however. Using the same tactics as the CIA, a group of British journalists paid local Afghans to lead them to a padlocked compound in the Sheragha Jama district of Kandahar, where they discovered a terrorist training camp that had been abandoned by the Taliban and al-Qaida as they rushed to defend Kandahar airport from attack by the Northern Alliance.

Documents had been piled up to be incinerated by the terrorists, but in their haste, they had not destroyed everything. In the corner of a small room, the British reporters found the plans to build a huge van bomb (the same exact type that had been used on the U.S. embassies in Kenya and Tanzania) to blow up Moorgate, in the heart of London's financial district. Worse yet, the instructions were all written in neat English, and accompanying them were notes on how to blend in with the Britons, bypass security, where to purchase bomb-making materials in the London area, and even directions on how to locate Moorgate through the business directory. The scope of bin Laden's multinational terrorist organization seemed wider than ever, and America wasn't the only nation in the crosshairs.

Take-Down of Mir Wais Hospital

Shortly before the Special Forces took Kandahar on December 7, Taliban and AQ wounded had gone to the Mir Wais hospital for treatment. Knowing that it was only a matter of time before American forces reached the hospital ward, sympathetic hospital workers smuggled in guns and grenades, secretly arming the wounded terrorists so they could make a last stand, or martyr themselves if necessary. Some were only slightly injured and fled while they still had time. When the Green Berets surrounded the hospital, six hard-core AQ were left in the ward, and they refused to surrender. They repeatedly said they would rather die than give up, and threatened to kill anyone besides Taliban and al-Qaida sympathizers who came into their part of the hospital. Still, even though the terrorists proclaimed they would rather die than surrender, two escape attempts had been made. One man was captured when he broke his leg trying to leap from a second-story window. Another tried to escape and committed suicide by holding a grenade to his chest when he realized they were surrounded and there was no way out.

One of the only qualified doctors in the hospital was a member of the Swiss Red Cross, and he talked two more of the cornered, hurt zealots into leaving with him so they could get proper "treatment." They walked right into the hands of SF, and were flex-cuffed and taken away screaming *"Insh'allah"* to warn the few who were left that it was all a ruse.

Kandahar was the Taliban's stronghold, and locals still had strong ties with them, even though they kept it a secret. Frustrated, the local *muj* "paramilitary police" blocked food deliveries in an effort to starve out the holed-up fighters. The plan failed. Food was still getting to the men inside the hospital—once again from sympathetic hospital staff. Fruit and bread were brought in at first, then only prepackaged foods as time went on and they feared anything else might be drugged or poisoned. Worse yet, the press was arriving in droves to report on the standoff, and their reports often had a spin on "fair treatment," resulting in growing sympathy among Muslims worldwide. The fighters were portrayed as poor, defenseless men who "had no other choice." One terrorist was even interviewed by an Arab newspaper, and he requested that Muslims everywhere "pray for him and his brothers" inside.

Lieutenant Colonel Dave Fox, aka RAMBO, was given the mission to end the standoff. The close relationship between the Green Berets and Commander Mamack would now pay dividends. The *muj* police force was set up by the Special Forces to provide martial law in the newly retaken city, so TASK FORCE DAGGER thought ending the standoff would be a good way to see just how well Fox had taught them. Now, RAMBO and the paramilitary police would have an opportunity to fight together. Governor Sharzai approved the operation, and planning began at once.

The "official" concept was simple: the RAMBO element would help with reconnaissance, negotiation, and fire support, while the *muj* would have the mission of assaulting the interior of the building. This "division of labor" made sense. The police were responsible for law and order in the city, and the Special Forces were going to do all they could to enable success, and prevent future uprisings among the Taliban-friendly populace.

*Un*officially, the Green Berets would conduct the interior assault with their Afghan counterparts and make it look like the Afghans of Kandahar did it all by themselves, although reporters on the scene could easily tell the difference between the two. It didn't matter, though; hopefully the locals would still fall for it, since they were all prevented from getting too close to the scene by strands of concertina wire.

One of Fox's majors, known as "Chris," was selected to be the negotiator. Without success, Chris used loudspeakers and native translators to repeatedly ask the al-Qaida to surrender.

On January 28, after close to a two-month standoff, RAMBO

decided it was time to rout out the cornered rats. The longer they waited, the more the press fed on the situation, and the higher the tensions rose in Kandahar. Something had to be done.

At 0330, the Green Berets geared up and ran through a dry run on what would happen with their *muj*. The uniform was standard SF door-kicking and room-clearing—full-battle dress CQB assault equipment, Second Chance armored vests, leg holsters, Kevlar helmets, and Oakley sunglasses—except for the New York Yankees hats that some of them wore, the NY Mets shirts that others wore, and the "I Love NY" pins that all of them wore. At 0800, they crept toward the Mir Wais.

The AQ inside spotted them, and a firefight broke out. As the *muj* ran and ducked for cover, several of RAMBO's commandos sprinted up and made it to the edge of the building. The terrorists were on the second floor and couldn't see them below. The Green Berets scaled the building to the second floor and crept along a ledge that ran just below the windows. Snipers were placed on surrounding rooftops to take out any terrorist who made the mistake of looking out the windows.

After the gunfire died down, the "police" took a chance and ran up to the building, joining the special operators who were on the ledge over their heads. They waited. Prayer time was at noon, and the men of RAMBO wanted to make sure "those bastards got one last chance" to say theirs.

As soon as prayer time ended, dozens of grenades were lobbed through the hospital's shattered windows, and the operators on the second floor ducked for cover.

"Fire in the hole!" one operator yelled to his mates as he stepped to the side cover of the wall.

Glass and concrete flew in a million directions as two dozen grenades went off simultaneously. White smoke billowed out the window frames.

Three more operators had already placed an explosive breaching charge on the door to the upstairs and detonated it at the moment the grenades went off, blowing the door down the hallway. Within seconds, the Berets on the top floor went in while the "police" stormed up the stairs from below.

Two terrorists on the top floor cowered under beds as they tried to spray the operators with bursts from their Kalashnikovs, missing them. The Green Berets returned fire, killing them instantly. Another one played dead, but was quickly executed by the *muj* when they spotted him reaching for a pistol.

Inside, it was utter devastation. Limbs and torsos were everywhere, the remnants of the AQ who had martyred themselves with grenades earlier. Still visible on the torsos were the Pakistani Army sweaters they had been wearing, the mark of the most hard-core AQ. The same kind of sweater John Walker Lindh had worn at the Qala-i-Jangi prison revolt. There were clouds of flies on the bodies that were already there from before, and the stench of rotting death was everywhere. The operators' boots made sucking sounds as they stepped through old puddles of coagulated blood. "Hey, this is what they wanted," one of RAMBO's men said, shaking his head.

Needless to say, none of the AQ survived. The al-Qaida terrorists had just had a lesson in close quarter battle, something the Green Berets excelled at. The problem with the international media and Muslim audience's growing sympathy had been swiftly resolved by "peace through superior firepower."

One thing that took longer to rectify was to repair the hospital to return it to functioning condition. According to special operators on the scene, it took months to gain appropriate funding for cleaning supplies and repair materials because of bureaucratic red tape.

Psychological Operations

After weeks of harassment and interdiction operations, the Special Operations Forces were retasked for other activities. After Special Operations and USAF Transportation Command assets helped fly the Marines into RHINO, the Central Command initiated a huge information campaign to inform the entire country that the United States *finally* had a conventional force on the ground.

Occupation and pursuit tasks replaced unconventional warfare as the main effort of U.S. forces in Afghanistan. All sorts of conventional tools were brought in to conduct raids on suspected al-Qaida pockets.

NATO and Allied Special Forces also flowed into Kandahar. No one wanted to be left out. Itching to get into the fight, the Navy SEALs set up their own Special Operations headquarters, under the command of Naval Captain Bob Hayward, and announced OPERATION KABAR would begin. Both the Naval Special Warfare Groups, CNSWG-1 on the West Coast and CNSWG-2 on the East Coast, sent teams. Commander, NSWG-1 sent SEAL Team 3, and Commander, NSWG sent SEAL Teams 2 and 8. One SEAL Delivery Vehicle Team (SDV-1) from the West Coast was also sent. The Green Berets, already in combat for months, fondly called it Operation KandyBar. Their biggest laugh was why SDV-1 was being brought in—SDV-1 conducts hydrographic surveys for possible amphibious invasions, using highly specialized top secret mini-subs. Afghanistan was land-locked, had no harbors, incredibly small rivers, and hadn't seen rain in six years.

Army Special Forces sent in Alpha Company, 1st Battalion of the 5th Special Forces Group (A/1/5), under the command of Green Beret Major Joe Whelan, Jr. Eventually, even Lieutenant Colonel Tim Sherwood's 3rd Battalion of the 3rd Special Forces was added to the mix, joining A/1/5 in the direct-action business.

A/1/5 went straight into combat. One of its first missions was on January 12, 2002, when it moved quietly into positions to observe a village. After ninety-six hours of continuous surveillance, they had formulated a plan. They pressed into the village late at night, sweeping up the seven men they had seen conducting illegal activities. In minutes they were on a helicopter flying away into the night. No lights, no shots.

The direct-action effort was effective in keeping AQ remnants off balance, and kept the remaining, hard-core Taliban deterred. It was clear that the U.S., the British, and the other allies meant business.

The teams ran day and night, hunting down every rumor that concerned the whereabouts of Osama bin Laden and Mullah Mohammed Omar. They were desperate to find bin Laden. Not everything was easy. During one assault by A Company of the 5th Special Forces Group, Staff Sergeant Ward was shot in the leg and had to be evacuated to the U.S. An Australian SAS trooper was not so lucky, however.

Trooper Andrew Russell was on patrol in the lead vehicle of a five vehicle convoy near Kandahar when his Land Rover hit an antitank mine. Severely injured, his mates immediately started treating his wounds while they called in a medevac.

Within twenty minutes, a medevac chopper was dusted off, and in the air. A U.S. Air Force C-130, with search and rescue Parajumpers on board was circling the area as well, and picked up the urgent message.

Overtaking the slower medevac chopper, the four PJs (one surgeon and three medics) parachuted into the site an hour later, and began operating on Russell. He was medevac'd by helicopter to Kandahar, but died shortly thereafter.

The Perth native was flown back to Australia by C-130 after a brief ceremony in Afghanistan, where bagpipes were played as his colleagues carried his body aboard the aircraft.

Russell left behind a wife, Kylie, and a baby daughter, Leisa. Australia's Prime Minister, John Howard, said "This young man died in the service of his country and in the fight against terrorism which is so critical to all of us and to our futures." Russell was posthumously awarded the Distinguished Service Cross, Australia's fifth highest medal.

Pursuit was hard business, and it was taking on a new dimension. Intelligence was developing which indicated that potentially large formations of AQ remained in the eastern part of Afghanistan. The AQ was "pooling," or regrouping in the vicinity of Tora Bora, Paktia, Khost, and other mountainous locations. The Green Berets would have to go in as small groups, gain intelligence, and then ferret out the terrorists. Just another day at the job.

"Stand Up and Do Something"

Back on September 12, 2001, Sergeant First Class Nathan R. Chapman was in Thailand with his A-Team. Via an urgent phone call from his peers at Fort Lewis, Washington, he and his mates heard of the attacks on the World Trade Center and the Pentagon. Normally the funniest man on the detachment, Chapman was beside himself with rage.

Entering the Army as a teenager, Chapman had immediately joined the Army's 2nd Ranger Battalion. Chapman was soon drifting through the air over a Panamanian airfield, as AK-47 bullets and tracers crossed the sky under him. Chapman did not fear as he looked down into the darkness below his parachute and floated directly through a hail of cracking enemy fire. Chapman and the Rangers landed safely. Panama fell, and so did Noriega.

As part of the Army's effort to help boost the esprit de corps and experience of "leg" units, Chapman was transferred to the 3/47th Infantry and was promptly sent to the Persian Gulf for Operation Desert Storm. Begging to return to special ops, he tried out for the Green Berets. After two years of selection and schooling, Chapman deployed to Haiti with Special Forces, culminating in three conflicts before his late twenties.

Chapman was cross-trained as a master communicator, sniper, and a light-weapons specialist. He was a charismatic and natural-born leader. He couldn't stand "sniveling pukes" or worrying over things outside his control. His infectious saying, at home and at work, was "Stand up and do something!"

Pacing and angry, he was irritated that he wasn't in the States and couldn't get the inside scoop about what was going on. Chapman had to find a way to get in on the action.

Three days later, Chapman was even more pissed off when he learned that the one Green Beret officer killed in the Pentagon was Major Cole Hogan, his former A-Team leader.

Nathan, when asked to volunteer to join his 5th Special Forces Group peers in Afghanistan, raised his hand for the fourth time. He wanted a piece of the al-Qaida. He was thirty-one years old.

On January 4, 2002, Sergeant First Class Nathan Chapman would be the first military man to die from enemy-inflicted wounds in Afghanistan. He was killed in an ambush in eastern Afghanistan; a CIA officer was seriously wounded in the chest during the gunfight.

Chapman and the CIA agent had been meeting with Afghan anti-Taliban forces near the town of Khost, close to the Pakistani border. After leaving the meeting they were ambushed in a "fast and intense" gun battle. Chapman didn't leave his partner, he didn't run, and he didn't relent. He stood up and shot it out until the very end.

At his funeral, the commanding general of the Army's Green Berets, Major General Geoffrey Lambert, said that he could see Chapman's legacy. "I see Amanda and Brandon, his children. I see a democratic Panama. I see a liberated Kuwait. I see a small girl entering school in Kabul. I see terror on the run," Lambert said.

"Major Hogan and Sergeant Chapman have, as we say, 'effected link-up' in the sky. They look down on their Green Beret brothers and wish us well in the just-beginning fight against this evil," the general concluded.

Later, after the State of the Union address in late January 2002, President Bush attended the reception for those invited on his behalf. The President sought out Chapman's widow, Renae, and, aside from the others in the room, quietly explained how much her loss meant to him and the nation.

No Kite Stompers Allowed

The Taliban had outlawed toys, and children were never allowed to play outside. After Kandahar Province was freed, toys came out into the open in greater and greater numbers each day. The Taliban specifically outlawed the flying of kites. Kites had been a simple joy so long denied that many of the younger children, seeing a kite for the first time, were absolutely mystified by the phenomenon. It was a simple truth recognized by all observers—Afghan children loved to fly kites.

Afghan children could not buy kites in packages; they built them. Out of string from the open sewers, sticks from bombed-out buildings, and plastic found floating on the streets, they built their kites, some of them virtual engineering marvels, others just crude endeavors.

Two Special Forces soldiers had recently arrived in-country for the first time. They were lookouts on the top of a building, which was their assigned security team position for the day. Unknown to them, a boy launched a kite in the square below. As the kite struggled to climb in the wind, it came over the edge of the roof and bumped into the back of one of the Green Berets, startling him.

The startled Green Beret raised his desert boot and crushed the kite under his heel, throwing it from the roof in disgust. His partner watched his teammate's actions, horrified and shocked.

Immediately after his partner tossed the kite over the side, the special operator reached for his MBITR radio and asked for Lieutenant Colonel Fox. He relayed the events he had just witnessed. The "kite stomper" was flown home to Fort Campbell the next day. Special Forces would not tolerate oppression of an indigenous people at any level, in any way.

To the Green Berets there is no higher calling than that of the words *De Oppresso Liber*—"We Liberate the Oppressed"—and no one would ever be allowed to violate that sacred oath.

CHAPTER 23

OPERATION ANACONDA

"There will be times of swift, dramatic action. There will be times of steady, quiet progress. Over time, with patience and precision, the terrorists will be pursued. They will be isolated, surrounded, cornered, until there is no place to run or hide or rest."

—PRESIDENT GEORGE W. BUSH,
Pentagon memorial service,
October 11, 2001

Into the Belly of the Beast

Gardez, Afghanistan

AQ and Taliban fighters were regrouping in the mountains of eastern Paktia Province, near the border of Afghanistan. A good estimate of enemy strength was difficult to determine, varying from as low as 150 to what was known to be a wildly inflated number of 4,000, depending on the sources of information.

Local Afghan tribesmen reported that many Chechens had arrived with their families after the fall of Kandahar. Some reported their homes were being confiscated, while others said they received payment for the use of their homes to placate them. CIA estimates of foreign al-Qaida in the area continued to vary from at least hundreds to more than two thousand.

Several things were clear: Al-Qaida was re-forming in the Shah-i-Kot Valley. They were on the move with their families, they had funding, and they had loads of ammunition and weapons.

Colonel Mulholland and the 10th Mountain Division's young commanding general, "Buster" Hagenbeck, worked closely with each other to determine what to do in response to this new intelligence information. They prepared their plan for Lieutenant General Paul T. Mikolashek's consideration.

Shah-i-Kot presented its own unique set of terrain-associated problems. It was a small village in a valley surrounded by mountains. Traveling southeast from Kabul you would pass through Logar, then on to Gardez. Because it was formerly a high-level Taliban route, the road was good, one of the few blacktop roads in all of Afghanistan.

Gardez was a den of thieves. The "good guys" in Gardez were all former Taliban, having only recently shaved their beards and removed their turbans. You could look at these fresh Northern Alliance allies and spot the newness of their Massoud hats. From Gardez, the Shah-i-Kot Valley was five hours by 4×4, and across dangerous terrain. The terrain went from desert sand to reddish clay, and the passes one had to travel through were ripe for ambush by the hidden Taliban and AQ forces. The safest way in was, of course, by chopper.

Identifying the al-Qaida leadership in the area was difficult. NSA, CIA, and ISA intelligence forces offered some possible answers. Jalaluddin Haqqani, the former Taliban minister of frontier affairs, was considered. Others identified Saif Rahman, an old anti-Soviet fighter, as the possible leader of the AQ presence in the valley. The British GCHQ was also now assisting the signals intercept (SIGNET) effort with their entire listening complex at Cheltenham aimed at Southwest Asia—including Pakistan. The Government Communications Headquarters, formerly known as the Code and Cipher School, was best known for its work at Bletchley Park decrypting German Enigma messages during WWII.

The likelihood of Osama bin Laden or Mullah Omar being in the valley was a strong negative. The intelligence community unanimously endorsed one conclusion: the AQ forces in the area were temporarily halted. Their ultimate goal was to escape to Pakistan, and the United States needed to act quickly before they fled, but there were little or no "big fish" there.

Meanwhile, al-Qaida was encouraging Afghans to join in a new *jihad* against the Americans and their allies. Appeals for support of their *jihad* were circulated by *shabnama,* or "night letters" that circulate covertly, a psychological-operations technique taught to the Afghanis by American CIA agents during the 1980s. *Shabnama* are similar to the "story books" carried from village to village in the Andes by the Peruvians suffering under the assaults of the Sendero Luminoso (Shining Path).

AQ was upping the stakes in the area for everyone by putting out "night letters" on specific Special Forces operators and offering prices on their heads. Al-Qaida was even offering $50,000 for virtually any foreigner killed, to include humanitarian aid workers and journalists. British and American Special Forces were valued at $100,000 in cash, and the American civilian military advisor to the Northern Alliance had a $250,000 price tag on his head.

Major General Hagenbeck and Colonel Mulholland arrived at the same conclusion: they recommended attacking the area with a tighter circle of security around it than had previously been established at Tora Bora. The encirclement and squeezing technique was appropriately entitled OPERATION ANACONDA. Hagenbeck agreed with General Franks that the operation was too large for Afghanistan's fragmented "National Army," actually the Northern Alliance, and the Special Forces. According to Franks, reduction of the Shah-i-Kot terrorist enclave to rubble was going to take "professional soldiers."

Franks and Mikolashek wanted the U.S. Army's conventional ground forces to take the lead—but with Special Forces support. Outranked by a bevy of stars, Colonel Mulholland finally agreed, giving his approval to Major General Hagenbeck and the 10th Mountain Division. The decision to use professional infantry was made based on historical data as well as a current intelligence analysis, and the fact that the conventional generals desperately wanted into the war. The conventional army, virtually left out of the conflict, were itching to get into Afghanistan on a division level. They wanted to show they could fight, and they also wanted to justify their budget and necessity in the future. So far the war had been a total SF op.

When the Soviet Union had tried to overtake the area, saturated with interlocking caves dug into the rocky mountainsides, they had lost 250 men in one day, including all eight helicopters used for infiltration. At hand was an opportunity to see if the U.S. could do better with its technology and Army techniques, tactics, and procedures.

Hagenbeck's troops from the 10th Mountain Division and the 101st Airborne Division began their planning. TASK FORCE DAGGER intensified the training of the small nucleus of local *mujahadeen* who had been hired. The force was basically light infantry and its commander, General Zia Lodin, led a contingent of soldiers from two ethnic groups. His troops had been recruited to become U.S. proxy soldiers, and the pay for each man was $200 per month.

Jack, an advisor to the Northern Alliance, sent a message to the teams on the ground letting them know that one thing they didn't count on, or possibly consider enough, was that Lodin's men had many foreign Taliban in their ranks. They were also more of a mercenary army than the Northern Alliance, and that severely irritated the NA's hierarchy in Kabul.

OPERATION ANACONDA was the biggest concentration of conventional firepower in the war to date, and a large concentration of manpower and firepower was what conventional generals were best at providing, regardless of the necessity. Franks' joint/combined operation numbered more than nine hundred U.S. soldiers, nine hundred Afghan *mujahadeen,* and hundreds more from Australia, Canada, Denmark, France, Germany, and Norway. Men from almost every SAS unit would join the American Green Berets, including British, Australian, and New Zealander, and Canada's elite and little-known JTF-2 counter-terrorist unit. Brigadier General Ken

Gillespie, National Commander of the Australian Force contribution to the U.S. coalition, and overall commander of the Australian Special Forces Task Group to Afghanistan, sent in all available personnel from the SASR, as the SAS was officially referred in Australia. Additionally, Britain had now deployed Tornado bombers armed with laser-guided bombs and Nimrod surveillance aircraft to assist the SAS forces.

Friday, March 1

Near Gardez, late in the evening, SHARK, the 5th Special Forces Group's command-and-control unit, commanded by Lieutenant Colonel Chris Haas, and two A-Teams, TEXAS 14 from the 5th Special Forces Group, and COBRA 72 from the 3rd Special Forces Group, began supervising the mounting of their special operators into a number of vehicles in the bitter cold. The Green Berets numbered thirty, and the Afghan force they were advising consisted of 380 newly recruited Pashtun fighters.

The convoy of Toyotas, Soviet-era trucks, and civilian vans began a long trek through the mountain trails toward a point approximately six miles from the first village in the Shah-i-Kot Valley. The Afghan force would orient its march toward the three villages of Sarhanekhel, Babadul, and Marzak.

Their mission was to push into al-Qaida–occupied areas and put pressure on enemy defenses, forcing the mainly Arab and Chechen AQ to pull out and head for the high ground. Around the valley, manning the high-mountain ridgelines, the 101st Airborne and the 10th Mountain Division, along with allied and other Special Forces and Afghan elements, were to seal off known routes of escape. The altitude was an issue, with some passes approaching ten thousand feet in elevation.

The 10th Mountain Division would focus on battle positions or objectives "Heather," "Ginger," and "Eve," named after porno starlets. SF figured if they couldn't have women in Afghanistan, they might as well name their objectives after them.

SHARK's formation was going to conduct an infantry maneuver called "movement to contact." Movement to contact is the act of moving in a secure formation, spreading out with scouts or "point men" in the lead, with side and rear security. A unit uses a movement to contact when the enemy situation is uncertain. The goal is to determine where the enemy is, engage him, and develop the situation via maneuver, ideally ending with the enemy's destruction. In OPERATION ANACONDA's case, the movement to contact would hopefully push the AQ forces within the contracting rings of the conventional coalition forces.

As SHARK's convoy moved slowly through the night, the pilots of the 101st were preparing to fly ANACONDA's ring into place. Other elements included Pakistan's border paramilitary units. They were supposed to use roads and vehicles to tighten the noose around the al-Qaida. Pakistan, faced with criticism over the AQ escapees during Tora Bora, assured the coalition's command they would try to seal sixty miles of their border.

The A-Team leaders and Haas realized that the next day was going to be a real test. With a newly formed Afghan force, they were going up against an AQ that was well trained, would definitely fight to the death, and was blocked in with no means of escape. According to their preliminary intelligence, SHARK and his teams knew that the enemy would number more than 150, that the terrorists would use caves in the area, and that they would be dug into the well-developed fighting positions used against the Russians. This was a place where American Special Forces had trained, equipped, and led Afghan *mujahadeen* so successfully against the Soviets. This was the place where the American Green Berets had chosen to destroy the Soviet army fifteen years earlier.

Colonel Mulholland was concerned. Large conventional operations opened the door for correspondingly large losses.

ANACONDA was going to test his men and the new Afghan
troops. The test would begin at dawn, or H-Hour.

Saturday, March 2

Haas and his two A-Teams entered the battle already
stretched out. The rocky and muddy trails from the village of
Zurmat had eroded the force during the night. Many of their
convoy's vehicles had become stuck in the mud or sand, and
some had broken down. They had covered the seven miles required to be at their phase line, the line of departure for the attack. However, much of their force was now dismounted and
on foot, which significantly slowed down their movement to
the objective. As they paused in their attack position, the
force was well arranged, with vehicles and men ready to
launch. In the darkness, they began to move closer to the AQ
line of defense.

The AQ hard-liners didn't wait for the assault. AQ attacked
them before dawn, slamming the anti-Taliban force's attack
positions with mortar and RPG rounds. A flurry of explosions began impacting around the entire group. The Afghan
forces were shocked at the degree of accuracy of the incoming fire. At first it looked as if the fire were mortar rounds
from a village, but they later identified it as coming from the
mountainside.

SHARK was pinned down and taking casualties. Over a
dozen Afghan troops were already wounded.

Hundreds of American, British, Canadian, German, and
other coalition troops were being airlifted into landing zones
much closer to enemy positions than anticipated. Intelligence
preparation of the battlefield was not looking as good as first
thought. Fortunately, only one landing zone was red-hot with
enemy, a considerable improvement over the total loss of Soviet helicopters in their failed attempt a decade earlier.

The U.S. had finally brought in Apache and Cobra attack
choppers. The 101st Airborne's Apache AH-64s arrived on

the scene and started pounding the suspected AQ positions. It was the first time they were being used in-country. Overhead, the JFACC's fighters and bombers were also responding as well. During the day more than eighty bombs would be dropped on the objective area.

It became evident that the AQ had set up in-depth defenses that would allow them to eliminate the infidel attackers, then withdraw to fight again, over and over, moving farther up the valley each time. Al-Qaida mortar positions were well concealed and unexpectedly accurate. It was clear that they had registered (prefired) their mortars to settle the base plates into the ground and test the trajectories and mortar charges so they would know exactly where their rounds would go. This was a highly trained and experienced enemy.

Some caves were better prepared than others. They included heavy dried-mud reinforcements and "range cards" showing distances and locations of all potential enemy positions and potential avenues of approach. A few of the al-Qaida fighters had state-of-the-art night-vision devices that enabled them to see just as well as the U.S. infantrymen after dark.

Meanwhile, the 3rd Brigade of the 101st Airborne Division (the Rakkasans) was joining the Special Forces and the 10th Mountain Division in the fight and learning firsthand that the AQ were hardened fighters. Their helicopter forces came under incredibly intense fire.

The 101st AH-64 Apache gunship pilots were unflinching. They flew directly into the face of AQ positions, literally nose to nose, knocking down the AQ as they returned fire. The AQ would level their heavy machine guns directly at the choppers as they flew toward the side of the mountain. A stream of enemy DSHK 12.7mm bullets ripped through the skin of one pilot's chopper and sent the ballistic glass flying into his cheeks.

Al-Qaida had come up with the not unique tactic of engaging choppers with RPG antitank rockets, similar to what the Somalis had done in Mogadishu in 1993. The RPG rockets were having a hard time penetrating the armor of the Super

Cobras and Apaches, but they were creating enough damage to ground the birds until repairs could be done.

Colonel Frank Wiercinski from the 101st Airborne Division was observing the fight from his command-and-control bird when an RPG hit his chopper. It failed to explode, but caused enough damage to make the Blackhawk set down. They were immediately attacked by AQ terrorists, who swarmed the chopper. Wiercinski and his security element killed eleven of the enemy as they held out for help. They fought a defensive stand until their extraction eighteen hours later.

One 10th Mountain Rifle Company landed in a location where the AQ could hit them with plunging fire from caves two thousand meters above them. The infantrymen's rifles and AT-4 rocket launchers were outranged and ineffective. They fought and hung on, using fire support to hold off the enemy until they could be pulled out by rescue helicopter under the cover of darkness.

The AQ played chess with tracer ammunition. Al-Qaida kept probing with small arms, a technique the Army calls reconnaissance by fire. By goading the U.S. into firing tracer rounds at them, they were able to see the glowing rounds and pinpoint their positions in the dark. The 10th Mountain unit fell for the trick at first, then quickly learned.

Once an AC-130 Spectre gunship came overhead, the 10th Mountain troops fired tracers exactly at the enemy location, and Spectre used their tracers' impact to focus their heavy fires. The 10th Mountain troops started waiting until Spectre was ready before they opened up with tracer fire. The AQ got all the tracers they wanted, as well as the 40mm grenades from above they hadn't counted on. The AQ in contact never fired back, giving the troops automatic feedback. It was working.

Other AQ forces were ducking and taking cover momentarily and then coming back seconds later full stride. It was clear that the enemy was using fire and counterfire and had battle rhythm, established over time, like World War II or Korean War veterans.

The AQ taunted American troops to illustrate their lack of fear. Clearly, the al-Qaida fighters were thrilled to finally fight the hated American infidels face-to-face.

In the valley below, TEXAS 14 and COBRA 72 still kept trying to push their troops forward. The Afghan fighters had never witnessed such accurate and devastating AQ fire, particularly from sources that couldn't be pinpointed. They hadn't even closed with the enemy yet.

Taking Blue Fire

CW2 Stanley Harriman, the second in command of COBRA 72, was calling on the radio from his vehicle in a dry streambed. The open area was cut with deep ravines and trenches in the sand. Moving through the valley, he and his men had just seen a truck near the head of the Afghan formation explode from a direct hit.

Luckily, the Afghan commanders were in a Toyota behind the troop transport. SHARK was still okay, as was TEXAS 14. That was about to change.

Suddenly, rounds hammered COBRA 72's position. One of them impacted near Harriman, wounding him. Others impacted directly in a nearby creekbed without warning. The driver thought the fire was coming from a house or compound, but the rounds were not being "walked in" by bracketing the target and then making adjustments—they were dead-on. The volume of incoming fire was huge, more than they expected from al-Qaida.

CW2 Harriman left his vehicle and ran among his force of seventy *muj,* yelling for them to disperse. They spread out immediately, an act that would save their lives. Rounds kept raining down on the column as sand flew into a cloud. Metal was ripping and tearing and flying apart as the bullets impacted around them. *Muj* soldiers were screaming as they were hit. Disregarding his own safety, Harriman ran back to his command vehicle, possibly to retrieve another radio or IR strobe to halt the air strike. He was hit again, fatally wounded; two of his Green Beret comrades were also hit but would survive.

Special Forces warrant officers were created in 1985 to replace first lieutenants on the A-Teams as the XO, or executive officer. Their numbers are few and although they are officers, they are far more specialized than most. They are the only warrant officers to command ground-maneuver troops.

Harriman had been an engineer sapper during Desert Storm. He since had learned French and Spanish, had become an officer, and met a woman he loved. His personal trinity was family, faith, and Special Forces. They were all priority one.

As he was dying from his wounds, Harriman stayed on his radio. Captain Matthew McHale, his team leader, who loved him dearly, was with him as he died. CW2 Harriman was the first Green Beret warrant officer ever to die in combat.

The Green Berets had one KIA and two WIA, while Afghan Commander Zia Lodin had over twenty wounded and eventually reported three KIA. TF DAGGER quickly learned the origin of the unusually accurate fire that had decimated the Afghan formation: CW2 Harriman had probably been killed by rounds from a USAF AC-130 Spectre gunship.

Two procedures were immediately implemented. The first was to place orange V-17 reflective panels on the roofs of all anti-Taliban and anti–al-Qaida vehicles engaging the enemy, and all supporting vehicles. The coalition aircraft would then be able to easily identify them as friendly targets. The second procedure was to allow Spectre and other aircraft to identify individual friendly forces on the ground, including Afghan soldiers, and remains classified.

Combat Ineffective

Commander Lodin, in spite of advice to the contrary from his Special Forces advisors, called off the assault and ordered his troops to pull back toward Gardez. The American advisors had to struggle to keep control of the Afghan forces as they retreated.

The Pashtun fighters were not willing to keep going. The fight was going to have to be waged by the conventional and Special Operations forces in the rings around the valley. Lieutenant Colonel Chris Haas began planning to reconstitute the unit in Gardez. With vehicles littering the valley, equipment strewn in the field, and more wounded to be found and evacuated, the Afghan troops were spent, and combat ineffective. It would take several days before Haas' troops could reenter the fight.

That night, Haas visited the teams and consoled his Special Forces troops. Many of them were despondent after being forced to turn back. The colonel explained that such things happen during guerrilla warfare. All the men knew what unconventional warfare entailed, but failure was failure. Their commander conveyed that he was simply damned proud that they had the courage to run directly at the enemy.

The movement-to-contact plan had failed miserably. The Pashtun anti-Taliban force was not prepared to fight with the spirit and courage of the Northern Alliance, even for $200 a month.

Mulholland rendered his reports about the loss of CW2 Harriman. The death of the highly respected, savvy, and inspirational leader hurt deeply. Haas tried not to focus on the loss of the chief, but found it difficult.

Haas later went to see the Afghan wounded, speaking in the smattering of Dari and Pashto he had learned through osmosis. Mulholland's heart went out to his new troops. His two wounded Green Berets and the body of Chief Harriman would soon be en route to Germany from Bagram airfield just north of Kabul.

A week later Afghan commanders groused to the press that the opening drive up the valley was botched. It was. The majority of the Pashtun force refused to go back into the fight. Al-Qaida was now free to focus only on the Americans in their midst.

Sunday, March 3

General Hagenbeck had serious obstacles to overcome. Three of his Apache AH-64s were already riddled with bullet holes. His maintenance crews did not sleep. By the next day they had all of them back up in the air except one. More U.S. air strikes began at dawn, and by the end of the day, the number of bombs dropped had been more than double the number of the day before, up to 190. AC-130 Spectre gunships were also working hard to spot and eliminate the enemy.

Units from Norway, Australia, Canada, Denmark, Germany, and France were now participating. Many were occupying blocking positions, effectively sealing the area. After encountering the initial enemy elements the previous day, the coalition was discovering the surprising strength of the AQ defensive preparations that had been laid out in advance.

Bringing in additional 10th Mountain troops, an MH-47E touched down in the Shah-i-Kot Valley. The LZ was supposed to be well behind the AQ defenses. The moment the men left the chopper, they came under immediate and intense RPG, machine-gun, and mortar fire. Sergeant Major Frank Grippe was wounded as soon as they ran off the tailgate. The AQ were firing everything they had, from machine guns to surface-to-air missiles and RPGs, at the aircraft.

The 10th Mountain Division soldiers hit the ground, seeking cover, and returned heavy volumes of fire to force the al-Qaida back into their positions, hoping to buy time for the men to regroup. Using their AT-4 "bunker buster" rockets, they pushed the enemy back toward their caves. Eventually, they were able to hold them back far enough to call in a medevac for the wounded.

Even though the same thing had happened to the 101st, there were no further American KIAs that day. However, the fight was so intense that thirty-four men were wounded. They weren't Special Forces, but they fought extremely well and were tough and innovative. They earned the respect of the Green Berets.

Although the going was extremely difficult for all concerned, by the end of the day battlefield reports were clarifying AQ strength: estimates were settling at more than 600, considerably more than the previous low estimate of 150.

Hagenbeck spent the night repositioning men from lower helicopter landing zones to higher ones in order to gain the advantages offered by the mountainous terrain.

Monday, March 4

At three in the morning, two Army Special Operations MH-47Es from the 160th NightStalkers, code-named RAZOR 3 and RAZOR 4, were approaching their LZ high in the valley. By now, the Navy's Special Warfare Group had brought SEALs into the operational area, and were supplying the SR, strategic reconnaissance teams for coalition Marines and Infantry. At one point there were 72 SR Teams, made up of two to four men, working in the Shah-i-Kot region. The idea was to put TASK FORCE 11 "eyes" on the ridgeline to see into the valley. At over ten thousand feet, al-Qaida were waiting, just like the *mujahadeen* had waited for Soviet helicopters, dug in and ready to pour fire into the air-assault assets.

Leaving from their staging area in Gardez, RAZOR 4 was inserting one team on the western side of the Shah-i-Kot Valley and had split from RAZOR 3. They would rendezvous in one hour after dropping off their teams.

RAZOR 3 flared out and landed on LZ Ginger on the eastern side of the Shah-i-Kot Valley. A six-man recon team of Navy SEALs with one Air Force combat controller ran out the back of the chopper and into knee-deep snow. Navy SEAL Neil C. Roberts was at the front of the team. Al-Qaida machine guns and RPG gunners opened up on them, and the dull black fifty-two-foot-long MH-47 jolted sideways from the impact of an RPG that ripped through both of its sides. The RPG was launched from so close that the rocket's warhead did not have time to arm. LZ Ginger was hotter than

Ginger Lynn in a triple-X film, and the SEALs were right in the middle of a nest of AQ terrorists.

The impact from the RPG was like a brick flying at hundreds of miles an hour, ripping through the aircraft. As it tore through the skin of the chopper, the round ruptured the chopper's hydraulic lines. Hydraulic fluid was spitting out like blood from a great black beast as the chopper's blades whomped through the thin air. The ramp was still down and the team was out in the snow. The men sprayed the enemy with small-arms fire, firing as fast as they could with as much as they could.

"Get out of here. We're taking fire! *Go! Go! Go!*" the crew chief screamed to the pilot.

"Exfil! Exfil! It's too hot!" screamed Roberts.

The team ran back onto the ramp firing to the left, right, and rear as bullets ripped into the chopper. The left-door gunner was emptying his machine gun into the dark.

"They're on. *Go! Go!*" screamed the crew chief to the pilots.

It was time to "un-ass the AQ." The pilots pushed full-throttle forward as they lifted the chopper off. The MH-47 wobbled and shuddered as it lurched up and down trying to gain altitude. The RPG round and machine-gun fire had destroyed electrical power to the controls and hydraulic fluid pressure.

Petty Officer First Class Roberts was still on the tailgate of the helicopter shooting as it took off jerking and lunging from the impact of small arms and the loss of hydraulic fluid. As the chopper strained to get off the ground and out of AQ range as fast as possible, it bucked and Roberts was thrown off the ramp and into the darkness below.

The left-rear crew chief lunged for Roberts, trying to grab him, but slipped on the hydraulic fluid spewing down the ramp and out of the chopper. Alexander slid right off the chopper's ramp and into the night behind Roberts.

"Fuck, we lost them, we lost them," the right-rear crew chief yelled. Just then he saw Alexander hanging over the tailgate's edge by his safety line. Slipping and skidding on the slick oil, "Got him, got him," he yelled again as he pulled Alexander back into the crippled bird.

The chopper started to buck and lose power as the pilots threw it into a dive down the mountainside, thinking one engine had failed. As the chopper dived into the dawn's early light, they realized it still had both engines and it was the hydraulic system failing. Leveling it out, the MH-47 crew kept the bird flying long enough to get out of the kill zone. It was a miracle.

Within minutes the crew chiefs told the pilots that Roberts had been thrown out. Immediately the pilots told the team they were turning around. It didn't matter if everyone died—leave no man behind!

Just then the controls started locking up from lack of hydraulic fluid. The crew chiefs started cutting cans of hydraulic fluid open and manually pumping it into the bird's circulatory system as the chopper barely held on. The controls started to come back, but there was no way the chopper was going to make it back up the mountain.

The controls kept freezing up as the twin-rotor chopper descended into the valley below, aborting their return and rescue attempt.

"RAZOR 4, RAZOR 4, this is RAZOR 3, over," they kept calling. It would do no good—the radios were out. At the same time RAZOR 4 was beginning to wonder about the other chopper, RAZOR 3 was late for their rendezvous, and that was not a good thing.

Four miles from the original firefight, RAZOR 3 hit the ground hard and the SEALs ran out and took up fighting positions, expecting another contact.

Finally calling back to TF DAGGER's FOB with their satellite radios, RAZOR 3 made contact. TF DAGGER relayed the message to RAZOR 4, which immediately headed to RAZOR 3's grid coordinate to pick them up. Forty minutes later, RAZOR 4 was on the ground again, and everyone from RAZOR 3 loaded into it.

The team quickly considered their three options. First,

head back to Roberts with everyone on board. That wouldn't work because the chopper would never make it to ten thousand feet with the weight of both recon elements and both crews. Second, leave RAZOR 3's crew there and head back to Roberts with all the SEALs from both choppers. Or, third, return to Gardez and get more men and choppers to rescue Roberts.

Their mind was quickly made up for them. Predators spotted dozens of AQ fighters less than a mile away and coming toward them. They left the disabled RAZOR 3 and headed to Gardez, where they would drop off the crew and return with both recon teams to rescue Roberts.

Meanwhile, more personnel were being generated to search for Roberts. An AC-130 Spectre was already overhead, and Predators were on the way to Roberts' position to get pictures that could be transmitted back to Bagram airfield, where RAZOR 1 and RAZOR 2 were departing. They would be carrying a quick-reaction force of U.S. Army Rangers and USAF combat controllers.

RAZOR 4 had already lifted off from Gardez and headed back to the spot where Roberts was last seen. As RAZOR 4 approached LZ Ginger, the Predator UAV's infrared lights malfunctioned and could not get a video picture to send back.

RAZOR 4 only needed to set down for half a minute, long enough for the dozen special operators to run off the back tailgate and into the snow. They hoped Roberts was still alive. It did not matter—he would be rescued one way or another.

As RAZOR 4 came in and flared out forty feet above the LZ, the pilots saw the muzzle flashes.

"Fuck me," the cockpit voice came forward.

"*Oh, this is going to hurt,*" the pilot thought to himself.

The machine-gun rounds were already punching through the nose of the chopper and ricocheting around the inside of the aircraft. Rounds crashed through the Lexan windshield. The chopper kept setting down through the bullets, and the team ran off the tailgate and into the snow, for the third time. No one looked for cover, no one got down; they just ran shooting into where they thought Roberts might be.

The combat controller, Technical Sergeant John A. Chapman, started killing AQ fighters behind cover as a concealed bunker position opened up on him. Chapman was hit with bursts of AQ gunfire and went down, permanently. He was dead, and the others were getting hit left and right.

RAZOR 1 and RAZOR 2 were already on the way, but it was a long flight from Bagram through rugged mountain passes down through Logar and across the Gardez Mountains into Shah-i-Kot. The Rangers on board knew little, only that a chopper was down. As RAZOR 1 and RAZOR 2 rescue forces closed and flew southeast into the valley, they got an intel update. They were to link up and extract a SEAL team that was pinned down.

The command element at Bagram had no idea what was going on. The radios were malfunctioning, the Predators were sending intermittent images, and the SEALs on the ground were fighting "commo blind."

With no information from the HQ at Bagram, the Rangers on RAZOR 1 went into LZ Ginger not knowing the SEAL team had retreated down the ridge. RAZOR 2 was on the other side of the ridge. RAZOR 1 landed at 6:30 A.M. and was immediately hit with an RPG round that tore through its engine and spewed fire and metal as it crash-landed. The ten Rangers on board, designated Chalk-1, ran down the ramp to seek cover as al-Qaida poured bullets into them. The right door gunner, Sergeant Philip Svitak, was killed almost immediately; the other door gunner was hit in the leg. Bullets punched through the cockpit windshields as they shattered the pilot's legs.

RAZOR 2 had lost commo with RAZOR 1 shortly before and had returned to Gardez. On the ground the senior Ranger on board grabbed the crew chief by the neck and started screaming.

"I don't give a fuck what your problem is, motherfucker. RAZOR 1 had only ten guys on it, that's half the fucking package."

"We have to get word from them where they are and if they need us before we head out," the crew chief explained.

"Listen, you fucking asshole, you're a fucking delivery service, you understand me, fucking delivery boy? You brought in half the package, half the fucking package. We're the other half that completes that package, and if something happened, those guys need us!" the Ranger sergeant screamed.

Just then RAZOR 2 got word that the other chopper was down. RAZOR 2 was finally back in the air with Chalk-2 and got to the ridgeline at 8:30 A.M. Dropped off two thousand feet lower on the ridge, Chalk-2 now had to fight their way up to their fellow Rangers. As the second wave of Rangers, led by Staff Sergeant Arin Canon, moved up the mountain, they dropped everything they could except ammunition, guns, and water. The firefight raged long and hard throughout the next hours.

The AC-130 Spectre gunship that had been overhead through the darkness was forced to leave when night lifted. RAZOR 1 would no longer have the security blanket provided by its 105mm howitzer or the advantage of night-vision goggles on the ground. A three-man medical team led by USAF Technical Sergeant Keary Miller was treating patients as al-Qaida fighters cut them down. Miller grabbed an M-60 machine gun off RAZOR 1's ramp and gave it to a crew member to hold the terrorists off. Several hundred miles away were two F-15E fighters, piloted by Major Chris "Junior" Short and Captain Kirk "Panzer" Rieckhoff. They were code-named TWISTER 5-1 and TWISTER 5-2.

Staff Sergeant Gabe Brown, pinned down on LZ Ginger, was on the air calling for help: "We're a downed helicopter under enemy fire!" Brown repeated his call and then yelled into his radio, "I need guns only, I need guns only, and need them *now!*" Brown, a combat controller on RAZOR 1, was now using the code name SLICK 0-1, which allowed the pilots to identify it as a downed chopper.

The two Air Force Strike Eagle tactical fighters heard the call for help and headed toward RAZOR 1 at more than a thousand miles per hour. TWISTER 5-1 and TWISTER 5-2 came flying in low and fast, screaming down on the crashed

MH-47 site as they slowed to 575 miles per hour. One of the F-15E's weapons release officers put his thumb on the trigger of the Strike Eagle's 20mm Gatling gun. The cannon was for air-to-air combat, meant to engage an enemy fighter during a supersonic dogfight. The pilot had never used his Gatling gun in an emergency close air support role before. He was willing to take the risk: there were Americans down and trapped, they would die if he missed, and they would die anyway if he didn't try. On the ground Gabe Brown, SLICK 0-1, was dumping magazine after magazine into the enemy advancing on their downed chopper, as he vectored the jets in. It took three passes to line up at the right angle to the enemy position.

Al-Qaida was eighty meters to the front of the downed chopper and still advancing when the M-61 A1 six-barrel 940-round Gatling gun ripped into the terrorists, sending flesh and pine bark splintering through the air. It was close, danger close, but TWISTER 5-1's weapons release officer, Lieutenant Jim Fairchild, had missed the SLICK 0-1's team and hit the enemy dead-on.

Ten minutes later the F-15E's Pratt & Whitney turbofan engines were out of gas. They would refuel in the air with a half tank of fuel and head back into the battle only twenty minutes later, guns blazing into the mountainside again. By the time the Rangers were charging the enemy, TWISTER 5-1 and TWISTER 5-2 were completely out of ammo. The pilots were frustrated because they couldn't do more for the boys on the ground, but they had done more than enough. However, the Rangers would not fight the rest of the way alone. The TWISTER pilots got on their radios and started cockpit-to-cockpit briefs of more fighters and bombers in other areas. Soon, fighters and bombers from all over were covering RAZOR 1.

Two F-16s came in to join the fight, as did a B-52 Stratofortress with JDAMs. When all the air assets were out of ammo and gas, al-Qaida was still shooting back. It was now up to the Rangers on the ground.

Bullets were slinging in every direction; "it was like *Black Hawk Down* in the fucking snow." The Rangers fought through the al-Qaida and eventually seized a bunker. Inside they found Roberts' body and two dead AQ terrorists. One was wearing Roberts' jacket.

By now, Sergeant Matt Bouillaut had led Bravo Three patrol of the Australian SAS up onto one of the nearby overlooking ridges. Battling freezing cold, snow, and al-Qaida rockets, Bouillaut's SAS team joined the defense by calling in airstrikes and blocking AQ reinforcements from reaching the downed helicopters on the other ridgeline. Although they were a substantial distance away, hypothermic, and unable to move in the brutal terrain, Bravo Three kept identifying AQ targets and calling in CAS to support U.S. forces pinned down.

It was now broad daylight, and all four teams had casualties—one pilot was critically wounded; others were dying or dead. Still, the fighting had subsided, thanks to the scores of five-hundred-pound bombs that had come in on AQ, and Chalk-1 called for medevacs and exfil.

"We need a SITREP on the PZ," headquarters radioed.

"The PZ is cold and we have URGENT SURGICAL conditions for medevac," Air Force Combat Controller Kevin Vance replied.

No sooner had Vance and the Rangers told command that the pickup zone was cold than another group of AQ fighters appeared. The AQ fighters started pouring machine-gun fire into the casualty collection area.

Senior Airman Jason D. Cunningham and the other medics were dragging more casualties to cover as they desperately tried to treat the wounded. The AQ fighters kept pouring lead into LZ Ginger. Cunningham kept exposing himself to fire as he used his medical skills to save lives. The Rangers had no choice but to just sit there and shoot it out. Luckily, Cunningham had convinced his command to allow the medics to carry blood packs, something that had not been allowed on previous operations. The Air Force pararescuemen were called PJs, short for "parajumpers." Cunningham's blood packs were saving wounded Rangers. Just then, bullets tore through the twenty-six-year-old PJ. Cunningham was hit in the abdomen and the bullet exited his pelvic area. He was losing blood rapidly; there would be no exfil attempt now.

Cunningham's blood left a red swath across the snow as his teammates dragged him to cover. The other medic from the 160th was also wounded. It was a fucking disaster.

Despite his wounds, Cunningham stopped his bleeding and continued to work on other patients, even as his condition grew more and more critical.

By 5 P.M. the sun was down and the weather was turning bitter cold as the wind whipped through the mountains. The men tore insulation from the walls of the downed helicopter to keep the casualties warm. They were all coughing up blood from the thin air, hypothermic, dehydrated, out of food, and low on ammunition.

At 6:15 P.M., Cunningham died in the snow. His blue eyes closed for the last time. He had hung on for hours. They had all hung on.

At 8:15 P.M., four choppers came in to exfil them. Three picked up the Rangers and SEAL Petty Officer Roberts. A fourth picked up the SEAL team on the other side of the ridge.

Seven special operators, Army Rangers, and Air Force Special Tactics airmen had died trying to save a Navy SEAL who was down. Seven men had lost their lives trying to recover one man. Several reporters questioned that. Apparently they did not grasp the brotherhood of Special Operations—it was the modern-day version of "all for one and one for all."

Jason D. Cunningham would later be awarded the Air Force's second-highest medal, the Air Force Cross, which had been established by Congress in 1960. Only twenty-two enlisted men had ever been awarded the medal. Twenty of the medals were awarded in Vietnam, with ten going to Air Force pararescuemen. Since Vietnam only two had ever been awarded, one to a PJ in Somalia in 1993, and now one to a PJ in Afghanistan. Everyone who had been on the mountain that day would say Cunningham deserved the highest medal the

Air Force had to give—the Medal of Honor. The PJs were living up to the creed of the Army Rangers and Green Berets. So were the SAS—Sergeant Matt Bouillaut was awarded the Distinguished Service Order for his actions and leadership during OPERATION ANACONDA.

Leave no man behind. Strength and Honor, as always, was the order of the day.

At the end of that day AQ might have lost up to two hundred men, but in terms of American lives it was the most expensive operation of the entire Afghan war.

Wednesday, March 6

The Green Berets had tracked a truck leaving the ANACONDA fight and heading toward the border of Pakistan. A fighter aircraft engaged the target. Although several of the fourteen killed were enemy, some were women and children, mostly Arabs. It appeared to be an unfortunate mistake. But what the U.S. forces didn't know at the time was that apparently the women were also al-Qaida, a rarity in bin Laden's forces.

Several days into the battle, more and more skirmishes occurred toward the *outside* of ANACONDA's ring. Al-Qaida sympathizers, including some from Pakistan, had crossed back into the mountains eluding the ANACONDA ring, and had reinforced the AQ under attack there. With AQ moving both in and out of the valley, Hagenbeck sent in three hundred more conventional combat infantrymen.

The Army AH-64 Apaches were worth their weight in gold, hunting AQ and supporting the troops on the ground. They continued to face direct enemy fire over and over until the number of enemy rounds in each aircraft forced it into a maintenance halt.

Five Apaches were inoperable and being repaired. Meanwhile, the U.S. Army and U.S. Transportation Command had done a great job of anticipating TF DAGGER's needs. They slammed additional Apaches on C-17s and sent them smoking into OPERATION ANACONDA, actually beating the formal request by TF DAGGER. A-10s and AC-130s from the U.S. Air Force along with bombers and carrier assets came, helping to pick up the slack by hitting known enemy locations. The A-10 Warthogs had been badly needed for five months and were finally in the battle.

As U.S. air assets pounded the enemy positions, problems continued to occur. The French deployed Mirage 2000 fighters into the battle in support of the Green Berets. COBRA 72 was calling in air strikes against AQ bunkers on the high plain of the valley. The first bombs almost wiped out the CAS team on the ground.

"Whoa, whoa, we're the good guys, dude," COBRA 72 called back.

"*Oui, oui,* sorry about that, I didn't precalibrate the laser guidance system," the Mirage pilot responded. The French had been lobbying hard to test their Mirage 2000s out in Afghanistan. They didn't seem to care much about the liberation of Afghanistan, or the defeat of terrorists, but they did care about selling the Mirage to the Middle East, and this was a chance to work out the bugs, and improve the precision-guided targeting systems. The first test would hopefully not be a precursor of things to come.

CAS became much riskier when the Green Berets spotted the worst possible scenario. Al-Qaida were now using orange panels in the mountains to identify themselves as friendly forces. Apparently AQ spies had infiltrated the Pashtun fighters from Gardez and passed the orange panels to the enemy.

Despite the confusion, the Green Berets were able to continue CAS and effective air strikes using additional target confirmation techniques. Al-Qaida started dispersing its forces. Nonetheless, the Pentagon announced at the end of the sixth day of combat that the number of AQ and Taliban killed in action had exceeded six hundred.

Secretary of Defense Rumsfeld announced that the United States would stay the course. Bin Laden and his AQ had killed thousands of innocent citizens of America and other nations. America was in a world war, and she was going for the jugular.

At Fort Bragg

Staff Sergeant Larry Wadsworth wore his Class-A dress uniform to Stanley Harriman's funeral. He couldn't button the coat because his arm was in a cast, and the wound on his throat kept his collar from being buttoned. He'd been with Harriman in ANACONDA. The shrapnel that had almost broken his leg made Wadsworth limp severely.

Before leaving the memorial service, Major Jim Burnside was asked if he could verify Chief Harriman's last words to see if the rumor sweeping Fort Bragg was true. Harriman had whispered, "I hope that this has not been in vain."

On the day of the funeral, Afghan women in Kabul were celebrating International Women's Day, faces uncovered, at a convention.

Afghan Forces Reenter the Fray

On March 7, Afghan forces from northern Afghanistan began to arrive in a staging area near Gardez. The U.S. had finally realized that the Pashtun fighters from the south were not going to engage their old compatriots the way the Northern Alliance would. The NA were itching to get into the battle and show the Americans that their courage and willingness to fight in the north would not be lacking in the south. General Fahim agreed with his chief of foreign military affairs, Abdul Wadood, now promoted to colonel, that it was time to send the NA into the south. The Northern Alliance could prove their alliance with the Americans, and why America needed to support them.

There was no lack of NA commanders volunteering for the task. After much deliberation and political positioning,

Fahim decided to send Commander Gul Haider. Haider was tough and seasoned. He had gained a wooden leg fighting the Soviets, and he had a well-equipped and ready-to-move army. His unit was mostly Tajik, an ethnic group underrepresented in Paktia Province. They had tanks, armored personnel carriers, and were loaded for combat. Once again, the Green Berets were to be their combat advisors.

Haider's column departed from Kabul with their Russian T-55 and T-62 tanks smoking diesel and running hard and fast down the road through Logar and into Gardez.

Local Afghan warlords were upset because Northern Alliance forces were now on Pashtun ground. Use of such troops in the south sent a message to all: the national government was flexing its muscle, and warlords needed to be on notice. An additional advantage was accrued by having the forces in Paktia Province. Northern Alliance troops hated the Taliban and AQ, and Tajiks would be less susceptible to corruption and less inclined to clandestinely support the AQ.

The Northern Alliance force would number one thousand, and was to be fully assembled on March 12, ready for combat.

Meanwhile, the U.S. kept pounding the AQ and shrinking the ANACONDA circle. The Special Forces, other than those in the valley, continued to work the ANACONDA ring. Fifty Afghan soldiers accompanied several Special Forces formations of three jeeps and two all-terrain motorbikes.

Field report calculations were starting to add up. Initial AQ strength was approximately eight hundred, and several hundred more reinforcements had snuck in to help.

By March 11, KIA figures were up to around seven hundred, and intelligence analysts claimed the number of enemy troops left in an area called the Arma al-Qaida base was reported to be two hundred, separated into two remaining pockets of resistance. AQ escapees probably made up the difference.

This time, the Afghan troops and the Green Beret combat advisory teams had good intelligence. The critical task for the advisors was to help Afghan soldiers force the AQ out of its remaining trench lines and into areas where they would be easy pickings. The operation was called OBJECTIVE REMINGTON.

Some of the local warlords began discussions of amnesty for the holdouts, to include escorts to the border of Pakistan. The Afghan culture of negotiation when an opponent had clearly gained the upper hand was not to be applied to the situation. Rumsfeld would have none of it; the coalition would finish the fight.

The local Afghan commander was still Zia Lodin, but now Commander Gul Haider was on the battlefield, and he wasn't going to give anyone amnesty. As they began the final assault, U.S. infantry and Canadian snipers were brought in to continue blocking escape routes. They brought intense bombing onto the trench line and the two pockets of resistance in the villages. Air power overwhelmed the remaining AQ, who gave up the trench line and ran into two small villages, where they sought refuge.

The villages virtually disappeared under a rain of ordnance, changing into piles of dusty brownish-red rubble consisting of logs, large rocks, mud, and dust. SHARK and their *muj* assaulted the towns virtually unopposed except for a few remaining diehards. As the Afghan troops and their Special Forces partners searched the villages, they found twenty-five bodies during the initial search.

Jack, an advisor to the Northern Alliance, was with Haider's troops, having been sent by General Gada in Kabul. Gada was the oldest of the *mujahadeen* commanders, and had it not been for his age, he probably would have been the defense minister. Fahim, now defense minister and overall commander of all Afghan forces, still consulted Gada on a regular basis, and kept him as one of his closest confidants.

With Jack on site, the Northern Alliance knew they would have a voice, and support in both the intelligence and medical arenas. Over the next days Jack operated on more than two dozen Afghan troops, often removing AQ bullets from wounded *muj* in the middle of the desert villages or on rocky hilltops. The *muj* would stand around in awe watching him

operate and stitch their wounds in the middle of nowhere. It was
a familiar scene to the Green Berets, who had used this sort of
medical assistance before in Vietnam to build bonds with the
Hmong, Montagnard, and other tribes fighting the Viet Cong
with them. Without fail, after each round of medical assistance,
the local Pashtuns also watching would voluntarily provide
him with al-Qaida intelligence.

Major Mark Schwartz

On March 12 in the Shah-i-Kot Valley, a unit of T-55 tanks
under the command of General Gul Haider mistakenly identified soldiers from the 101st Airborne as enemy troops, and
one of the tanks took a shot at the Americans' position. A potentially "green on green" incident was unfolding, and Major
Mark Schwartz, aka SHARK 95, immediately called a cease-
fire. He called the 101st Airborne's commander on the radio
and confirmed that there were friendly troops in the area.
Haider's infantry and tanks were told to withdraw before any
casualties were sustained. Schwartz's quick reactions saved
numerous lives, and according to Lieutenant Colonel Haas,
the senior SHARK officer, Schwartz "carried the day for the
SHARK element on more than one occasion."

Kill All You Can

Both operations, Tora Bora and ANACONDA, killed about
the same number of AQ and Taliban; however, the number of
escaping al-Qaida was still a problem.

Mountains are tough terrain, and fighting in them is extremely difficult and inexact. Al-Qaida had lots of time to
memorize every nook and cranny. They also had resources
that were not expected—satellite phones, laptop computers,
GPS, and even American/British PRC-117 radios. While
NSA was monitoring their communications, they were monitoring the coalition's communications. At night they would

escape with their gear and their KIA and WIA. Such was the art of counterguerrilla warfare, and in ANACONDA, the AQ were now the guerrillas, instead of the Green Berets and SAS.

The Culture of Pashtunwali

The al-Qaida were able to fade in and out of the Pashtun population and swim in its sea of the uncommitted rural populace because of ancient tribal practices in Afghanistan's nonurbanized and remote areas. The tenets of the tribal code are to give shelter to those in flight, protect anyone who seeks refuge, and avenge the death of your family members.

If a fleeing AQ or Taliban "brother" comes to your house for refuge, you must give it. If he stays in your house, you must feed and clothe him. If you kill a soldier, his family is obliged to kill you. The code of revenge makes a compelling argument for why the Northern Alliance granted amnesty to Afghan prisoners in the north.

Al-Qaida used the tribal code with ingenuity and impunity, and the Pashtun continued to harbor them.

Unqualified and Absolute ...

After the battle, General Franks visited Bagram airfield to award Purple Hearts and medals for valor to 10th Mountain and 101st Airborne Division troops. During his visit he stated that OPERATION ANACONDA was an "unqualified and absolute" success, having radically changed the landscape of the Shah-i-Kot Valley from an AQ haven to part of the new and free Afghan nation. Even though the final CENTCOM estimate of enemy KIA was approximately 520, Franks tried to steer judgment away from the body count. Several Green Berets later said that Franks and CENTCOM had inflated the enemy casualty figures to downplay the inherent failure of their conventional infantry operation.

General Franks had given official approval for the operation. There was little doubt that it had freed a large part of southern Afghanistan, and destroyed one of the AQ's last refuges. But Franks' decision to use conventional ground forces would probably be something he would sorely regret, resulting in more than a hundred casualties, and more Americans killed than Special Forces had lost in the past eight years. Franks' decision ended up costing the U.S. more lives in one day than any single combat mission since the disastrous Ranger and Delta Force raid in Mogadishu in 1993.

It had taken thousands of conventional troops and special ops forces to kill just a few hundred of the AQ. Working by themselves, one hundred Green Berets had killed tens of thousands in the first part of the war.

General Franks added, "I believe that future operations may well be the size of ANACONDA." The conventional army and its accompanying wisdom was again taking over.

Mulholland's Last Hurrah

Special Forces' participation in OPERATION ANACONDA had far exceeded that reported by most observers. Up to eight A-Teams and dozens of D-boys were engaged at one time, enough men in the operation for two company headquarters to get into the fight as well. The 3rd Special Forces Group had now been battle-tested in Afghanistan along with the 5th SFG(A). Colonel Mark C. Phelan and the 3rd Special Forces Group, reinforced by the 19th Special Forces Group, would carry on the fight in Afghanistan.

Pursuit of the AQ and the Taliban would continue. International peacekeepers would keep the lid on things in Kabul to buy time for the Afghanistan interim government to get on its feet. Early attention would have to be given to establishing a system to maintain law and order, passing and enforcing laws that encouraged investment and trade, and creating a national army. All of this would be incredibly difficult in a land of tribal hatreds and age-old customs.

The task would be left to others to handle such challenges. OPERATION ANACONDA was the 5th Special Forces Group and Colonel Mulholland's last hurrah.

CHAPTER 24

From Dagger
to Broadsword

*"Our goal is not to reduce or simply contain terrorist acts, but
our goal is to deal with it comprehensively, and we do not in-
tend to stop until we've rooted out terrorist networks and put
them out of business, not just in the case of the Taliban and the
al-Qaida in Afghanistan, but other networks as well. . . . As
we've said from the start of the campaign, this will not happen
overnight. It is a marathon, not a sprint. It will be years, not
weeks or months."*

—DONALD RUMSFELD,
Department of Defense briefing,
October 29, 2001

Mission accomplished, Colonel Mulholland sent the U.S.
Army Special Forces Command a short message on March 15,
2002:

–SECRET–
MESSAGE TRANSMISSION
**I have pulled the last 5th Special Forces Group
A-Teams out of Afghanistan. TASK FORCE
DAGGER no longer exists.**
END MESSAGE
–SECRET–

The 3rd and 19th Special Forces Groups had moved in
to replace Colonel Mulholland's 5th Special Forces Group.

They would continue operations in remote areas, prolonging the hunt. Mohammed Omar and Osama bin Laden remained on the run. The hunt remained ever-reaching, ever-present.

One way to find bin Laden was to seek out those who had close ties to him. Obviously this meant his top advisors, his military planners, and his financial lieutenants. One such man was Ahmad Sa'id al-Khadr, a member of bin Laden's closest circle of advisors. He was an Egyptian-born Canadian known as "al-Kanadi," Arabic for "the Canadian." Khadr was known to move money to fund terrorist operations through a Canadian relief agency known as Human Concern International.

He had also been on TASK FORCE DAGGER's ten-most-wanted list. Now he was on TASK FORCE 11's death list.

Khadr was believed to be going back and forth from Afghanistan to Pakistan, moving money, and staying in close contact with other top al-Qaida leaders. One of his sons, nineteen-year-old Abdul Rahman Khadr, had already been captured in November by TF DAGGER and Northern Alliance forces after the sieges in Kunduz and Taliqon. His family also had close ties to Mohamed Zeki Mahjoub, a member of al-Qaida's elite council, which picks potential targets and authorizes terrorist operations. In 1995, Khadr had been arrested by Pakistani authorities for his involvement in financing the bombing of the Egyptian embassy in Islamabad that year. Khadr had been released with the help of the Canadian government, which claimed he had not received "due process" from the Pakistanis. The Canadian Security Intelligence Service (CSIS) was not happy about this. There were also secret reports that al-Qaida had paid bribes to Pakistani officials for his freedom, and that the ISI had engineered the release. Bin Laden's fingerprints were everywhere.

In July 2002, operating on an intelligence tip from one of their paid informants, TASK FORCE 11 mounted an operation to capture Khadr. The plan was to swoop into the village where Khadr was hiding and descend on the house with Little Birds and the lightning-fast SOP of the D-boys, *Speed, Surprise, and Violence of Action*. The operation was to be small and fast. As a cover, another force would conduct a standard house-to-house search for weapons as part of the ongoing disarmament program. This would provide backup forces should the assault element run into problems or be engaged by a superior force. It was well known that bin Laden and his top men were constantly surrounded and protected by elite foreign soldiers, hard-core al-Qaida combatants. They were always heavily armed and outfitted.

The assault team hit Khadr's house on July 27, 2002. The planned ten-minute prisoner snatch turned into a battle, which lasted more than five hours.

Khadr's bodyguards fought hard, firing through gunports in the mud walls and hitting the TF 11 team with grenades and RPG rockets. When it was over, TASK FORCE 11 had control of the compound, and several prisoners. They did not have Khadr in custody, and five operators were wounded, including Sergeant First Class Christopher J. Speer, who was in critical condition with a severe head wound. They had captured Khadr's fifteen-year-old son, Omar al-Khadr; the younger Khadr had fought alongside the other al-Qaida terrorists and was both heavily armed and well trained.

Speer and the other wounded were flown to Germany for surgery. Chris Speer died on August 6, 2002, of head wounds received in the battle. Only days before the firefight, Speer, a combat medic with SFOD-D, had gone straight into a mine-field to save two injured Afghan children.

His death was not in vain; TF 11 was able to gain enough intelligence and information to pinpoint the locations of hideouts in Pakistan where the elder Khadr had been ferrying escaping al-Qaida terrorists from Afghanistan, including one of bin Laden's personal interpreters.

By the summer of 2002, the SEALs were having successes also, launching an airmobile assault on Mullah Kairullah's convoy. Kairullah was wanted for Taliban war crimes, and when the tip came, the SEALs had only twenty minutes from notification to briefing to airborne. One MH-53 Chinook launched with an AH-64 Apache for fire support. They were joined by elements of the Danish Special Forces and caught the convoy in open terrain. Ending with his successful capture, alive, the entire operation lasted less than two hours from tip-off to flex cuffs.

Mulholland's TF DAGGER boys were now home, reorganizing their teams, recuperating from a long, arduous trek from K2 to Kabul, and getting ready to topple the terrorist madman Saddam Hussein. Their missions, their promise, would now fall to the 1st and 3rd Special Forces Groups and TASK FORCE 11's D-boys. TASK FORCE 11 was now also known by the code name TASK FORCE SWORD, and they would need to cut a wider swath than DAGGER. A new task force was formed, called the Combined Joint Special Operations Task Force, and headquartered at Bagram Airfield.

Intelligence SNAFUs would continue, and in spite of the fact that TF DAGGER and TF 11 had the finest commandos in the world, they remained at the mercy of poor intelligence and conventional commanders. The CIA was still as inept as ever. They refused to deal with people they didn't like, even if those people had incredible intelligence. They had been willing to buy the surrender of Taliban commanders in the early days of the war, but they were unwilling to put "criminals" on their payroll for information. They would not hire or pay "bad guys" even if those bad guys had information that could result in the capture and termination of other bad guys, and the Agency was still overly political and inherently untrustworthy, not to mention rife with novice agents who had no experience in war and lacked courage. "Bad guys" seemed to be a subjective term open to interpretation by the agent or agents dealing with the situation. Several of the contract agents for the CIA, mostly former Special Operations soldiers, did not have this problem; they would deal with anyone as long as he could help them. To make matters worse, the FBI was continuing to interject itself into the conflict, in a long-running turf war for more funding and personnel. The CIA and FBI were now completely at odds with TF SABER and even refused to take bags full of intelligence materials that TF SABER had captured.

In September 2002, Special Operations Forces intercepted a satellite phone transmission and located Mullah Omar traveling through the desert near Kandahar by triangulating his cell-phone signal. NRO and NSA had worked together to pinpoint the signal and fired the information off to the Agency. Omar's Land Cruiser was finally in their sights. It took hours for the intel to be relayed to the Joint Special Operations Command and down to the ground commanders, however, and Omar's Land Cruiser was on the move and heading through the desert toward Pakistan. To make matters worse, once Omar was on the move, NRO satellites had problems tracking the Land Cruiser and soon lost it in the desert. The second-most-wanted man in the War on Terror had once again slipped away, leaving the special operators with their dicks in their hands and no power to move.

Rumsfeld had already moved to fix the intelligence problems. He authorized Special Operations Forces to operate using tactics and techniques normally reserved for the CIA. That meant they could conduct their own "source operations." In other words, they could hire, pay, and bribe their own intelligence sources, develop agents and assets with links to the enemy, and use a host of other techniques normally reserved for the CIA. Special operators could now recruit action agents (assets who had contact with the targets) and general support agents (assets who could act as spotters and recruiters of action agents and also work as interpreters, safehouse keepers, and collectors of intelligence materials). Not only could they recruit assets, they were now allowed to run their own agents and agent nets. SF was finally getting some of the operational latitude and authority that the British SAS and M16 regularly enjoyed. This was a huge advantage for the Special Forces and Delta operators, because they now had control over their intelligence. If bad intelligence got them killed or wounded, at least it was their own fault, not the result of being "forced to depend on some dweeb who just took off his polyester suit a week before."

They were also now authorized to conduct "coercive recruitment." That meant they could blackmail and threaten physical violence, if needed, to force a Taliban or AQ sympathizer or member to expose his cohorts. The Green Berets finally had another silver bullet in their arsenal of counterterrorism.

With Omar and bin Laden still on the loose, they were prepared to go anywhere in pursuit of the hunt.

The al-Qaida network spanned up to sixty nations, and the CIA was after it. The Agency's counterterror center in Langley, Virginia, increased its manpower to eight hundred analysts, technicians, and covert operators, a 100 percent growth in only a few months. MI6 continued to operate as it always had, with only slightly more funding, but a much greater sense of purpose. MI5, concerned with the internal security of England, now had a mission in Afghanistan. Several British citizens, fighting with al-Qaida, had been taken prisoner in Afghanistan, and others in Pakistan. MI5 intelligence identified 207 British-born Muslims that had left England to fight in Afghanistan, Chechnya, or with al-Qaida in a terrorist role.

With the help of the Green Berets and the D-boys, the Agency was turning over rocks everywhere, trying to take the network apart. They were in hot pursuit of finances and logistics, key personalities, and, most important, they were building archives that could be cross-referenced and matrixed with other intelligence inputs. Thousands of leads and suspects were being sorted out around the world.

Traditionally one of the worst functioning and most parochial of organizations, the FBI was energized, too. After years of disgrace and embarrassment, the FBI had convinced Congress to expand its counterterrorism workforce fourfold to four thousand personnel. It was typical FBI wisdom— "we only fucked up 9/11 because we didn't have enough money . . ." And, it was a typical American response—when faced with incompetence and bureaucracy, spend another billion dollars, and hire some more bureaucrats to fix the problem. Many claimed they were still out of their league, and FBI operations in Afghanistan were a joke with Special Forces operators. The FBI supposedly was sharing sophisticated cyber-crime and other domestic information more freely than before with state and local police departments.

But the NYPD and others kept complaining that the Bureau refused to share intelligence, frequently holding back a large percentage of the most valuable information. The NYPD was so incensed at the FBI's withholding of information and incompetence that they set up their own NYPD CIA—even sending former undercover narcotics cops, now retrained as undercover counterterrorists, into Afghanistan and Pakistan to conduct their own operations. Green Berets were more willing to help the NYPD operators because they were just regular guys like them, "neither pompous nor arrogant," said one. The Green Berets appreciated the NYPD more than the FBI because, like Special Forces, the NYPD had sacrificed lives in this war.

Yet the FBI was desperate to be included in the war, and they knew that inclusion meant more funding. Eventually they interjected themselves into Special Forces missions in Pakistan in a futile attempt not to be "left out of the party." The Bureau was once again trying to expand its reach, and many operators complained they were trying to set up their own CIA, and acting twice as arrogant.

Initially, what many in federal law enforcement agencies did not understand is that the main effort for victory would be hard, tedious intelligence work and you had to develop your sources based on friendship, not alienate them and treat them as potential adversaries. The Defense Intelligence Agency worked hard, and proved they were well suited for the job. Where others failed, the DIA excelled, using classified units like the Intelligence Support Activity, a supersecret arm of the Green Berets that specializes in gathering intelligence in dangerous situations and in denied areas of operations. ISA operators often went in as total civilians, completely undercover, with no resources, no support, and with no connection to any official organization. The Green Berets internally referred to them as the Northern Army of Virginia.

As the tedious work to paint a worldwide intelligence picture was under way, the Green Berets were moving to do what they could in other theaters.

Special Forces were covertly deployed to Yemen to work

for the ambassador, assisting an attempt to sort out the AQ presence in the northern part of the country. Colonel David P. Fridovich was leading the 1st Special Forces Group effort in the Philippines, while Colonel Charles Cleveland was preparing to send 10th Special Forces into the former Soviet republic of Georgia.

The Al-Itihaad Islamic group was ripe for examination in Somalia. According to some, Sudan was beginning to behave. Colombia had declared all-out war on the FARC, with implications for the U.S. still unclear. Mischief was still afoot in the Balkans. Odd things were happening in Paraguay. In Sri Lanka there was hope that the Tamil Tigers might stop fighting, and in Nepal the Maoist guerrillas had taken down one-third of the country. Indonesia, the Philippines, and Malaysia were all known to have significant terrorist targets. The Palestinian/Israeli struggle had reached new levels of chaos and breakdown, begging for an internationally imposed solution. Hundreds of Special Operations troops were covertly heading into other countries.

Iraq wasn't getting the message—America was on the warpath, and those that didn't join the fight, would find themselves on the wrong side of the fight. No one expected Iraq to assist in the War on Terror, but it was expected that they would "straighten up and and fly right." In fact, it appeared that Desert Storm had taught Saddam Hussein to be more watchful and keep greater secrecy. Special operators knew that if Saddam *ever* developed significant stockpiles of small nuclear, biological, or chemical weapons that they would eventually be in terrorist hands and the U.S. would pay the price. They also knew that Saddam already had WMDs, weapons of mass destruction, and might use them if backed into a corner.

At the 180-day mark after September 11, business was picking up and the Green Berets remained ready, George Orwell's "rough men waiting in the dark."

EPILOGUE:

Jack's Tora Bora Café

"If you want to join the coalition against terror, we'll welcome you in. . . . All I ask is for results. If you say you want to join us to cut off money, show us the money. If you say you want to join us militarily, . . . do so. . . . If you're interested in sharing intelligence, share intelligence."

—PRESIDENT GEORGE W. BUSH,
White House press conference,
October 11, 2001

"Where are all your men? You have come alone? How can you help us defeat our enemy with only one man? The Russians sent tens of thousands . . . Bush sends us one. . . . What kind of men are these Green Berets that will come alone?"

—GOVERNOR OF LOGAR PROVINCE
to Jack, January 2002

Jack sat back in the olive-green seat of a Russian MIG jet fighter and looked out over the Kabul skyline. Down below were the shattered buildings and dilapidated mud huts that made up Afghanistan's capital and largest city.

To the west, spanning out for miles he could see the ruins left by Hekmatyar's genocidal rocket attacks from before the Taliban's new reign of terror. Looking out to the south he could see the stadium where al-Qaida had tortured and executed their enemies. To the east were the mountain passes that had brought down so many Russian fighters and trapped so many tanks as the *mujahadeen* slaughtered the invaders, and where the AQ had murdered four journalists. As the sun

380

glinted off the black Lexan glass shielding his eyes, he turned to the north, and saw the devastation of the Shomali Plains— the mines laid by countless invaders, and the scorched earth the Taliban had left.

The crisp desert air dehydrated his face. He could feel the hard steel corners of his two Soviet 9mm Makarov pistols— one in a shoulder holster under his black field jacket, and the other tucked into the small of his back. His hand reached down and touched the ejection seat lever as he stretched his legs, pushing against the rough canvas seat pads.

His black-and-white-checkered Massoud scarf flew in the wind. . . .

Jack was sitting on the roof of the Mustafa Hotel. The ejection seat had been a gift from the Northern Alliance. It was all that was left of a Taliban fighter jet hit by U.S. bombers as they destroyed bin Laden and Omar's military airfield. The airfield was now flying the Northern Alliance flag and was being rebuilt by Jack and his men. Kabul had been free for more than six months, and Jack had now been in Afghanistan for more than eight months.

The Mustafa Hotel was owned by two Afghan-Americans, Weiss and Sol, and it was the only place in Kabul you could buy a pizza or a steak. It was also the only place in Afghanistan where you could drink vodka and pomegranate juice—in fact, vodka and anything. It was called Jack's Tora Bora Rooftop Café.

Jack lifted his glass off the table beside his ejection seat and raised it in the air. Sol and Weiss raised theirs in turn. They were also sitting in MIG seats, courtesy of Jack and the NA.

"SF is back." Jack smiled. "Strength and Honor! Here's to the boys from TF DAGGER. They're the best there ever was. I can only hope Americans will one day know exactly how many al-Qaida ragheads those guys really killed."

Weiss and Sol raised their glasses and joined the toast, although they knew nothing of what the words "TF DAGGER" or "SF" meant. Unlike most Americans, they did know that the Green Berets had sent tens of thousands of bin Laden's terrorists to meet Allah, and that alone renewed their faith in America and their hope for the future of Afghanistan.

"God, I hate it when a war ends," Jack quietly said as he stared at his drink. His teary eyes glassed over from the booze.

Most stories about the Afghan conflict start on September 11, 2001, but Jack's story began a long time before. That day he read the book *The Green Berets* in 1968.

Throughout the war, it seemed as though he was everywhere. Khoja-Bahaudeen, Kal-a-Khata, Taloqan, Mazar, Tora Bora, Kandahar, Gardez—from one conflict to the next, Jack was there. But was Jack one person, or several involved in the war on terrorism, all using the same JFK-style pseudonym?

One correspondent called Jack "Collateral Damage II," referring to the Arnold Schwarzenegger film in which a New York City fireman's family is killed by terrorists, sending him on a one-man war in South America.

Jon Lee Anderson of *The New Yorker* fondly referred to him as "Colonel Kurtz," a reference to Marlon Brando's rebel Green Beret character in *Apocalypse Now.*

Heart of Darkness

Jack had already been all over America's television sets when he helped save wounded *National Geographic* producer Gary Scurka in northern Afghanistan. But America's first real glimpse of who Jack was came through the eyes of Dan Rather of *CBS Evening News* and *60 Minutes II* fame.

Rather flew to Afghanistan in January 2002 to find Jack, and to investigate a story that Elizabeth Neuffer was writing for the *Boston Globe*—a story that Rather quickly learned would be the most far-reaching, wide-running story of the war.

CBS appropriately called it "Heart of Darkness," and it was America's first look inside al-Qaida. It was a look at their motives, their operations, their training, and their faces. Almost seven hours of video, captured by Jack, were released to the American public and the world. Jack named them the

8mm VideoX tapes, and they were images of terror Americans needed to see.

In an exclusive U.S. interview, conducted at what used to be the largest al-Qaida terrorist-training base in Afghanistan, Jack told Dan Rather, "I want my mom, your mom, everyone's mom, to see this. I want them to see inside the heart of al-Qaida, to know their evil, to know the blackness of their soul, and to know why this war must continue, why we have to bring it to their doorstep wherever they may be."

The Pentagon did not want the videos released. The U.S. Army Public Affairs Office called it irresponsible, borderline criminal, and completely in violation of U.S. objectives and policy. But, government officials are often out of touch with the heartbeat of America, and this situation was no different. The Department of Justice scrambled to draft a response. Rumsfeld, on the other hand, decided he liked it.

If any videos, any pictures, did justice to President George Bush's mission against terrorism, it was Jack's al-Qaida videos. There was the video of bin Laden himself admitting his complicity in the September 11 attacks, but that video was released by the U.S. government, and as a result was called into question by some people. They wondered what was cut out or possibly altered.

Jay Weiss, Rather's *60 Minutes II* coproducer on the piece, and Elizabeth Neuffer wondered out loud on numerous occasions, was the release of these tapes a Pentagon black op— the phrase for operations so secret that they are made to look as if the Department of Defense has no involvement? Or, was Jack a complete renegade? That remained the number-one question about Jack.

It wasn't just the *8mm VideoX* operation that focused the world's attention on al-Qaida's evil motives, or on Jack.

As the first waves of U.S. bombs were falling, Jack was helping deliver food and supplies to the Northern Alliance. By November he was helping the NA with aid shipments and advice. In December at Tora Bora, it was Jack who found documents in bin Laden's retreat that painted a vivid picture of his terrorist goals. When Afghans thought they had an armed assassin at Hamid Karzai's inauguration on December 22, 2001, it was Jack they called in to sort it out.

In January, Jack uncovered an al-Qaida plot to kill President Clinton. In March, standing in the middle of a Kabul street armed with a Russian assault rifle and six hundred rounds of ammunition, Jack held off Islamic fundamentalists for four hours as they tried to take eighteen foreign citizens hostage, keeping them at bay until Engineer Ali and the Northern Alliance arrived to back him up. By the end of March, Jack was in a Northern Alliance helicopter and on his way to the Nahrin earthquake, where the Associated Press photographed the lone American rescuing a little girl. She wasn't the first child he would save, or the last. By mid-April Jack was rebuilding Northern Alliance airfields, and by May he was back on the trail of more hidden al-Qaida commanders.

TASK FORCE DAGGER was long gone, as was the 5th Special Forces Group. The 3rd and 1st Special Forces Groups, and the 19th Group, a National Guard unit that had been activated, had since replaced them. Afghanistan was now free. Jack's mission was over. Yet still, he could not bring himself to leave Afghanistan and "Indian country." His adrenaline glands were not yet burned out, and this was the best high on the planet. Besides, al-Qaida was still there, the Taliban had changed their name—but were re-forming in Pakistan to return—and the Northern Alliance still needed a friend, maybe now more than ever.

It was almost June 2002, and things would be much harder now, more conventional, more static, and more political. The Green Beret pondered whether or not he should leave and return to Fayetteville, North Carolina. In the middle of negotiating for the surrender of AQ prisoners being held in the basement of a local Afghan commander, his mind was made up for him. His mother had passed away in New York.

One question would remain—how did Jack, operating completely independently of TF DAGGER and the Central Command, interject himself so completely in America's War on Terrorism?

Maybe there were dozens of guys called Jack running around Afghanistan, and maybe there was just one. Regardless of how many there were, or will ever be, regardless of who he was, Jack got results, and the Afghan generals often said he is the kind of American that our Afghan allies want to see more of.

Fort Bragg, North Carolina, 2003

John Bolduc's ring was now back in care of General Lambert, and Bolduc's retirement was finalized on December 31, 2002. With Bolduc's blessings Lambert passed the ring to Kevin Morehead, and two weeks later, just after the New Year, Morehead was the first Green Beret to infiltrate into Iraq to meet with resistance leaders.

Mulholland's Green Berets went into isolation, and started the entire process all over again. This time they would be going to a country they were well familiar with, Iraq. Once again, they were to be America's Jedi Knights in the War on Terror.

David Stirling's beloved 22 SAS began making preparations to insert into Iraq, and spearhead Tony Blair's military forces in the battle for Baghdad.

Kirk Harrington deployed to the command center for the Iraq invasion. In spite of his injured leg he wasn't about to sit on the sidelines again.

Major Mark Mitchell was promoted to Lieutenant Colonel, and took command of special operations in Southwest Asia.

General Tommy Franks finally got the war he was groomed for. His conventional forces performed admirably and his war plan for Iraq was implemented with precision and professionalism.

The U.S. Congress interrogated President Karzai, embarrassing America's greatest Muslim ally, and refused to give him the humanitarian and military aid that General Franks had personally promised the Afghans during the December 22, 2001 inauguration. President George W. Bush took it upon himself to call Karzai personally and apologize for Karzai's treatment while a guest of the United States. Meanwhile, the Congress and Senate continued to hold up the aid Afghanistan so desperately needed.

Geraldo Rivera was accused of disclosing secret war information on a Fox News broadcast and was promptly removed from Iraq by the U.S. Army.

Gary Scurka quickly convinced his bosses to send him in as the only imbedded reporter from *National Geographic* Television. It was an easy sell—there were no other volunteers.

Jon Lee Anderson, the fearless and dedicated *New Yorker* journalist, returned to England and began working on his third book.

Massoud's memory lived on, both in the hearts of the Northern Alliance fighters, and in legend, immortalized by Anderson in his stirring book of dispatches from Afghanistan, *The Lion's Grave,* which he wrote while reporting from the front lines, evading Taliban roadblocks and interviewing al-Qaida prisoners.

Elizabeth Neuffer once said, "The truth may be hazardous to those who tell it, but the truth is not dangerous, disinformation is. As I saw in Bosnia and Rwanda, it is propaganda that fans the flames of hatred." Neuffer, an award-winning journalist and friend of the Special Forces, was killed in Iraq in May 2003.

J. Cofer Black left his beloved CIA and became the U.S. Ambassador at Large for Counter-Terrorism. It was a terrifying prospect for countries that supported terrorists. He would never stop serving God and country and he never stopped wanting to see flies on bin Laden's eyeballs. When asked about diplomacy in the War on Terror, Black responded quietly, methodically, and without a glint of emotion, "All you need to know, is that there was a before 9/11, and there was an after 9/11 . . . After 9/11 the gloves came off."

Kevin Morehead, the last recipient of the ring from General Lambert, was killed in action during Operation Iraqi Freedom on September 12, 2003, near the town of Ar-Ramad in Iraq.

Jack returned to the desert. He was not interested in helping the Iraqis. His heart remained with the Northern Alliance, and he became an outspoken advocate for their support on American television. In Afghanistan, where he returned to, Jack is still known as simply "Jack," and always will be . . .

After-Action Reports

"Until you have him [bin Laden], you do not have him, so what is progress? Until he is no longer functioning as a terrorist, he is functioning as a terrorist. There isn't any 'progress.' You either have him or you don't."

          —DONALD RUMSFELD,
           Department of Defense briefing,
           October 25, 2001

"Al-Qaida in Afghanistan is finished, but our job is far from over. Now I want bin Laden, dead or alive, preferably dead. Keep him on the run. Hunt him. Hunt him to the ends of the earth, then send him to Hell. This is our mission; this is our debt to the American people, and to New York."

          —commander, U.S. Special Mission Unit,
           May 30, 2002

The Hunt for bin Laden

Author's note
September 11, 2003

When we finally finished updating this book today, I still knew several inalienable truths about the War on Terror. It is a war to destroy sophisticated organizations. Operations against one man are impossibly difficult—even Hitler eluded our capture in the end. But the fate of Osama bin Laden weighs on the American public, and I want his severed head on a stake as much as the next red-white-and-blue American.

On my journeys with Special Forces and other special operators, I continuously surveyed them both overtly and covertly to obtain clues to the fate or whereabouts of Osama bin Laden. During the Special Forces 50th Anniversary celebration, I closed many bars digging for insight. Many say that bin Laden was in Tora Bora before the fighting intensified, and that he had been positively located in a valley. Others say that the Canadian troops sent into the Tora Bora region to recover over twenty bodies from a bombing site in early May of 2002 was an indicator that Tora Bora was the military's last chance for a positive identification. Yet, the CIA was sure they had him in the Dehbala region on February 6, 2002, when they fired a Hellfire missile at a tall man with bodyguards.

Many have come to say, as has President Pervez Musharraf of Pakistan, that Osama is dead. Yet, Musharraf's pronouncement was followed a day later, on July 2, 2002, with an assessment that bin Laden is still alive by Afghanistan's foreign minister, Dr. Abdullah Abdullah. That assessment was restated by the foreign minister in August 2002.

Musharraf, trying to keep the lid on a violently anti-American country, wants U.S. scrutiny and troops out of the region. Abdullah, a close friend of the United States, and comrade of the assassinated Commander Massoud, wants the U.S. to remain.

However, in August 2002, new reports began to circulate. Osama bin Laden was alive and well, and preparing to rebuild his forces, continue his *jihad,* and wage a guerrilla war against U.S. troops in Afghanistan. According to Abdel-Bari Atwan, editor of the London-based daily *al-Quds al-Arabi,* bin Laden's minions will now "dig in and prepare to fight a war of attrition" against U.S. troops in Afghanistan. Atwan claimed that they will time their attacks to coincide with the planned U.S. attack on Iraq, in order to show that bin Laden remains the only Arab standing up to the United States.

By Christmas 2002, several audiotapes of Osama bin Laden had come out. All purporting to be his voice carrying the message of *jihad* to his followers, and flaunting the American hunt. According to Jack, every one of them was fake. It was well known in bin Laden's closest circles that he preferred to send his messages to the world via video, as he had always done in the past. Jack theorized that the purported audiotapes of bin Laden were a ruse by either al Jazeera television, al-Qaida members attempting to rally their forces, or a clever entrepreneur who sold them. Shortly thereafter, the Swiss *Dalle Molle Institute for Perceptual Artificial Intelligence* announced it was 95 percent certain that the tapes were fake. Two weeks before, the NSA had already issued a TOP SECRET/CODEWORD memorandum, saying it was 98.5 percent sure the tapes were fake.

I have been inside TASK FORCE DAGGER, to Uzbekistan, to Bagram, to Kandahar, to Kabul, to Pakistan, to Washington, D.C., to New York City, and to Fort Bragg, North Carolina, and the truth about bin Laden remains elusive.

Yet, I know the following: If Osama bin Laden surfaces physically, medically, financially, electronically, or in any other way . . . the Green Berets will execute him. They will hunt him, they will track him, they will hound him, and they will pursue him to the ends of the earth. They are America's avenging angels, and they will suffer, bleed, and die to bring their justice to bin Laden. They will continue to hunt al-Qaida across the face of the globe into the mountains, the valleys, and the remote regions where evil always hides.

Bin Laden's destiny, ordained by his psychotic attacks on America, will be to meet Allah personally, and every single U.S. special operator is working to make that meeting happen as soon as possible.

Murphy's Laws of Combat

"No plan ever survives the first contact—intact."
—Murphy's Laws of Combat

Blue on Blue

"Blue on blue" is a term that means friendly fire has killed friendly troops. "Fratricide" is another common term for U.S. forces killing U.S. forces. Realists understand that it has always happened, and that for the foreseeable future, in the fog and chaos of war, it will continue, but it doesn't make it any easier to swallow when it does. Green Berets were on the receiving end of friendly bombs in four locations in eighteen months; one in Kuwait, and three in Afghanistan. In Kuwait, USAF ground controllers called in Navy aircraft. The aircraft dropped its bombs before it was told to do so; 3rd Special Forces soldiers and others died.

In Afghanistan, at Mazar-e-Sharif, the USAF ground controller called for a bomb, giving his coordinates and those of the target. The aircraft "fingered" in the coordinates of the controller. Several 5th Special Forces Group soldiers were injured; dozens of Northern Alliance troops were killed.

In Afghanistan, near Kandahar, a bomb again hit the coordinates of the controller. Failure was reported to lie with the controller. Three men assigned to 5th Special Forces Group perished, along with numerous anti-Taliban Afghan soldiers.

During OPERATION ANACONDA, USAF aircraft engaged a Special Forces team and its Afghan allies, killing one Special Forces warrant officer from the 3rd Special Forces Group and wounding two others.

Blue-on-Blue Fact

For the past few years the Green Berets have been forced to take Air Force combat controllers with them since the Green Berets supposedly aren't qualified to call in U.S. Air Force CAS and other munitions. The Navy and the Marine Corps pilots don't have similar hang-ups and will fly in support of Special Forces troops.

In fact, Special Forces troops constantly acknowledge the fact that Navy and Marine fighter pilots will fly anywhere they ask, and bomb any way they want, as long as they just get to kill something. Master Sergeant Bolduc's team of Green Beret sergeants called in missions for three weeks and killed thousands and thousands of Taliban soldiers, without a single error.

During thousands of sorties (air combat missions) flown during the war, Green Beret sergeants made more than half of the requests for air support. Not once did a Green Beret sergeant call anything in on themselves, or their own troops.

Green on Green

"Green on green" is the term for warlords using fires of their own or of the U.S. against one another. The possibility of the warlords using U.S. firepower for their own ends is another battlefield reality that the A-Teams had to face.

There are several reported examples of warlords nominating targets that, when the A-Teams checked, were neither AQ nor Taliban; rather, they were merely anti-Taliban militias not loyal to the anti-Taliban warlord asking for the fire support.

Blue on Green

"Blue on green" refers to U.S. fires impacting Afghan allies or innocents.

On December 21, a convoy of tribal leaders outside Khost, heading toward Chairman Karzai's inauguration, was struck, resulting in more than twelve casualties, later determined to be friendlies. In Oruzgan Province on January 24, Special Forces soldiers assaulted two suspected AQ or Taliban compounds in a coordinated attack, killing fifteen and capturing twenty-seven, who were later released after Karzai's government revealed that the compounds contained neither AQ nor Taliban personnel.

Secretary of Defense Rumsfeld confirmed on February 21, 2002, that the earlier instances and the raid of January 24 were blue on green, and no systemic errors in the targeting process, mission planning, or mission execution were evident. More stringent and deliberate vetting of targets during transition and mopping-up operations appeared to be a solution.

An official from Afghanistan's embassy in Washington commented, "The overall campaign deserved an A-plus. These deaths are not monumental."

In Afghanistan, the war had its casualties, and the fact of the matter was that the collateral damage and unintended casualties of this war were far less and fewer than ever before, truly mistakes, and deeply regretted by all involved.

Blue on Red

"Blue on red" is the way it is supposed to be, and the experience in Afghanistan proved how lethal the Special Forces combined with USAF bombers and USAF/USMC/U.S. Navy fighters can truly be. Red forces are the enemy during service war games, also known as OPFOR (opposing force).

Tens of thousands of Taliban and AQ were destroyed by precision firepower because Special Forces could assist in finding targets. Had such weapons been available during the Vietnam War, an entirely different outcome may have resulted. Today, Special Forces teams along a "Ho Chi Minh trail," even in the densest terrain, would literally decimate any opposing army on the move. Their abilities were proven again in Iraq, where U.S. and British Special Forces units vaporized Republican guard units, leaving only burning remnants to face the coalition center sweeping across the desert.

Blue on White

"Blue on white" is the inadvertent killing of innocent civilians by U.S. forces. In March of 2002, Human Rights Watch research teams began surveying sites where civilian casualties may have occurred throughout Afghanistan. More than 300 alleged incidents across the country had been cataloged for investigation. Only a few are probably credible, and some may have been from Afghan heavy weapons, making exact findings impossible.

Nonetheless, Human Rights Watch's work is valuable. Precision weapons have lessened the suffering of innocents to a degree unimaginable only a quarter of a century ago. Careful scrutiny, open communication, and application of lessons learned can only be helpful as the Department of Defense strives to make combat more and more surgical, thereby lessening the threat to noncombatants.

Donald Rumsfeld

*"You can't deal with it [terrorism] through defense. The only
defense against terrorism is offense. You simply have to take
the battle to them."*

> —DONALD RUMSFELD,
> Department of Defense briefing,
> October 18, 2001

Fort Bragg, North Carolina

Many retired Green Berets were surprised that General
Franks agreed to give Special Forces a chance to show what
they could bring to a fight. That subject has been a definite
factor in the increase in revenue at the Green Beret Club at
Fort Bragg, North Carolina.

For months old-timers had stayed for an extra brew or
two, or three, launching and debating theories regarding General Franks' motivations. As Afghanistan vets started to flow
through the club offering their perspective, the old-timers
formed a consensus:

Rumsfeld wanted swift action, but everyone hesitated to
jump into a medieval combat zone with zero preparation—
everyone except the Green Berets. Neither Franks nor any
other general, however, wanted to tell Rumsfeld they weren't
ready for war. Two generals had already made that mistake
shortly after September 11.

Franks knew that Rumsfeld is not afraid to lead. He knows
that as secretary of defense he is legally in charge and that
he can organize his forces the way he wants. He has enough
confidence in himself and his team that he makes decisions
that are out of the box. Franks knew that Rumsfeld is also
not afraid to fire people. In fact, he is an exceptionally prag-
matic commander. When he sees what he thinks will work, he
does it.

He also limited the power of the military commanders to
give only mission *guidance*, and then turned Special Forces
loose. This allowed them to set up TASK FORCE DAGGER

and this created the conditions for TASK FORCE DAGGER to innovate, seek and pursue opportunity. It gave them operational and tactical agility unmatched in previous operations and wars.

Second, Rumsfeld understands the past. His appreciation of the Guam Doctrine, promulgated by the Nixon administration, was Franks' and Holland's guide for their operational concept to unseat the Taliban regime.

The doctrine, simply stated, is that we will aid those willing to fight tyranny with advisors and resources. When indirect warfare of this type is attempted, conventional forces are only planned as backup in case direct action is necessary.

Holland and Franks used the Green Berets because Lieutenant Colonel Dave Miller, on the verge of retirement, with nothing to lose, proved to them that there was enough unconventional warfare potential that they "might" succeed. It was an audacious plan. "Might" was good enough for the commander in chief, and they knew it was good enough for Rumsfeld.

Finally, Rumsfeld stood up for the troops and hated the enemy as much as any man on the ground fighting them. More than one Green Beret said he'd take Rumsfeld with him on a mission if he were even ten years younger. On January 24, 2002, when Special Forces attacked a complex that intelligence indicated was full of al-Qaida and Taliban, the men killed and captured were actually loyal to the Afghan government. The target identification turned out to be an intelligence/targeting/vetting failure. Rumsfeld took the heat, as good leaders do. Throughout the war, Rumsfeld protected the Special Forces soldiers who had attacked their objective, following their orders.

In the end, long after TASK FORCE DAGGER was gone, General Franks and the other conventional officers went back to their conventional thinking. U.S. forces began setting up permanent bases, fire bases in potentially hostile territory, and Franks called for peacekeeping troops throughout Afghanistan. Rumsfeld didn't hesitate to stand up and give his version, the unconventional version, the version that had worked before, and that Rumsfeld knew would work again.

In the end, the lessons of Vietnam and Afghanistan's prior history were lost on those conventional officers in command. They would build a powerful conventional presence that would ultimately lead to a reversal of roles—the Taliban and AQ would now be the guerrilla fighters and U.S. forces would now be the defenders. However, one man, at the very top of the food chain, Donald Rumsfeld, would "get it." In late August 2002, Rumsfeld would reject Franks' plans for U.S. peacekeeping forces, and direct the Green Berets to continue training a national defense force, whereby Afghanistan would develop their own peacekeeping force. Rumsfeld was engaging in SPARTAN, and allowing the Green Berets to do what they knew how to do; defeat terrorists and build nations.

Hamid Karzai had remained true to the Green Berets who saved his country, and insisted they, not the Department of State, be his personal bodyguards. In the first week of September 2002, al-Qaida and Hekmatyar attempted to assassinate President Karzai. The Green Berets saved his life once again. Even though the one shirtless American, looking like a complete slob, neither saved Karzai, or was a Green Beret, three days later, embarrassed by national news coverage of the ragtag, bearded commandos, General Lambert had no choice but to bow to the conventional wisdom of a career infantry officer, Lieutenant General Dan K. McNeil, who was now commanding the special ops troops in Afghanistan, and ordered their beards shaved, and all Green Berets back in uniform. A few days later General Franks ordered artillery into Bagram airfield to protect it. Conventional thinking had completely taken over the war. Conventional generals were destroying all that the Green Berets had accomplished.

But Lambert knew when to fight upstream and when not to. Still true to his unconventional roots, he waited until the next morning and made a private call to Afghanistan. "I know what my orders were, but we're dealing with politics here. Just grow the darn beards back until some fool gets photographed again and I have to order them off again." Lambert knew they must continue to operate unconventionally, or face the fate of the Soviet Conventional Forces.

As the first anniversary of September 11 approached, Rumsfeld was secretly taking steps to make sure *his* vision and the Green Berets' vision for the U.S. War on Terrorism would be followed. Lieutenant General Doug Brown would soon be selected to command a new force that would continue to fight America's war unconventionally. Control of the Afghan conflict would be taken away from Franks and the conventional generals, and put in the proven capable hands of the Green Berets.

Just days before this book was typeset, Donald Rumsfeld sent a confidential memo to each of the CINCs. As of October 22, 2002, there would be only one CINC, one commander in chief, and that would be President George W. Bush. Tommy Franks would now be just a "commander" and Bush, through Rumsfeld, would lead the war from this point on. The Green Berets were ecstatic.

A Perfect 10

Washington, D.C.

Bo Derek was in Walter Reed Army Medical Center. A veterans' advocate, she had heard of wounded Special Forces soldiers at the hospital, and dropped by to offer her support.

On arrival, she learned most of the Green Berets had moved back to their units for continuing care, and the one remaining was out on pass. The patient, a sergeant first class, had lost an arm. A small crowd gathered to peer over his shoulder to get a glimpse of Bo.

One tall young man noticed a small pin on the lapel of Bo's escort. It was a miniature Special Forces crest. An SF lapel crest meant instant camaraderie in the SF community. In the ensuing conversation, the escort asked the patient, "What's your name?"

"Sergeant First Class McElhiney," the patient answered.

The escort broke out laughing. "You shouldn't be here craning your neck to see Bo; she came here to see *you!*"

McElhiney replied in disbelief, "You're kidding."

For her support and volunteer work for veterans and Special Forces in particular, Bo Derek was later made an honorary Green Beret in a ceremony at the Special Forces 50th Anniversary Banquet in Fayetteville, North Carolina, on June 29, 2002.

To many soldiers in Special Forces, Bo is a modern-day version of actress-comedienne Martha "Colonel Maggie" Raye, who was a friend to American servicemen during World War II and Korea, and Green Berets during the Vietnam era.

The Green Berets had adopted Colonel Maggie as one of their own, and she was the first woman ever to be presented a Green Beret and given the right to wear it with her uniform. When Colonel Maggie passed away several years ago, she left her Special Forces mementos to the men of the Special Forces, who put them on display in "Maggie's Team Room" in the Special Forces Museum at Fort Bragg. While no one will ever take Maggie's place in the hearts of Special Forces, Bo Derek's unselfish concern for the operators in Afghanistan earned her a place in Special Forces history.

Black Berets—Issued Not Earned

General Eric Shinseki, the chief of staff of the United States Army, had honored 5th Special Forces Group by attending a ceremony to award over a dozen of the wounded their Purple Hearts and medals for service and valor.

General Shinseki was not exactly loved or respected by the Special Forces or Ranger rank-and-file. Prior to Afghanistan he had changed the Army's headgear policy and authorized all U.S. Army soldiers to wear the black beret, an exclusive symbol of the U.S. Army Rangers. Shinseki believed it would help the conventional Army's failing esprit de corps. Rangers and Special Forces troops believed that berets should be "earned, not issued." The controversy divided the lower ranks, who openly opposed it, and the general officers, who were forced to support the chief of staff's decision.

It especially incensed the airborne soldiers, who felt issuing berets to "legs" (nonairborne soldiers) was a slap in the face. E-mails, websites, and special-ops chat rooms abounded with cynical observations about the decision. "If Shinseki thinks a black beret will make his men better soldiers, then why not just issue a Medal of Honor to every swinging dick and he'll have an army full of heroes" was the message from one senior NCO.

The Air Force had already tried this type of material motivation when they started issuing leather jackets to flight crews to increase retention. That didn't work either.

Still, General Shinseki was a flag officer, and the chief of staff, and that deserved respect regardless of ideology. The men at the ceremony expressed that respect. Delta operators remembered Shinseki standing up for them against other generals during operational briefings. General Shinseki was introduced: ". . . and it is particularly fitting that General Shinseki be here today as part of this ceremony. He sat, years ago, as you are now, waiting to receive his Purple Heart for his wounds."

General Shinseki had earned his Purple Hearts, but many Rangers, paratroopers, and Green Berets wondered why their earned berets were not as sacred to him as those Purple Hearts.

The Real George W.

Walter Reed Army Hospital

Occasionally, a quiet and humble man brought his wife along to visit the wounded in Walter Reed Army Medical Center. In the rare moments when there was a small opening in his schedule, he would take the time to see his soldiers.

One day, on a visit, kept quiet as usual for security reasons, the couple paused to see a soldier whose distraught wife had just arrived. Laura Bush hugged her close, not knowing what else to do.

After eight long years of neglect and embarrassment, the U.S. military finally had a real commander and chief.

Expect Nothing

One night a 3rd Special Forces Group officer received an e-mail from his best friend, who was in Afghanistan. The e-mail was short and to the point. "If I buy the farm," the soldier wanted to know, "will my family be taken care of?" His friend's response was equally to the point. Should the "worst-case scenario come to pass," the wife and children left behind would be the officer's "first priority," his family's welfare "a personal mission, on the level of my own." It was all the soldier needed to know, and he had never doubted it; he just "needed to be sure."

The officer in the United States wouldn't ask what mission lay ahead to generate such a request, since it would be a security violation to ask or receive an answer. As he stared at the screen wondering, he reached for the phone. He dialed his friend's wife, just to check in and see if everything was okay.

The fact of the matter was that things were not okay for the Special Forces soldiers who were wounded and killed, or for their families. Most of the wounded would eventually be forced to medically retire, even if they wanted to stay in. It was a far cry from the days of Vietnam, when you might see a "Black Hat" Airborne instructor at Fort Benning with two wooden legs.

Servicemembers' Group Life Insurance would provide meager benefits for the family, and the best hope a soldier had was from guys like Texas patriot and philanthropist Ross Perot, who funded the scholarships for Colonel Nick Rowe's children when he was assassinated in the Philippines. Perot has always been a great friend to Special Forces. He had once hired legendary U.S. Army Green Beret Colonel Arthur "Bull" Simons, who repeatedly risked his life on rescue missions, and a group of Special Forces soldiers to rescue his employees in Iran, and Perot had thrown a California bash to unite Son Tay Raiders and former POWs during the seventies. In 2000,

Perot had funded a statue of Simons at Fort Bragg. There was no better friend to SF.

The Special Operations Warrior Foundation was created by Perot in 1980, after the Iranian hostage rescue attempt, as the Bull Simons Scholarship Fund to provide college educations for the seventeen children surviving the nine men killed or incapacitated at Desert One. Even still, it was underfunded. The only saving grace was a million-dollar donation given by Yankees principal owner George Steinbrenner after September 11. It nearly doubled the endowment, but even $2.7 million wasn't enough to go around; there were dozens of special operators dead by the time this book went to print. Mike McElhiney lost the use of his arms, and had to buy a specially outfitted car just to drive—his family had to pay for it themselves. After thirteen years of service, he gets paid less than $3,300 a month as a senior Special Forces soldier, and has to support a family of four.

Apparently, President Bush stepped in and allowed soldiers like McElhiney to stay on active duty. He was transferred to a Special Forces instructor position where he could teach the younger operators.

It was even worse for the Green Berets who left children behind. Mi Davis, wife of Jefferson "J. D." Davis, who was killed in action shortly before the fall of Kandahar, was a Korean citizen J. D. had met during a tour in Asia. They had been married for seventeen years. Mi and J. D. had two children, Cristina, age fifteen, and J. C., a boy, age twelve. Ten months after Master Sergeant Davis had been buried, his gravesite remained an unmarked grass plot. Mi struggled with everyone from the Department of the Army to the Veterans Administration to provide a headstone for this great American hero. She got nowhere. Finally, she threw herself on the mercy of her local congressman. It literally took an act of Congress to get Master Sergeant Davis a headstone for his grave. This wasn't the only insult she would suffer at the hands of bureaucrats. The Army had assigned a sergeant first class as the casualty officer for the Davis family. As dedicated as the man was, his rank carried zero clout with the staff pukes at the Pentagon.

He was not even able to tell Mi how her husband had died, only that the powers that be were working on a report, "to be released someday." The U.S. Army had no problem assigning colonels to write menus for headquarters staff, but they left powerless sergeants to fight for family survivors.

None of these heroes' wives were treated the way Americans would have expected or wanted. Their husbands were listed as "medically retired" instead of KIA, killed in action. This way, they would supposedly receive additional benefits for the children, but the benefits were insignificant compared to the losses that the families suffered. Of the three soldiers killed on December 5, Davis was the only one who left children behind. They were not even given dental care—J. C. had a mouthful of braces and Mi would have no way to pay for the dental program she needed. The Social Security Administration informed her that she would forfeit her benefits if she worked and earned more than $9,000 a year, an interesting catch-22 that made her a ward of the state subsisting at what many people would consider just below the level of poverty. Cody Prosser's wife would receive about $900 per month. The entire state of affairs surrounding the Green Berets killed in action sickened many in the community, yet the staff officers and generals kept a lid on the entire situation, cautioning the wives not to talk about their husbands or the secret missions in which they had engaged—including the way the Department of the Army dealt with survivors. When a chief warrant officer named Larry, who had fought in Tora Bora, returned to Fort Campbell, he learned of Mi Davis' problems. The CWO was Cristina and J. C.'s godfather. He supported Mi and fought the bureaucrats to straighten out her problems.

In the fall of 2002, Jack spoke to Mrs. Davis, and when he heard her story he had tears in his eyes. He spoke to Chris, my project coordinator, and me a short time later. "Tell this story, Robin," he said. "Tell the real story. Tell Americans exactly how fucked up this is for the survivors' families. Robin, they've got a task force for everything, from designing jeep seats to mess halls. They need a damn task force for the survivors, one central group to deal with wives and families, led by someone with some goddamn authority. I gotta believe if Bush or Rumsfeld find out about this, heads are gonna roll."

Dead and crippled Green Berets could expect little more than medals. On active duty, working twelve-to-eighteen-hour days seven days a week, they are paid less than a parking lot attendant in a major city. The families of the firemen who heroically died in the World Trade Center received millions of dollars each, by some accounts more than $8 million each, subsidized by the federal government and the City of New York. And they deserved every penny of it. But the Green Berets' families could expect nothing. The Green Berets would be left to rely on each other, taking care of their own wounded and dead as they had always done before.

The CIA didn't do much for Shannon Spann either. She and her three children, two of whom had been from Mike's first marriage, received a mere $275,000 in benefits.

The Special Forces' 50th Anniversary

Fayetteville, North Carolina
June 17–22, 2002

Prior to Afghanistan, it was readily apparent that there were two Special Forces communities—those who had served in Vietnam and those who hadn't. After the work of Special Forces in the Global War on Terrorism, a new unity emerged, and the veterans of Grenada, El Salvador, Desert Storm, Panama, Haiti, Bosnia, Kosovo, and many other conflicts were welcomed into the fold. The new bond was evidenced throughout a week of festivities celebrating the 50th Anniversary of the United States Army Special Forces.

The Reunion

In the third week of June 2002, at Fort Bragg and in Fayette-ville, North Carolina, the Special Forces community cele-brated the founding of the United States Army Special Forces.

During a weekend barbecue for the thousands who make up the SF community, Special Forces jumped into the fes-tivities with their new exhibition parachutes, the color of the Green Beret, with the Special Forces' teal-blue combat patch inside of each canopy. As the jumpers free-fell toward the ground, they pulled and the chutes opened to applause. The winds were gusting far above safe levels, but still they jumped. The last man down carried an American flag. Gust-ing winds drove him into the ground and his leg snapped like a twig. It didn't matter; he risked it for flag and country, and that is what they do.

Several men were Medal of Honor recipients. Their names were Gary Beikirch, Roger Donlon, Ola Mize, and Drew Dix. As generals, officers, noncommissioned officers, and soldiers approached them, they saluted, rendering the appropriate cour-tesy that many civilians are unaware of: anyone serving in the military salutes a Medal of Honor recipient first, regardless of rank.

The old-timers reached out to greet their young "brothers," and welcomed the modern generation of Special Forces war-riors. Unfortunately, several, like Dutch and Randy, had only just recently returned from Afghanistan, and the head-quarters staff (*aka* sewing circle) running the event said it was too late to register them—some things never change.

Colonel Aaron Bank

In the shade at the picnic, accompanied by his wife and beau-tiful daughters, was Colonel Aaron Bank, the founder of the United States Army Special Forces in 1952. His hundredth birthday was approaching, in November of 2002.

In the crowd, a resolution from the House of Represen-tatives was being circulated. The concurrent resolution, number 364, dated March 20, 2002, recognized Colonel Bank, the assembled veterans, and today's Green Berets fighting the Global War on Terrorism.

Recognizing the historic significance of the 50th anniversary of the founding of the United States Army Special Forces and honoring the "Father of the Special Forces," Colonel Aaron Bank (United States Army, retired) of Mission Viejo, California, for his role in establishing the Army Special Forces.

Whereas on June 22, 2002, the Special Forces Association will celebrate the 50th anniversary of the establishment of the first permanent special forces unit in the United States Army;

Whereas such unit was created in response to the advocacy of Colonel Aaron Bank (United States Army, retired), known as the "Father of the Special Forces";

Whereas Colonel Aaron Bank's service in the Office of Strategic Services and his experience leading resistance fighters against Nazi Germany convinced him of the need for permanent, elite units in the Armed Forces that would specialize in small unit and counterinsurgency tactics, intelligence operations, and the training of indigenous soldiers;

Whereas in 1952 the Army created its first special forces unit, the 10th Special Forces Group, at Fort Bragg, North Carolina, which would later be known for the distinctive green berets worn by its soldiers;

Whereas Colonel Aaron Bank was assigned as the first commanding officer of the 10th Special Forces Group;

Whereas the success of the United States Army Special Forces encouraged the incorporation of principles of force multiplication into the military doctrine of the United States and paved the way for the revitalization of special operations forces in the Navy, Air Force, and Marine Corps;

Whereas these special operations forces have helped revolutionize the conduct of modern warfare;

Whereas special operations soldiers have served with

bravery and distinction in every major military conflict in which the United States has been involved in the last 50 years and in innumerable covert operations;

Whereas special operations soldiers are sometimes called upon to conduct missions so secret that their bravery cannot be fully recognized;

Whereas special operations soldiers are playing a critical role in the war against terrorism; and

Whereas thanks to Colonel Aaron Bank and the thousands of United States Army Special Forces soldiers who have followed him, the Armed Forces are better prepared to conduct unconventional warfare and to protect the United States from developing threats: Now, therefore, be it

Resolved by the House of Representatives (the Senate concurring), That Congress—

recognizes the historic significance of the 50th anniversary of the founding of the United States Army Special Forces. . . .

honors the sacrifices made by United States Army Special Forces soldiers who have trained hard and acquitted themselves with honor by serving valiantly in battle, with many making the ultimate sacrifice to their country, many times in missions so secret that their valor may never be fully acknowledged.

The Memorial Ceremony

The hot summer sun beat down on the heads of those in attendance at the United States Army Special Operations Command Memorial and Stone Dedication Ceremony on the morning of June 19. As Colonel John Mulholland observed, TASK FORCE DAGGER was the spearhead, the unconventional arrow America had pulled from its quiver. OPERATION ENDURING FREEDOM was an umbrella for the oppressed Afghans. The families of soldiers slain during Operation Enduring Freedom held roses in their hands and wept for those who were lost.

General Franks was invited to attend. He was secretly

scheduled to fly into Fort Bragg that day. He never showed. It was the ultimate insult.

After the Stone Dedication Ceremony, in which memorial stones were placed in the walkway in front of the bronze statue of a Green Beret representing Mike Force and the 10th Special Forces Group (Airborne), the commanding general of United States Army Special Operations Command, Lieutenant General Bryan "Doug" Brown, stepped up to the podium and began to speak:

> Distinguished guests—flag and general officers, families, civilian friends of SOF, and a special welcome to Robin Moore . . . It is my distinct honor to welcome the Medal of Honor recipients that are here with us today:
>
> Colonel and Mrs. Roger Donlon and Colonel Lee Mize . . . and as you all know the ranks of our Medal of Honor recipients will grow by one when on the eighth of July President Bush will posthumously award Humbert Roque "Rocky" Versace the Medal of Honor in the White House . . . the last time "Rocky" was heard from, he was in a Vietnamese prisoner of war camp singing "God Bless America" from the top of his lungs in an isolation box. . . . Captain Versace was executed by the Viet Cong on 26 September 1965.
>
> The attendance by Colonel Aaron Bank and his wonderful wife, Catherine, and daughter Sandy as we memorialize the names on this wall today even make it more special for all of us. . . . Sir, it is a great honor to have you back at Special Operations Command, the unit you built.
>
> President Kennedy wrote to Bill Yarborough, "The challenge of this old, but new, form of operations is a real one and I know that you and the members of your command will carry on for *us* and the *free world* in a manner which is both worthy and inspiring. I am sure that the Green Beret will be a mark of distinction in the trying times ahead."
>
> President Kennedy was RIGHT . . . and he would be immensely proud of the amazing work being quietly accomplished by Special Forces, and all of our Special Operations

Forces, today in this war against terrorism . . . the skills and talents expected from them . . . *they have* . . . and are using them daily . . . as always, little fanfare . . . little recognition . . . little talk, but a lot of success. . . .

Today, we will take time to reflect our thoughts on the twenty-five brave men whose names we will add to our Memorial Wall. . . .

Twenty-five lives, spanning multiple wars, operations, and continuous military engagements, will forever be enshrined today on our Wall. . . .

An anonymous person once wrote a memorial to Special Forces soldiers and . . . I believe these words are appropriate as we remember all of our fallen USASOC soldiers. He simply wrote, "In memory of our fallen team mates, who were men of vision, *daring* to be different. Men which had confidence in themselves, trusted their comrades and left their fate to God . . . They were men of courage. . . ."

Today Army SOF is marching on, fighting better and stronger than ever before. However, the losses we have had to endure to get to this point are heartbreaking and gut wrenching, but we will not relent . . . and after every battle, after every year, we will be even better than before, always proving our comrades did not and never will die in vain. . . .

Today . . . as we reflect on comrades lost . . . the way I think all of us would really like to remember these warriors . . . is to also remember the kindness in their hearts and the smile you saw on their faces. . . .

Specialist Marc Anderson, 75th Rangers, a former schoolteacher who continues to make a difference by having diverted money from his own SGLI to one of his former students to help her continue her education. . . . Marc's father, a former Ranger, said Marc lived and died by the Ranger Creed. . . .

Master Sergeant Jefferson Davis, 5th Special Forces Group, Airborne, or J.D., as he liked to be called, had a smile from ear to ear every time he cruised on his Harley-Davidson. . . .

Ranger Private First Class Kris Stonesifer, laughing as he taught his father how to make pumpkin pies from tofu, surely one of the skills he learned in one of the many survival schools he loved to attend. . . .

Sergeant Philip Svitak, 160th Special Operations Aviation Regiment, known as "Sweet Chuck" to the guys in barracks . . . his NightStalker comrades say he always had a smile, he loved to laugh and he was always there when you needed him.

I met 75th Ranger Sergeant Brad Crose back in November 2001—he and I attended a Redskins-Seahawks football game in D.C., on Military Appreciation Day. He was having a good time with his Ranger buddies and flirting with the cheerleaders . . . the Redskins won that one. . . .

But that was a game, and as Eisenhower once said:

"The winning of freedom is not to be compared with the winning of a game . . . with the victory recorded forever in history. . . . Freedom has its life in the hearts, the actions, the spirit of men and so it must be daily earned and refreshed . . . else, like a flower cut from its life giving roots . . . it will wither and die. . . ."

Every time we look at the names forever cast in bronze on our Wall, we will remember sons, brothers, cousins, friends, husbands and fathers . . . our comrades . . . these are the names of men whose selfless service and devotion served a nation's purpose, our nation, . . . men who gave their lives for our freedom. . . .

I'm personally grateful, and our nation is eternally grateful to all of them, . . . and to all of you . . . the folks who will always remember the smiles of these heroes . . . our fallen comrades . . . the folks that have *never* forgotten that our freedom is a cherished but very fragile thing . . . and that it is worth fighting for. . . .

I received a letter, back in March, from a woman in Oklahoma in regard to Chief Warrant Officer 2 Stanley Harriman from 3rd Special Forces Group Airborne, that I would like you to hear. . . .

General Brown then read a letter from Anita Vreeland and closed with her final words:

> As we memorialize our comrades today, it's true that we formally say good-bye . . . but we also formally embrace them and their families forever into our Special Operations family.

As the tough and beautiful Major Kathleen Culp held Robin Moore's arm and looked on, she smiled as General Brown read her speech. The commanding general paused for effect, letting the words register in the minds of those in attendance before continuing:

> In Fayetteville we are blessed with a beautiful Veterans' Hospital and on the entrance gates it simply says . . .
> "The price of freedom is visible here."
> I would tell you as we all stand on Meadows Field and as we look at the wonderful statues of our heroes and the names on this wall, it is fitting that we internalize that same thought . . . as you look around today and forever at Meadows Field it is clear that . . . the price of freedom is visible here . . . it is visible on the wall, it is visible on the faces of our veterans that we are so fortunate to have come back and it is visible on our young men and women that are so ready . . . to stand on the wall for the defense of freedom. . . . Command Sergeants Major . . . call the roll.

In turn, the representative sergeant majors each came to the podium and read from a list the names that had just been inscribed onto the wall. Two soldiers, young paratroopers from the 82nd Airborne Division, raised a black veil as a band softly played "Taps," and after each name was read, a bell was tolled. After the last name was read, the families of those whose names were read came forward, and laid their roses at the foot of the monument.

Edmunds, John J., Specialist, 75th Ranger Regiment

Petithory, Daniel H., Staff Sergeant, 5th Special Forces
Group

Allison, Thomas F., Sergeant, 160th SOAR

Feistner, Curtis D., Major, 160th SOAR

Owens, Bartt D., Captain, 160th SOAR

Anderson, Marc A., Specialist, 75th Ranger Regiment

Svitak, Philip J., Sergeant, 160th SOAR

Stonesifer, Kristofor T., Specialist, 75th Ranger
Regiment

Prosser, Brian C., Staff Sergeant, 5th Special Forces
Group

Dorrity, James P., Staff Sergeant, 160th SOAR

Foshee, Jeremy D., Staff Sergeant, 160th SOAR

Rushforth, Bruce A., Jr., Staff Sergeant, 160th SOAR

Commons, Matthew A., Corporal, 75th Ranger Regiment

Romero, Daniel A., 19th Special Forces Group

Davis, Jefferson D., Master Sergeant, 5th Special Forces
Group

Chapman, Nathan R., Sergeant First Class, 1st Special
Forces Group

Egnor, Jody L., Chief Warrant Officer 2, 160th SOAR

Frith, Kerry W., Staff Sergeant, 160th SOAR

Harriman, Stanley L., Chief Warrant Officer 2, 3rd
Special Forces Group

Crose, Bradley S., Sergeant, 75th Ranger Regiment

Vance, Gene A., Staff Sergeant, 19th Special Forces
Group

The Ball

On the twenty-second of June, the Fayetteville Convention
Center was packed to capacity. Over three thousand members
of the Army Special Forces family were gathered to celebrate.

President Bush sent an inspirational video complimenting
the assembled body. At the end of the formalities, just prior to
retirement of the colors and singing of "The Ballad of the
Green Berets," the Army Special Forces announced the naming

of their patron saint, Phillip Neri, who was a warrior, a teacher, and was said to have had special powers at night. The first medal was awarded to Colonel Aaron Bank.

In the crowded ballroom, Dutch and Randy were watching with tired eyes after a night of seeing old friends and celebrating their fascinating journey to combat and back, bridging the time from learning the "Cotton-eyed Joe" in Wyoming to the week of the Fiftieth Anniversary of the Special Forces. Jack sat in the back of the room out of view and getting drunk. They had all snuck into the reunion after being told it was too late to register. After months of fighting Afghanistan, Jimmy Dean's security was no match for them, and they weren't about to miss the party. Chris Thompson sat with Laura and Ginny Hampton from Murfreesboro. Old retired sergeant majors like Al Schwarcbher, George Winder, Alsee Richardson, and Bud O'Donnell exchanged war stories and admiration for the new Afghan veterans. Major Jim Morris, author of *War Story,* watched with his old friend Colonel Bob Brown from *Soldier of Fortune* magazine.

The next morning, at the executive hangar in Fayetteville, several Green Berets were assembled. The group included Vietnam, El Salvador, and Afghanistan veterans. Lambert and the SF family had come to bid farewell to Colonel Aaron Bank, who was departing on an executive jet bound for California.

The SOF Truths

"In the missions ahead for the military, you will have everything you need, every resource, every weapon, every means to assure full victory for the United States and the cause of freedom."

—PRESIDENT GEORGE W. BUSH,
Pentagon memorial service,
October 11, 2001

For years, the United States Special Operations Command has trumpeted the four Special Operations Forces "truths" around Washington, D.C. The truths are said to be un-impeachable, transcend changes in technology, and are the definitive statements that clearly separate SOF from the conventional forces.

The four SOF truths are:

1. Humans are more important than hardware.
2. Quality is more important than quantity.
3. Special Operations Forces can't be mass-produced.
4. Competent Special Operations Forces can't be created *after* an emergency occurs.

The September 11 attacks brought those truths to the forefront of many discussions in Washington, D.C., USSOCOM, and the Army Special Operations Command at Fort Bragg, North Carolina.

Within thirty days, many were saying that Special Forces needed to be expanded to meet the requirements for the war on terrorism. Rapid expansion flies in the face of the second, third, and fourth SOF truths.

Special Forces simply can't be expanded quickly unless the Department of Defense wants Green Berets of lesser quality. There are several reasons why. When the Clinton administration shrunk the Army by approximately one-third, Special Forces stayed the same size as they were before the cuts. Since Special Forces only recruit from seasoned troops, the recruiting base has therefore shrunk an equal 33.3 percent.

In addition to recruiting, the extensive training program for Special Forces spits out a trained operator after approximately eighteen months to two years, depending on the individual's specialty. This reality means that even with a massive infusion of seasoned troops into the pipeline, facilitated by increasing schoolhouse resources, impact would be delayed by at least two years.

Attrition is also a critical factor for Special Forces personnel strength. The road for a Special Forces aspirant, usually with two years of previous Army service, is complex. The soldier must attend a selection-and-assessment course. In an effort to fill the force needed, graduation rates are already much higher than they were twenty years ago, running between 25 to 50 percent, depending on class composition. For those still in the running, approximately 90 percent will successfully complete Special Forces training. To finish their qualification, soldiers must also pass language school, and Survival, Evasion, Resistance, and Escape (SERE) school. Finally, the men receive the coveted Green Beret Special Forces tab for the left shoulder.

The only way to create Special Operations units quickly is to lower the standard of performance for the units involved. A good example is the Marine Corps reflagging of several standing units with some minor additions as an antiterror brigade soon after September 11. Regardless of bells and whistles, the unit will remain full of great, young, patriotic, boot-camp-trained Marines. However, the Special Operations community has no such quick remedies. The Green Berets need seasoned veterans, averaging thirty years old, stable, experienced, with foreign-language and specific expertise, trained in a multitude of special skills.

There was one other school of thought called "baby SF," not supported by the officer corps of the Army but by the real experts in unconventional warfare, that made a lot of sense. Around only for a short time after Vietnam, it allowed for the enlistment of new recruits, right off the street, at age twenty-one. By bringing these kids straight into the SF course, it allowed the instructors to completely mold them. It meant that they weren't corrupted with conventional tactics or wisdom. They had never had conventional training, and that made it easier to make them unconventional soldiers. But the "green army" feared them; they feared soldiers who had not been part of the establishment, and regardless of whether or not they could operate more effectively in an unconventional atmosphere, they only highlighted the wide separation of conventional and unconventional forces. The army had decided years ago that unconventional forces were no longer needed. Yet they were back, and needed now more than ever.

Reality Is Hard to Swallow

Many people in the Department of Defense have caught on to SOF's "Humans are more important than hardware" philosophy. SOF weapons, helmets, cold-weather gear, boots, rucksacks, nuclear, biological, and chemical warfare gear, and other equipment are all the rage in the conventional forces since their research-and-development efforts go toward developing the wherewithal to fight huge battles, as they should. The conventional forces now cruise SOF conventions to find the proper gear for their airmen and marines because it is so much cheaper than developing such gear within service budgets.

Unfortunately, USSOCOM never applied the four SOF truths to the U.S. Army Special Forces Command (Airborne). In fact, USSOCOM made it the lowest priority of fill for any of the bullet-slinging organizations in the military. The reason was twofold: Special Forces existed long before US-SOCOM or any of its components from the U.S. Air Force, U.S. Navy, or U.S. Army. After the debacles in Iran during the failed rescue of American hostages and inefficiencies in Grenada, many new units and structures began to try to resolve gaps in capability. The U.S. Army Special Forces were seen as a legacy, an albatross, and an impediment to progress. Generals tried to tone down their cowboy persona and renamed them the "Quiet Professionals."

A vicious cycle started. USSOCOM would give no new missions to Special Forces, and therefore, Special Forces needed no additional resources. Since Special Forces weren't adequately resourced, they weren't competent enough to receive new missions. A downward spiral had started, encouraged by the SEALs and U.S. Air Force SOF so they could compete for bigger and bigger slices of the SOF budget.

Each year the percentage of the SOF budget going to the Green Berets either stagnated or slightly dropped. Eventually, although much of the SOF budget is classified, only 4 percent of that budget went to the Special Forces Groups, even though they had the preponderance of forces in the SOF arena. The community had been taken over by "raiders" and Rangers, believing that a snatch, destruction mission, or a strategic reconnaissance mission was more important than fighting shadow wars with the CIA. It was also taken over by huge research-and-development mechanisms that changed focus from the point of the spear to conventional thought processes. Unending growth of high-dollar platforms adored by the military-industrial complex became the norm, including aerial platforms of all types and even SOF's own submarines.

After the Green Berets won the war in El Salvador, and established democracy in the war-torn republic, where now former FMLN guerrillas frequently win the seat of mayor in the capital, nothing changed. In fact, the USSOCOM historian was never even contracted to study the Special Forces' major accomplishment of the eighties. Special Forces' occupation of Panama for eleven months after military victory also lacks mention in most histories of the invasion.

Yet, something quietly altered the nature of the organization. In the early 1980s Special Forces became a separate Army branch for officers. When an officer joined Special Forces, he permanently chose a way of life, the profession of unconventional warfare. The same happened for the enlisted men and the warrant officers. With its limited budgets, the Special Forces organization began building a new core of officers and sergeants, working away, year after year, virtually unnoticed by the other special operators.

In fact, less than one year before Colonel Mulholland set up TASK FORCE DAGGER to sweep the Taliban out of power, senior SOF leaders met and agreed once again that Special Forces Groups were incapable of fighting in a sophisticated Joint Special Operations Task Force. The leaders of SOF had become victims of past perception.

With the rest of Special Operations a higher priority, isolation of the 5th Special Forces Group as they prepared to go to war in Afghanistan was interesting. The men were supposed to be packing to go to war. Instead, they were seeing the radios they would use in combat for the first time. The laser designators they had were limited in number, and those of the British SAS and the other SOF services were far more modern.

The great sadness was that the shortages spread to personal protective gear, like armored vests. In fact, SOF Air Force *maintenance men* had better communications equipment than the Green Berets. Worse, the two SF National Guard Groups, one battalion of which was sent to Afghanistan, didn't have any of the latest radios needed to do business. On the eleventh of September, Special Forces had only 48 percent of its SOF-funded radios.

Therefore, many Special Forces advocates are advertising the need for a Fifth SOF Truth: 5. Given that SOF truth #1 is true, humans deserve the requisite personal hardware to fight and survive.

SF had now shown what they alone could do and are now in the hands of the ultimate commander in chief, George W. Bush, and Donald Rumsfeld, to let them continue to do it, and give them the gear to do it.

OPERATION ANACONDA—5th Special Forces Group (Airborne)
Briefing Map: Summary of Special Forces Activities

April 2003

Secretary of Defense Donald Rumsfeld's fiscal 2004 defense budget request, awarded the U.S. Army's Special Forces Command a 20 percent increase in funding—$1 billion of a total award of $6 billion—and an 8 percent increase in personnel funding.

June 2003

In June 2003, only months after the victory in Iraq, Shinseki's terms as Chief of Staff finally ended. Instead of picking Franks, or a similar general, to replace him, Rumsfeld again signaled his displeasure with conventional officers. He requested that General Pete Schoomaker, a former Special Forces general, return to active duty from retirement to assume the position of Chief of Staff.

The Hunt for Saddam Hussein

Saddam Hussein was to enjoy the same destiny as bin Laden, a man on the run and without a country. Dead or alive, he remains on the hit list.

In March 2003, President George Bush gave Hussein seventy-two hours to voluntarily step down and allow a peaceful regime change. He refused.

Unlike the 1991 war, when General Norman Schwarzkopf virtually banned U.S. Special Operations Forces from conducting advance missions in Iraq and Kuwait, for fear of upsetting his delicate timetable, or grabbing his media spotlight, American and British Special Forces had already been in Iraq for three months when 300,000 coalition forces broke through the Iraq/Kuwait border and rolled across the country. Early on in the planning, retired General Wayne Downing had made it clear to Rumsfeld that Schwarzkopf's failure to allow his Delta Force commandos to starting locating Scuds ahead of time, was the single factor in preventing the destruction of the Scuds and the attacks on Israel and coalition forces. Rumsfeld made it very clear to General Franks that this time it would be different; special ops would be on the ground and working long before the first tank started its engine.

Colonel John Mulholland had put JSOTF-N, the Joint Special Operations Task Force-North, into action. By virtue of the vast geographical size of Iraq, about the size of California, JSOTF-N required every single available special operator to come on board. That meant Afghanistan and the hunt for al-Qaida would suffer for resources. However, it was also clear from intelligence that al-Qaida was in Northern Iraq, and they would be hunted and killed there too, just as they had been in Afghanistan.

Every available SAS operator forward deployed to their FMB, Forward Mounting Base, in Cyprus. The initial large-scale special operations missions, in December 2002 and January 2003, consisted of strategic reconnaissance. Eight four-man SAS teams were inserted by Chinook from Jordan and Saudi Arabia with the mission to conduct surveillance of Scud missile launchers in western Iraq. The Jordanian government allowed special operations forces to use their Azraq al Shishan Airbase to stage and launch from—they had not forgotten the Iraqi Scuds aimed at Israel in 1991, but mistakenly landing in Jordan. The primary goal was to ensure that the Scud launchers were in fact real and operational, rather than part of an Iraqi deception plan. Roughly one-third of the force exfiltrated one week later with the required intelligence. The rest stayed inside Iraqi-controlled territory to conduct deep penetration reconnaissance and help guide in additional forces in February and March.

Working in much the same way as they had in 1991, SAS operators dug spider holes in the desert, from which they would conduct long-term surveillance of opposition military forces. Placing remote battlefield sensors to monitor vehicles, convoys, and troop movement, they also used JSTARS battlefield reconnaissance planes to gather intelligence on Iraqi forces.

Other SAS and Delta Force teams started covert reconnaissance of command posts, communications bunkers, and military supply depots to ensure they had been properly identified by satellite imagery.

One squadron of the 22 SAS and one squadron of Delta Force protected the Iraqi oil fields from sabotage, ensuring that the environmental disaster of 1991 would not repeat itself. The CIA was back again with OPERATION U.S. DOLLARS, and paying off Iraqi commanders and Republican Guard officers to keep them from blowing the oil wells. Those that couldn't be bought off, and decided to follow Saddam's orders to burn the oil, were met with 7.62mm and .50 caliber bullets from Special Forces snipers. Even more important then the wells, which could be capped and extinguished if sabotaged, were the oil refineries, which would require expensive long-term efforts to put back on-line if blown up by Saddam's forces.

Other strategic targets requiring "special" protection included dams, power grids, and electric stations. The coalition would need these after the country was occupied. Their destruction by Republican Guard or Fedayeen forces could impeded the coalition advance, especially if dams were blown to flood the Euphrates or the areas being attacked. The potential for dam destruction was high enough to make the seizure of the Haditha Dam northwest of Baghdad a primary concern, and U.S. Special Forces not only seized it, but held it without reinforcements, and then eventually brought in the U.S. Army Rangers to occupy it.

The taking of Baghdad wasn't just bullets and blood. An extraordinary intelligence operation was conducted to lay the foundation for the takeover. Delta Force's Signals Squadron, working off public-works maps that the CIA had obtained, surreptitiously entered seven different communications switching systems. With access to cable, telephone wire, and fiber optics, satellite transmitters were installed sending back signals through the U.S. Space Command to the National Security Agency. Although the Signalers at Delta were highly skilled in wiretaps and communications surveillance, several of the operations were just too sophisticated and complex. SF operators infiltrated two civilian AT&T technicians, and passed them to Delta operators, who brought them into their safehouse to work on the system. British MI6 supplied a civilian technician with expertise on Chinese fiber-optic communications, as the Red Chinese had built much of Baghdad's communications infrastructure.

One month before the attack began, NSA was receiving so much intelligence and information, and had so many simultaneous wiretaps going, that the entire U.S. intelligence community was stretched to the breaking point just trying to sort out and translate the information. MI6 supplied several Farsi speakers who were infiltrated in and literally placed inside the underground tunnels, where they sat at the underground switching stations and junction boxes monitoring the calls, determining the importance, and re-transmitting the most important calls to the U.S. Space Command and National Reconnaissance Office.

JSOTF-N also put into play considerable PSYOPS, or Psychological Operations. While the use of PSYOPS was extremely limited in Afghanistan, in Iraq it was used extensively. The Special Forces Psychological Operations Directorate had developed a wide range of possible scenarios involving collateral attacks on Iraqi infrastructure, communications, financial networks, and the general populace. The U.S. Army's Special Operations Command forward deployed the entire 4th Psychological Operations Command and began the information and deception war. Operations ranged from dropping leaflets telling Iraqis how to surrender, to EC-130s flying Airborne Intercept missions transmitting President Bush's speech to the Iraqis. The Iraq government was literally freaked out to learn that American Special Forces could interrupt any communication, including Iraqi television and radio, and transmit across Iraqi frequencies, any message, at anytime, and without any possibility of interference by the Iraqis. Once the 4th PYSOPS Command started their information war, the Iraqis were completely powerless to stop it.

The CIA was doing much better this time around; their

green operators were no longer wet-behind-the-ears, having gained experience during the Afghanistan conflict. Their now experienced paramilitary forces were busy trying to build a Shiite resistance movement, but potential anti-Saddam guerillas were hard to convince; the West had deserted them and the Kurds before, leaving them to mass slaughter by Saddam's regime.

U.S. special operations forces, working once again for Mulholland and already with the Kurds in Northern Iraq, were bringing in airdrops of ammunition, food, and medical supplies, and working hard to convince the Kurds that there would be no repeat of their 1991 sellout. This time George W. Bush was at the helm, and America would finish that which his father had not completed.

Special operators in Baghdad, working as they had in Afghanistan, disguised as locals, began focusing on strategic targets and hunting senior Iraqi officials.

On March 20, one team spotted Saddam and his two sons heading for a bunker. Once again, bureaucratic delays would stifle a target of opportunity. By the time they got permission to fire the first attack of the war, almost two hours had passed. The Tomahawk missiles impacted the target, and the war began. Ten minutes after impact, the NSA monitored urgent Iraqi command radio traffic asking for emergency medical personnel for Saddam and one son. Their condition was believed to be critical. Like bin Laden, the entire incident would be clouded in secrecy and doubt. At first, it was believed that we had hit Saddam, and in fact, that he had been killed. As intelligence developed, it appeared that those hit may have been doubles.

The French, Germans, Russians, and Turks all refused to help. The French, Germans, and Russians were making too much money off their trading with Saddam. The French were even selling munitions, Mirage-2000 fighter jet parts, MIG replacement parts, and Roland shoulder-fired surface-to-air missiles to Saddam up until seven days before the war began, and only stopped when MI6 and ISA caught them red-handed. The Turks simply hated the Kurds, and a liberated Iraq brought with it the threat of a Kurdish territory, or even worse, a Kurdish state. As for the Russians, they were in it just for the money.

Tony Blair stayed the course and remained loyal to his American allies and the people that had perished on 9/11.

While "Baghdad Bob" was on Iraqi television announcing that American forces would never enter Baghdad, Green Berets, Delta Force, and ISA commandos were already swarming around Baghdad in taxis, Volkswagens, and Mercedes Benzes. They were Arab-speaking Green Berets of either Arab ancestry, or Hispanic descent, which allowed them to completely blend in.

Operators were sending back their information via LST-5 Satellite Radios and securing INMARSAT systems to the Central Command SCIF, Secure Compartmented Intelligence Facility, in Qatar, and to CIA Headquarters in Langley, Virginia, who would then forward the information to MI6. Several of the covert Baghdad teams had even hardwired into international phone lines and foreign embassy phone lines, sending reports, photos, and information via e-mail.

Delta, ISA, FOG, and *Increment* were already assassinating senior Baath Party members and forcing high-ranking Iraqi officials into hiding, where they found their command-and-control of lower forces severely limited by their own quest for personal survival.

The 22 SAS would repeat their most important mission of the 1991 Gulf War. Supplemented by Sabre teams from the 21 and 23 SAS, they infiltrated in by CH-53 and occupied the central corridor of western Iraq. In several cases Special Operations C-130 Hercules aircraft landed on desert roads, dropping their tailgates as the SAS raced off into the desert night in their modified Land Rovers, called "pinkies," equipped with M2 HB (heavy barrel) .50 Caliber belt-fed machine guns, and Bofors 40mm grenade launchers. This was the SAS at its best, screaming across the desert as they had against Rommel, hitting the enemy out of the darkness and disappearing again into the night. Their primary objective was to interdict and destroy Iraqi Scud units from firing on Israel and coalition forces.

The British SAS commandos were supported by Royal Air Force (RAF) Harrier GR7 jump jets deploying from Kuwait, and later deployed from the H3 airfield in western Iraq.

Staging from Camp Doha in Kuwait, 150 commandos from the Australian SAS, under the auspices of OPERATION BASTILLE, entered southern Iraq on the night of March 18 in long-range, specially designed jeeps in four-to-five-man teams. Skirting around Iraqi positions under cover of darkness, they pinpointed ballistic missile sites, command-and-control centers and oil wells. Within an hour of crossing the Iraq border, they started taking enemy fire as they blitzkrieged across the open desert toward Baghdad.

Almost simultaneously, a second group of Australian SAS was dropped into western Iraq by the 160th SOAR. On the 375-mile flight, deep behind enemy lines, the U.S. Special Operations' Chinooks struggled not only with terrain flying, to avoid Iraqi radar and air defense, but raging sandstorms that left them flying totally blind. They accomplished their goal, however, and inserted the Aussie commandos shortly before sunrise, where they rushed to link up with the first group.

After insertion and linkup, the Australians waited for two days in covered and concealed positions, until "A-Day," the March 20 start of the coalition's "shock and awe" bombing campaign. When the green light came on, the Aussies, poised on the outskirts of Baghdad, immediately began painting targets with laser designators, calling in devastating CAS from U.S. and British fighter-bombers. The primary goal was to quickly destroy any missile sites that might launch chemical or biological attacks on coalition troops or neighboring states.

Soon after, the Australian SAS conducted a lightning-fast raid on the Al Asad airbase, just west of Baghdad, calling in air support from a squadron of Australian F/A-18s. The giant airbase containing sixty MIGs hidden under camouflage netting, was quickly seized without the Aussies suffering even a single injury. One Iraqi MIG Fighter was later shipped back to Australia to be displayed at the Australian War Memorial.

Within minutes of conventional forces attacking Iraq, Republican Guard armor started blowing up. 5th Special Forces Group and the SAS were at it again. Using their SOFLAM equipment to conduct terminal guidance operations, precision-guided munitions were hitting dead-on over and over, only this time it wasn't one or two B-52s and a dozen fighters. This time the entire air armada of America and Britain had been sent into the sky. With upgraded global positioning systems and improved night-vision sights, the special operators were able to see their laser spots and engage targets at distances farther than three kilometers.

But it was not all guns and roses. Six days into the war, B Squadron SAS inserted teams by parachute just southwest of Mosul to probe Republican Guard defenses. Their Land Rovers were brought in later by RAF Chinooks. U.S. intelligence had indicated that the landing area was devoid of enemy forces. It turned out to quickly become hot. Two men got separated when the rest were exfiled, and ended up on a new mission—one to E&E, escape and evade Iraqi forces. Moving only at night, the two Sabre troops covered over sixty miles through hostile territory in just seventy-two hours. Three days later they were rescued. British sources quickly blamed the incident on bad U.S. intelligence, and it was, but the initial contact had been against only roughly fifty Iraq soldiers. U.S. special operators responded privately by remembering Davis, Petithory, and McElhiney in Afghanistan, where they stood alone on a hill against one thousand Taliban and al-Qaida terrorists. Although British and American Special Forces worked well together, there would always be rivalry when it came to skills and daring.

Navy SEALs and British SBS teams were in the southern port of Basra, mapping underwater mines, conducting EOD operations, and clandestinely sabotaging Iraqi defense systems. Under the command of now Commodore Bob Hayward, the U.S. Naval Special Warfare Group in Iraq, sent in the Navy SEALs to seize two oil terminals in the Persian Gulf preventing Saddam's forces from flooding the gulf with oil. These were floating platforms connected to shore with oil lines to load tankers in deep water, and anti-Saddam intelligence assets had indicated that they were to be sabotaged.

Tirkuk was quickly abandoned, and an area that pumped billions of barrels was virtually intact, with only one random oil well being set on fire. In fact, the Iraqis had managed to set only nine oil well fires in the entire country, thanks to the interdiction of coalition special operations forces. The Kurds, led by American Special Forces, came in without any resistance. In Biyara, Northern Iraq, Special Forces, working with the Kurdish resistance, had destroyed Ansar al-Islam, a militant terrorist group closely linked to Osama bin Laden and al-Qaida.

In just three short weeks, Baghdad fell to coalition forces. The city was remarkably empty and silent when conventional forces rolled in. Unknown to the world, it had been the quiet work of special operations forces in Baghdad, who had infiltrated everywhere, and set the stage for a low intensity takeover of the city. Saddam's supporters had either been recruited, bribed, or surreptitiously killed. Remarkably, not one special operator had been killed or captured during all this clandestine and covert activity.

The coalition casualty count stood at 101 U.S. KIAs, 11 MIAs, and 7 POWs; 30 U.K. KIAs; and zero Australian KIAs. The Iraqis had tens of thousands KIAs, and there were more than 7,300 Iraqi POWs held by the U.S. and 6,500 held by Britain. Still the fate of Saddam remained elusive, although it was believed that he was killed in the first pre-emptive "decapitation" strike by special operators in Baghdad.

Special Operations forces then began the next mission, bringing the remaining Iraqi war criminals to justice.

Just days after Baghdad fell, Delta Force seized Abu Abbas, one of the world's most wanted terrorists hiding in Iraq. Abbas had been the mastermind and leader of the 1985 hijacking of the cruise ship *Achille Lauro*, in which the handicapped U.S. citizen Leon Klinghoffer was shot and pushed overboard in his wheelchair, on Abbas' orders. Abbas, whose real name is Mohammed Zaidan, was a Palestinian radical who demanded the release of fifty Palestinians held by Israel.

Abbas and his four henchmen ultimately agreed to surrender in return for safe passage out of Egypt. They turned themselves in to Egyptian authorities and were allowed to escape Egypt in a plane bound for Tunisia. American fighter jets intercepted the plane, forcing it to land in Sicily, but Italian authorities released Abbas, claiming they lacked any evidence of Abbas' wrongdoing. Later Abbas was convicted in absentia by the Italian courts; he had already fled Italy to Tunisia, and ultimately, to Iraq, where he set up the headquarters of his faction of the Palestine Liberation Front (PLF) in Baghdad. Abbas operated his terrorist camp there for years, proving that Saddam was a major sponsor of international terrorism. The Italians had imposed five life sentences on Abbas, but it was a case of too little, too late—until he was snatched up and flex-cuffed by Special Forces in a midnight raid on the outskirts of Baghdad on April 15.

"Bringing Abbas to justice will send a strong signal to terrorists anywhere in the world that there is no place to run, no place to hide," said Klinghoffer's two daughters, Lisa and Ilsa, after learning of the capture of their father's murderer.

"It's an old score to settle," added former CIA counterterrorism chief Vince Cannisstraro upon learning of Abbas' capture.

Abbas was the second major terrorist found in Baghdad within the last year. The first was the infamous Palestinian terrorist Abu Nidal, who was executed by Israeli Mossad agents in the Baghdad hotel where he had been holed up, in August 2002. The Iraqi government officially declared Nidal's death a suicide—by a gunshot wound through the eye.

Chemical and biological weapons labs, torture chambers, mass graves, execution rooms, suicide bomber vests, bomb-making factories, and terrorists, were all found by special operations troops in Iraq.

One week later, it became clear to the world that Osama bin Laden had been in league with Saddam. Papers, marked

TOP SECRET AND URGENT, were found by the international press in the headquarters of the Mukhabarat, Iraq's intelligence service, revealing that an al-Qaida envoy had been clandestinely invited to Baghdad in March 1998. The purpose was to transmit secret verbal messages between Saddam and bin Laden, and arrange for bin Laden to personally visit Saddam. Documents were also found revealing how Russian intelligence had passed on to their old friends at the Mukhabarat, the details of conversations between Tony Blair and various leaders of allied countries.

The discovery has always been regarded as a fortuitous accident by the press. The *accident* had actually been arranged by the ISA and the MI6, who found the papers during their search of Mukhabarat headquarters during the previous week, and left them in the abandoned, bombed-out building shortly before the press arrived. . . .

Bush and Blair's crusade had been a righteous cause.

Still, the naysayers and opposing politicians complained that no weapons of mass destruction (WMDs) had been found. Therefore the war had been waged under false pretenses. The reality seemed to be mired in politics. Saddam had executed thousands of innocent people, tortured women, gassed women and children, assassinated his political opponents, supported terrorism with money, weapons, and safe havens, and embodied an evil that no decent man could ignore. That evil had been brought to an end.

In 1991 and 1992, Jack had uncovered shipments of nuclear weapons materials and SADMs, Special Atomic Demolition Munitions, or "backpack nukes," from Russia to Iraq, Iran, and North Korea. Weapons-grade U-235 uranium and six SADMs known to have reached Iraq were still missing.

The Green Berets and SAS continued their hunt.

Glossary

AK-47: a Soviet-manufactured assault rifle that fires 7.62×39 ammunition, also known as a Kalashnikov, after the Soviet inventor.

AQ: al-Qaida; the multinational terrorist faction led and partially funded by Osama bin Laden. Originally an Arabic word meaning "the Base." It is also spelled "al-Qaeda." We use the Dari spelling in this book.

A-Team: see also *ODA;* the standard, twelve-man teams that make up the U.S. Army Special Forces.

ATO: air tasking order; the means of distributing joint firepower assets around the battlefield in a prioritized and fair as possible method.

banzai: the suicidal charge of Japanese troops during World War II.

battlespace: a modernized term for "battlefield," it also implies the airspace above a battlefield.

BDA: bomb damage assessment; the KIA, WIA, and number of enemy vehicles destroyed after a bombing run. It can also mean battlefield damage assessment, when applied to damage caused by ground forces and aircraft.

BDU: battle dress utility; current terminology for military combat uniform.

B-52: also known as the Stratofortress; a USAF heavy bomber.

bombardier: the person who releases the munitions (bombs) from a bomber.

bounding overwatch: a military maneuver where one team provides cover fire while the other team "bounds" ahead toward the objective using cover and concealment.

BTR: a Soviet-made armored personnel carrier.

buzkashi: a game in which a dead goat is placed in the center of a field and surrounded by horsemen from two opposing teams. The object of the game is to get control of the carcass and move it to the scoring area. In some versions, there are no teams; every player is out for himself.

CAS: close air support.

CCT: combat controller, an Air Force CAS specialist.

CENTCOM: Central Command.

chai: Afghan green or black tea.

CIB: Combat Infantry Badge, a silver musket on a blue background with a silver wreath around it. Awarded for ground battle face-to-face with the enemy.

429

CO: commanding officer, usually a captain on a Special Forces A-Team.

C-Team: Special Forces area command-and-control element.

cuartel: Panamanian term for a military base.

DAT: defense attaché.

denied area of operations: an operational area either behind enemy lines, or in a hostile country where the operation is unauthorized and without permission.

De Oppresso Liber: Latin for "Free the Oppressed"; the creed of the U.S. Army Special Forces, the Green Berets.

EUCOM: European Command.

F/A-18: Hornet, a versatile, twin-engine, swept-wing fighter bomber used by the U.S. Navy and U.S. Marine Corps, usually aboard aircraft carriers.

F-14: Tomcat, a versatile twin-engine, swept-wing fighter bomber used primarily by the U.S. Navy aboard aircraft carriers.

FM: field manual.

FO: forward observer.

FOB: forward operations base; a location close to the forward edge of the battle area from which A-Teams can deploy and from which B- and C-Teams can provide logistical support.

FRG: the Family Readiness Group; a support group for the wives and families of Special Forces soldiers.

GPS: global positioning system.

guerrilla warfare: see also *UW* (unconventional warfare); a hit-and-run method of warfare used to inflict maximum damage with a minimum of weaponry and manpower.

gun run: a military term for a fighter plane diving close to the ground and using its cannons and machine guns to strafe the enemy on the ground.

headspace and timing: military slang meaning to make fine adjustments to something; originally it meant to adjust the M2 .50-caliber machine gun for firing.

HE: High Explosive (ammunition).

HEAT: High Explosive Anti-Tank (ammunition).

heavy-metal soldier: military slang for a soldier from a heavy, mechanized infantry or armor unit. More recently used for gear-laden commando killers.

helo: SF slang for "helicopter." Also *chopper, Huey, Hawk, bird,* and *slick.*

HUMINT: human intelligence (sources).

INMARSAT: international maritime satellite telephone/radio.

ISI: Pakistani Inter-Service Intelligence agency, vicious enemies of the Northern Alliance, and Pakistan's version of the KGB.

ISOFAC: isolation facility where Special Forces teams prepare for combat missions and remain until they deploy.

JDAM: Joint Direct Attack Munitions; an upgrade kit that turns conventional bombs into GPS-navigated bombs with an INS (inertial navigation system) kit that is retrofitted to the bomb. JDAM-equipped bombs can navigate to a target over fifteen miles away, regardless of weather conditions.

JFACC: Joint Forces Air Component Command.

jihad: a holy war against "infidels" declared by Islamic fundamentalists.

JMD: joint manning document.

KIA: killed in action; to be killed on the battlefield.

laze: to highlight or "paint" a laser signature on a target, so that a laser-guided bomb may use its guidance system to home in on it.

LBE: load-bearing equipment; the belt, suspenders, and system of pouches that enable soldiers to carry their basic load of equipment on the battlefield. Also called "web gear."

loya jirga: a council of representatives from throughout Afghanistan tasked with designing a new government after the fall of the Taliban.

madrasah: an Islamic schoolhouse, used for "educating" the Taliban in fundamentalist Islamic practices.

MANPAD: any man-portable, surface-to-air missile, including the Soviet SA-7 and the U.S. military Stinger missile.

Mark-19: an automatic, vehicle, or tripod-mounted, belt-fed 40mm grenade launcher used by the U.S. military.

MBITR: Multiband Intersquad Tactical Radio; a tactical handheld radio used by U.S. Special Operations personnel.

medevac: short for "medically evacuate" the battlefield, usually by helicopter.

M-4A1: a shorter version of the M-16A2 assault rifle, with a collapsible stock and a heavier barrel, favored by Special Operations Forces and vehicle crews. Includes a removable carrying handle and rails for mounting scopes and night-vision devices. Often includes an under-barrel, 40mm M203 grenade launcher as well.

MH-47: the MH-47 Chinook is a twin-turbine, tandem-rotor, heavy-transport helicopter specially modified for use by Special Operations Forces.

MH-60: or Blackhawk, the standard U.S. military transport helicopter.

mujahadeen (muj): typically, Afghan freedom fighters of the Northern Alliance. Also spelled *mujahideen* or *mujahedin,* both of which refer to Arab or Islamic guerrilla fighters in the Middle East.

mustang: an NCO who decides to become a commissioned, career officer.

NCO: a noncommissioned officer, or sergeant.

NightStalkers: nickname of the 160th Special Operations Aviation Regiment (SOAR), the air transportation and support component to the U.S. Special Forces.

Northern Alliance (NA): officially titled the United Front Military Forces, the *mujahadeen* or freedom fighters of northern Afghanistan.

NTC: the National Training Center, located in the Mojave Desert at Fort Irwin, California.

OCS: Officer Candidate School.

ODA: Operational Detachment Alpha; another term used in place of "A-Team" to describe the Special Forces' standard, twelve-man teams.

op: short for a military operation.

OP: observation post.

OPCON: operational control; in overall command of the mission.

OSS: Office of Strategic Services; the predecessor to modern-day Special Forces, their heyday was during World War II.

PaveHawk: the Special Operations version of the Blackhawk helicopter.

PaveLow: the Special Operations MH-53 helicopter for infiltrations.

PK: short for RPK, a Soviet-made, belt-fed light machine gun.

POW: prisoner of war.

QRF: quick-reaction force.

ROE: rules of engagement.

RPG: rocket-propelled grenade.

RPG-7: a Soviet-designed shoulder-fired, rocket-propelled grenade launcher.

SAS: the elite British Special Air Service; counterpart to U.S. Special Forces.

SEAL: Sea, Air, Land; the Navy/Marine Corps clandestine forces.

Sendero Luminoso: the Shining Path, a Peruvian terrorist group.

SERE: Survival, Evasion, Resistance, and Escape; the Special Forces acronym for POW situations, and their special-purpose school for dealing with capture by enemy forces and capturing enemy forces. It has also been modernized with the adoption of SERER, with the last *R* standing for "recovery," which is pickup by friendly forces after escape.

shabnama: "night letters," propaganda leaflets distributed under cover of night, and typically slid under people's doors.

SITREP: situation report.

SNAFU: situation normal all fucked up.

SOCJFCOM: Special Operations Command of the Joint Forces Command.

SOCOM: Special Operations Command, headquartered in Tampa, Florida.

SOF: Special Operations Forces.

SOFLAM: Special Operations Forces' Laser Marker; a lightweight, compact laser-target designator for laser-guided smart bombs/munitions.

SPARTAN: Special Proficiency at Rugged Training and Nation-building.

S-2: command staff, intelligence section.

Talib: of, or referring to, the Taliban; also *Taleb.*

Taliban: the Students (of terror); an extreme Islamic fundamentalist group linked to the al-Qaida in Afghanistan. They seized control of the country in 1996.

TASK FORCE DAGGER: The 5th Special Forces Group task force headquartered at K2 air base in Uzbekistan and commanded by Colonel John Mulholland.

TLAM: Tomahawk land attack missile; a subsonic cruise missile that attacks targets on land, and can be fitted with a conventional unitary warhead (TLAM\C), a nuclear warhead (TLAM\N), or a submunition dispenser (TLAM\D).

TOC: Tactical Operations Center.

UAV: unmanned aerial vehicle; a remote-controlled surveillance aircraft.

UHF, HF, VHF: radio frequencies—ultra high, high, and very high.

USASOC: United States Army Special Operations Command, headquartered at Fort Bragg, North Carolina.

USSOCOM: United States Special Operations Command, McDill, Florida.

UW: unconventional warfare; see also *guerrilla warfare*.

VOA: violence of action.

WIA: wounded in action; to be wounded on the battlefield.

XO: executive officer, usually a warrant officer on a Special Forces A-Team and second in command.

ZPU-2: Similar to the ZU-23-2, except that it fires Soviet 12.7mm ammunition. All variations, the ZSU, ZU, and ZPU, were referred to generically in Afghanistan as ZSUs or "Zeus."

ZSU-23-4: also called "Zeus" by Afghans, it is a Soviet-made tracked, armored, self-propelled antiaircraft vehicle with four 23mm cannon barrels mounted on a central, tanklike turret.

ZU-23-2: also called "Zeus" by the Afghans, it is a Soviet-made antiaircraft weapon similar to the ZSU-23-4 except that it has two 23mm cannons on a towed carriage. The Taliban and AQ frequently mounted ZU-23-2s on defensive positions, on hills, and on the backs of trucks so that they could use them against personnel.

Bibliography

Prologue: The War on Terror
Reuel Marc Gerecht, "The Gospel According to Osama Bin Laden." *The Atlantic Monthly,* January 2002.
Robert C. Coon, e-mail from the U.S. Army War College entitled "Terrorists" quotes Ralph Peters from his book *When Devils Walk the Earth.*

Chapter 1: The Tiger Roars
Ahmed Rashid, *Taliban.* New Haven: Yale University Press, 2000.
Lyrics from "The Ballad of the Green Berets," © 1966 Barry Sadler and Robin Moore. Published by Sizemore Music, PO Box 681041, Fort Payne, AL 35968.

Chapter 2: Striking at the Heart of Evil
Robert Burns, "Commander Contemplated Suicide Missions to Stop Sept. 11 Terrorists." Associated Press, August 30, 2002.

Chapter 4: The Dogs of War
Peter Finn in the *Washington Post,* on January 18, 2002, reported the release of the prisoners by the Bosnians and LTG Sylvester's comments.
Jerry Seper, "U.S. Eyes Saudi File on Terror Targets." *Washington Times,* February 25, 2002.

Chapter 6: The Flag and the Ring
"Lord of the Rings" and "One Ring to Bind Them" are both references to J.R.R. Tolkien's *Lord of the Rings* series of fantasy books.

Chapter 7: TASK FORCE DAGGER
Andrew Bushell, "U.S. Paid Off Afghan Warlords for Help." *Washington Times,* February 7, 2002.
Robert Burns, "Rumsfeld: CIA Was Involved Early." Associated Press, February 13, 2002.
Mark Mazzetti, "On the Ground: How Special Ops are Hunting al Qaeda." *U.S. News & World Report,* February 25, 2002.
Douglas Waller, "How the CIA Fights Its New War." *Time,* November 5, 2001.

Massimo Calabresi and Romesh Ratnesar, "Can We Stop the Next Attack?" *Time*, March 11, 2002.

David S. Cloud, "Caught Off-Guard by Terror, the CIA Fights to Catch Up." *Wall Street Journal*, April 15, 2002.

Chapter 8: Northern Alliance—General Dostum

Robert Young Pelton confirms the Dostum quote in Chapter 9 in "The Legend of Heavy D & the Boys (or, How the Green Berets Learned to Stop Worrying and Love the Warlord)." *National Geographic Adventure*, March 2002.

Jeffrey Schaffer of the Associated Press described in detail the farewell ceremony conducted by General Dostum and Captain Mark Nutsch, January 20, 2002.

The photo of a Green Beret participating in a *buzkashi* match was seen worldwide. The AP photo was by Maxim Marmur.

Chapter 9: Northern Alliance—General Fahim

Barbara Hall, "The Story of ODA 595." *The Drop* (magazine of the Special Forces Association), Spring 2002.

Chapter 10: Northern Alliance—General Baryoli

"One Ring to Rule Them All" is a reference to J.R.R. Tolkien's *Lord of the Rings* series of fantasy books.

Kirk Spitzer, "Green Berets Outfought, Outthought the Taliban." *USA Today*, January 7, 2002.

Ray Carbone, "A Hero's Welcome." *Foster's Daily Democrat and Sunday Citizen* (Dover and Laconia, New Hampshire), February 10, 2002.

Chapter 11: Northern Alliance—General Atta

Donatella Lorch, "The Green Berets Up Close." *Newsweek*, January 14, 2001.

Chapter 12: Northern Alliance—Commander Khalili

"Buddha Statues to Be Rebuilt." *USA Today*, April 11, 2002.

Chapter 14: Northern Alliance—Ismail Khan

Afshin Valinejad, "Afghan Warlord's Iran Office Closed." Associated Press, Tehran, February 11, 2002.

Tyler Marshall, "Iran Casts Shadow on the Afghan Political Map." *Los Angeles Times*, January 24, 2002.

Peter Baker, "Warlord Gets Money, Arms from Iran, Afghan Aides Say." *Washington Post*, February 7, 2002.

"If You Want a Mercedes, Try Herat." *The Economist*, January 26, 2002.

Amy Waldman, "Mystery Men Held by U.S. Are Afghans." *New York Times*, March 14, 2002.

Amy Waldman, "Courted by U.S. and Iran, an Afghan Governor Plays One Side Off the Other." *New York Times*, April 3, 2002.

Borzou Daragahi, "Iran Courts Afghan Business." *Washington Times,* April 4, 2002.

Pamela Constable, "Afghan Officials Say Forces Foiled Sabotage." *Washington Post,* April 5, 2002.

Chapter 15: The Qala-i-Jangi Uprising

An article relaying eyewitness accounts of the events surrounding the loss of Mike Spann was published in *Time* magazine, December 17, 2001.

Robert Young Pelton, "The Legend of Heavy D & the Boys (or, How the Green Berets Learned to Stop Worrying and Love the Warlord)." *National Geographic Adventure,* March 2002.

Tonya Spann Ingram, "Traitors and Terrorists Should Pay the Consequences of Their Actions." *Army Times,* April 8, 2002.

Matthew Campbell, "First Person: The Battle of Qalai Janghi." www.foxnews.com/story/0,2933,39912,00.html, December 2, 2001.

Alex Perry, "Inside the Battle at Qala-I-Jangi." Time.com, December 1, 2001.

Jennifer Harper, "CNN, Hollywood Air Afghan Accounts." *Washington Times,* July 30, 2002.

Chapter 17: Attack in the South—Karzai

Thomas Shanker, "Conduct of War Is Redefined by Success of Special Forces." *New York Times,* January 21, 2002.

Peter Finn relayed the first comprehensive report regarding the amazing story of Captain Amerine and his A-Team in the *Washington Post,* December 11, 2001.

Sean D. Naylor continued his quality reporting of Special Forces activities for the *Army Times,* December 24, 2001, discussing the impacts of Tarin Kowt.

Rowan Scarborough, "Karzai, A Team Turned the Tide of War." *Washington Times,* January 22, 2002.

Chapter 19: Attack in the South—Kandahar Falls

Rowan Scarborough, "Karzai, A Team Turned the Tide of War." *Washington Times,* January 22, 2002.

Ray Carbone, "A Hero's Welcome." *Foster's Daily Democrat and Sunday Citizen* (Dover and Laconia, New Hampshire), February 10, 2002.

Chapter 20: Tora Bora

Susan B. Glasser, in her article in the *Washington Post,* provides first-rate on-scene coverage. December 12, 2001.

Dennis Steele, "Afghanistan Phase 2: Hitching Up for the Long Haul." *Army Magazine,* February 2002.

Susan B. Glasser, "The Battle of Tora Bora." *Washington Post,* February 17, 2002.

Ed Vulliamy in New York, Jason Burke in Peshawar, and Paul Harris collaborated and provided valuable insight during the heat of the fight. *Fayetteville Observer,* December 9, 2001.

Vivienne Walt, in *USA Today,* December 18, 2001, reported that most caves were dry holes.

Bradley Graham and Edward Cody, "2 Top Al Qaeda Fighters Caught." *Washington Post,* January 9, 2002.

Cesar G. Sorian reported the raid near Khost that resulted in the capture of two Taliban or AQ suspects. *USA Today,* January 22, 2002.

General Cao Van Vien, *The Final Collapse.* Washington, D.C.: U.S. Army Center of Military History, 1983.

Mark Mazzetti, "How Special Ops Forces Are Hunting Al Qaeda." *U.S. News & World Report,* February 25, 2002.

"Bin Laden in Hiding Near US Missile Strike." UPI, February 13, 2002.

Kathy Gannon, " 'Holy War' Force Said Regrouping, Al-Qaeda, Taliban Fighters Urged to Strike at U.S." Associated Press, March 2, 2002.

David Folkenflik, "War News from Rivera Seems off the Mark." *Baltimore Sun,* December 12, 2001.

David Folkenflik, "Reports of War Draw Fire to Fox." *Baltimore Sun,* December 15, 2001.

David Vest, "Turn, Turn, Turn." *Counterpunch,* January 1, 2002.

Bob Steele, "Geraldo's Story: Truth or Consequences." *The Poynter Institute—Bob Steele's Talk About Ethics,* www.poynter.org/talkaboutethics/122101.htm, December 21, 2001.

The Project for Excellence in Journalism, "Return to Normalcy? How the Media Have Covered the War on Terrorism." www.journalism.org/publ_research/normalcy1.html.

AIM Report, 2002 Report #01, Reed Irvine—editor, January 31, 2002.

Jim Rutenberg, "At Fox News, the Colonel Who Wasn't." *New York Times,* April 29, 2002.

Chapter 21: Flags over the Embassy

Kevin Dougherty was the first to report the private 5th Special Forces Group flag-raising ceremony. *Stars and Stripes,* European edition, December 15, 2001.

"SF Soldiers Bury Pieces of WTC" originally appeared in SFA Chapter 38's newsletter, *The Beret.*

Chapter 22: Occupation and Pursuit

Rowan Scarborough, "Karzai, A Team Turned the Tide of War." *Washington Times,* January 22, 2002.

Ellen Knickmeyer, "Strike Finishes Hospital Standoff." Associated Press, January 29, 2002.

Susan Sevareid, "Troops Count Abandoned Ammunition." *Boston Globe,* January 4, 2002.

Thomas Shanker, "In Kandahar, New Mission for 'A Team': Make It Safe." *New York Times,* January 7, 2002.

Comments by the secretary of defense and the chairman of the Joint Chiefs of Staff reflected favorably on the simultaneous raid conducted against two suspected AQ/Taliban buildings. Fox News, January 24, 2002.

"Captured al Qaeda Documents Show Broad Reach of Terrorist Interests, Activities." *Washington Update,* May 2002.

Chris Stephen, "Startled Marines Find Afghan Men All Made Up to See Them." *The Scotsman,* May 24, 2002.

Chapter 23: OPERATION ANACONDA

Kathy Gannon, " 'Holy War' Force Said Regrouping, Al-Qaeda, Taliban Fighters Urged to Strike at U.S." Associated Press, March 2, 2002.

Vernon Loeb, "Army's Mountain Division Mops Up." *Washington Post,* March 3, 2002.

"U.S., Afghans Launch Attack." *Fayetteville Observer,* March 3, 2002.

Michael R. Gordon, "This Time, American Soldiers Join the Fray." *New York Times,* March 4, 2002.

Vernon Loeb and Bradley Graham, "American Troops Play Greater Role in Latest Offensive." *Washington Post,* March 4, 2002.

Tim Friend, "U.S. Assault Largest of War." *USA Today,* March 4, 2002.

Jonathan Weisman, "Battle Is Fiercest Yet, and It Won't Be Last." *USA Today,* March 5, 2002.

Kathy Gannon, "Villagers Heeded Warning, Fled." Associated Press, March 5, 2002.

Jim Drinkard and Jonathan Weisman, "War's 'Dangerous Phase.' " *USA Today,* March 5, 2002.

Jonathan Weisman, "War's Deadliest Day." *USA Today,* March 6, 2002.

Sean Naylor, "U.S. Trick Silences Al-Qaeda Taunts." *Army Times,* March 7, 2002.

Kathy Gannon, "Troops Battle on Hills, in Caves." Associated Press, March 8, 2002.

Barry Bearak, "Kabul Rushes 1,000 More Men to Join G.I.'s on Battle's Sixth Day." *New York Times,* March 8, 2002.

Peter Baker, "Afghans Bolster U.S.-Led Force." *Washington Post,* March 8, 2002.

Lutfullah Mashal, "An Escalating, High-Altitude Showdown." *Christian Science Monitor,* March 8, 2002.

Dave Moniz, "U.S. Troops Try to Block Enemy Escape Routes." *USA Today,* March 12, 2002.

Jonathan Weisman and Vivienne Walt, "U.S., Allies Press Last Holdouts." *USA Today,* March 13, 2002.

"In Anaconda with Special Forces." UPI, March 14, 2002.

Evan Thomas, "Leave No Man Behind." *Newsweek,* March 18, 2002.

Mike Phillips, Tim McGirk, Michael Ware, Alex Perry, Sean Scully, Mark Thompson, and Rahimullah Yusufzai, "Assault on Shah-I-Kot." *Time,* March 18, 2002.

Kathy Gannon, "U.S., Allies Control Valley." Associated Press, March 14, 2002.

Charles J. Hanley, "Colonel's Black Hawk Goes Down Early." Associated Press, March 16, 2002.

Paul Haven, "Franks Calls ANACONDA a Success." Associated Press, March 19, 2002.

Geoffrey Mohan, Bone Tempest, John Daniszewski, and Richard Cooper, "Anaconda." *Los Angeles Times,* March 31, 2002.

Ilene R. Prusher, "Afghan Nomads Cloaked Al Qaeda." *Christian Science Monitor,* April 4, 2002.

Beth C. DeGrasse and Edith B. Wilkie, "To Build Peace in Afghanistan." *Washington Post,* April 5, 2002.

Ron Martz, "Franks: No U.S. 'Hot Pursuit' into Pakistan." *Atlanta Journal-Constitution,* April 4, 2002.

Missy Stoddard, "News from Home Hit 3rd Group Hard." *Fayetteville Observer,* March 19, 2002.

Chapter 24: From Dagger to Broadsword

Douglas Waller, "How the CIA Fights Its New War." *Time,* November 5, 2001.

Massimo Calabresi and Romesh Ratnesar, "Can We Stop the Next Attack?" *Time,* March 11, 2002.

After-Action Reports

Cesar G. Soriano, "Coalition Forces Examine Possible al-Qaeda Graves." *USA Today,* May 8, 2002.

Michael Georgy, "Bin Laden Reportedly Back at Helm of al-Qaeda." Reuters, August 27, 2002.

Eric Schmitt, "After January Raid, Gen. Franks Promises to Do Better." *New York Times,* February 8, 2002.

Tom Bowman, "U.S. Chases Shadows in Afghanistan." *Baltimore Sun,* February 25, 2002.

Jonathan Weisman, "Rumsfeld Admits Allies Were Killed." *USA Today,* February 22, 2002.

Thomas Shanker, "Conduct of War Is Redefined by Success of Special Forces." *New York Times,* January 21, 2002.

Chip Cummins, "Human-Rights Group to Estimate Civilians Killed in U.S. Campaign." *Wall Street Journal,* February 7, 2002.

Special Forces' 50th Anniversary memorial speech, LTG Brown, USASOC CG, c/o Major Kathleen R. "Kaz" Culp, CG speechwriter, June 19, 2002.

Appendix

Memorial Funds, Charities, and Nonprofit Groups

To help the children of Sergeant Chapman:
SFC Nathan Chapman Children's Memorial Fund
PO Box 620020, Dallas, TX 75262-0020

To help all SOF personnel:
Special Forces Survivor Fund
6911 Green Hill Place, Tampa, FL 33617-1720

To help with college educations:
Special Operations Warrior Foundation
PO Box 14385, Tampa, FL 33690
www.specialops.org

Special Operations Association:
Chairman, Scholarship Committee
4401 Park Road, Alexandria, VA 22312
www.specialoperations.org

To help the Northern Alliance and to fight al-Qaida:
US Counter-Terrorist Group
PO Box 691, Fayetteville, NC 28302-0691
www.counterrgroup.org

To help the people of Afghanistan:
Afghanistan Relief Organization
PO Box 10207, Canoga Park, CA 91304
www.afghanrelief.com

Index

Photograph Credits

Photo Pages 1–2: The Hunters
Horse charge: courtesy of US Counter-Terrorist Group
ATV assault: courtesy of TASK FORCE SABER
NA MI-8 chopper: courtesy of the Northern Alliance
Special Forces Ring: courtesy of The Hunt for bin Laden Group, LLC
Hindu Kush: courtesy of US Counter-Terrorist Group
SF Hunter Team: author's personal collection

Photo Pages 3–4: The Hunted
World Trade Center: copyright © 2001 by Spencer Platt/Getty Images; grateful acknowledgment is made to Spencer Platt and Getty Images for permission to reproduce this photograph
Osama bin Laden: file photo, U.S. Department of Defense
Mullah Omar: file photo, U.S. Department of Defense
Al-Qaida 1: courtesy of PBS News.tv, *8mm VideoX* archive
Al-Qaida 2: courtesy of PBS News.tv, *8mm VideoX* archive
Al-Qaida 3: courtesy of PBS News.tv, *8mm VideoX* archive

Photo Pages 5–6: The Command
General Brown: courtesy of U.S. Army Special Operations
Colonel Bank: courtesy of Major Kathleen Culp
Colonel Mulholland: author's personal collection
General Yarborough: courtesy of General William Yarborough
Major Brigham: courtesy of US Counter-Terrorist Group

Photo Page 7: The Northern Alliance
Commander Massoud: courtesy of Colonel Wadood, Northern Alliance
Massoud commanders: courtesy of J. K. Idema
Mujahadeen praying: courtesy of Lloyd Francis, www.07d.net

Photo Page 8: Northern Afghanistan—the Hunt Begins
K2 base in Uzbekistan: courtesy of a confidential source
SF pack mission: courtesy of a confidential source
Streets of Khoja-Bahaudeen: courtesy of J. K. Idema

Photo Pages 9–10: Shomali Plains—with General Fahim
MH-47 over Shomali: courtesy of the Northern Alliance
Mulholland and TIGER 03: courtesy of a confidential source
Bagram tower: courtesy of US Counter-Terrorist Group

Al-Qaida prisoners 1: courtesy of a confidential source
Al-Qaida prisoners 2: courtesy of a confidential source

Photo Pages 10–11: Mazar-e-Sharif—with General Dostum
JDAM explosion: courtesy of U.S. Army Special Operations
TIGER 02 and Robin Moore: author's personal collection
Refugees receiving aid: courtesy of Abdul Khalili, www.afghanrelief.com
Wounded soldier: courtesy of 1st SFOD-D/TASK FORCE 11

Photo Pages 12–13: Kal-a-Khata—with General Baryoli
Scurka wounded: courtesy of US Counter-Terrorist Group
Afghan refugees: courtesy of US Counter-Terrorist Group
HDR food packs: courtesy of TASK FORCE SABER
Kal-a-Khata frontlines: courtesy of US Counter-Terrorist Group

Photo Page 14: Bamian—with Commander Khalili
Green Berets on roof: courtesy of U.S. Army Special Operations
ZSU AA gun: courtesy of U.S. Army Special Operations
SF A-Team: courtesy of a confidential source

Photo Pages 15–16: Mazar-e-Sharif—with General Atta
Mujahadeen on roof: courtesy of J. K. Idema
Captain "Ally": author's personal collection
Spectre gunship shell: courtesy of JSOTF/TF DAGGER
Green Berets and cash: courtesy of a confidential source
General Wasiq: courtesy of J. K. Idema

Photo Page 17: Kandahar—with Commander Sharzai
Green Berets with exploded truck: courtesy of COBRA 72
JDAM the dog: courtesy of Sergeant First Class Jeff Bright
SF A-Team and *mujahadeen*: courtesy of COBRA 72

Photo Pages 18–19: Kandahar—with Commander Karzai
President Karzai: courtesy of J. K. Idema
Petithory's Privy: courtesy of Sergeant First Class Jeff Bright
Mir Wais hospital raid: courtesy of U.S. Army Special Operations
Karzai and TEXAS 12: courtesy of a TEXAS 12 family member

Photo Pages 20–21: Tora Bora—with General Hazrat Ali
"NYPD" on tank barrel: courtesy of PBN News
Green Beret with AQ computer: courtesy of a confidential source
Green Berets with AQ mines: courtesy of a confidential source
Commander Hazrat Ali: courtesy of US Counter-Terrorist Group
AQ cave: courtesy of a confidential source

Photo Page 22: Gardez—with Commander Gul Haider
Hotel Gardez: courtesy of a confidential source
SF A-Team with General Brown: courtesy of a confidential source
Green Beret operating: courtesy of the Northern Alliance

Photo Page 23: OPERATION ANACONDA
COBRA 72 with SAS: courtesy of a confidential source
SF team in Shah-i-Kot: courtesy of a confidential source
160th SOAR (ABN): courtesy of U.S. Army Special Operations

Photo Page 24: "When the last Angel has fallen . . ."
Mike Spann's funeral: courtesy of the Central Intelligence Agency
Staff Sergeant Cody Prosser's funeral: courtesy of the Department of Defense, Arlington National Cemetery
Shawna Prosser: courtesy of the Department of Defense, Arlington National Cemetery
Sergeant First Class Chapman's funeral: courtesy of the 1st Special Forces Group
Burying pieces of the WTC: courtesy of the 5th Special Forces Group

NO ROOM
FOR ERROR

The Covert Operations of America's
Special Tactics Units from Iran to
Afghanistan

by Col. John T. Carney Jr. and
Benjamin F. Schemmer

"This is one of the most compelling and
comprehensive accounts I've seen of
special operations missions all over the
globe."
—William S. Cohen
Former Secretary of Defense

"America and the world need to know
what kind of people defend us and who
are the real heroes."
—Caspar W. Weinberger
Former Secretary of Defense

Published by Presidio Press
Available wherever books are sold